THE LIFE AND LIES OF PAUL CROUCH

UNIVERSITY PRESS OF FLORIDA

Florida A&M University, Tallahassee
Florida Atlantic University, Boca Raton
Florida Gulf Coast University, Ft. Myers
Florida International University, Miami
Florida State University, Tallahassee
New College of Florida, Sarasota
University of Central Florida, Orlando
University of Florida, Gainesville
University of North Florida, Jacksonville
University of South Florida, Tampa
University of West Florida, Pensacola

University Press of Florida
Gainesville · Tallahassee · Tampa · Boca Raton
Pensacola · Orlando · Miami · Jacksonville · Ft. Myers · Sarasota

THE LIFE AND LIES OF PAUL CROUCH

COMMUNIST, OPPORTUNIST, COLD WAR SNITCH

GREGORY S. TAYLOR

Printed in the United States of America on acid-free, recycled paper.

This book may be available in an electronic edition.

19 18 17 16 15 14 6 5 4 3 2 1

Library of Congress Cataloging-in-Publication Data

Taylor, Gregory S., author.
The life and lies of Paul Crouch : communist, opportunist, Cold War snitch / Gregory S. Taylor.
pages cm
Includes bibliographical references and index.
ISBN 978-0-8130-4920-5
1. Crouch, Paul, 1903–1955. 2. Informers—United States—Biography.
3. Communists—United States—Biography. 4. Cold War—Biography.
5. Communism—United States—History—20th century. 6. Anti-communist movements—United States—History—20th century. I. Title.
E748.C949T39 2014
363.25'2092—dc23
[B]
2013038959

The University Press of Florida is the scholarly publishing agency for the State University System of Florida, comprising Florida A&M University, Florida Atlantic University, Florida Gulf Coast University, Florida International University, Florida State University, New College of Florida, University of Central Florida, University of Florida, University of North Florida, University of South Florida, and University of West Florida.

University Press of Florida
15 Northwest 15th Street
Gainesville, FL 32611-2079
http://www.upf.com

For Grandma, Darren, Becky, and Thomas

CONTENTS

FIGURES

ACKNOWLEDGMENTS

This book was made possible by the support and assistance of any number of individuals. If I failed to thank you at the time, I hope this acknowledgment makes up for my oversight.

My entire family has been supportive of my academic and intellectual endeavors from the beginning, and I can never thank them enough for all they have done.

My many friends and colleagues at Chowan University not only served as sounding boards and read early drafts of the manuscript but also encouraged me along the way and put up with my constant allusions to the work. It is with the most heartfelt thanks that I acknowledge my gratitude to David Ballew, Dean Lawson, William Bradley, Emily Isaacson, John Parnell, Bruce Moser, Amy Wethington, J. Brabban, Ken Wolfskill, Danny Moore, and M. Christopher White. Special thanks go to Georgia Williams, Linda Hassell, Sarah Bonner, Rachel Peterson, Tarshae Ellis, and the entire library staff at Chowan University who put up with my constant requests for often hard-to-acquire material and always succeeded in procuring it. I would be remiss if I failed to thank my students for their interest in my work and for the great assistance of Kimberly Smiley-Hicks who helped organize the bibliography.

The many archivists at the Hoover Institution Archives, the University of North Carolina, and Wilkes Community College made my research trips fruitful and enjoyable, and I cannot thank them enough. Finally, many thanks to Sian Hunter, Shannon McCarthy, Nevil Parker, freelancer Elizabeth Detwiler, and the entire staff at the University Press of Florida who made this project possible and whose suggestions and vision dramatically improved the work.

INTRODUCTION

THE MOST DANGEROUS MAN IN AMERICA

American history is full of ideologues. Indeed, the nation was created, in part, by men and women who were true believers in their cause and the righteousness of it. But true believers also can be dangerous, especially when they see the world only in black and white. Such a Manichean perspective blinds them to the positive possibilities of a competing worldview and makes compromise nearly impossible. The dangers of such individuals and their ideological purity are only increased when they have benefactors who hope to reap gains from such rigidity. Former special counsel to President Richard M. Nixon and convicted Watergate felon Charles "Chuck" Colson described well these circumstances when, in discussing the Nixon White House, he wrote: "A holy war was declared against the enemy. . . . *They* who differed with *us*, whatever their motives, must be vanquished."[1] From Colson's perspective, *we* were right, and not only were *they* wrong—*they* were evil, un-American, and had to be destroyed.

Historian Richard Hofstader agreed that such a perspective is dangerous, and he worried that it creates a paranoia in which the ideologue sees the world in "apocalyptic terms—he traffics in the birth and death of whole worlds, whole political orders, whole systems of human values. He is always manning the barricades of civilization. He constantly lives at a turning point: it is now or never in organizing resistance to conspiracy. Time is forever running out. Like religious millenarians, he expresses the anxiety of those who are living through the last days."[2] For Hofstader, what made these ideologues so dangerous was not just that they saw the world as a struggle between good and evil but their belief that that struggle needed to be won immediately. Thus, not only was room for negotiation or compromise lacking—there was not even time for debate.

Columnist Max Lerner took this definition a step further to explain what happens when such a paranoid worldview permeates an entire era: "People feel surrounded by deceivers and betrayers, by false leaders, by ideas which are formless threats, by men who personify those threats to us. From this it is only a small step, in a distorted mind, to resolve to remove the threat and kill the idea by shooting the man. It becomes an egomania—the delusion that because the time is out of joint it is one man's role to set it right by his action."[3] Although writing about the 1970s and the climate that created Arthur Bremer, the man who shot former Alabama governor and U.S. presidential candidate George Wallace, Lerner easily could have been talking about the subjects of this work—the Communist fear that capitalism was leading the world to ruin in the 1920s and 1930s or the anti-Communist fear that the American way of life was under threat by the Communist menace in the 1940s and 1950s. In each instance, the fear of the enemy and the belief that the enemy's threats were imminent led many Americans to accept the idea that the world was so out of order that anything—legal or illegal, moral or immoral, right or wrong—was acceptable to bring about *their* destruction.

The Communists of the 1920s and 1930s, for instance, believed they were performing righteous deeds to protect the working man, and the nation as a whole, from the evils of industrial capitalism. They were convinced that the nation was heading off the rails and that capitalists with their store-bought politicians were purposefully ruining the nation for their own benefit. They believed that the United States had been forced into World War I by capitalists desiring to profit from the war and viewed the Espionage Act of 1917 and Sedition Act of 1918 as evidence that capitalists and politicians would brook no dissent in the drive for those profits. The arrests of the Wobblies, "Big" Bill Haywood, and Eugene Debs, as well as the Red Scare of 1919–1920, seemed to confirm the Communist perspective. The Great Depression offered further evidence that capitalism was the root of all evil, and that view only was inflamed by the outbreak of World War II, which many Communists understood as yet another capitalist war. McCarthyism and the Cold War, meanwhile, cemented the idea that capitalists were willing to go to any lengths to protect and ensure their profits. Communist ideologues helped sell such a "paranoid" worldview, and in the process won thousands of converts who believed capitalists were evil and un-American. Such paranoia led them to judge every action with evil intent and to justify for themselves the right to destroy the nation and the entire capitalist system.

Anti-Communists, by contrast, believed it was the Communists who were leading the nation into dangerous depths; and they had plenty of evidence for this perspective. The anarchist bombs of 1919, the radicalism of the New Deal, the Manhattan Project spies, the spread of Communism into Eastern Europe, the "fall" of China, and the Korean War all seemed to demonstrate the Communist threat. Anti-Communists therefore attacked the Communist Party for its internationalism, for undercutting the incentive toward innovation and hard work, and, most important, for being subversive and un-American. To protect the nation from such dangers, they prodded the U.S. Congress and the executive branch to crush the party through the aforementioned Sedition and Espionage acts, Red Scares, and McCarthy era. They even looked the other way as American citizens lost their First, Fifth, and Fourteenth Amendment rights, and often their jobs and reputations, simply because of their political perspective. Individual ideologues helped sell this worldview as well, and in congressional hearings, courtroom testimony, and literary efforts they described Communism as the greatest threat the nation ever faced—one that needed to be destroyed regardless of the means.

The problem with all of this, as Colson, Hofstader, and Lerner well note, is that neither side in this ideological struggle acknowledged the legitimacy of the other. While they understood the opposing ideologies and agendas, there was no willingness to compromise and no willingness to accept that *they* might have a valid ideal or worldview. *They* were different; *they* were wrong; *they* were evil; *they* were going to destroy America; and so, *they* had to be destroyed. The end result, sadly, was that neither side won and the nation as a whole lost. The Communist Party was decimated, the anti-Communist forces were pilloried, traditional American values were disregarded, and thousands of individuals had their lives destroyed in the name of political purity.

Such an outcome helps explain the continued fascination with the Communist and anti-Communist movements in American history. Countless books from countless perspectives have sought to better examine the origins, impacts, and membership of each ideology. One way historians have attempted to understand all of this is to study one person who, at different times in life, was a member of each camp. What attracted the individual to each side, what factors led them to abandon one for the other, and what were the implications of their decision? There are numerous examples of such individuals, specifically those who once were Communist zealots only later to become anti-Communist activists. Indeed, dozens of individuals fall within this subset.

Louis Budenz, for instance, joined the Communist Party of the United States of America (CPUSA) in 1935 as a result of the party's announced determination to fight off the fascist threat of Nazi Germany. During a decade within the party, he served on the National Committee and as editor of the Communist Party's newspaper the *Daily Worker*. He quit in 1945 as a result of policy changes he believed benefitted only the Soviet Union, and not the working class or Communist Parties worldwide, and joined the Catholic Church. In 1946 he began to testify for the government against his former comrades. Throughout the 1940s and early 1950s he was a useful and highly paid informant despite having what one contemporary called a "latex memory" and what another called a "readiness to elevate hearsay to the status of authoritative facts and an expansive disregard for the niceties of actual Party affiliation." He testified thirty-three times over a twelve-year period and later claimed to have earned some $70,000 for his anti-Communist revelations.[4]

Elizabeth Bentley also joined the CPUSA in 1935, inspired by its fight against fascism, its struggle for social justice, and its camaraderie. Unlike Budenz, Bentley not only served the party, she also became a spy and spent nearly a decade passing along sensitive government information to her Soviet spymasters. She quit in 1945 after conflicts with those spymasters, and on November 7, 1945, began a series of debriefings with the FBI during which she named some 150 spies. Bentley proceeded to testify publicly in several trials against those she named, published a book about her life entitled *Out of Bondage*, and eventually converted to Catholicism.[5]

In 1925 Whittaker Chambers joined the Workers (Communist) Party of America (WPA), one of the predecessors to the CPUSA. He later claimed to have embarked on his Communist career "because he [was] driven to despair by the crisis of history through which the world [was] passing." He believed that the capitalist world was dying while

Communism promised mankind a new and better life. Determined to be a part of that renaissance, he joined the Communists and used his literary talents to write for the *Daily Worker*, the *New Masses*, and other party publications. Like Bentley, he also became part of the Soviet spy network, delivering documents from government workers to his Soviet contacts. Disturbed by the violence of Joseph Stalin's regime, Chambers left the Communist Party in 1938. A decade later he testified in the infamous Alger Hiss case, named the State Department employee as a Communist, and subsequently published *Witness* about his experiences in the party and as an informant.[6]

Harvey Matusow offers one final example. Fresh from the military and seeking the camaraderie he had left behind, he joined the CPUSA in 1947. He grew dispirited with what he perceived to be the dictatorial nature of the Communist Party, but also began to fear being caught up in the growing Red Scare. As a result, in 1950 he contacted the FBI and offered to provide information. He remained in the party as a government informant, but members quickly exposed and expelled him. Despite that, he spent the early 1950s testifying against party members and gained fame for asserting that Communists had infiltrated the State Department, CBS, the *New York Times*, and the Boy Scouts. In 1955 his testimony ended when he admitted to perjury, a crime for which he served forty-four months in prison.[7]

As should be obvious, these four individuals share a number of similarities. All joined the CPUSA in search of political and personal benefits. They saw something wrong with the world, believed capitalism was the cause, and were willing to take the radical step of becoming a Communist in order to fight for the dramatic reordering of society. At the same time, all sought a sense of self from their work in the Communist Party. They became part of something larger than themselves and enjoyed the friends and close relationships such a perspective engendered. Joining the party was consequently a near religious experience; it promised hope and salvation and brought together a diverse lot unified around a specific set of beliefs. That Bentley and Budenz became Catholics after they left the party only seems to magnify this point.

Beyond the personal and political, they all achieved some level of success within the Communist Party. They remained members long enough to move up the ranks and gain some insight into the inner workings of the movement. Once they came to see beyond the utopian propaganda of the party's public pronouncements, however, they grew outraged at the lack of freedom, the lack of intellectual autonomy, and the subordination of all things to the needs of the USSR. Indeed, with the exception of the intellectual Chambers, they initially had little real appreciation for the intellectual underpinnings of Communist ideology. They understood the Communist Party's struggle against fascism, militarism, racism, and imperialism, and its support for economic and social equality, but had little understanding of the finer points of Marxist-Leninist ideology.

They thus failed to appreciate, for instance, that Marx's theory of surplus value asserted that the bourgeoisie stole from the working class its fair share of the value of their industrial productivity. In practice, such a belief would have required factory owners to pay workers the entire value of the goods they produced, which would have destroyed the profit motive and capitalism as we know it. They failed to appreciate that Lenin's theory of democratic centralism demanded absolute obedience once the party had made a policy decision, and consequently forbade any dissent and required members to parrot the party line regardless of their personal beliefs. They also failed to understand that Lenin's theory of the vanguard party, which called for the creation of a small group of professional revolutionaries who would lead the overthrow of the established government, required some level of secrecy on the part of the party elite and all but assured some level of revolutionary violence. Once they learned these hard truths, all four quit the Communist Party in disgust.

Not only did they quit, each completely reversed their ideological compass. They turned on their former ideology and comrades and viewed all they had once believed as evil, dangerous, and un-American. They eventually grew so fearful of what the Communist Party could do that they offered their knowledge and insight to the federal government, which was desperate for information amidst the Red Scare and McCarthy era of the 1940s and 1950s. But it was more than a patriotic or ideological move that led all four into the anti-Communist camp. Once again the moves seem personal—a means of cleansing themselves of the sins they committed while in the party. Their testimony became a purgative, of sorts. At the same time, they all found a new sense of camaraderie within the anti-Communist movement as they joined the ranks of those fighting to save the nation; and those ranks were much larger, much more popular, and much better paid than were the Communists.

There are many more who fit this description and share these similar traits; yet few former Communist informants can match the topic of this work—Paul Crouch. Crouch became a Communist in 1924 as a result of his sympathy for the working class and his sense that capitalism had failed. He spent seventeen years in the Communist Party as an organizer in Virginia, Utah, North Carolina, Alabama, Tennessee, and California. During those years he traveled to Soviet Russia, trained members to infiltrate the military, organized strikes, encouraged union activism, and published countless screeds against American capitalism. He believed to his core in Marxist ideology, followed the party line obediently, and willingly put himself and his family at risk to implement that ideology. Although he had the occasional moment of uncertainty, he believed what the Communist Party put forth and worked hard to realize its agenda with the clear knowledge that he was serving a foreign master.

However, after one too many policy shifts that seemed to have more to do with serving the USSR than affecting the needs of the proletariat, Crouch left the party during World War II. Once out, he remained apart and largely silent for five years. During that time, he, like the other aforementioned Communists, made the decision to turn on the party and testify against his former comrades. This decision did not come easily, but financial incentives, the desire for fame, vengeance, fear, and a true change of heart made his choice easier. Crouch realized he could live well as an informant—indeed much better than he ever had either in the Communist Party or out. He reveled in seeing his name in lights and appreciated that the national fascination and fear of Communism meant an informant was assured of press coverage. He also recognized the opportunity to avenge perceived slights the party had inflicted on him, both while he was a member and after he had left. At the same time, he understood that his fame would protect him from the perceived dangers that came with testifying. Finally, he truly came to view his past behavior as improvident and to believe that his former comrades were destroying America. He therefore determined to testify in part to save the nation. That he sold this testimony only serves to further confirm his new worldview: he had become a capitalist.

In 1949 Crouch joined the ranks of the ex-Communist informants, testifying against the party, and becoming wealthy and famous thanks to his claims that union leader Harry Bridges, atomic scientist Dr. J. Robert Oppenheimer, and comedic actor Charlie Chaplin were Communists. He even asserted that Communists had attempted to infiltrate the Roosevelt White House during the Depression. Eventually, however, he ran out of new, useful information. Fearful of returning to the poverty and obscurity from which informing saved him and committed to the belief that his former ideology truly was evil, he simply made up his subsequent testimony. Like the aforementioned Matusow, he lied. Protected from cross-examination by the rules of congressional inquiry and from a growing chorus of media accusations by the very government he served, Crouch ruined countless lives until his charade was unearthed in 1954. He died the ensuing year, before suffering any legal consequences for his perjury.

Crouch clearly shares traits with his fellow former Communist informants; yet few were as ideologically pure during their days in the party or as ruthlessly effective during their time on the witness stand. That such an individual has remained free from historical inquiry seems astonishing. Indeed, the few historians who reference Crouch use descriptors that seem to demand further inquiry: Sarah Brown labels him "a pathological liar"; Griffin Fariello calls him "one of the more brazen liars in the business"; Ellen Schrecker describes him as "a voluble ex-Communist whose enthusiasm outweighed his veracity"; David Caute dubs him "one of the most brazen and colorful liars in the business"; and according to Alex Lichtenstein, in the list of important ex-Communist informants, Crouch comes in third behind only Whittaker Chambers and Elizabeth Bentley.[8] Yet none of these historians have gone on to examine Paul Crouch in any real detail.

There are a number of possible reasons for the failure to pursue his biography. First, Crouch indeed was a pathological liar. Despite leaving behind a treasure trove of archival material, the reality of that material is problematic. Corroboration is key for the historian; yet for certain moments of Crouch's life there is almost no way to verify his assertions. What to believe and what to reject is thus a significant issue in addressing Crouch's life. To address this problem in as neat a manner as possible, I have presented those moments of Crouch's life for which there is little corroboration exactly as he "remembered" them in his archival record. Nearly every one of those remembrances reemerged in later years as a weapon used by Crouch's enemies to discredit him. Therefore, I revisit his questionable assertions later in the book and present the problems many have with his biography in that manner. This may not be the best method for presenting Crouch's life, but it helps clear one of the hurdles of his biography.

A second issue that may have warned off historians is that Crouch not only lied about himself, he also lied about others—often on the witness stand. Unlike Bentley, Chambers, and countless other former Communist informants, Crouch committed perjury and undermined the judicial and investigative process. Thus, anti-Communists hated him for his role in destroying the Red Scare and the informer system by offering real, obvious evidence of its abuses. They also hated him because his lies called into question the legal judgments of many of those against whom he testified. Communists and fellow travelers, of course, loathed him as a result of his willingness to turn on the CPUSA and align himself with anti-Communists and the political right. They also attacked him for subverting the judicial process—but for a different reason. They were disgusted by his belief that the Communist threat was so great that it had to be destroyed regardless of morality, legality, or the destruction of innocents; such a justification smacked of fascism. As with his personal lies, I have addressed the lies he told about others within the context of the backlash he faced as opponents gathered and cataloged his countless errors in order to appeal court decisions and undermine the entire Red Scare era. Once again, I revisit much of his questionable testimony later in the work.

That political sympathy for Crouch is hard to find is obvious, but so too is personal sympathy. Although he had a difficult life, he is not an easy man for whom to feel sorry. Crouch was an egotist who put himself and his ideology first. Everything else, including his family, placed a distant second. Indeed, reading his unpublished autobiography "Broken Chains" one gets the sense that he lacked any real empathy. He was the center of every action and the cause of every event, and he rarely thought about others or the impact his efforts or perspectives might have.

His callous disregard for the impact his lies had is clear proof of egotism; but so too is how he treated his family. His long-suffering wife Sylvia, who also served the party, frequently was left alone to raise their two children while he worked as a Communist organizer for a small pittance that left them in near constant poverty. Crouch also dragged his family all over the nation with little regard for their social or economic needs. The shy and discreet Sylvia eventually grew fed up with the unending travel and its impact on the children's education and demanded they settle down. Crouch was never one to stop moving, however, and he continued to travel and move the family during his time as an informant. Although Sylvia also served as an informant, and this work dramatically improved the family's finances, Crouch's self-centeredness remained evident. Indeed, when crisis hit he showed a marked lack of sensitivity or compassion. His son Carl struggled throughout his life with hemophilia and ultimately succumbed in 1951. Although Crouch surely suffered for the loss of his only son, his autobiography includes no note of sorrow or remorse. This absence of emotion might also help explain his lack of friends. He had few intimates, other than his wife, and it seems that those who knew him best kept the rather prickly and self-centered Crouch at arm's length. This is a rather sad assessment of the man, but serves yet again to explain why he has remained unexamined.

Despite these biographical issues, Crouch's life is a useful historical tool and serves as a perfect example of the aforementioned dangers of ideological certitude. As a Communist he viewed capitalists as evil and un-American and worked to destroy the system for the betterment of the working class. Although he frequently saw evidence that the CPUSA was not all that it seemed to be, and frequently hurt those it promised to help, Crouch the Communist ideologue ignored those issues and saw only the positive side of his ideology. After his transformation into an anti-Communist he acted much the same. He came to imbue his new belief system with near religious powers to save the nation from the Communist menace and did everything he could, including lie, to help bring forth that salvation. As both a Communist and an anti-Communist, therefore, Crouch viewed *them* as evil, believed *they* were leading the nation to a quickly approaching ruin, and determined that he had the obligation to do anything to stop *them*.

Crouch's life provides insights into larger issues as well. From him we can better appreciate what attracted many Americans to Communism in the 1920s and 1930s. His experiences also offer insight into the Communist Party's actual agenda and the means by which it sought to implement that agenda. The fact that the agenda often was guided from afar and served the needs of the Soviet Union also becomes apparent, as do the machinations of internal party politics. Of course, his decision to leave the party offers a prime example of what drove many from the Communist movement, while the struggles he faced after leaving demonstrate the lingering consequences of Communist Party membership as well as the struggles many Americans faced in the immediate aftermath of World War II. Finally, Crouch's time as an anti-Communist provides a fascinating and unique view of the Red Scare and McCarthy era. Such a view helps explain why former Communists joined the assault on their former comrades, how the government used those informants, and why the American public willingly believed the testimony of people they would have once considered the enemy.

Crouch thus offers some important perspectives on American history. Despite such a historically significant life, however, to dub one individual, especially one few people recognize, as "the most dangerous man in America" is rather provocative. History is littered with "dangerous" men, and the very essence of the label is pejorative and open to debate. So let us end the debate immediately. Is Paul Crouch truly "the most dangerous man in America"? Literally, he is not. Far more powerful and dangerous men have had far greater an influence on American history. But figuratively, the answer is yes. Crouch's life is a symbolic representation of the dangers that arise when ideologues come to dominate the political scene, when paranoia becomes widespread, and when fear leads to a belief that the enemy must be destroyed by any means necessary. Crouch was part of such a development and helped engender it from two divergent ideological perspectives. We can learn much from him, and it is to that instructive life that we now turn.

1 CHILDHOOD AND YOUTH, 1903–1924

Wilkes County is a quiet community in northwestern North Carolina. Located between the Blue Ridge and Brushy mountains, and watered by the Yadkin River, it has maintained a low profile throughout its history despite being named after British radical John Wilkes. Formed in 1778, and populated by those seeking the religious or political freedom that its relative distance from colonial centers of power provided, the county has since enjoyed but few flirtations with history. It provided its fair share of soldiers to the Revolutionary War (most notably for the Battle of King's Mountain), hosted a young Daniel Boone, became the home of Chang and Eng Bunker (the famous Siamese Twins), and was the birthplace of long-time West Virginia Senator James Byrd and NASCAR legends Junior Johnson and Benny Parsons. As noteworthy as all of these individuals are, there is one person whose historical impact on the nation far exceeds that of anyone else from Wilkes County. His name is Paul Crouch.

Paul Michael Crouch was born on June 24, 1903, in Moravian Falls, North Carolina, which is located in the southern part of Wilkes County. He was the first child from the union of Isaac Milas Crouch, a Baptist minister and Civil War veteran, and Emma Brewer. Isaac was born on January 15, 1847, one of twelve children raised by Eliphalet and Alicia Crouch. He joined the Confederate Army at the age of eighteen, in January 1865, but had little interest or enthusiasm for the Confederate cause, viewing the conflict as needless, and was pleased to return to Wilkes County without seeing combat. In 1872 he married Ann Caroline Laws who gave Isaac three sons, John, Harrison, and William, and five daughters, Dora, Rosa, Mattie Iona, Lula, and Effie. Ann died on September 22, 1897, at the age of forty-two, leaving Isaac alone to manage the sizeable household. He did so briefly but in 1899 married thirty-one year old Emma Brewer, whose descendants allegedly included a Spanish uncle who was a member of Tennessean William Walker's expedition to Nicaragua in 1855. She gave birth to Paul four years later.[1]

By the time Paul was born, his half-brother John already had achieved some fame as the author of *Historical Sketches of Wilkes County*. The book, published in 1902, includes a history of the county as well as numerous biographical sketches of notable inhabitants. Other relatives made names for themselves in the publishing field as well. R. Don Laws, a relative of Isaac's first wife Ann, published *Yellow Jacket*, which according to historian Glenda Gilmore attracted over 200,000 subscribers and was a "Republican paper filled with anti-Catholic diatribes, pro–Ku Klux Klan editorials, and sneers at 'nigger equality.'" James Larkin Pearson—Crouch's neighbor, distant relative, and future North Carolina Poet Laureate—put out a Socialist paper called *The Fool-Killer* as a form of rebuttal. It offered "'Idiotorials,' sympathy for the theory of evolutionism, scorn for religious hypocrisy, and hard-hitting jabs at capitalism."[2]

Surrounded by this literary heritage, Crouch grew into an inquisitive young boy. Despite that, he lacked a formal education until the age of eleven when he enrolled in elementary school after the family settled in Dockery, North Carolina, in the northern part of Wilkes County some ten miles west of Wilkesboro. Crouch quickly blossomed in school. He was influenced toward the plight of African Americans after reading *Uncle Tom's Cabin* and developed a hero worship for Spartacus. As the son of a Baptist preacher, he also read the Bible, attended weekly church services, and accepted Baptist theology. It was religion, however, that also led Crouch to his first bit of rebellion. As a teenager he broke from the Baptist Church after he asked why certain things were sins and other were not, and neither his father nor fellow church members could provide an adequate explanation.[3]

Crouch's time in Dockery was thus highly formative. It also was enjoyable. As he described it years later: "Commercialism had not destroyed the instinctive and genuine hospitality of the mountain people."[4] Even the onset of World War I did little to trouble this idyllic existence, although the enlistment of his half-brother John began to impress on the teenaged Paul that there was a wider world beyond Wilkes County. By 1918 and the end of the war this impression grew, as new roads and the appearance of tourists brought new people and ideas into the area. The newly created infrastructure and influx of visitors also stole the tranquility of the county. Accordingly stuck, like many Americans at the time, between the pull of modernity and the loss of some idyllic past, Crouch desired to escape. Still too young to do so on his own, a fifteen-year-old Paul was ecstatic when Isaac announced plans to move the family to Vermont.[5]

Isaac believed Paul had an intellectual gift that needed to be nurtured and decided to move the family north to take advantage of better schools. The move proved a failure almost from the start. A railroad strike prevented the family from completing the journey, and they abandoned their plans for Vermont and settled instead in Dover, Delaware. Crouch enrolled in school and settled into tenth grade. Of more interest to Crouch than schooling, however, was his first contact with immigrants and the political ideologies they brought with them.[6]

This was not the best of times in American history to be an immigrant or a believer in a radical political ideology. The economic convulsion after World War I pushed nearly four million workers to the picket lines in 1919 alone, and from longshoremen in Seattle to steelworkers in the Midwest to police officers in Boston, it seemed no one was immune to the strike wave. While these strikes achieved little of economic value, they did inflame public passions. Those passions were inflamed even further as politicians and businessmen, looking for an easy and noneconomic explanation for the labor unrest, pinned the blame on "Bolsheviks." Good Americans would not behave this way, the argument went, and the only explanation was that the evil that had infected Russia two years earlier with the October Revolution had made its way to the United States. This assessment gained greater credence in September 1919 when disenchanted members of various radical groups met in Chicago and formed what would become the Communist Party of the United States (CPUSA).

That September meeting of American radicals quickly dissolved into sectarian skirmishing and the creation of two Communist political organizations. Since organized Communism was far from a reality, it was up to other groups to provide evidence for the supposed Bolshevik threat. That evidence first erupted in April and June 1919 when anarchists sent out a series of mail bombs to the likes of J. P. Morgan, John D. Rockefeller, and Attorney General A. Mitchell Palmer. The bombs did little damage, although the wife and housekeeper of U.S. Senator Thomas Hardwick of Georgia were injured by one, and anarchist Carlo Valdinoci died when the bomb he personally delivered to A. Mitchell Palmer's house exploded in his face.

Although the bombs did no major damage, the threat was real, and the fear they instilled was only increased when those responsible for the bombs sent out a message: "War, Class war, and you were the first to wage it under the cover of the powerful institutions you call order, in the darkness of your laws. There will have to be bloodshed; we will not dodge; there will have to be murder: we will kill, because it is necessary; there will have to be destruction; we will destroy to rid the world of your tyrannical institutions."[7] Determined to prevent this violence, in December 1919 and January 1920, Attorney General Palmer authorized massive nationwide raids on radicals and radical groups. Police and federal agents arrested over 3,000 individuals in what became known as the Palmer Raids. The only ones to suffer any lasting punishment, however, were 556 people who were deported. Mostly members of the Union of Russian Workers, the group also included infamous anarchists Emma Goldman and Alexander Berkman, who had tried to kill Henry Clay Frick during the Homestead Steel Strike in 1892.

The Red Scare, as this wave of fear was called, continued despite the relative failure of the Palmer Raids; the dread of radical and foreign groups thus lingered. In November 1919 members of the Industrial Workers of the World (IWW or the Wobblies) were attacked and murdered in Centralia, Washington, and in 1920 anarchists Nicola Sacco and Bartolomeo Vanzetti faced a kangaroo court for their alleged roles in a murder and robbery in Braintree, Massachusetts. As a sign of the times, the killers of the Wobblies escaped justice while Sacco and Vanzetti were executed.

It was into this politicized and polarized world that Crouch was first exposed to the realities of radical politics. Although intrigued by socialism, Crouch initially opposed the use of violence implicit in the ideology taught him by the immigrants with whom he met. They explained to the impressionable teen, however, that the institutionalized violence American workers and radicals faced, as evidenced by the crushed strikes and Red Scare, meant that violence might indeed be necessary to save the working class. Crouch seemingly bought into this assessment and ultimately described his political education in Dover thus: "Those events probably did more than anything else to bring me closer to the Communist point of view on the question of revolutionary struggle for power."[8]

Crouch's political education took a detour in 1921 when Isaac, who had grown to loathe the cold weather, put aside the object of educating young Paul, purchased a home in Florida, and led the family south to warmer climes. When they reached their new Florida home, however, they found it burned to the ground from a recent fire. They rented a nearby house for a short time, and Crouch's introduction into the ways of the wider world continued. This time the education had to do with race. Crouch was marginally aware of racism while growing up in North Carolina, but with few African American neighbors he had little understanding of the depths of the American racial dilemma. That understanding deepened dramatically when he discovered a "segregated newspaper" in Florida with the byline "Whites Only—Niggers Read and Run."[9]

Race was not the only factor that affected Crouch's development in Florida, so too did the books he read. By his teenage years Crouch already was reading various works by Karl Marx and Friedrich Engels, as well as tracts by Ludwig Feuerbach and August Bebel. His favorite work was Edward Bellamy's socialist classic *Looking Backward*, with its utopian vision of the future. Crouch adored the book, and in February 1921 he set out to become a writer. The result was a short story entitled "The Enchanted Mountain." The story tells of Thomas Cameron who longs for adventure and so takes a walk in the woods. He soon discovers gold dust covering the path along which he walks. He follows it deep into the forest although parrots along the way chirp: "Not all that shines is gold!" Cameron considers going back, but the lure of gold proves too strong and he continues on. The path eventually leads him to a mountain apparently made entirely of gold except for a red spire on top. He learns later that the spire possesses the unique ability to reverse a person's sense of direction. Unaware, and mesmerized by the gold, he continues forward. As he approaches the mountain, however, it turns from gold to black. Terrified, he tries to run away, but the spire had reversed his sense of direction and instead he runs ever closer, eventually entering the mountain through a cave. Unaware of the changed senses, he tries over and over to escape, only to venture ever deeper into the mountain. Cameron eventually enters a well-lit hall deep in the cave, whose walls are covered with hideous pictures. As he examines the pictures he falls through a trap door that drops him into another hall—this one full of skeletons and spiders and lighted only by the green eyes of dragons.

Although terrified, Cameron stops to think about his predicament and soon realizes that he always was going in the wrong direction. He thus decides to try going in the direction opposite from which he really wants to go. It works, and he slowly makes his way out of the hall. As Cameron retreats he realizes he cannot find the trap door through which he fell and, while contemplating his next move, he discovers a young woman with whom he immediately falls in love. She informs him that she had been a magic student until she was captured by the dragons. She has used her skills to keep them from eating her, but they keep a close eye on her, preventing her escape. She also tells him that she has the power to turn people into spiders but does not have the power to figure out the direction problems. Since Cameron already has solved that mystery, he explains it to her. She then changes both of them into spiders and they escape through cracks in the mountain. When they emerge, she changes them back into people and they flee. The two marry and live together happily, if modestly, remembering that "all that shines is not gold."[10]

While a rather prosaic effort, the story does contain some interesting elements. Crouch's developing worldview and perspective clearly are evident. The world, he perceived, was not always what it seemed. Dangers lurked everywhere, evil was a constant threat, and buried far from the beauty of the outside world were untold horrors and misery. He also made it clear that people could be tricked into thinking they were acting properly (or heading in the right direction) when actually they were doing the exact opposite. This made the world that much more dangerous as the difference between right and wrong proved less distinct than one might hope. The criticism of greed also is obvious, as what leads Cameron to the haunted mountain in the first place is his fascination with the gold. The couple's future happiness, by contrast, comes when they determine to eschew the glitter. Coming from a future Communist, this work by a seventeen year old is rather prescient.

Related elements also strike a chord. The first is the power of the mind. Cameron realizes the reversed sense of direction after stopping for a moment to think about his predicament. Likewise, the girl, oddly unnamed, keeps away the dragons thanks to her magic training. Despite the power of the mind, what ultimately leads them to freedom is magic. While the intellect proved useful, it was the girl's ability to turn them into spiders that allowed them to escape. It is as if Crouch already was looking for something mystical to solve the world's problems; possibly a philosophy like Communism that not only claimed to explain all of history but also offered a magical cure and a utopian future that was almost too good to believe.

Crouch's development in Florida consequently included not only a growing sense of the nation's inequalities but also a growing fascination with the written word. Not for the last time would he use this fascination, and his imagination, to create a little fiction.

Despite this intellectual development, by late 1921 the family realized Florida had little to offer and gave up its great adventure to return to North Carolina. Crouch, by then eighteen, intended to go to school to become a teacher. Financial constraints, however, forced him to take work at the Arista Cotton Textile Mill in Winston-Salem. There he received his first experience as a member of the proletariat and came to appreciate more fully the underlying causes of the radicalism about which he had learned in Delaware. Crouch and his fellow "lint heads" worked six, ten-hour days per week for twelve dollars, of which five went to rent. He found the work hard and the low pay frustrating but enjoyed his fellow employees. Determined to help his coworkers and, undoubtedly, himself, Crouch made his first effort at union organizing. While the low pay and long days were hard enough, the impetus for his effort was the "stretch out," by which Crouch and his fellow workers were expected to do additional work without an increase in pay. Crouch achieved little as an organizer, however, as the workers feared his radical talk and preferred bad jobs to being unemployed. He was similarly unsuccessful as a worker. Within a year of taking the job at Arista he developed an abscess on his leg that forced him to quit.[11]

This would not be the last time health issues would plague his employment record, but it may have been one of his worst ailments as the wound took a year to heal. When finally healthy, Crouch returned to the labor market hoping to avoid the dangers of mill work; he thus sought out new avenues for employment. He first took a secretarial job at Brown and Williamson Tobacco, but that job also proved more taxing than he preferred. Deciding to put his intellect and literary skills to use, in March 1923, he took work at *Pearson's Paper* of Boomer, North Carolina. Edited by James Larkin Pearson, the paper, formerly known as *The Fool-Killer*, offered Crouch his first real journalistic opportunity.[12]

As associate editor, Crouch helped Pearson run the paper but also found time to write several articles. In March he published "A Preachment on Prophecy," in which he argued that despite the magnificent advances mankind had made over the previous several decades, life had not become any easier.

> Look at it from any way you please—from any angle you please—and it is an unusual time. From the angle of scientific progress it looks like the world is making rapid strides ahead. And it is. Men have made great discoveries and developed great inventions. And these things have piled in on top of each other so fast that we can hardly keep track of them. Machinery has taken place of hand labor and production has been speeded up. Thus the necessity for actual human labor has been reduced—theoretically, at least. It OUGHT to follow as a natural result that the business of living would get easier from year to year. It OUGHT to follow that the people would have time to develop their minds and enjoy life as never before. But—what do we see? The awful reality is that the business of living gets harder and harder for the masses. . . . A few get the benefit and live easy, but the masses of the common people feel the pinch more than ever.[13]

The only possible outcomes of the situation, he contended, were for man to destroy the system and start anew or for the system to destroy itself and mankind in the process. Clearly the revolutionary lessons he had picked up on the family's travels inspired the diatribe, but Crouch also was speaking to the growing masses who had come to fear that industrial development and modernization were not creating the utopia industrialists had promised.

In May 1923 he authored an article entitled "The Goose-Step," in which he reviewed Upton Sinclair's book by the same title. Crouch raved about Sinclair's assault on how business had taken over university life. More important, he came out in full support of a League of Youth in which young Americans, and indeed all who were "young and unprejudiced in mind," would organize to "break down the barriers of autocracy, militarism and ignorance which are retarding the progress of the world."[14] Clearly the older generation had failed, and it was time to give the younger one a chance. Although less radical than the previous essay, this one was clearly a product of the time and shows some sympathy for the Lost Generation's critique of a world gone mad.

A month later Crouch published a third article entitled "Thoughts from Here and There," in which he once again examined the troubles of the age. He argued that capitalism was the cause of the world's problems but that the working class remained too weak and divided to implement socialism. As such, he wrote, "I prefer to think that the present troubles of the world are going to destroy the corrupt features of our modern life and thought, and pave the way to a GOLDEN AGE where the selfish nature of man will be eliminated by the working of an unseen spiritual force. Then, in an earthly paradise, the UNIVERSAL BROTHERHOOD OF MAN will become a reality and not a dream."[15] It seems Crouch no longer believed man had the capacity to save the world. Things had gone too far; it was time to let the world destroy itself and start over.

Crouch continued the article by invoking Jean-Jacques Rousseau to explain why this course of events was acceptable. Arguing that civilization brought no real benefits to mankind, Crouch asserted that the end of modern society and the requisite starting over would not be that bad: "Primitive man," he wrote, lived a life free from modern worries. While he admitted that civilization had provided man with various forms of entertainment, he asserted that the only ones who benefited were the elite. The average wage-slave had little time or money to enjoy such benefits and lived a life far worse than the primitive. All the more reason to let this world end—we could return to a time when life was simpler and no man was exempt from happiness.[16]

In dozens of similar essays, Crouch attacked organized capitalism and religion while supporting vegetarianism, Esperanto (which he was learning to speak), and various other New Age concepts.[17] Indeed, it seems that Crouch still looked to save the world through that combination of intellect and magic he wrote about in "The Enchanted Mountain." While the quality of his writing and the content of his articles remained immature, the work at *Pearson's Paper* demonstrates a young man honing his journalistic voice.

For some that voice showed real potential, and in late 1923 he accepted a new job at the *Sentinel* of Statesville, North Carolina. Work at this newspaper offered Crouch a great opportunity for intellectual and political musings as a lazy editor allowed him to do most of the work. He wrote an editorial about the first issue of the Communist newspaper the *Daily Worker*, as well as a memorial on Lenin's death, and generally moved the paper to the political left. For a time the editor failed to notice the new course of his paper, but once alarmed to such radicalism he took back control of the editorial page and fired Crouch.[18] By early 1924 Crouch again was unemployed and his journalistic career was on hold.

Disenchanted, out of work, and without a clear career path, Crouch pondered his future. He then remembered the opportunities and experiences his half-brother John had enjoyed during World War I and decided to make the military his vocation. He enlisted in the U.S. Army in 1924. Sworn in, in April, Private Crouch, serial number 6346392, did his basic training at Fort Bragg, North Carolina, and received additional instruction at Fort Slocum, New York. He saw himself as a barnstorming pilot and signed up to serve in the Army Air Corps. Prior to training, however, he contracted the mumps and was quarantined for three weeks. During that time he read magazine articles about Hawaiian and Polynesian life and decided to serve in the Pacific. He subsequently rescinded his application for the Air Corps and requested any job that would get him stationed in Hawaii. Perceiving his literary background as useful, the military granted his request and transferred him to Hawaii to serve as publicity agent for Division G-2, Military Intelligence of the United States Army.[19] The transfer marked the beginning of Crouch's ideological career, but it was not the career he had envisioned.

Crouch's childhood and early adulthood clearly give some clues to his future development. He was affected by the plight of others and was determined to improve the world. Open to radical ideas and philosophies, he believed that there was a better world out there, even if it meant destroying the current one. At the same time, there is a clear sense that there were mystical forces in the world that, if properly understood and embraced, could save mankind. Such are the beliefs of the ideologue: that there is something wrong with the world, that it needs to be totally remade if not destroyed, and that there is a power, or an idea, that has the ability to save humanity. Crouch was on the path to becoming an ideologue, but he had yet to find the specific ideology to which he would attach himself. Oddly, it was in the military that he would find it and embark on the first part of his ideological journey.

2 THE HAWAIIAN COMMUNIST LEAGUE, 1924–1927

Paul Crouch turned twenty-one in 1924 but had yet to find his calling. Failed efforts as a textile worker and journalist left him unfulfilled, rudderless, and uncertain of his place in the world. The military seemed a sound choice for such an individual, and indeed Crouch would find both his calling and his ideological center while serving in the U.S. Army. Shockingly, that calling and center was Communism. Although he would suffer for this decision, his time in Hawaii launched him into a seventeen-year career as a Communist organizer. It also turned him into an ideologue.

The Hawaii to which Crouch was heading had a tortured history with the United States. The Reciprocity Treaty of 1875 recognized Hawaii as a sovereign nation but ceded Pearl Harbor to the United States. In 1887 the treaty was expanded and the United States received the right to build a permanent naval base at Pearl Harbor, much to the chagrin of many native Hawaiians. After the overthrow of Queen Liliuokalani in 1893 and the creation of a republic in 1894, there was a growing demand in America for annexation. That finally came in 1898 during the Spanish American War when the islands became American territory. American businessmen took advantage of the new territorial status to purchase vast tracts of land and establish sugar and pineapple plantations. Largely worked by Japanese, Chinese, and Filipino immigrants, the plantations made vast sums for their owners and shareholders, but low wages and long hours provided little benefit to the workers. To help pacify the workforce, but also to defend the Pacific from the growing power of Japan, the U.S. military spent millions outfitting Pearl Harbor and building additional barracks and installations throughout the islands. The Schofield Barracks, constructed in 1909, were the largest army post of the era.

It was to this land of wealth, poverty, and military might that Crouch sailed in 1924, full of excitement and expectation. During the voyage that anticipation only increased when he met a fellow soldier named Fred Creque, who also had more than a passing interest in Esperanto and radical politics. The two became fast friends and spent much of the voyage in deep conversation, only to depart for different parts of the military's large base in Hawaii.

Crouch's job in the Military Intelligence Corps was rather easy and consisted mainly of rounding up news reports from throughout the islands. It also gained him extra food rations and made him exempt from retreat and reveille. Unfortunately, the extra time those benefits afforded got him into trouble. The first part of his trouble resulted from his political statements. Early in his enlistment several soldiers claimed Crouch was a Communist who had attempted to convert them to the ideology. They reported their complaints to a Lieutenant Colonel Murphy, who brought in Crouch for questioning. Crouch claimed Murphy was a devout Catholic who feared all things radical and despite a complete lack of political acuity determined Crouch indeed was a Communist. He was confined to his quarters and fully expected to be discharged. By this point, his desire to make the military his career had waned and the thought of being sent home was appealing. Much to his surprise, however, he was not discharged but rather reassigned on the island. The military determined he was a good soldier who simply needed to keep his political views to himself. He was thus placed with the 21st infantry as the regimental supply clerk.[1]

This transfer led to Crouch's second set of troubles—his associations. The transfer reunited him with Fred Creque, and the two, along with other friends, resumed their political discussions. One of this group was Walter Trumbull, also known as "Bull the Bolshevik." Trumbull was a native of Boston, a graduate of MIT, stood about 5 feet 6 inches tall with a stocky body and black hair, and once received a six month suspended sentence for promoting and inciting sabotage. Another member of the group was Roderick Nadeau who shared the other member's radicalism. The small group, with Crouch, Creque, Trumbull, and Nadeau as the leaders, formed an Esperanto club they dubbed La Homaro, meaning "the humanity," and under its guise talked politics. Although they often held meetings while hiking in nearby mountains, they just as often met on base, and as a result the club soon became well known amongst the soldiers of the 21st. By 1925 nearly seventy-five men had joined this loose association of army radicals.[2]

The third problem Crouch faced was the rise of local issues that caught the attention of La Homaro. On April 1, 1924, Filipino sugar plantation workers on the island of Oahu walked out on strike. Under the leadership of Pablo Manlapit, the strike quickly spread to other islands and dragged on for months. While the workers demanded better wages and working conditions, author John Reinecke contends the "strike should be viewed as a social protest more than as a 'pork chop' economic struggle" with calls for more equitable treatment, an end to racism, and an appreciation of Filipino culture being as important as calls for improved wages and conditions. The plantation owners cared little why the workers walked out, only that they did not damage the crops. They subsequently requested aid, and the police soon arrived to protect the sugar harvest. Their presence, however, led to violence. On September 9 the "Battle of Hanapepe" erupted leaving four police officers and sixteen Filipino strikers dead. During the next two days police arrested 130 Filipinos, more than 100 of whom would serve time in prison for their roles in the battle, and searched the homes of countless others to round up weapons. Police and National Guardsmen remained in the vicinity to maintain peace until the end of the month when the strike collapsed and the workers returned to the fields as impoverished and exploited as ever.[3] The members of La Homaro were well aware of the strike and the plight of the Filipino workers. Believing they were witnessing the greed and racism of American capitalism firsthand, these likeminded soldiers discussed the strike and their support of it.

Not all of those attracted to the group, however, were as selflessly concerned about the plight of others. Many were more concerned with their own misery as soldiers. This misery manifested itself in a second contemporary event, one that occurred much closer to the soldiers' home. On February 8, 1925, while patrolling on guard duty, U.S. Army Private Franklin Van Gelder shot and killed fellow soldier Corporal Willard D. Crumback. Van Gelder was charged with murder and faced a court-martial that became the focus of the barracks' attention. The trial opened on March 23, with the prosecution claiming Van Gelder planned the murder as a means of getting off the islands. Witnesses testified that prior to the shooting Van Gelder said he "wanted to get out [of Hawaii] even if he killed somebody" and asserted that he had asked what happened to a sentry who killed a man while on duty. Others reported that the night of the shooting he said, "I have a hunch I'm going to use my gun tonight. Dead men tell no tales. If anything happens, say nothing."[4]

Van Gelder claimed he shot because Crumback refused to halt and had threatened him. The pathologist, however, testified that two of the bullets hit Crumback in the back and followed an upward trajectory. The wounds were not consistent with a victim standing erect but rather suggested Crumback either was crawling on the ground or running away, bent over as he fled. Presented with such damning testimony, the court-martial quickly rendered a verdict of guilty of willful and premeditated murder and sentenced Van Gelder to a dishonorable discharge and life in prison with hard labor.[5] Many of the soldiers in La Homaro sympathized with Van Gelder's desire to get off the islands. They believed army discipline was more severe in Hawaii than on the mainland and rued their enlistment.

The combination of native strife and military concerns thus encouraged the group, which had remained relatively discreet and discussion oriented, to act on its beliefs. In mid-February 1925 Crouch, Trumbull, and Nadeau wrote letters to local newspapers in support of the Filipino strikers and in defense of Communist ideology. On February 15 the *Honolulu Advertiser* published a letter to the editor by Crouch, in which he attacked the paper for an editorial it had run three days earlier. The article had argued that proof of Communism's failure was that famed anarchist Emma Goldman had "begged for the privilege of getting back on capitalistic soil" after her exile to Russia in 1920, and that she was "in England now, cured forever of bolshevism." Crouch explained that Goldman, as an anarchist, was no real friend of the Soviets. He further defended Communism by arguing that it was a system that precluded idleness, allowed people to choose their labor, and prevented the accumulation of great wealth by individuals that was accompanied by the impoverishment of millions. He concluded his essay by arguing that the Soviets were peace loving because "there is no possibility of the government going mad with slaughter since the government is the people (the WORKING people) and their wishes are carried out."[6] Crouch's letter included his military affiliation but made no mention of La Homaro.

The next day the *Advertiser* carried yet another letter from Crouch entitled "A Bolshevik Defends his Views." In this letter Crouch focused first on the strike. He attacked the paper for siding with the landowners who produced no wealth yet lived well by exploiting their workers. Crouch rejected such a world and argued that "the workers have a much better right to the ownership of the land upon which they work than the parasites who live on the sufferings of other men." He then called for the creation of a Communist society that "gives honor ONLY to those who contribute something to the world for the benefit of ALL." After a brief synopsis of Communist ideology and an assertion that Russia had improved dramatically under Soviet rule, he concluded his diatribe with a challenge: "Print this if you dare. If you don't the writer and many others will be forced to believe you are afraid of the truth."[7]

The *Honolulu Advertiser* was not "afraid of the truth," as it printed the letter, nor did it let Crouch's statements go unanswered. On February 18 the paper printed a letter from an unnamed soldier who eviscerated Crouch and other members of La Homaro who had written letters, for taking food, money, and training from the United States military at the same time they were attacking it. He called their statements "a breach of oath and of allegiance, detrimental to military discipline, [and] an insult to the soldiers of America and to our flag." He suggested they be court-martialed "and sent Emma Goldman's way."[8]

Individual soldiers were not the only ones upset by the letters. Military authorities quickly determined to infiltrate and break up the group and assigned Corporal Eugene Fisher the task. Crouch and Trumbull later claimed that Fisher's spying was so obvious they refused to allow him to participate, although Creque asserted that Fisher indeed was a member and that he, not Crouch or Trumbull, was the only one to express suspicion. Whoever was suspicious, Fisher's presence did not diminish the club's enthusiasm. Instead, under the slogan "Hawaii for Hawaiian Workers—The World for Communism," Crouch, Trumbull, and the others threw off the cover of La Homaro and announced the existence of the Hawaiian Communist League. The newly public organization quickly penned a letter to the Communist International (Comintern), the organization that sought to unify the various national Communist parties in the global struggle against capitalism, and requested admission and recognition as an official organization within the international Communist movement. The letter read:

> Executive Committee
> Communist International
> Moscow
> Union of Soviet Socialist Republics
>
> Comrades:
>
> Greetings to the Communist International from the class conscious workers and soldiers of Hawaii.
>
> Knowing that unity is essential for the success of world revolution, the class conscious workers and soldiers of the Hawaiian Islands have organized themselves into the Hawaiian Communist League.
>
> The Hawaiian Communist League wishes to take its place in the world movement for revolutionary Communism and to enable us to co-operate with our comrades in other lands in the fight against capitalism, we desire to affiliate with the Third International [the Comintern].
>
> The Hawaiian Communist League accepts the principles and regulations of the Communist International without reservation and will co-operate to the full extent of its ability in the movement to free the workers of the world from the chains of capitalism.
>
> The members of the Hawaiian Communist League have been very active in a publicity movement for the purpose of presenting the facts about Russia to the Hawaiian proletariat for bringing all class conscious workers into a common movement. Of course this is meeting with opposition from the capitalistic forces and the immediate future promises some very important developments.
>
> The condition of the workers in Hawaii is much worse than in America and the European countries and practically all the land is in large plantations which employ Japanese and Filipino labor. Strikes are very frequent and there is good field propaganda.
>
> The Hawaiian proletariat desires to take its place with the revolutionary parties of the Communist International.

All mail for the Hawaiian Communist League should be sent to the secretary, Roderick P. Nadeau, 21st Infantry Band, Schofield Barracks, Hawaii.

Hawaiian Communist League
The Executive Committee,
Walter M. Trumbull, Roderick P. Nadeau, and Paul Crouch.[9]

The letter never made it to the Comintern, however, as military intelligence, which clearly knew more about the group than members believed, seized it. Based on the letter, the previous letters to the newspaper, and any information provided by Fisher, on February 17, 1925, military authorities rounded up league members. Most were discharged for the good of the military, although a few retained their positions or were reassigned pending discipline. Crouch and Trumbull, however, were singled out as the ringleaders and each faced court-martial proceedings. Crouch was charged with failing to obtain a charter for a secret society and violating the 96th Article of War by convincing others to join an illegal organization and advocating the violent overthrow of the federal government. The specific charges read: "First—Organizing a secret society having for its object revolutionary communism in violation of Section 4214, revised laws of Hawaii, 1915; Second—Advising and persuading another soldier to join said secret society; Third—Writing a letter to the Third International, Moscow, Russia, applying for affiliation by secret society and stating that the society believed in revolutionary communism and in the principles and regulations of the Third International; Fourth—Stating in the presence of other soldiers that he favored the overthrow of our Government by revolutionary means if necessary."[10] Trumbull faced the same charges on counts one, two, and three, but the fourth count was replaced by the charge that he had violated the 62nd Article of War, which prohibited the use of disrespectful language against the United State and its flag. According to the court, Trumbull once said, "The president may be all right as an individual, but as an institution he is a disgrace to the whole god damned country."[11] He was further accused of saying, "I'm sick and disgusted with the whole damned country, everything and everybody in it. I wish I could get where I would never hear the name of the United States again. Flag and country are a disgrace to humanity."[12]

Despite the fact that the Hawaiian Communist League had yet officially to join the international movement, the Workers (Communist) Party of America's newspaper *Daily Worker* made the arrest headline news. Claiming the U.S. military was using Hawaii as a staging ground for a future war, the paper alleged that Crouch and Trumbull were imprisoned merely for "correcting misstatements about Soviet Russia" in an effort to prevent that war. The paper further alleged that the two were confined illegally and held incommunicado, were "being treated abominably," and faced death sentences merely because of their political persuasion. It also defended Crouch and Trumbull's innocence and alleged that Fisher had never been admitted to the group and his testimony would therefore be "either manufactured or stolen." Worse still, the paper accused the military of deliberately trying to "suppress all publicity with regard to the case" because it understood the American working class would not stand for such outrages.[13]

Young Worker, the organ of the Young Communist League (YCL), joined the fray when it alleged that the two were being used by the military "to scare the class conscious soldiers." The paper asserted that Crouch and Trumbull's arrest and brutal treatment was an "attempt to impress upon soldiers the fact that they have 'no political rights' and that they should be nothing but cannon-fodder in times of peace as well as war." The paper argued that the military was afraid class-conscious soldiers like Crouch and Trumbull would educate other soldiers about the real nature of war and capitalism and would thereby convince them to join with the proletariat against the warmongering bourgeoisie. Fortunately, the paper concluded, the very effort to quiet Crouch and Trumbull served as its own lesson.[14]

The *Honolulu Advertiser* saw the case differently and argued that the reason Crouch and Trumbull were arrested was because the real goal of the Hawaii Communist League was "the overthrow of the government by revolutionary means."[15] They were not accused of holding certain beliefs, the paper asserted, but rather of seeking to act on those beliefs in violation of state, federal, military, and civilian law.

In reality, since 1920 American Communists, following the lead of the Comintern, had forsaken the goal of the immediate overthrow of the government. The Second Period, as the era from 1920 to 1928 would be known, foresaw an extended period of capitalist stabilization. As such, Communist parties worldwide were expected to work on party building rather than fomenting revolution. The *Advertiser* clearly was not aware, or interested, in that development, and like many Americans of the era, viewed Communists as a true national menace and believed Crouch and Trumbull got exactly what they deserved.

As the journalistic war raged, the case against the two continued apace. After a brief trial and deliberations that lasted less than half an hour, the court-martial convicted both men on all counts. The court found Crouch guilty of violating Hawaiian state law (count one) for "having organized a secret association without having first procured a license." The court also convicted him of violating the 96th Article of War (counts two, three, and four) by "having advised Corporal Eugene M. Fisher to become a member of the Hawaiian Communist League; of having written a letter through the U.S. mail to the Third International at Russia; [and] of having said orally and in the presence of other soldiers that 'a majority of common people will be hard to swing into the red column.'"[16] The court determined that Trumbull had violated state law and the 96th Article of War for similar reasons and that he violated the 62nd Article by speaking ill of the president. On April 4 the court sentenced Crouch to forty years' hard labor and Trumbull to twenty-six years' hard labor.

Trumbull, who testified on behalf of Crouch at the court-martial, later claimed that Crouch took the harsh sentence in stride. He maintained that after he testified, the hearing continued briefly and then the jury dismissed Crouch so it could deliberate.

> He came out of the court room. He says, "Well, Trumbull, they are going to deliberate on the case now and find out whether I am guilty or not and how much I get. They have been hearing this thing for six days now so I guess it will take quite a while to decide." Inside of five minutes they called Paul Crouch back into the court room and handed him his sentence, and they tell me he got a fair trial. The evidence of six days was decided in inside of five minutes. . . . He came out of the court room a second time after they had handed him his sentence and he had a grin on his face from ear to ear. I thought he had been acquitted. I said, "well, Paul, how did you get out?" "Oh, I only got 40 years."[17]

While Trumbull's version smacks more of braggadocio than reality, the men clearly faced an unfriendly court.

However the hearing actually transpired, the court-martial justified the harsh sentences by claiming that both men "were concerned in plotting before coming to the islands" and had joined the military for the sole purpose "of fomenting revolution, both in the garrison and among the civil population of Honolulu."[18] The *New York Times* offered additional justification for the harsh sentences when it noted that while the presence of agitators in the military was rare, their threat was real. The paper explained that military authorities believed the danger was especially high in Hawaii since it was a bastion of American defenses in the Pacific. Communist infiltration in Hawaii therefore threatened the entire nation. The paper also noted that recent military maneuvers on the islands increased the potential danger and implied that Crouch and Trumbull were spies. Although there was no evidence of such action, the paper explained that "the almost unprecedented sentences imposed were viewed here as indicating that there was more behind the case of the two men than an ordinary plot of malcontents."[19]

Although journalists and pundits justified the sentences, on April 11 military officials in Hawaii announced that "the sentences are excessive and probably will be very materially modified."[20] Despite that, the Communist press used the sentences to stir up further outrage. On May 5 the *Daily Worker* labeled them "illegal." According to Crouch, who wrote to the Communist paper, the illegality came from the fact that "according to accepted military law, no one is subject to state or territorial law for his conduct on a military reservation, especially in so far as political matters are concerned. Politically speaking, the military reservation is not a part of the territory, and even if the Hawaiian Communist League had been a secret organization (which it was not) there would have been no violation of section 4214, revised laws of Hawaii, as all acts of the league mentioned in the court-martial were on the U.S. military reservation."[21] Crouch thus ignored counts two, three, and four and alleged that the violation of Hawaiian law (count one) was bogus because as soldiers whose actions occurred on a military base, he and Trumbull were not subject to civilian law.

The *Daily Worker* took on the remaining charges by claiming the Hawaiian Communist League was not a secret society, as evidenced by the fact that members used letterhead when corresponding to Hawaiian newspapers and the Comintern. The paper also noted that writing a letter to the Communist International in no way violated military provisions or articles of war. It further alleged that Crouch had been misquoted when he was accused of supporting the violent overthrow of the government. The paper claimed he supported gaining power legally through the political process and statements that he, or any Communist, supported the overthrow of the government through force and violence were false.[22] The Communist press asserted that the case was illegal and poorly presented and as such failed to demonstrate real guilt.

After denying the propriety of the charges, the *Daily Worker* next took on the testimony of Corporal Fisher. It alleged that Fisher "was told by the army intelligence department at Schofield barracks to go as far as he liked, and employ any means he desired to 'get something' on the Communist soldiers." Ignoring Creque's testimony that Fisher was successful in this effort, the paper alleged that "he was such a blundering ignoramus, the league members knew him for a spy and refused to admit him." The paper contended that Fisher never had access to the league and never knew what the membership or leadership truly believed. As such, he was in no position to make the accusations asserted in his testimony. The paper further alleged that the testimony Fisher provided was "so childish that any intelligent person could see at once that the 'evidence' was an obvious false concoction."[23] It also ignored the fact that Nadeau had turned state's evidence during the court-martial and actually corroborated much of Fisher's testimony and instead depicted Fisher as the sole prosecution witness who acted as a tool of the capitalist oppressors.

The Communist press used the idea of capitalist oppression not only to defend the two men but also to counterattack. On May 7 the *Daily Worker* claimed, "The army officers are guarding well the profits of their imperialist masters, which are gouged out of the oppressed dark races in Hawaii."[24] The real criminals, to the Communist mind, were the capitalists who robbed Hawaii and the workers of great wealth and the military authorities who supported such theft. Crouch and Trumbull's "crime" thus was nothing more than attempting to prevent that theft.

Crouch and Trumbull bolstered such assertions with additional letters to the *Daily Worker*. Crouch combined the issues surrounding his arrest with the Filipino strikers and the discontent on the military bases that led to the Van Gelder case to demonstrate that soldiers were simple "tools of American imperialism." Such imperialist exploitation was most obvious in Hawaii where soldiers were being used to crush working-class revolts and otherwise maintain the capitalist status quo. Soldiers in Hawaii were used in such an egregious manner, he claimed, because there was no opportunity for them to desert. Echoing Van Gelder, he noted that whereas soldiers on the mainland could go AWOL, troops in Hawaii were virtual hostages. According to Crouch, "If soldiers on the mainland were subjected to the same injustices that their comrades in Hawaii are forced to endure, the army would not exist for a week." The result of "such brutality and injustice" in Hawaii was "that the rank and file of the army is on the verge of revolt."[25]

To address these injustices, and indeed to solve the problems of the proletariat worldwide, Crouch called for the creation of "a union of soldiers, sailors, and marines," whose purpose would be education. Once soldiers learned how the world truly worked and realized they shared values and concerns with the working class and subject peoples, the exploitation of each group would cease and the glories of a socialist utopia would arise. This effort would be difficult, he warned his readers, as capitalists and politicians feared an educated working class and would do all they could to stymie its intellectual growth. Crouch portrayed the sentences given to himself and Trumbull as evidence of such capitalist determination but expressed faith that the working class would prevail and the United States would soon follow Russia on the path to socialism.[26]

Although such assertions and editorial vitriol made good propaganda, the *Daily Worker* eventually refocused the debate on the two men and their sentences when it got hold of the trial transcript. The editors dissected what they claimed to be a series of lies, fabrications, errors, and omissions. They alleged there were nineteen errors in Trumbull's transcript and fifty-nine in Crouch's, with many more "probable errors" not yet counted, 90 percent of which were favorable to the prosecution.[27] Crouch eventually received a copy of the transcript and issued a point-by-point refutation. Among the errors he noted were cases in which the "government invents [an] answer," "manufactures nonsense," destroys defense evidence, and covers up their own stupidity. Specifically, Crouch asserted that the government made up the following interactions:

> Q: Do you believe there are times when rule by a minority against the wishes of the majority is justified?
> A: Yes; during a time of national emergency it is the duty of the

> minority to enforce any measures that may be necessary for society, such as compulsory military service and labor against a man's wishes.
> Q: Do you believe in compulsory military service?
> A: Not unless it is necessary.
> Q: When would you consider it necessary?
> A: National defense or to prevent a minority from obtaining power.

Of this section Crouch wrote, "The above rot is . . . manufactured testimony. I said nothing that resembled this nonsense or expressed such absurd ideas. How could a minority use compulsory military service to prevent itself from obtaining power? Perhaps the government 'stenographer' thought one minority would use force against another minority while the majority was a disinterested observer!"[28]

Crouch also complained about the following interaction:

> Q: Now, what was your feeling at the outbreak of the Russian revolution?
> A: I was glad to see an autocracy overthrown.
> Q: In what respects were you not pleased?
> A: I considered the violent outbreak at first to be based on no sound foundation and I believed that the Russian Communists were starting prematurely.

Of this Crouch wrote, "Perverted imagination! I said nothing about 'no sound foundation' or that the 'Russian Communists were starting prematurely.'"[29]

Finally, Crouch complained that many prosecution errors were omitted or corrected to make the military appear less inept. He noted that in the following interaction the official transcript read: "Q: Did you ever hear of the I.W.W.?" Crouch claimed the actual conversation was: "Q: Did you ever hear of the International Workers of the World? A: I never heard of the International Workers of the World, but I have heard of the Industrial Workers of the World." The *Daily Worker* published the analysis of the trial transcript and concluded that the military made such edits because otherwise "Crouch's testimony would have hurt the government as it showed the absurdity of the court martial."[30]

The combined efforts of Crouch, Trumbull, and the Communist press seemed to pay off as workers and unions nationwide came out in support. The Council of Machinists in Pittsburgh issued a formal resolution that read in part, "RESOLVED, That we, the Machinists of District No. 6 voice our severest protest against the high-handed savage unjustifiable court martial that condemned Privates Crouch and Trumbull to inhuman sentences that amount to a living death in a military prison—demand the immediate release of the aforesaid soldiers, and the punishment of the officers responsible for their imprisonment."[31] The Labor Defense Council of Chicago gathered petitions and resolutions calling for the release of Crouch and Trumbull, as did the Capitol City Lodge No. 459 of the International Association of Machinists in St. Paul, Minnesota. The Western Progressive Farmers of Washington State joined the chorus when it passed a series of resolutions that denounced federal corruption and capitalism, criticized the sentences imposed on Crouch and Trumbull, and demanded their immediate release. World War I veterans in Ohio, members of the Young Workers League in Philadelphia, young Russian workers in New York City, the Millinery Local Union No. 48 and the Cigar Makers Union No. 225 in Los Angeles, and the national ACLU also supported the two men.[32]

Amidst the journalistic war and the growing sentiment in support of the two soldiers, on May 10 military authorities reduced Crouch's forty-year sentence to three years and Trumbull's twenty-six-year sentence to one year. The two men remained confined in the 27th infantry guardhouse on the Schofield Barracks until final arrangements were made to send them to Alcatraz, where they would serve out the remainder of their sentences. Military authorities rejected the idea that the reductions were the result of the protests and resolutions, claimed they were a normal part of military justice, and reminded people that almost as soon as the initial penalties were imposed officials announced the expectation of reductions. Crouch, Trumbull, the Communists, and their assorted allies did not buy the contention, however, and argued that it was a smoke screen. The military, they alleged, hoped the reduction would stop the bad press and make people forget the real reason the two were in prison—for supporting Communism.

Crouch, Trumbull, and their allies did not forget, however, and despite the reduced sentences the struggle continued as the two men determined to appeal. On May 18, G. W. Wright, president of the Honolulu Central Labor Council, visited Crouch and Trumbull in prison and offered assistance. Wright informed the two soldiers that the council itself would not take a stand on the case but told them that he would do all he could to help. As a part of that, Wright met with attorney John Matthewman about appealing the decisions and getting the two tried in a civil court. Matthewman and his substitute, Fred Patterson (who took over when Matthewman was required to travel to the mainland), took up the appeal and focused their efforts on what they claimed were a series of "errors and irregularities" in the original trial.

The attorneys claimed, as Crouch had all along, that the two soldiers violated "no law or military regulation." The writs of appeal also alleged that the court-martial had been incompetent and did not have jurisdiction to hear the case. Furthermore, the appeal claimed the trial was "not carried on in accordance with the rules and regulations prescribed for general court martial by the military authorities of the United States," but proceeded "without due regard to the rights" of Crouch and Trumbull. As such, the writs charged "That said detention of imprisonment of [Crouch and Trumbull] is illegal and without authority or justification of the law and is in violation of the constitution of the United States." Oddly, the *Honolulu Advertiser* added an additional justification for retrial when it noted that during the court-martial evidence emerged that Captain George Van W. Pope had looked over the Hawaiian Communist League letterhead and gave his "tentative approval for printing" it on the army press.[33] Such approval, the paper intimated, precluded charges against the men.

As the lawyers worked on the appeal, Crouch, Trumbull, and their allies realized that the continuation of the case would be costly. Therefore, they created a legal defense fund and urged people to donate. In an effort to influence donations, attorney Patterson tried to demonstrate the larger implications of the case. He told the *Honolulu Advertiser* that "Neither Crouch nor Trumbull are fighting for freedom to save their own skins. Theirs is a fight for free speech and free thought." Despite the effort to broaden the meaning of the case, donations were meager, and a week into the campaign less than $150 dollars had been raised. The *Daily Worker* subsequently issued a second appeal for funds, requesting an additional $200 to save the two men from capitalist prison.[34]

With money slowly trickling in, the appeals continued apace, and on June 24 a federal court issued writs of habeas corpus to Major General Edward Lewis, the commanding officer of the U.S. Army's Hawaiian branch, requiring him to produce Crouch and Trumbull at a 2:00 p.m.

hearing on June 25. The hearing, held before Federal Judge John T. DeBolt, was anticlimactic as Lewis failed to appear. Defense attorney Patterson moved that Judge DeBolt throw out the case, but he refused and instead held over the appeals until July when Federal Judge William T. Rawlins would preside.[35]

The hearing finally began on July 16 in front of Judge Rawlins, but only Crouch remained. (Trumbull determined to delay his appeal and wait until he was in California, where he hoped to find a more sympathetic court.) Both sides presented their cases, with the defense claiming the court-martial was "unfit" to hear the charges as evidenced by the forty-year sentence. Attorney Patterson argued, "Any man's mind that was so warped that he was willing to sentence Crouch to jail for 40 years was not fit to sit in any court where the life and liberty of another individual was in jeopardy." Prosecuting attorneys Colonel Frederick Brown and Charles Parson rebutted Patterson's claims by asserting that the forty-year sentence "was only an interlocutory sentence" and that the court should recognize the final sentence of three years as the true finding, thus demonstrating the competency of the court-martial.[36]

Judge Rawlins had little interest in either argument, however, and instead focused on jurisdiction. Rawlins asked Patterson, "What authority has this court to interfere with a properly organized military court?" Patterson responded, "You are the bulwark between the military court and the rights of an American citizen." Rawlins did not buy the argument and asked again, "Just how can this court interfere? You maintain that I'm a reviewing authority." Realizing he was losing the argument, Patterson ignored the judge's query, returned to the idea that the court-martial was biased, and argued that the judge needed to correct that bias. As Patterson expressed it: "The army court in sentencing Crouch showed their animus to be such that they were not fit to sit in judgment. Why, when I first read of the communist soldier, I thought he had guns and cannon hidden under his bed to foment a revolution. I thought that actual steps had been taken to start a revolution."[37] With the judge's question left unanswered, court adjourned for the day.

The hearing continued the next day, July 17, with prosecuting attorney Brown taking on Patterson's charge that Crouch was no threat to foment revolution. Brown noted that while Crouch claimed to want a bloodless revolution, he understood that "any other method" might be used to achieve his goal. Brown alleged that "any other method" referred to violence. He continued: "I can conceive of nothing more injurious to army discipline than such propaganda. This is revolutionary propaganda from within, where soldiers are supposed to protect the country against violence, rather than foster it—propaganda of the most dangerous sort."[38] The hearing dragged on throughout the rest of the day with both sides arguing over Crouch's rhetoric and only ended when Judge Rawlins called for the hearing to continue on Monday, July 21.

After both sides presented their final statements on that Monday morning, Judge Rawlins deliberated briefly and then rejected Crouch's appeal. Rawlins argued that he had no jurisdiction to hear the case and was in no position to rule. Such was still not the end of the case, however, as ten days after Judge Rawlins's decision, Crouch won the right to appeal to the United States Ninth Circuit Court of Appeals in San Francisco. Famed labor lawyer Austin Lewis took the case on retainer from the WPA's legal wing, the International Labor Defense (ILD), and went to work fashioning yet another appeal. As the appeal thus continued, the military announced its intention to send Crouch and Trumbull to Alcatraz on August 8.[39]

While awaiting the move, and despite the hardships he was suffering, Crouch remained devoted to the cause of Communism. Indeed, he announced that "While in Alcatraz, we will study and prepare ourselves in every possible way for more efficient service to the cause of the working class after our release."[40] In a letter to James Larkin Pearson, Crouch wrote, "I know that you are not a Communist. But I believe that if you had seen a few of the evils of capitalism I have witnessed, you would be a 'Red.'" Although still devoted to the cause, he was concerned about how his arrest affected his family. He specifically feared that his father had been "duped" by the capitalist press into believing the worst of him and asked Pearson to write an article about his character that would correct the wrongs that were being told about him.[41]

As Crouch kept in touch with family and friends, they kept in touch with each other. Crouch's father sent Pearson a series of letters in which, quite the opposite from what Crouch feared, he expressed his pride in Paul's willingness to go to prison for his beliefs and explained that he had received several pieces of correspondence in a similar vein from others who were equally impressed by his intellect and moral fortitude.[42] In return correspondence, Pearson agreed that Paul was an intelligent and upright young man but wrote "I do regret that he has had to fall in with that extreme crowd of ultraradicals, Communists and Industrial Workers of the World." He also criticized Communists for their irreligion and concluded "I wish Paul wouldn't go too far."[43] Crouch's father agreed with Pearson's fear that Paul might go too far and admitted "Paul has been too radical for me." He then sympathized with his son's worldview, however, and wrote, "You may think I am a Bolshevik I am not, but I am in sympathy with the working class. This thing of oppressing the poor will come to an end by and by. Read James fifth chapter and the whole bible favors the poor, and the rich is warned to look after the poor."[44]

As their families and friends dealt with the prison sentences in their own ways, Crouch and Trumbull continued to defend themselves as they awaited their removal to Alcatraz. The *Daily Worker* published an article Trumbull wrote in which he told the story of a sympathetic soldier in the Schofield Barracks who wrote a letter to the *Honolulu Advertiser* protesting their arrest and punishment. The letter never made it to the paper but was intercepted by military intelligence. The letter writer, Trumbull claimed, was imprisoned for his effort, demonstrating how absolute was the power of the military and how fearful military authorities were of allowing the development of any kind of working-class consciousness. Despite that, in a separate article, Trumbull claimed "I can safely say that four fifths of the enlisted personnel of the post are ready and willing to learn all about Communism. They are extremely friendly to us." The *Daily Worker* picked up on this theme of military support for Crouch and Trumbull and told the story of a young soldier in Los Angeles who proudly read several Communist publications to keep abreast of their case and the larger struggle against capitalism.[45]

Crouch made similar assertions in his letters. He wrote a short essay in the *Young Worker* in which he reiterated the idea that the military, like capitalists in general, understood the need to keep the working class divided to ensure its continued strength. Only education could overcome this division and convince the soldiers that they had a shared interest with the workers, and he called on the YCL to be a part of that educational effort. In an article for the *Daily Worker*, Crouch demonstrated the power of such knowledge. He claimed that the effort of the Filipino plantation workers, whose strike had helped start the entire episode, was evidence that "the masses are waking from their long sleep and the coming of a new social order is as inevitable as the dawn of a new day." He argued further that the struggle was proof that "capitalist imperialism is not secure" and Communism would soon emerge triumphant.[46]

The propaganda blitz did not stop the wheels of justice, however, and on August 8, 1925, the two men were loaded on board the U.S.S. *Cambrai* for the trip to California. They arrived in San Francisco on August 14 and immediately were transferred to Alcatraz. From their new prison the two men awaited their appeals and continued their Communist propaganda. Crouch was especially prolific and in December wrote a letter to the *Young Worker* in which he asserted that making speeches and passing resolutions against capitalism, militarism, and imperialism was not enough. He demanded action and offered some suggestions. He called on Communists to attack the Citizens' Military Training Camps, which provided private citizens with military training without the obligation of active duty service, as the beginning of domestic fascism. He also called for the creation of "Red nuclei" in every military unit to help spread Communist doctrine and for the formation of an intramilitary Communist organization that would unionize soldiers, sailors, and marines. He further urged soldiers who were sympathetic to the Communist cause to inform the party press of conditions in their units and to expose "the brutalities that would arouse the working class."[47] These efforts against the military, he argued, attacked one of the main struts that upheld the capitalist system and would speed along the day of its demise.

Crouch made similar suggestions in April 1926 when he again penned an article for the *Young Worker*. He wrote that he was appalled that the nation's soldiers and workers remained "asleep," thereby allowing capitalism, militarism, and imperialism to ruin the world. He demanded that people rise up and fight: "We must make war against war." Since religion and nationalism had lost their "potency" for pacifying the working class, he claimed, militarism was the new tool used by the capitalists to try to keep the international proletariat divided and weak. Only when workers and soldiers united and destroyed capitalism, he argued, would war and imperialism end and the Communist utopia arise.[48]

By this point Communist leaders realized that Crouch and Trumbull were useful for purposes well beyond their immediate predicament. In December 1925 the *Young Worker*, running short of money, ran a fund-raising campaign that included an ad with the heading "Paul Crouch

Speaks From His Cell." In the ad Crouch wrote, "Enclosed you will find $2. This is for the $5,000 BUILD THE LEAGUE FUND. I regret that I cannot give more, but you will doubtless understand my financial circumstances. I pledge myself to contribute not less than ten percent of my total earnings to the League and its official organ after my release." The ad concluded, "Can you be silent in the face of such loyalty?" In April 1926 the *Young Worker* included a similar ad in the form of a letter from a French soldier. Entitled "Letter from a French 'Paul Crouch'" the writer offered international solidarity as well as twenty-five francs in support of the paper. Three months later the paper ran a review of the wealth Hawaiian agriculture produced, described the exploitation under which the workers who produced that wealth lived, and concluded by informing the readers: "The terrible condition of the working class in Hawaii inspired Crouch and Trumbull to begin organizing a Communist Group. Their first attempt met with failure. But it will not be long before the work of these comrades will be taken up by the Hawaiian workers and together with the workers of the U.S. will fight against imperialism."[49]

While the Communist Party benefitted by broadening the propaganda campaign, the continuing rhetoric surely did little to win the sympathy of the justices hearing Crouch's appeal, and it was no surprise when the Ninth Circuit Court unanimously upheld his conviction in June 1926. The justices ruled against every element of the appeal and proclaimed the court-martial was held fairly, in keeping with territorial and federal law.[50]

By the time the court ruled, Trumbull already was a free man. He was released in February 1926 and quickly demonstrated that prison had done little to cool his Communist ardor. He took to the lecture circuit and traveled the nation recounting his case and spreading the Communist cause. In May he was in Detroit where he regaled the crowd with his exploits and tales of the court-martial. For instance, he assured the crowd that he and Crouch knew what they were doing all along and expected to get caught: "Now Crouch and I knew absolutely that we were going to get a court martial. We expected we would get death sentences. . . . We were not concerned about that. We did not hesitate the cost. We wondered how much our action would be worth to the movement, and after having found out we made our move unhesitatingly."[51]

He also spent a good deal of time specifically talking about Crouch. He informed the crowd that Crouch's parents were poor, "old and crippled, unable to work," and argued that labor owed them for their son's efforts. In an attempt to raise money for the parents, Trumbull informed the crowd that he had a message from Crouch that he would only read after they had donated five dollars. When he finally had the money, Trumbull first told the audience of an event he learned about mere months before his release:

> Now three months before I was released a thing happened to him that is really significant. It shows the kind of Bolshevik he is. He was called up before the commanding officer and the commanding officer says to him, "Paul Crouch, you [*sic*] father and mother are in danger of going to the poor farm. They are in danger of being shut away because they are unable to support themselves. They need you at home. Now we will offer you your freedom with no strings attached to it. We will offer you your back pay in the army for one entire year. We will also offer you free transportation home. Over and above that we give you an Honorable discharge. . . ." And Crouch says, "Well, what is all this being given to me for?" They tell him, "You are to sign a statement to the effect that you repudiate all Communist views that you have held heretofore, and furthermore you will devote the rest of your life to the smashing of the Bolshevik power wherever it exists wither in the United States or any other country." Crouch says, "I am to sign a statement like that?" And the officer says, "Yes, and allow us to print it in the Capitalist press." Paul Crouch folded his arms, he looked at that officer, he said "Damn you, you are not talking to me." That's the kind of Bolshevik Paul Crouch is.[52]

As the crowd roared its approval, he then turned to Crouch's specific message. Trumbull informed the audience that he visited Crouch before he left Alcatraz, and Crouch said, "Comrade Trumbull, if you get the chance to talk to the comrades on the outside I wish you would give them this message from me. I will spend the rest of my life in Alcatraz California, rather than do anything that would be detrimental to the cause of the working class."[53]

Trumbull spread the word far and wide and enjoyed a brief moment of celebrity during his speaking tour. Even after the fanfare faded, Trumbull continued his radical ways for decades. He served briefly on the ILD National Committee in Gastonia, North Carolina, during the infamous 1929 strike of the Loray Mill and later headed an ILD office in Charlotte. He continued to travel and speak, served as the district organizer for the Young Workers League in Detroit, was national secretary of the Workers Ex-Service Men's League, and was an active member of the Anti-Militarist Committee of the Communist Party, which had as its goal the infiltration of the military to weaken national security and enable a socialist revolution. In 1940 he took his efforts a step further and organized a failed bid for the United States House of Representatives from the 21st District in Pennsylvania on the Communist Party ticket.[54]

Crouch, meanwhile, remained imprisoned in Alcatraz. In later years he described his time in prison and noted that while Alcatraz was not yet "the Rock" of later fame, "the death-like silence and rigid discipline of the whole place" certainly left a lasting impression.[55] He also explained that he applied for membership in the WPA while incarcerated but was informed that he could not join until he got out. Despite that, Communist leaders did try to alleviate some of his suffering and even found him a "relative" in San Francisco who was allowed to visit him in prison. The woman, Beatrice Siskand, claimed to be his cousin and brought him food and cigarettes as well as news from the outside world. Despite having lost his religious faith as a teen, Crouch found additional comfort from a friendly chaplain who brought him proscribed magazines (such as the *New Republic* and the *Nation*) and helped him sign up for a Russian language correspondence course through the University of California, Berkeley.

Crouch also continued his correspondence with James Larkin Pearson. In November 1926 Crouch informed the writer that prison life was not too bad as it gave him time to read and think. He claimed to have read O. Henry's biography as well as the Russian classic *Fathers and Sons*. He asked Pearson to send along additional reading material and signed the letter "Your Bolshevik friend." Despite trying to keep upbeat, Crouch later admitted that he spent most of his time in prison working on the rock pile, in the laundry, or in the tailor shop, and trying to avoid the homosexuality he found rampant and disturbing in the prison.[56]

As Trumbull toured and Crouch did his time, the Communist press continued to use the two for its own gain. In 1927, *Labor Defender* author Manuel Gomez declared Crouch a "prisoner of the class struggle," whose example would soon be followed by other soldiers who came to realize that they were mere tools of capital. Once those soldiers realized that the capitalists for whom they fought were actually their enemy and the workers and colonial natives they were sent to oppress actually were their allies, the class and race-based repression of the capitalist era would come to an end. Gomez argued that this was the greatest fear of the imperial capitalists, who already had grown "panicky" as a result of the likes of Crouch and Trumbull. The Young Workers League took this critique a step further and authored a formal resolution. The "Communist Demands for Servicemen" iterated twenty-one points including better pay and food rations, free uniforms, a reduced work day, the rights to join political unions, to free speech, and to elect officers, and a prohibition on the use of soldiers as strike breakers. The same resolution called for soldiers to refuse to fulfill their duties until such changes were instituted and urged them to "refuse to act as policemen for Wall Street."[57]

When the resolution failed to find mass support, the Communist press returned to well-trod ground and told the stories of various soldiers who followed in the footsteps of Crouch and Trumbull and joined the Communist cause. The *Young Worker* included an essay by George Pershing in which he described his arrest for destruction of property while serving in the military in Hawaii. He too was transferred to Alcatraz where he met Crouch and Trumbull, who convinced him to become a Communist. The press also played up the story of John Porter, a deserter from the U.S. Army who joined the Communist Party and was made an honorary member of the presidium of the World Congress of the Young Communist International. Porter would go on to partake in a number of strikes—including the 1928 effort in New Bedford, Massachusetts—but eventually was arrested and turned over to the military. Porter used his court-martial to espouse Communist rhetoric and not surprisingly was convicted and sentenced to two and a half years' hard labor. Despite allegedly being brutalized while in prison, Porter remained firm in his beliefs, and the Communists packaged his story with Crouch and Trumbull's to attack the military and its alleged support for American capitalism.[58]

The Communists also used Crouch and Trumbull to oppose promilitary propaganda. Claiming the military had issued a pamphlet in which it explained to recruits all the benefits of military life (job security, assured wages, free meals, free medical care, technical training, and the overall benefits of a job that would produce a healthy body), the

Communists counterattacked. The *Young Worker* first turned the assurances of the military on their head, noting that unemployment, low pay, hunger, lack of medical care, and jobs that ruined mind and body were exactly the capitalist-created problems against which the Communists fought. In other words, the military's propaganda proved the Communist allegation that capitalism was evil. The paper then alleged that even if one accepted all the good things the military offered, it meant selling one's soul and learning to become a murderer: "Be a soldier. Learn how to use a bayonet. Learn how to jab a fellow's guts out of his body. Learn how to use poison gas and hand grenades." The paper finally noted that as a soldier those people one would kill were fellow members of the working class. Their deaths did nothing to help the individual American soldier and only served to prop up the capitalist system, thus ensuring more violence and slavery.[59]

While the Communist press used Crouch for its own purposes and may well have lamented him his freedom, there is no doubt that he was relieved when he was released from prison on June 1, 1927. Now twenty-four and world famous, at least among Communists, Crouch had some important decisions to make. Was he going to become a member of the WPA now that he was free? Was he going to devote his time to the cause for which he had served three years in prison? Or, was he going to listen to his father and Pearson and avoid going "too far"?

For Crouch, the decision was not particularly difficult. He clearly had found his ideological center and emerged from prison a devout Communist. He had suffered for his faith and yet never questioned its righteousness. Communism was the only path to salvation and was worth all the pain. At the same time, all the world's evils and all the horrors he had suffered had been caused by capitalism. It had disrupted his idyllic hometown, infected his leg, crushed workers fighting for their humanity, and sent him to prison. There was nothing good that had come from this ideology, he believed, and it—and all who supported it—needed to be destroyed. By 1927, Crouch the Communist ideologue had been born.

3 "PAUL CROUCH, BOLSHEVIK," 1927–1932

Free from prison and a true believer in Communism, Crouch accepted his party card and became a full-fledged member of the Workers (Communist) Party of America upon his release in June 1927. He would spend the next fourteen years as an active Communist organizer, deftly following the ever changing party line and surviving amidst a nation that continued to view Communism as un-American and dangerous. During the first five years of his active Communist life, he traveled nationwide, spoke about his experiences in Hawaii, visited Russia to witness the glories of the first socialist state, and spent brief periods in New York City, Massachusetts, Delaware, Virginia, and North Carolina trying to expand the party's membership. Although Crouch would face his moments of doubt, his faith in Communism got him through the darkest hours and confirmed his ideological fervor.

Upon leaving prison and formally affirming his membership in the WPA, Crouch joined an organization in turmoil. The two parties that formed in the aftermath of the 1919 foundational meeting in Chicago eventually unified, at the behest of the Comintern, and in 1921 organized as the Workers Party of America, which in 1925 became the Workers (Communist) Party of America. Although unified, sectarianism remained a problem. Within the party two groups predominated, corresponding to the struggles in Russia to succeed Lenin, who died in January 1924. Charles Ruthenberg and Jay Lovestone led one faction, which allied itself with Nikolai Bukharin, while William Z. Foster and James Cannon supported Stalin. This division and the factional struggle played out during the rest of the decade, with the Foster group emerging victorious thanks to Stalin's victory in the Soviet Union, but in the meanwhile it distracted party leaders.

There were other problems as well. In 1923 the Communist Party boasted some 15,000 members. Of that number, however, only 5,000 spoke English and only 46 percent were members of trade unions. Believing that both issues were hindering the party's efforts, in 1925 leaders announced a program of "Bolshevization," which aimed at creating the vanguard of which Lenin had written. By demanding ever more from members, focusing more on trade union efforts, and expanding the American base of the movement, party leaders hoped to create a highly trained and skilled phalanx that could better seize power. The excessive organizational demands this campaign made on party members, however, decimated the membership rolls, with numbers falling from 16,325 at the start of the year to 7,213 in October. When Crouch formally joined the WPA in June 1927, membership remained below 9,000. Worse still, there were few African American members, females comprised less than 20 percent of the membership, and the party remained geographically centralized in the urban, industrial Northeast and Midwest.[1]

There was one final problem as well. As the Soviet leaders came to realize that the worldwide revolution they had expected was not imminent, they announced the aforementioned Second Period—the era of capitalist stabilization—and the subsequent need to expand party membership, to find willing allies, and to defend the Soviet Union. In the United States, that led the party to end calls for revolution and instead to focus on reforms for the betterment of the working class. As Jay Lovestone explained: "We might talk ourselves blue in the face about our holy cause, about the wonders of Communism, about the necessity for shouldering guns against capitalism and yet not enhance the revolution by an iota. But let us talk to the workers about their long hours, their disemployment, their hardships and the why and wherefore of these, and they will be ready listeners and doers."[2] Although such talk previously was disparaged as "economism" by none other than Lenin, who believed a focus on reforms within the existing system was anathema to the revolutionary nature of Marxism, by the time Crouch took his party card it was established policy.

Historians Harvey Klehr and John Earl Haynes, however, assert that "this tactic inherently had a large element of subterfuge to it." As they explain it: "immediate demands would win support for Communists from the masses of workers. This support would give Communists power; power in trade unions and power in politics. Communists would then use this power to advance the revolutionary cause by whatever means were expedient." The element of subterfuge came from the fact that "only the initiated Communist party members knew the ultimate intentions."[3] This too caused the party problems. Although the new, and seemingly more benign, Communist Party won new followers to the cause with their calls for reform, when members learned of the truly revolutionary agenda they fled.

Thus, the Communist Party in the 1920s was young, small, faction ridden, unsure of its founding principles, and willing to lie to win converts and power. Despite those problems, Crouch jumped in enthusiastically. He did so for many of the same reasons that the four individuals mentioned in the introduction joined. First, he had few friends and sought out the camaraderie of the party. Rarely in his massive archival collection does he mention any close acquaintances, with the exception of James Larkin Pearson who was his cousin and his elder by twenty-five years. His parents were older when he was born, the family moved frequently, and Crouch seems to have been unable to establish close relationships. As such, the Communist Party was a perfect place for him to enjoy personal associations that he had never before appreciated. Crouch also clearly saw the world as endangered. His early literary efforts attest to that, and his association with socialists in Delaware seems to have urged him to the Communist cause. That he had already suffered for the movement, for his efforts in Hawaii, further confirmed to him that the cause was just. Crouch also enjoyed the notoriety that came with being a Communist; he had published a number of works while in prison and seemed to relish seeing his name in print. Indeed, his personal archival collection includes a mass of clippings and newspaper stories about him. Regardless of the nature of the reporting—positive or negative—Crouch loved the exposure, and being a Communist in the 1920s was a good way to ensure such coverage. Finally, although Crouch liked to think himself an intellectual, he had only a minimal education and was not nearly as smart as he claimed. As such, joining an organization that told members what to think and believe makes sense. Although Communist ideology is complex, the average member simply needed to learn and be able to parrot the party line. Crouch was willing to do so and in the process could feel intelligent without having to think for himself.

He received some unexpected support for his new endeavor from James Larkin Pearson, who fulfilled Crouch's request and published a short article about him not long after his release. Entitled "Paul Crouch, Bolshevik," the poet first described Crouch's father as an old-time school teacher with a "long patriarchal white beard and a benevolent, not to say saintly, countenance. Paul's mother is a woman of more than average intelligence, with a quick and natural temperament." Of Crouch he wrote that although he received little formal education, he had rounded up enough knowledge to challenge college professors and had developed enough writing skills to mark him out as a "rising literary star." Unlike many young men, Crouch did not drink, smoke, chew tobacco, or use profanity and was uninterested in sports or gossip. Instead, he focused on "the bed-rock problems of existence." Pearson further asserted "that he was a dreamer and idealist [who] could not be doubted for a minute," although he acknowledged that "'practical minded' folks would have said that he was 'nutty.'" Pearson concluded his assessment by asserting that Crouch was "a creature of destiny, with a mission which must claim his whole attention. He must solve the problems of the world. He must save society from the effects of its own folly. He must live and die for his cause."[4]In a later remembrance, Pearson added that "instead of knowing how far to go and when to stop, Paul Crouch made a beeline for the reddest thing he see [*sic*], and never stopped until he landed with both feet in the camp of the Russian Bolsheviks."[5]

Pearson was more correct than he knew. Crouch indeed was a dreamer and an idealist, although those ideals shifted over time. He also certainly headed for the "reddest thing" he could find, believed himself a literary figure, and clearly viewed his mission in life as one to save mankind from itself. Similarly, many throughout the years would describe him as "nutty." By contrast, the idea that he "could not be doubted for a minute" was about as far from the truth as possible. Crouch had only an imperfect relationship with reality, and at times one wonders whether he knew what the truth was. All of this will become apparent, and at the time he left prison not even Crouch knew where his future lay. For the moment, all he knew was that his present was with the Communists.

After a short rest in California to recuperate from his years in prison, Crouch agreed to go on a nationwide tour for the Communist affiliated All-America Anti-Imperialist League. On July 18, 1927, his comrades in California gathered to celebrate Crouch's freedom and his forthcoming trip. An invitation for the event informed people that the tour upon which he was about to embark had been delayed by illness, which was the result of "the cruel military prison regime where he spent his three year sentence."[6] Now recovered, the party celebrated his return to health and the beginning of his new career.

After the fête, Crouch embarked from Los Angeles and spoke formally in Detroit, Cleveland, Toledo, Philadelphia, Pittsburgh, Scranton, Baltimore, New Haven, New York, and Boston, as well as in countless small towns in between, under the slogan: "Bring back all American military and naval forces from foreign territory!" Although technically opposing imperialism, Crouch focused his talks on the horrors of military service and the abuses he and other "agents of imperialism" suffered. He urged soldiers and workers to fight against American militarism and the capitalist desire for another war, and he argued that the only way to prevent such a war was through a class-conscious alliance of soldiers and workers. According to the press, countless soldiers and former soldiers complained that Crouch actually understated the horrors of military life and after the speeches regaled him with their own stories. According to Crouch, it was not merely soldiers who supported him; while in Plentywood, Montana, in the extreme northeastern part of the state, he discovered that "the sheriff and most of the county officials" were Communist sympathizers and came out in support of his speech.[7]

While in Chicago in the midst of the tour, he sent a letter to James Larkin Pearson in which he updated his itinerary and offered his assessment of the Communist Party's future in the American South. He told Pearson that he was anxious to reach Southern workers but feared that "for religious reasons, it would be very difficult to organize the Workers Communist Party in the South." He continued on this irreligion bent by criticizing Pearson for the religious nature of many of his poems: "Personally, I think the religious ideas expressed in many of your poems does [*sic*] more harm to the success of your work than everything else. Ninety-nine per cent of the THINKING WORLD today is militantly anti-religious; and even one religious poem would make them throw aside the book in disgust. To fight for religion in intellectual circles today is about as practical as to defend Evolution in Tennessee."[8] In a subsequent letter Crouch asserted that he rejected religion because there was no scientific basis to it. He argued that scientific advances had necessitated changes in religion that religion had failed to make. As a

Figure 1. Paul Crouch pictured in his military uniform during his 1927 nation-wide tour. Courtesy of the James Larkin Pearson Library, Learning Resources Center, Wilkes Community College, Wilkesboro, N.C.

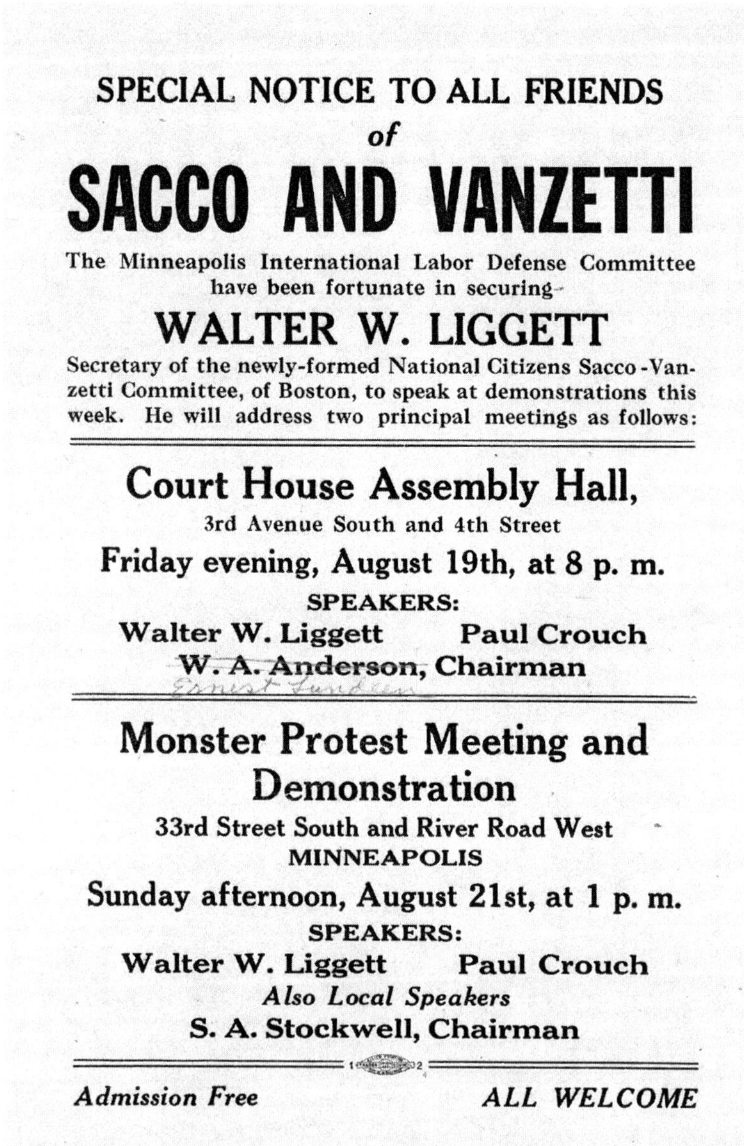

SPECIAL NOTICE TO ALL FRIENDS
of
SACCO AND VANZETTI

The Minneapolis International Labor Defense Committee have been fortunate in securing

WALTER W. LIGGETT

Secretary of the newly-formed National Citizens Sacco-Vanzetti Committee, of Boston, to speak at demonstrations this week. He will address two principal meetings as follows:

Court House Assembly Hall,

3rd Avenue South and 4th Street

Friday evening, August 19th, at 8 p. m.

SPEAKERS:

Walter W. Liggett Paul Crouch

~~W. A. Anderson~~, Chairman

Ernest Lundeen

Monster Protest Meeting and Demonstration

33rd Street South and River Road West
MINNEAPOLIS

Sunday afternoon, August 21st, at 1 p. m.

SPEAKERS:

Walter W. Liggett Paul Crouch

Also Local Speakers

S. A. Stockwell, Chairman

Admission Free *ALL WELCOME*

Figure 2. Poster announcing Paul Crouch's speech in support of Sacco and Vanzetti, August 19, 1927. Courtesy of the James Larkin Pearson Library, Learning Resources Center, Wilkes Community College, Wilkesboro, N.C.

EVERYBODY ATTEND

LAST DAY OF DEMONSTRATION

Thirty-six Hours Before the Time Set for

EXECUTION OF SACCO AND VANZETTI

PROTEST MEETING AND PICNIC FOR TWIN CITIES

SUNDAY, AUGUST 21ST, 1 P. M.

at Picnic Grounds, 33rd Street South and River Road West, Minneapolis. Three blocks south of Lake Street. Take any Selby-Lake car and get off at River Road West and walk three blocks south.

PAUL CROUCH

Just released from U. S. Disciplinary Barracks at Alcatraz, Cal., will be chief speaker

OTHER SPEAKERS:

Chairman: S. A. STOCKWELL

ERNEST LUNDEEN — LEWIS J. DUNCAN

J. F. EMME — EMIL S. YOUNGDAHL

Come in Crowds and Protest!

By Mass Solidarity Rescue the Doomed Men!

Stay the hand of the executioner! Sacco and Vanzetti must not die!

Auspices: International Labor Defense

Figure 3. Poster announcing Paul Crouch's speech in Minneapolis, Minnesota, August 21, 1927. Courtesy of the James Larkin Pearson Library, Learning Resources Center, Wilkes Community College Wilkesboro, N.C.

result of this failure, religion had devolved to mere superstition and had reached the point where "the word 'god' has become synonymous with a man with a long white beard . . . a Santa Claus for overgrown children."[9]

Crouch then moved from religion to more practical matters and argued that while religion might make organizing the South difficult, labor issues offered an opening. He informed Pearson, "there should be a good field for the All-America Anti-Imperialist League, the International Labor Defense and the Trade Union Unity League. Conditions for the workers in the South are very bad, and they are poorly organized. We can take the lead in organizing the workers under militant and honest leadership." Crouch then concluded by assessing his concerns about internal party issues, informing Pearson that the biggest problem the Communist Party faced was "the conflict between the European and American elements." He said he preferred the Europeans due to their "revolutionary traditions," but complained that their phraseology was incomprehensible to American workers and needed to be Americanized.[10] This letter thus demonstrates Crouch's true devotion to Communism. He was not merely along for the ride to enjoy the speeches and tour. Already he was planning future efforts in places where he would not be regaled as the conquering hero. At the same time, his idealism is clearly visible as he saw a problem within the party but papered over it.

Of more immediate interest than these musings on the future was his speech, in which he again focused on his time in Hawaii and his claims that the job of the military there was to suppress the natives and facilitate American imperialism. On October 1, 1927, he told a Chicago throng:

> While stationed in Honolulu, Hawaii I found it impossible to act in the traditional way as a good watchdog of American imperialism there. I could not believe that it was my supreme duty to suppress the demands of the Hawaiian people for freedom from foreign (American) rule. Talking matters over with other soldiers, I soon found that I was not the only one who felt that way about it. Walter Trumbull and myself, together with others, decided to organize the Hawaiian Communist League which would fight for the cause of the Hawaiian people, for Hawaiian independence. For that "crime" against imperialism, both Trumbull and I were court-martialed, and sentenced to Alcatraz military prison.[11]

Like a good Communist, Crouch warned his audience that the military served the needs of the oppressor class and asserted that only unity from below could prevent the nation from being destroyed by the rapacious capitalists and their agents of destruction—the politicians and generals.

From Chicago he headed to New York City, where flyers appeared in working-class districts announcing his speech, set for October 14. One explained that most people had no idea how bad life was in the military, so Crouch was making it his object to spread the news of military misery. Another explained his prison term but noted that "the working class of the United States protested and *FORCED* the War Department to reduce my sentence to three years," thus reminding his readers that they had the power to affect change should they chose to do so.[12] Calling them "buddies," Crouch encouraged New Yorkers to hear him speak on the horrors of military life and the power of the working class.

The Bureau of Investigation (BOI), the forerunner to the FBI, had been aware of Crouch's tour and rhetoric from the beginning and trailed him for much of the trip. This was especially true after his arrival in

New York City, at which point BOI boss J. Edgar Hoover informed the War Department that the purpose of the tour and the speeches was "to spread so-called anti-imperialist propaganda and to attempt to organize party nuclei in the Army and Navy."[13] As evidence, Hoover passed along an essay published in the June 1, 1927, issue of the *Young Worker* in which Crouch demanded real action from the nation's youth. Specifically, he called for greater efforts to educate workers about the true principles of Communism and the true goals of the American military. He also reiterated his call for the creation of a union of soldiers, sailors, and marines that would carry Communist propaganda into the military. Hoover offered an additional essay from the journal's September 15, 1927, issue in which Crouch attacked the American Legion. Calling it "the Fascisti of the United States," he alleged that while the legion claimed to speak for ex-soldiers, it really served the interests of the capitalists. In fact, he asserted that its goal was "to enslave the workers and make America safe for the next imperialist struggle."[14] Crouch used such rhetoric in his New York City speech—and indeed throughout the remainder of his tour—but neither the BOI nor the War Department yet took any action. They were, however, building a record that would later come back to haunt him.

Largely unaware that the government was watching his every move, Crouch ended his speaking tour with his first visit to North Carolina in more than three years. Prior to his arrival at his parents' home in Hays, just north of Wilkesboro in central Wilkes County, Crouch sent Pearson publicity for his final speech. Crouch begged Pearson to use his pull to get the publicity in local papers to ensure a good turnout. He then turned to politics and informed Pearson that everyone he had talked to who had visited Russia was enthusiastic. He asserted that under the Bolsheviks the country enjoyed a 20 percent increase in industrial output, while workers benefitted from an 11 percent annual increase in wages, as well as unemployment insurance, illness payments, and two weeks of vacation each year. All of this, he argued, was clear evidence of Communism's success. He then informed Pearson that recently he had "made a very Revolutionary talk" in which he attacked pacifists, declared that force must be used to meet capitalist force, and that "the next imperialist war must be converted into a civil war and a Revolution by the workers." Fearing he had gone too far and scared Pearson, undercutting his propaganda efforts, Crouch quickly assured his old friend that he would not talk that way in North Carolina where "They are ready only for the 'milk' of working class ideology."[15]

Pearson was not scared by such rhetoric and succeeded in getting the *Wilkes-Journal Weekly* and the *Wilkes Patriot* to publish a press release about Crouch's speech. The *Wilkes-Journal* entitled the release "Paul Crouch, Local Boy, Tours Country," while the *Wilkes Patriot* headlined it "Famous Radical to Visit Home Here Soon." The release itself called Crouch "an internationally known rebel soldier" and described his previous speeches and attacks on American militarism.[16] The publicity helped attract a small, receptive audience, but it also created some antagonism. The night prior to the speech the Ku Klux Klan exploded a bomb and burned a cross in front of the family home.

Crouch later responded to the attack with an essay in which he argued that the Klan was a tool of the capitalists who sought to weaken the working class by keeping it divided along racial lines. The Klan and its capitalistic allies, he argued, feared Communism because it threatened to unify the workers. To prevent that unity, Klansmen resorted to violence to keep him quiet. Crouch refused to be quiet and told his readers that the Klan represented only a small percentage of Southerners and was doomed to fail despite its alliance with the capitalists.[17]

The *Wilkes Patriot* also responded negatively to the speech, although unlike the Klan it did so obliquely. Without actually mentioning Crouch, the paper ran an editorial two weeks after the speech in which it questioned why "in the world there are teachers of radicalism and anarchy." The paper said it understood such politics in Europe, where the workers were poorly paid, but argued that there was no reason for it in America. To prevent such nonsense from catching on, the paper urged the nation's teachers to criticize radicalism as un-American and to promote patriotism in the classroom.[18]

The speeches complete and the political handwringing aside, Crouch took some time to relax. He initially worried that his parents would be outraged by his politics, but they welcomed him home with open arms and, as he wrote years later, had "no criticism to make of my course in life."[19] Crouch thus enjoyed the homecoming and reminiscences with his parents and recuperated after years in prison and a hectic speaking schedule.

Seemingly energized, and certainly confirmed in the righteousness of Communism, he soon returned to New York City to attend the national WPA convention and begin work as a party functionary. Crouch enjoyed a certain celebrity status at the convention, but that status brought with it responsibility and party leaders assigned him two tasks. First, he spoke to the Fourth National Convention of the Young Workers League in New York City in November 1927. His "Report on the War Danger and Anti-Militarist Work" sounded much like the speeches he gave during his tour. He argued that antimilitarism must be at the forefront of the Communist effort but that many comrades ignored it or subordinated it to other mundane matters. He asserted that a new war was imminent and would emerge either as a result of American efforts in Latin America or China. The greatest threat, however, was a Western war against Russia. In any case, Crouch argued that Communists should not advocate for peace but rather work to expose the imperialist nature of the coming war. He further argued that the United States was actively preparing for a war, economically and ideologically, and that American youth were being primed for it through militaristic programs such as ROTC. To meet those threats, he called for the education of party members about the danger of American militarism and urged direct agitation among young workers and soldiers to inform them about the rising threat of a capitalist war. Specifically, he reiterated his calls for the creation of a union of soldiers, sailors, and marines and for a focus on National Guardsmen. The guard was an especially important focus, he contended, as a result of its use as a strike-breaking force. He concluded by encouraging party members to join the military and win soldiers to the cause one at a time.[20]

Task number one completed, party leaders assigned Crouch to attend the upcoming Ninth Plenum of the Executive Committee of the Communist International in Moscow. He spent four months in Russia, from December 1927 through April 1928, on a trip arranged by the Soviet trading company Amtorg. Crouch traveled on his own legally obtained passport, sailing first to Istanbul on an Italian vessel chartered by the Soviets and from there to Novorossiysk. He remained in this South Russian port town for a week while his papers were processed, and he then traveled to Moscow. During this leg of the journey, from the United States to Russia and from Novorossiysk to Moscow, Crouch shared passage with George

Mink. Crouch described Mink as a former taxi driver from Philadelphia, a heavy drinker, promiscuous with women, and a man of "gangster characteristics." Crouch quickly grew sick of hearing Mink's boasts that he was a big shot and that all the Soviet leaders knew him, but he then saw Mink in close contact with Solomon Lozovsky, at the time head of the Red International of Labor Unions (RILU) and later soviet vice-commissar of foreign affairs, and learned that all the American delegates to the RILU knew that in order to get anything done they had to go through Mink. After a meeting with Soviet officials, Mink also showed Crouch a wallet stuffed full of cash and told him he was on his way to the United States to spend the money organizing American sailors.[21]

Although Mink seemed a powerful individual, Crouch did not care for him and spent much of his time in Novorossiysk and on the journey northward examining firsthand Communism in practice. What he saw was a mixed bag. He claimed that the food was plentiful but of limited variety and that there was little choice of clothing, although it did keep him warm. He was surprised at the overall low standard of living, although Bolshevik leaders assured him that the standards were higher than the Russian people had ever before enjoyed. Crouch also toured factories, and, while he found them old, ill equipped, and unproductive, he believed that the working conditions were good: there was no stretch out, the workers enjoyed free medical care, sick pay, paid vacations, and reduced-rate meals. He was saddened to see the lack of cars, poor laundry services, and that basic supplies—such as pens, watches, and alarm clocks—were luxury items. He also was concerned to discover that there was no democracy in Russia; that people did not have the right to demonstrate and that prisoners had no right to bail or free defense council. Disappointed, but ever the ideologue, he wrote off these problems as the growing pains of a young socialist state struggling to survive amidst a sea of enemies, both internal and external.[22]

Crouch also visited military bases on the trip north. While he noted that the military barracks were similar to those found in the United States, he believed the Soviet military was much different from the American model he had grown to hate. Most notably, he claimed there was a lack of distinction between the enlisted men and officers. He said soldiers did not salute, all men ate together, and overall there was a general "social equality of officers and enlisted men." In subsequent writings he admitted this equality disappeared before long, but Crouch claimed that as late as 1928 it remained. Soviet officials also allowed him, as a former soldier, to attend the Frunze Institute. Known as "the West Point of Russia," professors taught Crouch about guerrilla and civil warfare tactics, while he educated the Russian students about the United States. Officials there made him an honorary officer in the Red Army, and BOI files indicate that he was awarded the title "Professor of Military Sciences and Tactics for the Communist Party, United States Section."[23]

As the trip to Moscow continued, Crouch wrote further observations to his friend James Larkin Pearson. He told the author, without any real way of knowing, that there were more bookstores in Rostov-on-Don than in New York City, despite the fact that it had only 450,000 residents. He also quite dubiously claimed that Moscow had more bookstores than any city in the world and that this was proof of a high literacy rate. He further described the beauty of the music, art, and architecture of the country, and he asserted that most Russians knew more about Americans than vice versa. Of the working class, he claimed that workers had an eight-hour day, soon to be reduced to seven, and that those under eighteen worked six hours but were paid for eight while no one under sixteen worked. These same workers, he contended, got better food and had better working conditions than did American workers and they had more intellectual opportunities and real freedom of speech. He further claimed that sick workers could go to the Black Sea or the Caucasian Mountains to recover. He admitted that the standard of living was lower than in the industrial northeast but argued it was much higher than in Wilkes County, and he wrongly asserted that Russian farmers gained more than industrial workers as a result of the revolution. All of this would have been news to the Russian people, but Crouch was so firmly in the grips of Communism that he saw only what he wanted. Indeed, Crouch concluded his letter to Pearson by noting that he wished he could stay in Russia, but he realized that the American Communist movement needed him, and he would dutifully return once his trip was complete.[24]

What makes all of these observations, and indeed much of the story, problematic is that Crouch made them despite the fact that he admittedly had trouble finding people who spoke English. At the same time, the little Russian he had learned while taking correspondence courses at Alcatraz proved so poor that Crouch himself noted he was unable to communicate with virtually anyone for the first week of his visit. He eventually discovered a young girl who spoke English and briefly served as his tour guide, and he later befriended several Russians who spoke Esperanto. Those relationships enabled him to communicate a little more freely, but language remained a problem throughout his visit.[25]

Despite the hardships, Crouch was intrigued by what he saw during the trip north. That journey complete, he checked in to the Lux Hotel in Moscow where he shared a room with a Young Communist International representative from Turkey. While waiting for the plenum to begin, and despite the lingering language issues, Crouch visited the Lenin School, where budding young Communists from around the globe could receive an education in Marxist theory. While there, he described to students his experiences with oppressive capitalism. He also met with an array of Communist icons, including Mikhail Tukhachevsky, then commander-in-chief of the Red Army, future Marshal of the Soviet Union, and in 1937 victim of Stalin's purges; Lenin's widow Nadia Krupskaya; German Communist leader Klara Zetkin; and "Big" Bill Haywood, leader of the Industrial Workers of the World and an expatriated American who fled the United States in 1921 following his conviction for violating the Espionage Act.[26]

The meeting with Tukhachevsky was especially important. They met with three other members of the Soviet General Staff and discussed the military, Communist efforts in the Caribbean, and the struggle in Latin America. The military leaders first expressed interest in learning from him about American military tactics and strategies. From there they made some significant criticisms and suggestions, many of which sound curiously similar to the rhetoric of Crouch's Anti-Imperialism speeches. Specifically, Tukhachevsky and the others expressed their frustration with the failure of American Communists to infiltrate the military, criticized American efforts to train members in the military arts, and instead suggested that American Communists join the National Guard and regular army where they would get military training for free. The Russians also suggested focusing on the Navy and getting members jobs in military industries. They further demanded that the American Party train soldiers to complain about every little problem so as to create divisions between officers and enlisted men, to create clubs and various organizations as a secret way of winning soldiers to the party, and to encourage members to work hard and study in the hopes of becoming officers. The Soviets then urged Crouch to oversee these reforms and promised him a return trip to Russia for additional military training once the efforts in America were underway.[27] The discussion next turned to Communist efforts throughout Latin America. The Russians urged Crouch and the Americans to focus on Panama, because of the canal, and Florida, especially Miami and Key West, for their proximity to the Caribbean. The idea was that from these southern outposts the Communist Party would be able to destroy the Panama Canal and influence the overthrow of Central American governments.[28]

The conference with the military complete, Crouch next met with various Soviet and European Communist leaders, including Krupskaya and Zetkin. He later claimed that in talks with these individuals a general consensus emerged that a crisis of global capitalism was imminent and that the Communist parties of each country needed to make concerted efforts to take advantage of that crisis. Specifically, he claimed: "It was agreed by all the leaders present that at the coming World Congress a program should be formulated which would make it clear to the Communist parties of every nation that Communism could not be realized by peaceful means, but only by the armed destruction of capitalist governments through civil war and by setting up of a Soviet government in each country."[29]

In reality, Crouch had no role in the creation of this new policy. Prior to the February 1928 meeting of the Ninth Plenum, Bolshevik leaders were still fighting to determine Lenin's successor. The policy shift Crouch describes was part of Stalin's campaign against Nikolai Bukharin and the "right opposition," which helped pave the way for Stalin to institute formally his dictatorship. Eventually known as the Third Period, the new policy foresaw the end of the Second Period (the era of capitalist consolidation) and the beginning of the collapse of the capitalist system. As defined and clarified over the ensuing years, the Third Period envisioned an era marked by "the increasing growth of the general crisis of capitalism and of the accelerated accentuation of the fundamental external and internal contradictions of imperialism leading inevitably to imperialistic wars [and] to great anti-imperialist revolutions in colonial countries."[30]

These wars and revolutions, the theory went, would result in "either dictatorship of the bourgeoisie or—the dictatorship of the proletariat; either economic and political slavery or—to put an end to capitalist exploitation and oppression."[31] In either case, it meant the "radicalization" of the working class. To ensure they won the ensuing class struggle, the Comintern encouraged Communists worldwide to resist fascism, which they viewed as the consequence of the dictatorship of the bourgeoisie, to attack other political parties, especially leftist groups who pretended to side with the working class but actually were "social fascists" and class enemies, and to organize united fronts from below in order to ensure broad working-class support for the struggle. Thus with an uncanny sense of timing, international Communist leaders predicted the international crisis of the Great Depression mere months before it erupted, issued a coherent policy platform in preparation for that crisis, and, in so doing, energized the revolutionary nature of international Communism.

It was at the Ninth Plenum that the announcement of the Third Period was made and formally adopted, but any sense that Crouch was part of a revolutionary new idea is far from the truth.[32] He simply was parroting the new Communist Party line. Although Crouch clearly exaggerated his role in creating this new policy, he did not exaggerate his acceptance of it. Despite being a radically new worldview, Crouch, like a good ideologue, accepted the change.

Crouch had a little more trouble accepting events that transpired a few days later, after he gave a speech before the Young Communist International. The day following his speech he was appalled to learn that the Soviet newspaper *Pravda* (Truth) reported him saying things he had not said. When he questioned others about the story he was informed that while he did not say the things attributed to him, he "should have said them."[33] Frustrated, Crouch left Moscow for several weeks, during which time he traveled to the Tambov region and watched military exercises with the Budenny Cavalry Division.[34] While there, Crouch was photographed in a Red Army uniform and later explained that he wore the uniform while speaking to the division and for a week hence while touring other military installations. He suggested later to congressional investigators that he believed the reason his picture in a Red Army uniform was important to the Soviets was because it "illustrate[d] the Communist policy that the loyalty of all Communists throughout the world, whether civilians or in the armed forces, must be unquestionably true to the Soviet Union."[35]

At the time, he was not concerned with the geopolitical implications of his picture—although he would have agreed—and continued his travels to Nizhny Novgorod (Gorky) and east to the Urals. He was impressed with the sheer size of the country and appreciated that it, along with the cold temperatures, provided the nation with a cover for its industrial shortcomings should another war erupt. He also came to realize that there were many in the country who opposed the Bolsheviks. Those opponents, he argued later, were unorganized and fearful because "if any group held a public meeting for the purpose of opposing or criticizing the Moscow government in any fundamental respect, everyone connected with such a demonstration could be sure of years in prison, if not death by shooting as the penalty."[36] Despite realizing this lack of democracy, the trip reinvigorated Crouch, and he returned to the plenum once again devoted to the Communist cause. Not for the last time would he call his faith in Communism into question, but, as would so often be the case, his faith overcame any rational objections.

Crouch ventured back to Moscow where he took part in sessions dealing with the expansion of Communism into the American South. Party leaders believed Communist efforts in the South would not only inspire African Americans to rise up in revolt but also would stimulate a global rebellion of the oppressed. The Soviets, as supporters of that rebellion, believed they could then guide the rebels toward Communism. More important than the desire to enter the South was the Soviet belief that they knew how to make the Communist Party palatable to Southerners who heretofore had demonstrated little interest in Communism. The new policy, created by RILU General Secretary Solomon Lozovsky and written up with Crouch's help, was deemed "national self-determination."

According to this policy, Communists were to view African Americans as doubly exploited: as workers and a segregated minority. The depth of that exploitation meant they would never be able to achieve equality within the system; their only hope was to create a separate black state. Lozovsky believed poor Southern whites would willingly join this new state since they too were exploited as workers and suffered the lower wages resultant from segregation. The new interracial workers' state, he asserted, would consist of the Black Belt region of the American South, a territory that Lozovsky defined as stretching from coastal Maryland though eastern Texas.[37]

Although he helped craft the program, Crouch was skeptical. As a Southerner he understood the depths of the racial problem in America and appreciated that few poor whites would be willing to grant any real political power to African Americans. Nor would they be willing to join them in a new state as coequals. He also appreciated how poorly the concept of secession would go over in general and was astute enough to understand that African Americans did not want to leave the United States but rather sought freedom and equality within it. Despite those concerns, he accepted self-determination as the new party line and prepared to return home to implement it.

According to historian Cedrick Belfrage, by this point the Soviets were all too ready for his departure. Despite Crouch's claims that he was a key player during his Moscow sojourn, Belfrage asserts that Crouch's time in Russia was far from stellar. Citing an unnamed "American teacher at the [Lenin] school," he argues that Crouch refused to study or do any real work and that "the Russians found his behavior so odd that after a few months they gave him money to go home."[38] Regardless of his actions or behavior, Crouch had spent four months in Russia and departed the socialist utopia ever more committed to the Communist cause.

Crouch traveled through Poland, Germany, and France, before finally setting sail for America in April 1928. Once back in the United States, he took a brief rest at Camp Nitgedaiget, a Jewish/Communist-affiliated camp in Beacon, New York. Not only did his time at the camp allow him to rest, it also provided him time to think and to meet new people. Among his thoughts was a plan to create a "small colony of radical writers and 'intellectuals' in North Carolina." He even wrote a letter to Pearson asking what he thought of the idea. Crouch then suggested that he might return to North Carolina and buy the home and land of Pearson's father so the two could work together on publishing a newspaper and organizing the colony.[39]

By this point Pearson had grown concerned about Crouch's radicalism and in August 1928 responded to the letter by expressing those worries. He wrote that while he respected Crouch's intellectualism, he was afraid of his revolutionary nature and feared that if they remained too close he [Pearson] would be dubbed a revolutionary. He wrote that he wanted to remain friends and believed Crouch was brilliant but stated emphatically that he would agree to work together on joint publishing projects only if Crouch dropped his revolutionary beliefs. Pearson concluded by urging Crouch to return to the church and leave all things in God's hands: "Any effort by men or by nations to leave God out will result only in disaster."[40]

While stung by this rejection, Crouch remained committed to the Communist cause. Indeed, his faith deepened as a result of meeting numerous individuals at Camp Nitgedaiget who had suffered for their beliefs. Among those he met were a refugee from Poland who had needles stuck in the bottom of his feet and water pumped through his nose while incarcerated, and an American who had opposed World War I and subsequently was brutalized in prison. The suffering of these individuals only confirmed Crouch in his belief that government was the cause of mankind's problems. He even wrote Pearson another letter in which he informed the journalist that if others understood the horrors governments perpetrated in the name of freedom, they too would demand a revolution.[41] In other words, Crouch's time at the camp further assured him of his faith.

Refreshed and confirmed in his revolutionary nature, Crouch returned to active party work as Director of the Communist Apparatus for Penetrating the Armed Forces of the United States. As a part of his duties, he began teaching military tactics in Communist schools. Up and down the east coast he taught Communist students various methods to "combat police and national guards during street riots and demonstrations."[42] He also worked to infiltrate the U.S. military based on the policies he had discussed with Tukhachevsky and others in Russia. This later task proved rather difficult as it involved finding Communists who could both pass the physical requirements of the military and could be released from other party work for this new assignment.

Despite that difficulty, he achieved early success thanks to Fred Taylor from Wilkes-Barre, Pennsylvania. Taylor was the first Communist to enlist in the military with the sole intention of using his time in the service for propaganda and party building purposes. He "enlisted in 1929 . . . and established civilian contacts in Panama, maintained correspondence through the underground channels which we established, served his enlistment without detection, and returned to the United States."[43] Crouch also claimed some success in the Navy, where after only a few weeks' effort he recruited ten sailors aboard the *USS Oklahoma*. These sailors carried out Communist propaganda once at sea and were able to arouse some level of discontentment among their fellow sailors.

Finally, Crouch turned his attention to the National Guard, where he enlisted 200 Communist Party members. Thus relatively successful in this military endeavor, Crouch continued his work until January 1930 when Trumbull succeeded him, continued the policies, and placed even more Communists in the military.

The BOI already had a file on Crouch, but these new efforts amid the military caused the bureau yet more concern and resulted in more surveillance. Agents tailed Crouch and noted his every action, from the shaves he received at a local barber, to the lunches he ate, to the several meetings he attended. They also noted his alias, Karl Fontel, and his residences in New York City and Hays, North Carolina. In the late summer of 1928, J. Edgar Hoover sent the Military Intelligence Division of the War Department two notes explaining the more important facts BOI surveillance had gleaned. The first letter noted Crouch's teaching itinerary, including talks and writings in which he urged "the naval forces of the United States to use their naval training to defend the 'rights of the working class.'"[44] The second noted that agents witnessed Crouch in New York City's Central Park taking pictures of soldiers drilling there. They also saw him take pictures of army war planes that were flying over the park at about the same time.[45] Neither the BOI nor the military were ready yet to take action against Crouch, but his efforts clearly concerned Hoover and the military brass.

Not only did these efforts amid the military concern the federal government, they also concerned Communist Party leaders. Several members found "his tales on the tall side," and came to consider him a braggart and a liar whose self-promotion ran counter to the needs of the party.[46] Not everyone believed his tales of meeting with Communist bigwigs in Moscow, nor did everyone believe his "success" in infiltrating the military. Indeed, several of his comrades believed Crouch was lying about all of it. Others, by contrast, were concerned with Crouch's apparent machinations to influence the intramural struggles then wracking the movement. In 1928 the American Communist Party remained split as a result of the continuing struggles in Russia to succeed Lenin. Crouch tried to remain separate from the internecine conflicts, but his work in the military unexpectedly dragged him in. Specifically, on several occasions party leaders accused him of trying to convince members to enlist in the National Guard or the regular army as a means of keeping them from being a part of the intraparty struggle. In other words, leaders believed Crouch surreptitiously was taking sides and trying to weaken his opponents by putting their supporters out of commission in the military.[47]

The intraparty struggle eventually ended once Stalin emerged triumphant. While Crouch emerged relatively unscathed, those who had backed other candidates soon found themselves on the outside looking in. Among them was Jay Lovestone, who in early 1929 was removed from his position as party leader as a result of his support for Nikolai Bukharin and his belief in American "exceptionalism," which rejected the Third Period application to the United States. Earl Browder eventually replaced Lovestone as leader of the newly renamed Communist Party of the United States of America, a position he would retain until 1945. Initially Crouch was pleased that the strife was over and accepted the removal of Lovestone and the accession of Browder as justified: "My reaction was that Lovestone's decision to fight the CI was treason to Communism, and I could not go along with it."[48]

In other reminiscences, however, Crouch said that the ouster led to his growing realization that under Stalin the Communist world would brook no dissent. He also realized that he too had become caught up in the shady world: "And I was beginning to learn that as an American Communist 'leader,' I was just a parrot echoing the voice of the master in the Kremlin. But as a disciplined Communist, I still believed in Moscow's infallibility, and in the final goal of the movement of which I was a part."[49] Once again, Crouch seemed to call his faith into question, but its pull on him persisted and he remained firmly convinced of the righteousness of Communism.

In July 1928 Crouch was freed from such political and personal concerns when Communist Party leaders sent him to cover a strike in New Bedford, Massachusetts. The strike erupted after textile manufacturers announced a 10 percent wage cut. Two unions, the Textile Council and the Textile Mill Committee, represented the workers, who were divided by skills, ethnicity, and goals. The Textile Council consisted of skilled Anglo-Saxon workers who simply wanted wages returned to their prior level. The Textile Mill Committee consisted of unskilled French Canadian workers who wanted wages increased 20 percent above the prior level, as well as a forty-hour week, the end of the stretch out, and the end of child labor. Although divided, both unions picketed the mills when management attempted to bring in replacement workers. The pickets turned violent, drawing in the police and costing the strikers public sympathy. Eventually, after more than six months out, the workers returned to the mills when management reduced the wage cut to 5 percent.

The Communists supported the strikers and hoped to gain new members from their midst. The party achieved little, however, and Crouch stayed in Massachusetts but briefly playing no role in the strike. He instead returned to New York City after the strike ended and was made head of the All-America Anti-Imperialist League, succeeding Manuel Gomez. In this capacity Crouch dreamed big and made plans to send one hundred party members to Nicaragua to aid Augusto Sandino and his rebel forces who were then fighting a guerrilla war against American occupying forces. The plan failed, however, due in part to cost and logistics.

Undaunted, but with his goals diminished, Crouch decided to attack imperialism via his literary skills. He thus wrote and released a statement attacking President Herbert Hoover's seven-week trip to Latin American as an example of American heavy-handedness in the region. He argued that the goal of the United States was imperial expansion and that Hoover's trip was evidence of it. He called the United States the most aggressive of all imperial powers and pointed to Latin America as the center of the imperial struggle. He asserted that international rivalries would lead to another world war, yet also argued that imperial powers were afraid of Soviet Russia for having inspired the colonial masses to rise up. He concluded that the only way to defeat the imperialists was through the unity of workers, farmers, and members of the exploited races and classes worldwide.[50]

Even this diminished literary attack on imperialism dissipated, however, when Crouch faced a new round of legal difficulties in early 1929. In January, Massachusetts state officials sought an extradition order to remove Crouch from New York so he could face charges for his role in the 1928 New Bedford strike. As his lawyer addressed the issue, Crouch briefly fled to Washington, D.C., in hopes of avoiding arrest. He soon returned to New York City, however, and was duly arrested on conspiracy charges along with several other Communist Party members. In a letter to Pearson about the arrest, he assured his old friend that his only connection with the strike was his effort to organize a defense committee for John Porter, the aforementioned deserter from the U.S. Army who

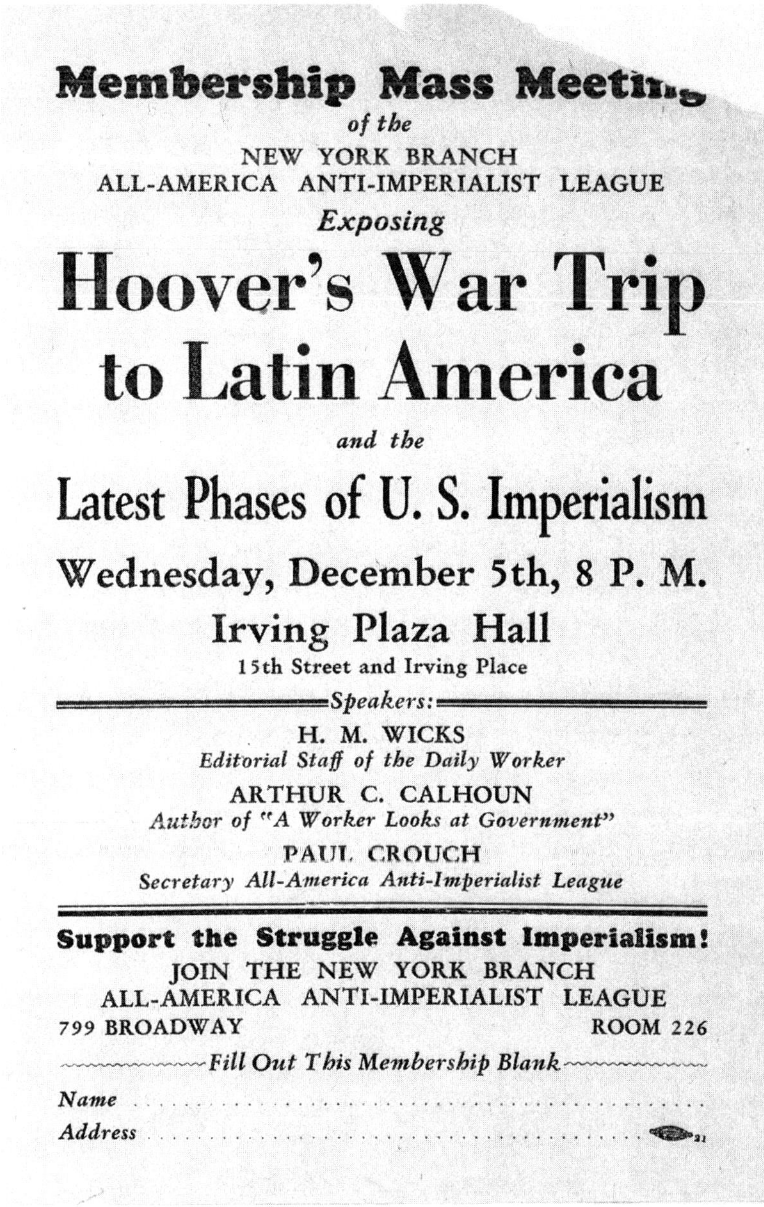

Figure 4. Poster announcing Paul Crouch's speech opposing President Herbert Hoover's trip to Latin America, December 5, 1928. Courtesy of the James Larkin Pearson Library, Learning Resources Center, Wilkes Community College Wilkesboro, N.C.

joined the Communist Party, partook in the strike, was arrested, turned over to the military, court-martialed, and sentenced to two and a half years' hard labor.[51]

Crouch's lawyers ignored this claim and appealed the extradition order to New York Governor Franklin Roosevelt on very different grounds. Specifically, they asserted that Crouch's actions did not warrant extradition. After meeting with Crouch and his lawyers, Roosevelt agreed with their contention and rejected the extradition request. According to BOI files, the reason Governor Roosevelt rejected the extradition order was that Crouch had remained in the city of New Bedford and the state of Massachusetts for an extended period after the strike and then returned peacefully to New York. He thus did not "flee" the state, as was required by law to force an extradition. Although the governor sided with Crouch on this legal issue, he said of the man himself: "I denounced the defendant publicly as a scoundrel, but I refused to permit the office of Governor of NY to be as a court for the collection of bad debts."[52]

Despite the personal critique, Crouch claimed this decision in his favor led him, yet again, to question his faith in Communism. He had long assumed that Roosevelt, like all politicians, was beholden to capitalists, bankers, and their moneymen. If, Crouch surmised, Roosevelt could buck his capitalist overlords in this individual case then maybe his other assumptions about capitalism were wrong. As he wrote years later, "My reaction to that meeting with Franklin Delano Roosevelt set in motion the forces that long afterward would take me out of the Communist movement."[53]

Freed from the immediate threat of prison, and only briefly shaken by the kindness of capitalist politicians, Crouch remained a busy and devout Communist throughout the remainder of the decade. He worked beside Whittaker Chambers as a columnist for the *Daily Worker*, acted as an official in the National Communist Campaign Committee, and served as editor of the *Young Worker*. He also remained in charge of the All-America Anti-Imperialist League. Having failed to achieve much as leader of the league, however, in October 1928, party leaders sent Crouch to Delaware, Virginia, and North Carolina to campaign for the Communist Party's presidential ticket of William Z. Foster and Benjamin Gitlow. While giving an open-air speech in Wilmington, Delaware, Crouch and African American Party figure Richard Moore, a candidate for Congress from the 21st district of New York, were arrested. Police removed Moore from the stage while he was speaking, and when Crouch took his place to continue they arrested him as well. On the way to the station the police taunted the two Communists by saying: "We told you that no more red meetings would take place in Wilmington." The taunt proved true, as a judge agreed to drop the disorderly conduct charges after Crouch and Moore promised not to hold any more meetings.[54] They did not, but they did pass out flyers and succeeded in getting the candidates on the ballot.

That accomplished, Crouch continued on alone to Virginia and his home state of North Carolina. He failed to get the candidates on the ballot in either state and realized the near complete absence of Communists in the South. Despite that absence, when he returned to New York he reported that the incipient industrialization around Charlotte made North Carolina the perfect place for the Communists to begin a Southern campaign. He also lobbied for Fred Beal, who had led the Textile Mill Committee during the New Bedford strike, to serve as lead organizer. Party leaders were pleased to learn that Crouch was not alone in his assessment. Fellow traveler Scott Nearing, leader of the Communist-led National Textile Workers Union (NTWU) Albert Weisbord, and party leader John DiSanto also urged the Communist Party to make North Carolina its base of operations in the South. As a result, in December 1928 the NTWU announced plans to send Fred Beal to North Carolina to organize the textile mills surrounding Charlotte.[55]

As Beal prepared for his organizational efforts, Crouch debated with James Larkin Pearson about the chances for the party's success. Pearson argued that the Communist Party's views on race doomed it. He believed that whatever good the Communists might offer Southern white workers, they surely would be turned off by the call for racial equality. Crouch rejected Pearson's contention, ignored the fact that he had similar concerns when the Soviets originally presented to him the idea of self-determination, and asserted that William Z. Foster and Scott Nearing had addressed race successfully during their tours of the South. He further argued that the party planned to send a black organizer south and asserted that "Not even the KKK can stop us!!" Then, as if to reassure himself, he added that he rejected the idea of black inferiority, said he worked with African Americans every day, and condescendingly explained, "I find them in every respect very intelligent."[56]

Crouch kept busy in New York as Beal worked to prove him correct.

He kept an eye on events in his home state, however, especially when workers at the Loray Mill in Gastonia, many of whom Beal had organized, went out on strike in April 1929 to protest management's firing of several union members. When the strike turned violent, Crouch requested he be allowed to help. Party leader Robert Minor agreed, and Crouch spent several weeks in Gastonia giving speeches and otherwise trying to aid the Communist cause. In late April he led the first of several groups back to New York City to raise money for the NTWU and the workers' strike fund. As a part of the fund-raising drive, on April 29 he described to the urban audience the punishing exploitation the poor rural workers endured. Because of the Communists, however, the strikers had grown self-aware and were fighting to overcome that exploitation. Success was within their grasp, he claimed, and he begged his audience to support the campaign.

In spite of the success of the several trips, problems soon ensued. Among them was infighting between Crouch and Karl Reeve, a representative of the International Labor Defense then serving in Gastonia. Reeve had a litany of complaints about Crouch, but what outraged him the most was Crouch's interaction with a local prostitute named Ruby MacMahon whose father and brother were deputy sheriffs. Crouch outraged the men when he tried to take Ruby on the trip to New York City. Although the family prevented her from making the excursion, Reeve accused Crouch of consorting with her and telling her secrets about the strike and the Communist Party. Reeve feared the outraged family and the breach of security threatened the strike, and he demanded party leaders do something with Crouch. Nothing came of the event, and Crouch remained in the region.[57]

He managed to infuriate others, however, as a result of his association with another woman, this one named Sylvia McMahon. Born on August 18, 1907, Sylvia hailed from Sevier County Tennessee, where her family had lived for more than a century. She grew up poor, poorly educated, and isolated—Pigeon Forge, the town nearest her home, lay some five miles away. In 1921 the family moved to Gastonia so as to work in the mills. Sylvia took a job as a spinner and worked twelve hours a day for $7.70 a week. When Fred Beal arrived and began to organize the NTWU, Sylvia joined. As she explained years later: "The Communists came and organized a strike against the mill where I was working. They talked about higher wages and better working conditions. When the workers struck, I struck too, and I joined the party. I thought then that they were working to help the underprivileged class of people."[58] Although Sylvia was of a more acceptable socioeconomic station than Ruby, the simple fact that Crouch was attracted to her upset strike leaders who believed the middle of a strike was no time for romance. Local leaders once again complained to national figures, who subsequently ordered Crouch back to New York City in June.

Away from the strike and the lures of Southern women, Crouch wrote up an assessment of the campaign. He asserted that many strikers had returned to the mill as a result of "a capitalist reign of terror," reported hearing "much talk of lynchings," and asserted that "it is widely and semi-officially announced that the first speaker at any future meeting in Gastonia will be shot down immediately."[59] The assessment proved prescient as at 10:30 p.m. on June 7, Gastonia Sheriff Orville Aderholt and a group of deputies and mill security invaded the tent colony where the remaining strikers were living after having been evicted from their company-owned homes. A shootout erupted injuring four men and fatally wounding Sheriff Aderholt. Police eventually arrested sixty Communist officials for the murders. Crouch was back in New York during the shootout but quickly returned to Gastonia to provide what help he could. There was little he could do. The strike pitifully wound down, and those charged with the murder of Sheriff Aderholt faced American justice. The number of defendants eventually fell to seven, and after an eventful trial all were convicted of second degree murder.[60]

Crouch ultimately expressed mixed feelings about the strike. He lamented its loss but blamed the defeat on factionalism, "stupid official orders," and "blundering tactics." But he also believed the campaign had opened the eyes of Southern workers to their exploitation and the role Communists were willing to play to end it. Thus, while questioning how his ideology was implemented, he remained committed to it, continued to believe in its righteousness, and felt assured that it promised a better future.[61]

Although Crouch's vision of the future remained rosy, his present was not so bright. The stress of the campaign, the general hardships of his job, and the difficulties of his several trips to Gastonia seriously affected his health, and he contracted pneumonia. After recovering, the party determined to send him to a less taxing assignment and ordered him to a YCL school in Waukegan, Illinois. There he taught twenty-three students the rudiments of Communist ideology and organizing. Among his students was the aforementioned Sylvia McMahon, with whom Paul was smitten in Gastonia. Their interaction as student and teacher only furthered the affections the two had for each other, and they became close. When the schooling ended they moved as a couple to New York City where they married in September 1929.[62]

Despite his new familial ties, once the couple settled in the city Crouch began to look for a little more excitement after the rather commonplace assignment as a school teacher. That excitement actually found him when Nicholas Dozenberg entered his life. Born in 1882 in Riga, in today's Latvia, Dozenberg moved to the United States in 1904 and in 1919 joined the Communist Party. He held dozens of different positions in the party and in 1927 was recruited by the Soviets as a spy. It was as a spy that he approached Crouch. Dozenberg introduced Crouch to the head of the Soviet secret police in the United States who asked him to place YCL members in State Department jobs from which they could acquire information.[63] Crouch was about to become the leader of a spy ring.

Before he could embark on this new career, however, two events sidetracked him. The first was the onset of the Great Depression. Despite the announcement of the Third Period, American Communists were caught unawares by the stock market collapse and the ensuing depression. In fact, it was not until February 1930 that the CPUSA finally determined on a response, and it did so only after Comintern prodding. Specifically, Comintern leaders ordered the American party to expand the "methods and pace of their work by concentrating their chief attention on the problems of the preparation and the carrying out of MASS REVOLUTIONARY ACTIONS OF THE PROLETARIAT—strikes, demonstrations, etc." More succinctly, Communists were to "fight in the streets."[64] American Communist Party leader Max Bedacht explained the change more clearly. He appreciated that "the economic crisis [would] not automatically bring the workers to building barricades," and called for the party to move away from "the dominating tendency of a propaganda sect to that of a revolutionary Party of action."[65] He called for the party to hold demonstrations, incite violence, do battle with the police and other agents of capitalism, and convince the masses that revolutionary socialism was the only route to social and economic security. Spying on the federal government, by contrast, took a back seat.

It was not simply global economic issues that changed Crouch's focus, so too did domestic issues. Sylvia became pregnant in early 1930 and they went back to North Carolina for her benefit. On September 13, 1930, the young couple welcomed their first child, Tanya, into the world. Two years later on January 18, 1932, their son Carl was born. Sadly, Carl soon was diagnosed with hemophilia, an affliction with which he would struggle for the rest of his life. Sylvia spent the early 1930s away from party work raising the children. Crouch did not.

Neither the changed international circumstances nor family life slowed him down for long. Crouch remained active in the Communist Party and in correspondence demonstrated that he remained as committed a Communist as ever. In June 1930 he wrote Pearson that the ends justified the means and, as such, he said he was willing to do anything to help the Communist cause. He assured Pearson that he hated violence and "would not like to kill a chicken," but argued that when you see a snake you must kill it. As such, he was willing to kill the snake that was capitalism. He further explained himself by arguing that only after the snake was dead would peace finally descend on the world: "Do you expect the workers to fold their hands and be satisfied to see their children grow up as human food for the gigantic industrial machine of capitalism, or for use as cannon fodder in wars caused by capitalist competition?"[66]

Crouch eventually admitted that he was not the murderous type and explained that what he really wanted to do to help the revolutionary cause was to produce books workers actually would read. He noted, "Looking Backward, no doubt, had more readers in the United States than Das Kapital." Crouch hoped to join the ranks of revolutionary writers so as "to portray the lives and thoughts of the masses and to aid as much as possible in producing literature that will tend to awaken their class consciousness."[67] While Crouch would do his fair share of writing, none of it approached *Looking Backward* or *Das Kapital*. The rest of his boasts to Pearson, however, proved much closer to the truth.

According to the BOI, Crouch returned to Russia in 1931 "for a post graduate course on Communism."[68] Newly educated, he would spend the next decade working across the country as a Communist organizer. As he spread the Communist message, he taught workers about the evils of capitalism and assured them that the only way to improve their lives was to destroy the capitalist snakes, thus opening the way for workers to seize control of the means of production and distribution. That organizing work, like all he had done in his first four years as a party functionary, would only deepen his faith in the Communist cause. Despite the occasional question or hesitation, Crouch was firmly committed to the ideology, adhered to it diligently, accepted the changed courses as required to meet the needs of an ever-changing world, and yet he still believed in its mystical powers to solve mankind's woes. An ideologue he remained as he ventured out on the second phase of his life as a Communist organizer.

4 DISTRICT ORGANIZER, 1932–1937

Healthy, educated, and reenergized, the family Crouch embarked on an eventful era, spending the years from 1932 to 1937 in Virginia, Utah, and North Carolina. Building on the ever deepening Depression, and intent on winning people to the Communist Party by fighting for the needs of the poor, Crouch found his element organizing the proletariat. As Cedric Belfrage notes, he was "a man from headquarters who could describe Russian marvels in a North Carolina accent, and as a serious sufferer from stomach ulcers, Crouch was welcomed by local comrades with awe and sympathy."[1] This charisma, charm, and shared sense of sacrifice made him relatively successful in his new incarnation as a Communist organizer.

In March 1932 the party sent Crouch to Norfolk, Virginia, where he took over as Section Organizer. When Crouch arrived he discovered only a single Communist in the city, but taking advantage of the Depression, he quickly found success organizing Unemployment Councils. The councils demanded an end to the eviction of unemployed workers, a 25 percent reduction in rents, and the use of the city's $300,000 budget surplus to offer $5 per week in relief as well as $2 per week in child support. Members also participated in a rent strike, during which people refused to pay their rent and moved the furniture of evicted individuals back into their homes or apartments. According to Crouch, those efforts won the Communist Party one hundred new members and thousands of letters of support. Even better, the rent strike ended victoriously when the city agreed to make cash payments to the unemployed to help them keep their homes.[2]

The efforts outraged many, however, and the party and councils soon faced a negative reaction from landlords, politicians, and other city authorities. At one meeting Crouch attempted to address forty audience members only to be arrested after uttering "Ladies and Gentlemen." Although no charges were filed, the official harassment continued. Sylvia, who had returned to active organizing efforts after some time away to raise the children and was serving as the local Unemployment Council secretary and a YCL organizer, was arrested and fined $25 for dragging furniture back into the homes of evicted people. Rather than pay the fine, she demanded a trial and used it to describe the horrors of unemployed life. The jury found her not guilty. Law enforcement, however, refused to give in.[3]

Using the alias Fred Allen, Crouch sent a letter to J. Louis Engdahl, head of the ILD, in which he described these continued enforcement efforts. He reported on an "intensive terror campaign against the Communist Party in Norfolk," which he alleged was organized by the "War and Navy departments, immigration authorities," and the local police. Crouch informed Engdahl that while a few arrests occurred, the local authorities were determined to use extralegal means to rid the city of the Red presence. According to his report, "Chief of Detectives Nowitsky told me: 'If I bring charges against you I could not make them stick and the judge would be forced to dismiss them. But you will not be allowed to stay in Norfolk, I guarantee you that—We will find means to get rid of you." The means, Crouch then proceeded to describe. He reported that in Portsmouth, Virginia, where a small unit had been formed, "comrade Bren K. Lacka" had been beaten up while two police officers looked on. Days later, he reported, Detective Nowitsky and a sizeable force of immigration authorities raided the Communist Party headquarters in Portsmouth without a warrant. The police searched everyone and examined their "citizenship papers [and] army discharge" notices.[4]

It was not simply the local authorities, however, who were aware of Crouch's efforts. The presence of Communists near the Norfolk naval yards also aroused the attention of the BOI. A bureau report from June 5, 1932, noted that Crouch again was agitating among ex-servicemen and was trying to convince them to join the Bonus March then congregating in Washington, D.C. The report claimed he "was using the same old propaganda that the Government owes them a living and if they go to Washington they will have to be looked after." It also noted that Crouch had been very active and that twenty-five to thirty former soldiers were expected to attend the march.[5]

Local party leaders were aware of the surveillance and grew frustrated by the continual harassment from both local and federal authorities. Unsure how to proceed, Crouch asked national Communist Party leaders whether or not he should "take an offensive attitude against the terror." Although no advice was forthcoming, Crouch decided it was best not to challenge local, state, or federal authorities and instead used the persecution to inspire his fellow Communists. He explained to them that the persecution was yet more evidence of the evils of capitalism and that they should take the abuse as evidence of their success.[6] The struggle thus invigorated both Crouch and his fellow party members.

Crouch and the Communists in Norfolk demonstrated this growing vigor and faith when they took a new tact in their local struggle with the publication of a newsletter called the "Norfolk Worker." The first issue went public with the same stories of which Crouch told Engdahl. The paper claimed that on March 17 workers in Norfolk tried to stage a rally in support of striking auto workers in Detroit but that the police "intimidated, searched and threatened those who came through the police lines and entered the hall." The paper further noted that Crouch was arrested "for reading a statement protesting against this terror and taken to the police station." It then described the subsequent assault on Lacka and invasion of the Communist Party headquarters. That such violence took place during peaceful meetings, the paper alleged, was proof that all workers faced the threat of the capitalist bosses—not just those who were on strike. The paper called on the entire working class to put aside their petty differences and join together in the larger struggle against the capitalist menace. As the "Norfolk Worker" put it: "Do not let the bosses use one section of the workers against another."[7]

In August, Crouch and local party members moved from protests and journalism to electoral efforts. They succeeded in getting national CPUSA leaders William Z. Foster and James Ford on the Virginia presidential ballot and got "Comrade S. W. Milligan of Portsmouth," an African American clergyman, on the ballot as a candidate for the 2nd Congressional District (Norfolk). As part of the election campaign, Crouch rented the Norfolk City Auditorium for a speech by Foster on October 17 and worked to get the speech broadcast on the radio. Those efforts were expensive, however, and he requested money from the national party to help cover the $100 in fees. Crouch also asked for help in getting other speakers for the electoral campaign, noting that while he had some good local volunteers they were not great orators, and his voice could only hold out for twenty minutes as a result of various ailments. He concluded by noting that the party was doing well raising money and distributing campaign literature and hoped this evidence that the locals were doing their part would inspire the national Communist Party to help out. Days later, however, Crouch grew worried that Foster would not speak, and he asked for assurance from national leaders that Foster would do so. In an effort to ensure this visit, Crouch noted that the party already had raised $50 toward the cost of the campaign events. On the last day of September, Crouch sent off another letter to the national election campaign committee in which he noted that the previous week the party held an outdoor rally on a small farm outside of Norfolk and was planning another rally in Suffolk, Virginia, for the coming week. Crouch announced that a new Communist Party unit had been formed in Suffolk and that the campaign was going well, but he still needed money, "white speakers" for future rallies, and an assurance that Foster would speak.[8]

Crouch's concerns deepened in early October when he realized that local segregation laws forbade an interracial event. If whites and blacks were to attend the scheduled rally, they had to sit on opposite sides of the venue and the Communist Party was required by law to provided ushers who would keep the races to themselves. Failure to do so would result in a $500 fine for the organizers, and individuals who crossed the color line were subject to a $25 fine. Worse, party lawyers assured him that holding an integrated event would give the police the justification they needed to break up the speech. Crouch was thus in the dilemma of acceding to local segregation laws in order to ensure that the speech by Foster was heard or of defying the law, upholding the Communist Party's traditional opposition to segregation, and having the affair broken up. Crouch asked for advice from the national party.[9]

Party leaders eventually responded by encouraging Crouch to hold the meeting in an integrated fashion. They also informed him that Foster would not speak but that *Daily Worker* editor and candidate for the U.S. Senate from Pennsylvania, Harry Wicks, would. Wicks did indeed give the speech in Norfolk, and he used it to urge people to vote for Communist candidates. More important, he called on those present to put aside their racial antagonisms and join together as workers: "Any party which does not raise its voice for the 12 million Negroes of this country is no workers' party, no organization of the masses."[10] The CPUSA was just such a group, he claimed, and pointed to the integrated audience as evidence that the working class could get beyond race and work together for the greater good. Although the speech indeed was integrated, police did nothing to break it up, and, according to Crouch, "from that moment the law calling for separate seating of Negroes and whites in public meeting places . . . was a dead letter in Norfolk."[11] Although a rather sizeable exaggeration, Crouch and the small party units in southeastern Virginia were proud of their efforts.

That pride was wounded, however, when Virginia scrubbed the Communist Party's congressional candidate S. W. Milligan from the ballot claiming he had not met the state's legal standards. In a frantic effort to make up for that loss, the party determined to focus on the presidential campaign. Crouch convinced Joe Clayman, S. W. Milligan, Martin Butts, H. Alterman, Allen Clark, Cornelius Brock, and William Emerson to stand as electors for the party's presidential ticket of Foster and Ford. There was little need for the electors, however, as the Communists managed only eighty-six votes. Crouch claimed that simply getting the candidates on the ballot and registering a few votes was evidence of Communist activism in and around Norfolk, but national party leaders were not impressed. Worse, the recurring issue of Crouch's health popped up in the days before the election, and he began to complain about various illnesses and ailments.[12]

Despite those problems, both organizational and health related, Crouch continued to work, and in late 1932 he tried to organize black marine workers, attempted to foment a dockworkers strike, and sought to create Unemployment Councils in Newport News, Virginia. None of the efforts achieved much, except for two arrests in November. On November 10, 1932, Crouch appeared before a judge on a charge of "trying to start a riot between the Negros and the police." The day before the trial Crouch sent a letter to national party leaders informing them of the case, the expected result (a $500 "peace bond"), and the continuing financial needs of the district.[13] Much to his surprise, Crouch was acquitted of the riot charges. In mid-November he faced another court case on criminal syndicalism charges. Although the BOI reported finding among his personal papers "instructions from Moscow to stop scrap iron shipments to Japan through strikes, sabotage, and any other means," the charges were dropped and he returned to organizing.[14]

Although he escaped jail, Crouch grew to fear that physical violence would replace official harassment. He warned national party leaders that increased violence was imminent and that Mayor Phillip H. Mason, who previously tried to prevent bloodshed, recently had warned that "those putting back furniture will be shot down." This fear deepened when flyers soon appeared throughout the city reading "WARNING: Communism will not be tolerated in Norfolk. The Ku Klux Klan Rides Again!"[15] The warnings soon came true as several local Communist Party members were beaten and assaulted.

Worn out by the constant threats, violence, and hectic activism, in late December 1932 Paul, Sylvia, and the kids took a vacation and stayed with his parents in Hays, North Carolina. Although the break was scheduled for two weeks, Crouch was still in North Carolina two months later. He kept in touch with national party leaders throughout the extended vacation, however, and in February 1933 penned a handwritten letter to the party secretariat. In it he addressed his belief that he had become too well known in Norfolk to achieve any additional gains as an organizer and that it was time for him to begin organizational work in another state. He suggested the secretariat talk with Walter Trumbull and others who could judge his abilities and where those abilities could best be used. For his part, Crouch suggested that he serve where he could work with former soldiers and where his legal and journalistic skills would be of most use. He informed party leaders that he was ready to return to full-time activism anywhere in the nation, "except malarial sections," and assured them that "my rest here has resulted in considerable gain in weight and health improvement—but I am very anxious to be back on active duty in the army of the working class as soon as possible." He concluded by noting that he would need a little extra money to take care of his children, Carl having been born in 1932, but that he and Sylvia generally did their best to reduce expenses as much as possible.[16]

The party agreed with much of Crouch's letter and transferred the family to Utah in the spring of 1933. The Crouches arrived in Salt Lake City to find 200 Communists as well as a growing number of Trotskyites. By this point, Stalin had destroyed all of his opponents and was firmly in control of the Soviet Union. Most of those opponents had been killed, but Leon Trotsky had eluded Stalin's grasp and was enemy number one. Since the CPUSA took its cues from the Soviet Union and supported Stalin, party members viewed the Trotskyites as traitors to the cause of organized Communism. As a result, one of Crouch's first efforts in Utah was to break up a speech by Trotskyite leader Max Shachtman, who was scheduled to speak in Salt Lake City. Crouch and several party members heckled him and otherwise worked to prevent Shachtman from speaking. Crouch later claimed to feel remorseful for his actions, but praise from national party leaders helped assuage his guilt, and he turned to a more important task—organizing coal miners.

Crouch focused this effort on the mines of Carbon County (southeast of Salt Lake City) and ordered Communist Party member Charles Weatherbee to the region first. Initially, Weatherbee, along with locals Charles Guynn and his wife Ray, were able to make only minor inroads through the National Miners Union (NMU). The NMU, a Communist-affiliated union, had arrived in early 1933 but achieved little. When Crouch appeared on the scene he dramatically increased propaganda efforts on the union's behalf. They started a union paper called the *Carbon County Miner*, plastered the county with flyers announcing the union and its goals, and held several union meetings which attracted nearly 1,000 attendees. These efforts focused on the town of Helper, a largely Slavic community that was also known as the "miners town" or "foreigners town," as distinguished from the nearby town of Price, which was the county seat and the "coal operators town." Reports note that the residents of Helper welcomed Crouch and the Communists and packed his first meeting, which was held in "Millerich Hall, a Serbian-owned building."[17]

Although attentive and interested, and certainly outraged by the sagging mine economy of the Depression era, it was only after operators at the Standardville mine reduced wages that workers expressed real interest in the NMU. The union responded by calling a strike, which quickly succeeded with the company restoring the wage scale and reducing rents on company homes during the summer months when the mines were at their slowest. That success encouraged the NMU to formally incorporate in Helper, and on May 28, 1933, it did so. Charles Weatherbee presided over the meeting, which included as one of the speakers Paul Crouch. According to news reports passed on by a "spy" from the National Guard, Crouch railed against the New Deal, especially the low wages paid in the make-work programs, and claimed such wages were evidence that Roosevelt was in bed with big business. He also alleged that programs like the Civilian Conservation Corps were a ruse and were not meant to help workers but rather served to get them in uniform and familiarize them with guns and organization. Such agencies, in other words, were part of a move toward domestic fascism. After the meeting, the NMU formed a local committee that laid out the union's specific demands, including lower rents, higher wages, cash payment every two weeks, a miners' checkweigh man, recognition of the union, and permission for laid-off miners to remain in the company owned homes.[18]

The union formally established, Crouch and his fellow Communists, as well as union leaders, set out to spread the word. This was especially important as the United Mine Workers of America (UMWA) also had a presence in the region and NMU organizers wanted to make sure workers joined the "correct" union. The UMWA had been rather dormant in Utah, but with the appearance of the NMU and the growing sense of union activism, it sprang to life. According to Helen Papanikolas, who studied the union efforts extensively, it was local officials, notably the mine owners, mayor, and American Legionnaires in Price, who supported the regeneration of the UMWA believing it was more moderate than the NMU and could offset its activism and power by winning away workers.[19]

Despite those efforts, the NMU drew ever larger crowds. Crouch was part of the reason for that success, as his experience as an organizer had trained him how to win over the masses. He won huge applause for his attacks on the UMWA, which he claimed had sold out to the mine owners. He also won accolades for his attacks on the Reconstruction Finance Corporation, which he claimed was allowing operators to pay in script in violation of state and federal law; on Hugh Johnson, head of the New Deal's National Recovery Administration, for allegations that he was filthy rich; and on Roosevelt's Secretary of Labor Francis Perkins for her alleged lack of concern and understanding of the poor. Sylvia also did her part talking to the wives of mine workers, strengthening their resolve and training them how to behave in the event of a strike or violent demonstration. Union representatives, by contrast, spent much of their time trying to downplay the Communist presence and assuring workers that all the union wanted was better wages and working conditions, not the overthrow of the government. Both efforts worked, and on July 9 some 800 workers attended an NMU rally at which they learned that Labor Day was to mark the start of a general strike should union demands not be met.[20]

The call for a general strike encouraged some miners to embark on wildcat strikes, and in early August miners in nearby Mutual, Utah, went out. The workers demanded recognition of the NMU and that owners hire local miners and stop hiring workers from afar. The mill agreed to the latter demand but not the former, and workers accepted the compromise and returned to work. While management may have hoped that the concession would preclude a general strike, such was not the case. Union leaders made clear that the Labor Day strike was to go forth as planned unless owners agreed to all the union's demands.

Such talk, as well as the success in Mutual, led to even more wildcat actions. On August 23, 215 miners at the Spring Canyon mine walked out. Fearing this was the start of something larger, Sherriff Marion Bliss requested Governor Henry Blood send in the National Guard. The governor refused, even as the strike spread to three mines at Gordon Creek. Local officials grew increasingly nervous as the strike wave continued to spread and they resorted to extralegal measures to convince the governor to send help. Crouch's car was broken into and copies of the *Young Worker* were stolen and sent along to the governor as evidence of the Communist presence. NMU headquarters were similarly raided, and Communist literature allegedly discovered there also was passed on.[21] The NMU responded by sending two signed petitions to the governor asserting that the strike was peaceful.

Despite the petitions, the governor ultimately acceded to the demands of the mine owners. To keep the peace he sent in two detachments of the guard and deputized nearly three hundred locals, many of them UMWA members. The first National Guard unit arrived on August 24, with the second arriving a day later. Despite their presence, union efforts continued, and on August 26 NMU protests organized pickets in front of the Gordon Creek mine. Deputies soon arrived. When the picketers refused to move, the squad fired tear gas. As the mob broke up amid the smoke, police arrested sixty-eight, including Sylvia Crouch, on charges of rioting. Police held Sylvia until 9:00 p.m., but upon her release she quickly made her way to the Spring Canyon mine where another picket line had formed. She informed the miners of what had happened at Gordon Creek and encouraged them to fight back should the deputies arrive.[22]

Despite Sylvia's warning, the 400 picketers in Spring Canyon were no match for the deputies who arrived early the next morning. Eight canisters of tear gas broke up the crowd, and deputies arrested 210. Those arrested were taken to the local jail and, according to reports, were left without food, water, or blankets for twenty-four hours. Outraged by these events, union leaders ordered the general strike to begin. In response, deputies patrolled local roads for the stated purpose of keeping out guns and ammunition. At the same time, however, the deputies arrested dozens of union leaders and Communists on charges of criminal syndicalism. Guynn and Weatherbee were among those arrested; Crouch managed to avoid arrest, although warrants for him were drawn up. The arrests and charges did little to stymie the strikers, and on September 11, 400 of them protested in Price to demand the release of their leaders and to push for the union's demands. Police confronted the protestors and demanded that they disperse. When they did not, officers lobbed in tear gas and then fired water cannons into the crowd. As the mob broke up, police arrested dozens. Among those they captured was Sylvia Crouch.[23] She was released on $5,000 bond, and the charges were later dismissed.

Among those they missed was Paul Crouch, who was present at the protest despite the warrant. Missing Crouch infuriated the police. On the ensuing evening, 100 deputies, without legal warrants, descended on Helper and broke into thirty boarding houses, hotels, and homes of known union supporters looking for him. They failed to find Crouch.[24] Local officials were frantic as a result of this failure and passed an ordinance banning future public meetings. Meanwhile, a local judge set September 16 as the start of the syndicalism trial for Weatherbee, Guynn, and Crouch, who remained at large.

The continuing chaos in and around Carbon County delayed the trial long enough for Crouch to surrender to local authorities on September 20, 1933. Although faced with charges of criminal syndicalism, he was freed on $10,000 bail and waited for his case to go to court. Before Crouch would be heard, however, the court would first hear Guynn's case, which commenced on October 5. He was convicted quickly but appealed, claiming that the jury foreman, R. L. Loveless, had been a deputy during the strike. His appeal went forth as Crouch's case began, but when an appeals court overturned the Guynn verdict and ordered a new trial, local authorities agreed to drop all charges as long as the men left the county. They did.[25] One of the reasons they did so was because all the while they were fighting their legal battles the UMWA had been negotiating with mine operators. By the end of October the union had signed an agreement that called for higher wages and recognition of the union. Most miners accepted the agreement and returned to work.

Although the "wrong" union won, Crouch labeled the campaign a success. The miners gained some improvements and party membership rose from 200 to 300. Despite that, at a conference of national Communist Party leaders held in Denver not long after the strike, Pat Toohey, the party's representative to the Comintern, criticized Crouch's efforts in Utah. Toohey had nothing to say about Crouch's organizational achievements but instead attacked him for "failing to expose the demagogic character of Roosevelt and the New Deal."[26] Considering Crouch's rhetoric during the strike, the charge may seem unfounded. Crouch, however, had not attacked the president personally, in large part owing to Roosevelt's 1929 decision not to extradite him back to Massachusetts. The Communist Party had no such sympathy for the president and viewed him as simply another capitalist politician and the New Deal as simply another capitalist ploy to undermine the working class. According to historian James Ryan, there was an additional reason for this hatred: "[CPUSA leader Earl] Browder despised FDR for stealing the working class from the workers' parties."[27] Roosevelt achieved in one hundred days what the Communists had tried and failed to do over the course of thirteen years—win the support of the workers.

As for the president's policies, the CPUSA had more substantive arguments. Browder argued that the New Deal's main features were "trustification, inflation, direct subsidies to finance capital, taxation of the masses, the economy program, military and naval preparations, [and] militarization, direct and indirect, of labor," and he even went so far as to define it as a program that paved the road toward American fascism.[28] The party also assailed the Agricultural Adjustment Administration (AAA) as an institution designed to help "the kulaks, the bankers, and the mortgage companies" and attacked the National Industrial Relief Act (NIRA), despite Section 7(a) and its provisions allowing for collective bargaining, as "a capitalist attack against the living standards of the masses" that was created solely to destroy labor unions and empower the corporate elite.[29]

Compared to such vitriol, Crouch's rhetoric was rather measured, although hardly worth a public rebuke. Crouch wanted to rebut the charges, but he remembered his scolding in Moscow as well as the expulsion of Jay Lovestone and held his tongue fearing that Toohey was speaking on behalf of more powerful members of the party. Crouch desperately desired to remain a Communist and accepted the public censure, deserved or not. And while once again made aware of the fact that democracy did not exist in the Communist Party, he remained too fully wrapped up in its grasp to do more than stew in private and request a new assignment.

That new assignment was slow in materializing. Crouch left Utah toward the end of 1933 and spent the rest of that year and early 1934 "hopping from one industrial town to another with time in Massachusetts, Rhode Island, Pennsylvania, Virginia, the Carolinas, Georgia, and Alabama." He even went to New Orleans and played a minor role in the formation of a Share Croppers Union branch in the Mississippi Delta.[30] None of that was what Crouch really wanted to be doing, however, so he was pleased when in the summer of 1934 the Communist Party named him District Organizer for CPUSA District 16, which included North Carolina and Virginia.

Crouch arrived in District 16 at a crucial time. First, the local party was reeling from serious internal squabbles that drove away nearly two-thirds of its membership and created bad blood between those who remained. Second, despite its initial vitriol, the CPUSA had finally realized that the New Deal actually offered opportunities for radical action. Specifically, it came to appreciate that Section 7(a) of the NIRA enticed workers to join unions, including Communist unions. Indeed, by the end of 1934 membership in Communist-led unions rose from 25,000 to 100,000, in large part thanks to the fervor for unionization the New Deal inspired.[31] Even better, the New Deal engendered labor unrest; 1933 saw three times more strikes than had 1932, and 1934 was even more active.

Determined to heal the rifts caused by the squabbles, grow the party, and take advantage of this increased labor activism, Crouch decided to focus his organizational efforts on textile workers. He believed their agitation over wage cuts and their recent talk of striking made them prime candidates for Communist Party activism. He worried, however, that District 16 was unprepared to lead a strike and decided to draw workers into the party and then make the move toward activism.

The first part of that effort was to relocate the party headquarters from Charlotte to Greensboro where it would be closer to the mills. He then sent party activists throughout the district to recruit new members. In July 1934 he and Sylvia joined the effort and made their way to Danville, Virginia. Police arrested Paul while he was distributing Communist leaflets and charged him with vagrancy. Judge C. K. Carter dismissed the charges after Crouch began to spout propaganda during the trial, and while the arrest increased the Communist Party's notoriety it did little to bring in new members.

In fact, the effort could have cost the party, as Danville police implemented a blockade to round up other Communist organizers. The resourceful Sylvia, however, was able to avoid the cordon and continue Communist efforts in the city. As the press reported her efforts years later: "Once, when there was a strike in Danville, Va., and police had blocked off the roads to prevent Communist agitators from bringing in party propaganda to stir up the workers, Mrs. Crouch took her baby in her arms, packed an innocent looking suitcase full of party literature and travelled on a bus past the police lines."[32] Despite Sylvia's daring, the efforts to expand the party base proved lacking. External events, however, were about to offer the Communists in District 16, and Paul Crouch in particular, the greatest organizational opportunity since the Gastonia strike of 1929.

The events centered on the 1934 General Textile Strike. 400,000 textile mill workers up and down the East Coast walked out on strike in September 1934 to protest the stretch out and low wages and to demand recognition of the United Textile Workers Union (UTW). The Communists did not start or even inspire the strike, but Crouch saw an opportunity to expand the party's presence and worked to insinuate the Communists into the campaign. To facilitate that effort, on September 11 Crouch staged a series of mass meetings. Speakers at these meetings found few willing converts, however, as the failure in Gastonia lingered in the workers' memories. More problematic than the failed meetings was the constant harassment. Police in Concord, North Carolina, arrested Crouch and Communist organizer Caroline Drew and confiscated a wide array of propaganda. Police in Gastonia, North Carolina, arrested

Sylvia and Communist organizer Belle Weaver for illegally distributing handbills within city limits.[33] Police in Charlotte arrested Crouch on the steps of the Mecklenburg County Courthouse after he tried to give a speech without a permit.[34] In each case the organizers escaped prison, but the lost time and propaganda undercut the party's efforts.

The lost propaganda points to yet another problem the Communist organizers faced—the lack of a unified base. Only about half of the textile workers in District 16 actually participated in the strike. Although that put the number of strikers in the region near 100,000, it also meant that the strike was incomplete. It was not simply the fact that some workers continued to produce that concerned the Communists, and the UTW as well, but that some struck plants continued to operate thanks to replacement workers. Among the flyers the Concord police seized was one which asked, "Why are these Concord mills not COMPLETELY closed 100 percent?" and answered, "It is because we have not had real mass picketing—stopping every scab who tries to enter the mills!"[35] The flyer further urged the strikers to refuse arbitration, to remain strong, and it encouraged them to take their wives to the pickets for additional moral support.

A related problem was that the working class in general remained divided. The National Guard, which North Carolina Governor John Ehringhaus had called out to protect the mills, consisted largely of working-class men who were being forced to pacify the strikers and protect the replacement workers. A second confiscated flyer addressed this issue and urged guardsmen not to defend the replacement workers or otherwise facilitate the strike breaking efforts: "Tell your officers you will not shoot down striking workers!"[36]

The inability of the Communists to proffer their agenda and the failure of the working class to stick together ultimately doomed the strike and the Communist hope of benefitting from it. The workers soon returned to the mills defeated, and the Communists returned to their headquarters having gained few new converts. Crouch admitted failure. After examining the situation, however, he believed he understood why the Communist Party failed and how to correct course. He determined that the party failed to achieve much in the strike because it remained too weak, it refused to ally with the UTW and other non-Communist unions thus weakening the base, and it had underestimated the workers' militancy.

To address those issues and correct course, Crouch ordered district units to spend more time educating their members. He organized weekly education classes with question-and-answer sessions, increased training for local leaders, and created Marxist libraries. He also demanded the Communist Party expand and called for doubling membership, expanding the number of units, and increasing circulation of the *Daily Worker*.[37] Crouch believed such efforts would strengthen the party and give it the stability needed to succeed when the next organizational opportunity arose.

In late November, two weeks into the new program, Crouch expressed frustration with the results. Although there were fifteen units scattered throughout District 16, he believed the district remained weak and had failed to embark on the reforms he had devised. He was more frustrated, however, with the growing problem of infighting and his inability to stop it. Danville, Virginia, section organizer James Crews, for instance, complained that area textile organizer Claud Clark was disrupting party meetings, while Clark accused Crews of ignoring his ideas and engaging in "factional maneuvers." Crouch proved unable to resolve the dispute and asked national Communist Party leaders for advice. He received no response, but local organizer Jim Weaver suggested Crouch order Clark into a mill. This would separate the two men and save the party the $8 each week Clark was being paid. This financial gain was as important as ending the squabbling, Weaver asserted, as Clark was an "inefficient organizer" whose salary could be better spent in support of poor families. Crouch agreed and took Weaver's advice.[38]

Crouch realized that his failures during the General Textile Strike, the lackluster growth of the district, and the infighting he could not solve did not place him in a good light. The resultant fear that he might lose his job, combined with the rigors of organizational work and being a father, caught up to him in late 1934, and he began to complain about health issues. In a letter to national leaders on November 20, 1934, Crouch complained that he had a "serious cold last week and then relapsed developing into grippe."[39] Five days later he returned to a discussion of his illness when in another letter he reiterated his previous complaints about the grippe, noted that he had been bedridden for days, and added that he had a stomach ulcer as well.[40] In December he continued his complaints: "Extremely poor health of the DO has been a retarding factor in all aspects of the work. If we had sufficient forces I would ask for a leave of absence for a few weeks, and it may become absolutely necessary. Apparently, chronic appendicitis and badly run down condition, also colds and attack of flu. Need an early and thorough medical examination. Medical service here very expensive and unreliable—no sympathetic doctors."[41] Communist Party leaders ignored his pleas for a doctor and a vacation, but undaunted, Crouch tried again when on February 21, 1935, he asked for "two weeks' vacation to be taken soon, at a time we can arrange best to have Dist. Work taken care of—financed by Dist. For three years I've not had three days in succession away from work except when traveling on official business or so ill I had to stay in bed. After a couple weeks' vacation I think I will be ready for more intensive work."[42] Crouch did not get the rest he requested and returned to organizational work.

Among that work was an additional effort to correct the district's problems. In February 1935 Crouch set new goals for the first half of the year including the recruitment of one hundred new Communist Party members and twenty-five new YCL members. He also ordered all party members into a union where they were to work to win new adherents to the Communist cause. Finally, he demanded an end to infighting and ordered all party members to obey orders and abide by the decisions made.[43]

Crouch received some help in this effort to strengthen the district thanks to yet another policy shift by the Comintern. In 1935, realizing that capitalism might not fall anytime soon, that workers and farmers were more interested in bread-and-butter issues than revolution, and that Hitler and global fascism were the real international threats, Stalin announced the end of the Third Period and beginning of the Popular Front. This new policy sought to expand membership by dropping the Communist Party's revolutionary rhetoric and organizing alliances, or united fronts, with left wing groups and unions. With the slogan "Communism is Twentieth Century Americanism," the Popular Front, according to historian James Ryan, "signaled the Communists' decision that defense against reactionaries had become paramount and that the offensive toward socialism had to be postponed indefinitely."[44] Although an obvious, pragmatic, and dramatic move to the political center, Communists saw this as a temporary change in policy designed to attract members and address the growing international threat.

Crouch accepted this policy shift as he had the others. Soon realizing that it fit in well with his agenda for growing District 16, he began to implement the Popular Front program. One front campaign instituted by Crouch during the strike wave that carried into the Popular Front era was an attempted alliance with the Socialist Party. During the strike Crouch had suggested to national head of the Socialist Party Norman Thomas that the two groups put aside their ideological differences and work together for the masses. He proposed a joint program calling for the repeal of state sales taxes, state funded unemployment insurance, and the easing of ballot restrictions.[45]

Thomas already had rejected an alliance with the national CPUSA and similarly rejected Crouch's proposal. Crouch responded to the rebuff by accusing the Socialist Party of putting its needs ahead of the workers. He then worked to undermine it by stealing away individual Socialist Party members, with the result that North Carolina state secretary of the Socialist Party Alton Lawrence and state committee member Hazel Dawson both applied for membership in District 16 of the CPUSA. When informed of their application, national party leaders instructed Crouch secretly to enroll them as Communists. They would then maintain their standing in the Socialist Party and could pass along information that might benefit the Communists in their struggle for support among the working class.[46]

Crouch achieved similar results with his campaign for a united front with unions. He first made an effort to ally with the UTW. The two groups were unable to ally during the General Textile Strike and actually spent a great deal of time attacking each other as the enemy of the working class. Despite that, after the strike failed UTW leader Francis Gorman agreed to work with the Communists. Although Crouch now had what he wanted—a united front with labor—he decided to dominate his new ally. He ordered Communists to join the UTW and work from within to seize control. That effort continued until 1937 when Crouch sought an alliance with the competing Textile Workers' Organizing Committee (TWOC). The committee refused Crouch's proposal, however, and publically ridiculed the idea. That public pronouncement outraged the UTW, which ended its alliance and left the Communists with little to show for their united front efforts with labor.[47]

Crouch was a bit more successful with a third united front campaign—this one with churches. Despite the CPUSA's well-known atheism, during the General Textile Strike several churches in District 16 had allowed Communist speakers to appeal for aid from the pulpit. Crouch hoped to expand that effort and approached a number of ministers to ask if they would allow party members to spread their antiwar message. Several ministers accepted the offer, and Crouch and others spoke out against militarism in general and the Italian invasion of Ethiopia in particular. James Ford, an African American national Communist Party leader and former vice-presidential candidate, also participated in this united front campaign and in January 1936 spoke at large church meetings in Charlotte, Durham, and Greensboro.[48] The party won few substantive gains as a result of this effort but succeeded in spreading its message through a rather unique forum.

One final campaign of this sort was the renewal of the Communist Party's work with the unemployed. Efforts through the Unemployment Councils had abated during the General Textile Strike, but in 1935 Crouch decided to revive the groups as a means of demonstrating the party's continued support for all workers—employed or not. The work with the councils received a boost when Cabarrus County, North Carolina, reduced relief aid by a third and ceased grocery relief. The county's Unemployment Council blasted the move and criticized the wealthy politicians who made the decision as heartless and vindictive. The council then demanded the county provide $5 of relief per week for each unemployed worker and $3 per week for dependents, offer free books, milk, and hot lunches for school children of the unemployed, and end evictions. In an effort to force the county's hand, the Unemployment Council called for supporters to elect an executive committee in each neighborhood that would organize mass efforts to prevent evictions and to form tenant leagues that would give renters more power to negotiate with their landlords.[49] Counties throughout District 16 engaged in similar activities and made similar demands—but with little success. Despite that failure, the overall efforts of the united front campaigns demonstrated to national party leaders that Crouch was making up for his previous failures. He was overseeing an active district, had solved the infighting that had previously plagued the unit, and seemed to be maturing as a leader.

All of the old problems reappeared with a vengeance, however, when in May 1935 Crouch again began to complain of health issues. This time, rather than ask for a vacation, he simply informed party leaders that he was going to take a few days off to recover. As Crouch recuperated, Jim Weaver decided it was time to address Crouch's constant illnesses and their impact on the district. On June 8, Weaver sent national Communist Party leaders a letter in which he addressed his concerns.

> Comrade Crouch is, and has been, in very bad physical health, which of course makes for a tremendous handicap to his effectiveness as District organizer. In addition to being in bad health himself, so is his wife, Comrade Sylvia Crouch, and the two kids. None of them seem to ever be well, and with doctor bills, etc. it's a constant drain on party finances without resulting in any organizational results. Comrade Crouch is a sick man and not able to be in charge of a party district. I lay much of his ineffectiveness to this fact—his poor health.

Weaver went on to note that recently Crouch missed an important unemployment meeting in Greensboro and that "I as well as a number of other leading comrades in the District are quite discouraged with the outlook of Comrade Crouch's work as well as with previous results." He then recommended giving Crouch "a few months to rest and recuperate" and concluded that "other comrades down here feel the same way," and they would be "quite discouraged with our outlook if Comrade Crouch is to remain as D.O."[50]

Weaver showed Crouch a copy of the letter, and Crouch, in a letter to the national leaders, acknowledged the veracity of the complaints. He urged the party to appoint a new District Organizer and recommended that his replacement be a Southerner and a "*PROLETARIAN*." Baring a replacement, he asked for additional time off to recover. Party leaders agreed that his health was a hindrance to organizational efforts but were not ready to replace him, so on July 15 they granted him a month-long vacation.[51] Fred Gray acted as interim District Organizer.

When Crouch returned from his sabbatical he was furious with Gray. He alleged that "Comrade Gray has the most sectarian ultraleft position on all political questions, confused ideas of all sorts, and his organizational work is extremely poor."[52] He further alleged that Gray had failed to collect dues, keep records, or attend meetings, and had ignored recruitment efforts and the Unemployment Councils. Crouch quickly stripped Gray of all his powers, publically castigated him, complained to national party leaders that if Gray "is kept here much longer he will completely wreck the District," and demanded that he be reassigned.[53]

Gray responded by accusing Crouch of factionalism and ignoring his organizational duties. Specifically, he charged that Crouch failed to travel and oversee the entire district, failed to address work among the unemployed, failed to acknowledge some of the problems the district faced, and had constantly butted heads with his subordinates. Key to this friction with fellow party members, he argued, was that Crouch refused ever to admit he was wrong. Gray concluded his letter by asserting that Crouch remained ill despite the month away and that it was his illness that was the source of these failures. He thus urged Communist Party leaders to remove Crouch for his health and for the good of the district.[54] Although Gray proved correct in his assessment of Crouch's health, he lost the struggle and was reassigned.

Crouch remained District Organizer for two more years but achieved little. He did run for governor of North Carolina in 1936, along with party member Anna Williams who ran for lieutenant governor. Sylvia served as their campaign manager and proved rather adept. She convinced radio stations in Greensboro and Durham to broadcast their speeches statewide and made great use of a newly purchased printing press to distribute masses of flyers and pamphlets. The candidates benefitted most, however, from outside forces. On October 2 radio stations WPTF in Raleigh, WSOC in Charlotte, and WWNC in Asheville broadcast a speech by Communist Party presidential candidate Earl Browder. Then on October 25 the party's vice-presidential nominee James W. Ford visited Durham.

Ford spoke to some 500 supporters and opened his remarks by declaring the rise of domestic fascism the real issue of the upcoming election. He said he was alarmed at the domestic dangers the nation faced and feared "the forces of reaction are destroying all the things that Jackson and Lincoln fought for."[55] He moved on to deny the oft-made claim that Communists sought the revolutionary overthrow of the government and reminded the audience that he and thousands of other Communists had served loyally in the U.S. military. He then concluded his speech by reminding his listeners that Communists only wanted what was fair for the average worker: unemployment insurance, pensions and aid for the elderly and sick, better schools, a more progressive tax system, and racial integration.

After the speech Ford dined with University of North Carolina (UNC) English professor Dr. Eston Everett Ericson. This interracial dinner outraged many, and for months the state was awash in demands that the university fire him. Ericson kept his job, and the Communists basked in the free publicity the dinner and public outrage created. Despite that notoriety, the electoral results proved dismal. Browder and Ford won only 79,315 votes nationwide, with only 110 coming from District 16. Crouch and Williams did even worse, registering not a single tally.[56]

That result seemed to embody perfectly the fact that Crouch had done all he could in District 16. In September 1937 national Communist Party leaders agreed and transferred him to Birmingham, Alabama, where he would organize workers and edit the *New South*, a new Communist journal. Although a demotion, Crouch was excited by the opportunity to return to journalism, and the family hoped that a more moderate workload would keep him healthy.[57] At the same time, despite all he had been through in the previous five years, Crouch remained as devoted as ever to the Communist cause. The health issues, the internecine squabbles, the undeserved criticisms, the failed campaigns, the dramatic policy shifts: none of these affected his faith. Focused on the salvation of himself and mankind, Crouch either ignored or justified those issues that called his Communist ideology into question and pushed forth as determined as ever toward the socialist revolution.

5 QUESTIONING COMMUNISM, 1938–1947

Still enthralled by the siren song of Communism despite failure, illness, and brief moments of doubt, Crouch left his Carolina home for Alabama in 1937. The next decade would prove as challenging as any period in his life, and his faith was tested like never before. While he remained devoted to the cause for much of that era, the tests became ever more severe and by 1942 finally proved too much. As war clouds brewed, opened up, and eventually exploded on American shores, Crouch dropped the rose-colored glasses and saw his ideology for what it really was. The ideologue would finally escape the chains of the ideology, but freedom would prove as perplexing as anything he faced as a Communist Party member.

Crouch arrived in Alabama in part to oversee the establishment of a new magazine entitled the *New South*. Its purpose was to influence liberals and progressives and, as such, after the first two editions and despite being funded by the national CPUSA, the magazine did not note it was a Communist organ. Among the liberal and progressive issues Crouch covered in the paper was the formation of the Southern Conference for Human Welfare (SCHW). The group called for shorter hours, worker compensation laws, desegregation, abolition of the poll tax, antilynching legislation, aid to farmers, uniform federal voter registration laws, state level graduated income taxes, and state level Wagner Acts to protect unions from management meddling.[1]

Crouch did more than cover the SCHW; he was one of six avowed Communists to attend its first organizational meeting held on November 20, 1938, in Birmingham, Alabama. Despite the presence of twelve additional "covert Communists," as well as Crouch's future assertions that "behind the scenes a CP steering committee was constantly busy" and that everything the SCHW did "had the approval of the Central

Committee [of the CPUSA]," the reality was more prosaic.[2] Indeed, Southern party leader Rob Hall claimed at the time that Communists played only a minor role in the meeting. As Thomas Krueger, author of the SCHW history writes in *And Promises to Keep*, "the Communist party . . . took a friendly interest in the Southern Conference, nothing more."[3]

Even Crouch, when writing about the organizational meeting for the *New South*, asserted,

> Southern progressives are proud of the South, of the splendid role played by our ancestors in the Revolutionary War and the establishment of our Nation. They are proud of the scenic beauty and the great natural resources found in the South. It is because they love the South that they wish to abolish illiteracy, poverty and starvation and disease from our land. There are differences of opinion on details, but there is no reason why a common program cannot be worked out for improving the conditions of the Southern people and making our South a better place in which to live with conditions inferior to no other part of the Nation.

He continued,

> The abolition of poverty, equality of opportunity, and intelligent use of resources and means of production can only be achieved through fundamental changes of the economic system for which the South and the Nation are not yet ready. But considerable improvement is possible now, and a minimum program upon which all progressives can agree will do much to raise the Southern people above the starvation level and to give them such cultural and material advantages as are enjoyed in other sections of the country.[4]

Crouch perceived that the SCHW would serve the interests of the Southern working class and bring together the various liberal groups who hoped to help that class. He did not view it as a revolutionary organization. This perception would change, and his association with the SCHW would have future consequences, but in 1938 it was only one of several issues keeping Crouch busy.

He also stayed busy dealing with internal party squabbles. This time, however, Crouch was not the cause of the squabble but rather the one to help quash it. In 1938 he learned that a Georgia Communist member was gossiping about the party, spreading rumors about its activities, and otherwise undermining its efforts. Crouch met with Southern party leader Rob Hall and then traveled to Georgia to meet with state leader "Comrade Taylor" to determine who the gossip was and how to handle him. Crouch later claimed to have discovered the culprit and, after so doing, to have debated with Communist Party leaders as to how to punish the wayward member. He alleged that two Soviet agents participated in the discussions and suggested the member be killed. Crouch "pointed out the unfavorable repercussions which might follow," so the agents suggested the author be given the opportunity to travel to Russia for "training," with the understanding that people who made such trips rarely returned. Crouch opposed that option as well, and the group ultimately decided simply to expel the rogue member.[5]

While the Soviet agents may not have been happy, American Party leaders were pleased enough with Crouch's actions to send him to Mexico in 1939 to meet with international Communist leaders. Paul and Sylvia stayed six weeks, during which time they learned of the Nazi-Soviet Non-Aggression Pact, which was signed on August 23, 1939. Crouch, and indeed most party members, initially were shocked by the alliance. A fundamental premise of the Popular Front was antifascism, and yet the Soviets had just signed a treaty with the fascists. The pact thus caught American Communists off guard.

The party's first response was a rather convoluted claim that the pact strengthened Poland, weakened Germany, and offered "a wonderful contribution to peace."[6] The *Daily Worker* praised the treaty because it "not only tremendously limited the direction of the Nazi war aims, but thereby bolstered the possibilities for peace in the world."[7] When World War II erupted a week later, on September 1, 1939, the Communists kept to their antifascist tradition and denounced the Germans, praised the British and French, and demanded that the United States do everything in its power to help Poland and prevent the further spread of fascism.

In reality, American Communists had no idea how to react to the new international situation; they were waiting for some word from Moscow. On September 12, 1939, they finally heard from the Soviets via shortwave radio. The message shocked the party almost as much as the treaty and the outbreak of war. The Soviets informed the CPUSA that the war was not part of the struggle against fascism that the Communists had been waging for the last several years. Instead, like World War I, this war was simply another imperialist struggle. As such, Communists worldwide were to oppose both sides and demand peace.

Initially, American Communists offered only meek platitudes denouncing the war; it was not until October 1939 that they become openly critical. This change may have had something to do with the fact that on October 23 Earl Browder was arrested for passport violations. Almost immediately upon his arrest, the CPUSA dropped all restraint and attacked President Roosevelt as a warmonger, asserting that he was leading the nation into an unnecessary war for the benefit of big business. As the war progressed, the Boats for Bases deal, Lend-Lease, and the Atlantic Charter provided the Communists more ammunition and elicited claims that Roosevelt was aping Hitler and driving the United States toward a military dictatorship. As a result, they sought to undermine the war effort by informing the Allies that "The Yanks Are Not Coming!"[8]

The CPUSA thus returned to a Third Period mindset early in the war years, bitterly attacking the president and refusing to work with any organization that supported him or the war effort. As Fraser Ottanelli writes, the move "undermined the credibility of the CPUSA as an indigenous radical organization."[9] Harvey Klehr concurs and notes, "the Nazi-Soviet Pact ended the most successful era in American Communist life, clearly demonstrating that loyalty to the Soviet Union took precedence over any and every other consideration for the entire Party."[10] Realizing that ideology was irrelevant and all that mattered was the whim of Stalin and the needs of the USSR, many American Communists grew outraged and abandoned the party. Crouch was unable to make that break and accepted the shifts and the Communist justifications for them. This is not to say that he was not perplexed by the moves; he simply submitted to them.

Crouch left Mexico and returned to Alabama and his work on the *New South* in dramatically altered global circumstances. His personal circumstances also changed, although not as abruptly, when in late 1939 he was promoted and transferred to Tennessee to serve as state secretary. Crouch succeeded Ted Wellman in that position, whose great success had been to organize approximately a dozen Communists within the Tennessee Valley Authority (TVA) in Knoxville. As described by Aaron Purcell, those individuals were young and well educated but worked at the lowest levels of the TVA. Despite that, or maybe because of it, they were able to interact with and help organize both white- and blue-collar workers within and without the authority. During the last few months of Wellman's tenure, however, the group fell apart as the individuals took different jobs or returned to college. Crouch believed many simply quit the Communist Party as a result of the Non-Aggression Pact and the shifts resultant from World War II.[11]

It was not simply TVA workers who fled, however, so too did regular Communists. Party units in Knoxville and Norris, some twenty miles northeast of Knoxville, dissolved shortly before Crouch arrived. Crouch also discovered that Wellman had made little effort in the rural areas of the state, although he soon learned about one farm outside of Knoxville where the party stored materials and another farm outside the city that was selected as a hideout should the government go after state party leaders. He also learned that most African Americans had fled, leaving only six active members. Crouch thus arrived at a difficult time for the Tennessee party. He found only seventy-five to eighty members statewide, with only fifteen less-than-enthusiastic members in Knoxville, another fifteen in Chattanooga, and thirty more in Nashville.[12]

Crouch did not find the cupboard entirely bare, however. Of those who remained, most were Russian or Polish immigrants who had a long history within the larger revolutionary tradition and accepted the twists and turns of international diplomacy. He further claimed there were six "newspapermen" in the party and that Communist activity in Nashville, centered on historically black Fisk College, remained vigorous. Additionally, he found twenty-five Communists in Monteagle, most of whom were associated with the Highlander Folk School, the labor training center founded in 1935 by Myles Horton. Crouch also claimed that Chattanooga was a "secondary Communist center" because the city generally tolerated Communist activism. As he put it years later: "The party attached a good deal of importance to Chattanooga because the local authorities didn't interfere with it and it was able to carry on its affairs. The party could rely on its constitutional rights in Chattanooga much better than in any other southern city."[13]

Despite some bright spots, Crouch had plenty of work to do to rebuild the party. His first effort was to expand the unit at Fisk College, where he claimed "there was a very active branch of the Communist Party . . . composed principally of white professors." There were only two or three student members, however, the most active of whom was Esther Cooper who served as an organizer for the Southern Negro Youth Congress, a Communist-dominated civil rights organization. Edwin (Ed) McCrea, a native New Yorker who attended St. John's College and NYU and would later go on to organize unions in Winston-Salem, North Carolina, and Memphis, Tennessee, ran most of the meetings at Fisk College, but Crouch frequently attended as a speaker.[14] Although the unit never grew particularly large, its presence and activism remained a bright spot for the Communist Party under Crouch's leadership.

Crouch also worked to win back the TVA employees who had left at the start of the war. He was pushed in this effort by Earl Browder, who "emphasized that the party would show off its full resources to concentrate in building the branch, the organization at TVA." Crouch later explained, "I called a number of meetings, attended by as many as a dozen TVA employees, after my arrival, all former party members. I tried to get them to return to the party, but I met a barrage of questions on the international situation that I could not answer to their satisfaction, and they did not return."[15] Unlike the efforts at Fisk College, Crouch proved unsuccessful in stimulating any Communist Party growth among workers in the TVA.

Undaunted by that failure, and in an effort to expand the CPUSA into new realms, Crouch returned to journalism and published the *Knoxville Volunteer for Peace and Democracy*. The sole issue, December 1939, described the CPUSA as "a small American political party always found in the front ranks of the workers in their drive for better conditions." The paper focused most of its attention on the international situation and complained that Roosevelt was trying to get the nation involved in World War II to help big business. Included in the issue was a visual representation of this claim with a cartoon depicting a man in a suit and top hat, with a dollar sign on his side, pushing Uncle Sam off a cliff into the swirling waters of war. By contrast, the paper played up the Communist Party's opposition to the war and support of the Non-Aggression Pact as proof that Communists were not going to play capitalist games and had decided to sit out this war.[16]

The journalistic campaign also fell flat, however, and Crouch realized that as important as were international issues, local concerns remained preeminent. He thus focused much of his energy in that direction in 1940 and 1941. During a meeting at the Ross Hotel in Chattanooga on

May 26, 1940, the Communists determined the best way to demonstrate their domestic agenda to the people of Tennessee was to run for political office. Crouch, therefore, planned a run for the U.S. Senate, but that run was contingent on getting on the ballot. On September 9 and 10, 1940, he appeared before the Tennessee State Election Commission in Nashville in an attempt to do just that. Despite his assurances that Communists did not advocate the seizure of power through force and violence, the Commission barred him, and indeed all Communists, after determining that the CPUSA sought the violent overthrow of the government.[17]

When the electoral angle failed, Crouch turned back to the SCHW, which in 1940 held a conference in Chattanooga. Crouch attended and took with him several members in the hopes of demonstrating that the Communist Party was not alone in its struggle for equality. That effort also failed, however, as the conference got sidetracked on international issues. Specifically, the delegates debated Lend-Lease, and, while Crouch and his fellow Communists were vocal in their opposition to it, most liberals supported the president's plan to aid the British. The debates did little to inspire the Tennessee Communists who joined Crouch at the meeting, and they came away believing their local needs were being subsumed by the war effort.[18]

As a result, Crouch returned to Knoxville more determined than ever to focus on local concerns. In late 1940 he began a campaign against the poll tax and also laid plans to expand into Memphis. As a part of that first effort, Crouch tried to get Knoxville radio station WROL to broadcast a speech by James Ford on the issue of the poll tax, but the station refused despite party threats to sue. No suit was forthcoming, and instead Crouch began to create a united front with other organizations that supported the abolition of the poll tax. The Communists, along with the NAACP, the American Federation of Labor (AFL), the Congress of Industrial Organizations (CIO), the League of Women Voters, and the SCHW formed the Tennessee Commonwealth Federation, which called for the end of the poll tax as well as civil rights, union rights, and democracy. The federation achieved some success and by April 1941 had convinced several counties in eastern Tennessee to abolish the poll tax. As that campaign progressed, national party leader Robert Minor informed Crouch that he was aware of the efforts, praised his leadership, and said that national leaders were "very much intrigued in what you told us about the poll tax fight and the very important work being done."[19]

Minor also referenced Crouch's suggestions for a move into Memphis and gave him the go-ahead to do whatever he saw fit. Due to the fact that Crouch was an open Communist and that Memphis was well known for its endemic anti-Communism, Crouch had Ed McCrea, who was not publicly affiliated with the party, do much of the organizing work. His efforts soon resulted in the creation of a small group in the city. The Memphis Communists focused much of their activity on civil rights. They organized to help protect African Americans being abused by the city's police force and worked to spotlight the continued threat of lynching. More important, the effort in Memphis reinvigorated the movement statewide. By early 1941 the state Communist Party numbered some 150 members, while the party committee in Tennessee consisted of: Ed and Beatrice McCrea (Nashville), Sam Reece (Knoxville), Simon Kaset (Chattanooga), "Eliz." (Monteagle), Dr. Addison (Red) Brown (Chattanooga), Francis Martin (Knoxville), and members-at-large Esther Jackson née Cooper (Nashville) and Harry and Mary Lou Koger (Memphis).[20]

Of the overall workings of the state party, Crouch noted "All of the party activities in Tennessee were conducted on a semi-underground basis. Meetings were kept small. Committee meetings often were held in cars parked by the side of the road. Instructions were given that party members were not to be mentioned in correspondence. Very little material was sent or received from the national office by mail." He further summarized the situation in Tennessee as follows: "Large distribution of these hand mimeographed [flyers], intensive training of members in operations of it [the mimeograph machine], storing of large quantities of mimeograph papers, stencils and ink, meeting regularly with the reserve organizer, giving him all the information so that he could take over at any time the operation of the party."[21] The state Communist Party, in other words, was active, developing a propaganda machine and, despite the need to remain secretive, was doing well.

At the same time Crouch was achieving some organizational success, however, he also found time for new experiences. Due to the help of Ed McCrea, diminished expectations from the national CPUSA, and a brief extended period of good health, Crouch was able to meet and associate with non-Communists for the first time in years. As he enjoyed this leisure and the resultant new associations, he also began to ponder his position within the Communist movement: "Always until then I had taken the Communist movement for granted to such an extent that I could not understand why anyone was not a Communist. Now . . . I carefully studied the views expressed by these new friends, and drew them out on various topics, with no thought of trying to convert them to the C.P. I was surprised to find that most of them were getting much more out of life than the average party member whom I had known."[22]

With these thoughts lingering, in April 1941 Crouch and family were ordered to move yet again, this time to Oakland, California, where Paul became a member of the county committee for the Communist Party of Alameda County. The operations in Tennessee were left to Ed McCrea. Crouch saw this transfer as a promotion, as the Oakland shipyards were essential to war production and the University of California, Berkeley, was the center of a great deal of scientific and military research. Indeed, by the time Crouch arrived the Communist Party already had established a close relationship with several scientists and engineers at UC Berkeley and had implemented a policy in support of striking the shipyards.[23] Crouch planned to continue and expand those programs, and he expected to be busy.

The Federal Bureau of Investigation (FBI), as the BOI was renamed in 1935, noted that Crouch's first appearance in California was a speech on June 28 in which he talked about the Soviet Union. Bureau records also note that a riot erupted when sailors tried to break up the meeting but that the fighting stopped after a band played the "Star-Spangled Banner." A week later, on July 6, Crouch spoke at Hermann Sons Hall on "Socialism vs. Fascism" with similar results.[24] Crouch gave dozens of speeches throughout 1941, and, while the membership rolls of the Alameda County Communist Party increased to about 300, none of his efforts led to strikes in war industries. One reason for this failure was that most workers were opposed to the Communist Party. Despite their desire for better wages, they viewed the party as un-American for its attacks on President Roosevelt and its opposition to the war. A second reason for the failure was yet another dramatic policy change that occurred not long after Crouch arrived.

On June 22, 1941, Germany broke the Nazi-Soviet Non-Aggression Pact and invaded the Soviet Union. Although the CPUSA had opposed American intervention in the war since its inception, with the motherland now at risk such a platform no longer made sense. As with the initial outbreak of the war, party leaders were left on their own. California state party leader William Schneiderman wanted to ramp up strike and sabotage efforts in response to the invasion, but the national CPUSA rejected that policy and decided to wait for orders from abroad.[25] International Communist leaders eventually ordered the American party to support the war and call for immediate American intervention. The Communist slogan thus changed overnight from "The Yanks Are Not Coming!" to "The Yanks Are Coming!" In other words, once again the CPUSA was forced to make a dramatic policy shift to fit the needs of the Soviet Union. Crouch accepted the changed platform and dutifully burned all of the local party's antiwar material. Not everyone was so accepting, however, as hundreds of party members fled and potential allies shied away.

Despite such problems, Crouch remained busy as the Communist Party was kept on high alert and leaders prepared to go underground at a moment's notice. Convinced that once the United States entered the war the government would crack down on the party, Communist leaders stopped issuing dues books, stopped keeping membership records, and held numerous meetings to train leaders on how to hide mimeographs and other such devices so the party could remain viable even with leaders underground. As a part of that, and in an effort to compartmentalize the Communist Party to protect it from possible arrests, county organizers, including Crouch, were not allowed to know the names of other organizers or the members of other county units.[26]

Crouch spent much of 1941 teaching the members of the Alameda Communist Party the global objectives of the Communist movement, the means of reaching those goals, the problems the party would face in its underground efforts, the methods of creating illegal leaflets, and other strategies for underground operations. He also worked to grow the party and focused on the county's growing immigrant population. He did this in part with bilingual advertisements. A flyer inviting people to the twenty-fourth anniversary of the Bolshevik Revolution to be held in Oakland on November 7, 1941, for instance, focused on the local Hispanic population and was titled "Pueblo Espano, Amantes de la libertad, Paz y Justicia," and signed "Partido Comunista." Crouch also reached out to the Japanese community. Indeed, he later asserted that he found the perfect individual for organizational work among the Japanese, a young woman named A_____, whom he believed could "be trained quickly for mass leadership in a pro-democratic movement." Much to Crouch's chagrin, however, state party leaders rejected the idea of working with the Japanese and showed little interest in attracting local immigrant or ethnic groups.[27]

Something more substantive came from another of Crouch's efforts, although the repercussions would not be felt for more than a decade. Crouch later asserted that it was while in California that he first came to know that Dr. J. Robert Oppenheimer was a Communist. Crouch explained that in August 1941, "by decision of the Communist Party leadership, a joint meeting was arranged of two units of the Communist Party, both units of a special section of the Party in which extra-ordinary precautions were taken. These units were (1) a unit of top professors of the University of California; (2) the unit of the Communist Party at the Radiation Laboratory of the University of California." Kenneth May was in charge of the special section, and he once took Paul and Sylvia to a house party in Berkeley. At the party, there occurred a closed meeting in which only CPUSA members were allowed to participate. Crouch said that Oppenheimer was at the meeting and that "he showed a remarkable understanding of Communist and Marxist teachings."[28] During later testimony, Crouch asserted that during the meeting one of the key issues discussed was stepping up efforts to infiltrate the Radiation Lab.

Crouch claimed that at the time he did not know who Oppenheimer was even though after the meeting they talked about personal issues. It was only after the gathering broke up and May was driving Paul and Sylvia home that he learned that the man with whom he had talked was "a very famous scientist." This was not the only such meeting, and Crouch eventually testified that he met Oppenheimer numerous times over the next several months at various Communist Party affairs. Crouch also claimed that at similar get-togethers in August and September 1941 he met Dr. Clarence Hiskey and Dr. Joseph Weinberg, both scientists from the University of California soon to be attached to the Manhattan Project. Also present were California party leaders Steve Nelson and William Schneiderman.[29] At the time, Crouch thought nothing of the meetings or the associations with Oppenheimer, Weinberg, Hiskey, and the others. The object was to aid the Communist Party and the Soviet Union by accessing American scientific secrets. A decade later, however, such an objective was treason, and Crouch would find himself in the middle of legal wrangling surrounding all the aforementioned individuals.

Those issues lay in the future, and as 1941 came to an end Crouch had more personal matters to deal with. In his words: "In the fall of 1941 I found myself increasingly disgusted with the CP and was torn inwardly by a growing realization that I was working for an organization completely dominated by men who had no regard whatever for the American people, and who respected no laws of human decency."[30] Crouch later wrote that he came to realize that the Communist Party's "purposes were evil and that it had no regard for the fundamental rights of humanity and nothing but contempt for real democracy." He further added: "I made that difficult decision to break with the Communist Party only because I was aware that my own future and that of my children would have no meaning if Stalin were victorious and subjected the world to the ruthless Soviet dictatorship. . . . The victory would mean a return of the world to slavery, tyranny, and unbridled despotism."[31] The ideology, in other words, had finally been exposed to Crouch as something sinister. Its hold on him was loosened, and he decided it was time to be free of the movement that had been the center of his existence since 1924.

At the same time Crouch was questioning his ties to the Communist Party, it seems that the party was questioning him. Cedric Belfrage notes that Crouch's California comrades "soon began complaining of his Marxist ineptitude: his reading seemed to consist mainly of the *World Almanac*, and he devoted much time to playing the jukebox in a bar and staring at the wall. Everyone felt sorry for him and his wife because of their son doomed by hemophilia; Nelson and others donated blood and visited them with toys and gifts; but inevitably comrades voted to oust him. They continued chipping in for medical expenses while Crouch drifted away."[32] Despite such sympathy, Belfrage contends that as Crouch was falling out of love with the party, it was reciprocating.

The Communist Party was not yet ready to sever ties completely. In November 1941 Crouch asked to be released from organizational activities so he could seek private employment. Despite Belfrage's contention, California party leader William Schneiderman was unwilling to lose Crouch; he rejected the request and ordered Crouch to continue his party work. Although a perfect example of the lack of democracy within the Communist Party, Crouch accepted the decision and carried on. Not long after, in late November, Sylvia took a good paying job with the Western Die Casting Company. Buoyed by the good money Sylvia brought home, Crouch pushed aside his unhappiness with the party and continued on with his organizational work. He was further buoyed after Pearl Harbor, when the Communists came out even more fervently in support of American intervention, which finally could be sold as benefitting the United States, not simply the Soviet Union.

Just days after Pearl Harbor, on December 11, 1941, Crouch demonstrated his continued allegiance to the Communist cause when he authored a report on the Alameda County party. He focused first on the status of the party and noted that there were 374 members (up from 329 in the summer) who composed forty-one branches (up from thirty a year earlier), of which nineteen were territorial, ten were industrial, and the others were focused on language groups, professions, or other specific entities. He then praised the effort to have regular meetings, the increase in the number and size of branches, and the improved trade union work. After that, he called on members to reexamine the party to find its weaknesses and strengthen them. As part of that, he demanded more information on membership, education, and recruiting. He also expressed his worry about insufficient contact with the larger political elements in the region, about not having a workers' school, the isolation of leaders from the working class, poor team work, and poor relations with the YCL. To address those issues, he offered nine proposals for improvement: adding two new members to "mass work of the Party"; weekly meetings of the county committee; recruiting more women; reorganizing the unit to be more efficient; strengthening leadership; abolishing administrative committees to allow county organizers to make more decisions; creating a new party in Hayward, southeast of Oakland; improving contact with the YCL; and getting section organizers to send in their meeting agendas a few days early so local leaders could all be on the same page.[33]

All seem sensible suggestions, and Crouch continued to be a good soldier despite his unhappiness with the Communist Party. He was thus outraged when, in mid-December, he learned of an important meeting to which he was not invited. Irate that he was not allowed to leave the party and yet was being excluded from important decisions, he determined to quit. Once again Schneiderman refused to accept this defiant act and instead informed Crouch that he had been reassigned to Los Angeles. Crouch refused, citing his desire to work outside the Communist Party as well as the need for Sylvia to remain in her position with Western Die. By this point Sylvia also had made clear her unhappiness with the constant upheavals and demanded that the family remain stationary so as to ensure the children a more stable family life and a better education.

Schneiderman had little interest in such domestic affairs and was livid at this insubordination. He thus demanded a meeting with Sylvia. Of the meeting Crouch later wrote: "When she walked into his office he stormed at her: 'Don't you realize that this isn't a request? Don't you know this is a party order? You have *got* to go!' She replied that she didn't care whether it was a party order or not, that she wasn't going. Schneiderman turned red with rage. Such audacity was unheard of in the C.P." Unsuccessful in intimidating Sylvia, Schneiderman had another meeting with Paul, during which he verbally abused him and then expelled him from the party. Crouch later reflected that while it was a bit shocking to be kicked out of the organization of which he had been a member for seventeen years, he was happy to be free.[34]

That happiness took some time to overcome habit, however, and Crouch later admitted that he continued to pay his dues, although sporadically, for another year and only stopped for good in 1943. He also explained that Steve Nelson, who replaced him as Alameda County organizer, personally visited him often in 1942 and 1943 to try to win him back. Despite the expulsion, Nelson, at least, viewed Crouch as a useful member and tried to entice him to return. In 1943 he even sent Crouch a dues book, which Crouch kept and would later present as evidence to the federal government.[35] Despite those temptations, Crouch refused to return.

Free from party work, pay, and discipline for the first time in seventeen years, Crouch looked for employment, which was plentiful as millions of men joined the armed services in the aftermath of Pearl Harbor. He easily found work, first in February and March 1942 with the Union Oil Company at Rodeo, just north of Oakland, and then in April with the Acme Furniture Company in Oakland. He eventually accepted a more permanent job with the United States Steel Corporation in Alameda, where he remained throughout the war years. He quickly joined the newly formed United Steelworkers Union, CIO Local 1789, and in July 1944 was elected to the union's Board of Trustees, a tenure that would last until January 1945.[36]

Not surprisingly, he did not serve in the military during the war, although like all American men he was classified, receiving a 3-A designation on April 30, 1942, which provided him with a deferment because of his children. A month prior, in March, he had signed an affidavit stating that he was not and would not become a member of the Communist Party. With this assurance, and the knowledge that he was no longer a party member, in October 1943 the FBI office in San Francisco announced that it was removing Crouch from its "key figure list" and urged headquarters in Washington, D.C., to do the same. Thus employed, free from the Communist Party, free from military service, and free from FBI surveillance, Crouch spent the war years relatively quietly in California. He remained at U.S. Steel, Sylvia remained at Western Die, and the family enjoyed a brief period of peace and stability.[37]

They remained in California until January 20, 1945, when Crouch led them to Brownsville, Texas. It is unclear why they left California as the war entered its final year, but the move may have had something to do with Crouch's earlier desire to be a barnstorming pilot in the military. Whatever the reason, Crouch took a job with Pan American Airlines and the family moved to south Texas where they continued to live in relative peace if not prosperity.

Despite the move and the wishes of the California branch of the FBI, the bureau continued to monitor Crouch. The FBI noted that he lived on Morningside Drive in Brownsville, worked as a mechanic and painter for Pan Am, and made $1.23 per hour. The bureau also learned that in 1946 the Transport Workers Union of America (TWUA) began organizational efforts among the Pan Am workers. Crouch initially hesitated joining the union due to its alleged affiliation with the Communist Party, but he eventually took a card with Local 504. Bureau records note that he was elected secretary of the Executive Committee of the Brownsville local and that in the summer of 1946 he traveled to Mexico with TWUA leaders Maurice Forge and Ed Beck. Crouch later claimed that it was during this trip that the two union leaders learned he was "the Paul Crouch" and bombarded him with all variety of questions relating to his years in the Communist Party. Crouch obliged, in part because he had not yet publicly announced that he had quit.[38]

During a subsequent trip to New York City for the TWUA, Crouch claimed to learn that fully three-fourths of the executive board of the union was Communist. He also was surprised when a number of those Communist board members, who were aware of his departure from the party, pressured him to rejoin. He refused and, according to the FBI, did his best to avoid contact with all Communist Party members. Despite that effort, in late 1946 Crouch was elected a delegate to the Texas CIO convention, and while attending the meeting he became acquainted with Ruth Koenig, a Texas Communist Party state organizer who tried to woo him back to the party. During a subsequent trip to Houston for the union, he again ran into Koenig, as well as Southern organizer Nat Ross, both of whom encouraged his return. Crouch rebuffed all such efforts and instead focused on the union, including an unsuccessful run for president.[39]

Although his postparty life seemed to be going well, in spite of the persistent recruiting by the Communists, it soon turned for the worse. Son Carl nearly died from a brain hemorrhage in late 1946, and the family was still recovering from that near tragedy when on January 3, 1947, Pan Am fired Paul for making false statements on his employment application. According to the FBI, the specific lie was his statement that he had never been a member of the armed forces, when he had, although it was more likely his Communist background that upset the company. Union leaders, at least, opposed the firing and tried to help. On January 4, 1947, M. L. Edwards, president of the TWUA local 504, demanded that Crouch be reinstated because "he did a remarkably wonderful job at negotiating in interests [of] all workers and it would be a disgrace to permit railroading of this outstanding union leader."[40] The appeal had no effect, however, and Crouch was out of a job at a difficult time in both the family's and the nation's history. The family needed money to cover Carl's medical bills, and, with millions of soldiers demobilizing, jobs were tight. Crouch thus found himself without a job, without an ideology, and in desperate need of money. This was not how he had envisioned his postparty years, and he feared for the future.

That future eventually would turn rosy, but only after several years of struggle and strife. Such turmoil, however, was commonplace for Crouch. He had endured a tumultuous existence during World War II, spending time in Alabama, Tennessee, California, and Texas. For most of that era he willingly acceded to the dramatic policy shifts the war years forced upon the CPUSA, but by 1942 those shifts proved too great even for a true believer, and he left the comfort of the ideology that had guided him for seventeen years. Sadly, leaving the Communist Party did not mean he had left its grasp. Whether being hounded to return or fired for prior membership, Crouch realized he could not easily escape his past. Worse, he soon came to learn that the American public did not believe a Communist leopard could change its spots. If he had been a devout Communist, what he needed next was a public exorcism to demonstrate the end of that devotion. That excision would take some time to occur and, when it did, Crouch would end up simply exchanging one ideology for another. As the immediate postwar era quickly evolved into the Cold War, Crouch, the former Communist ideologue, would become as ardent and prolific an anti-Communist ideologue as the nation had ever seen. A new era, in other words, had dawned for the nation and for Crouch.

6 "THEN CAME THE CONVERSION," 1947–1949

Without an ideology to which to cling, and frequently without a job to feed his family, Crouch suffered through the late 1940s. He eventually took advantage of the growing Red Scare to become an informant for the U.S. government against his former comrades in the CPUSA. He first volunteered for such service out of vengeance and in the hopes of earning money to supplement his meager income, but eventually he bought into the anti-Communist ideology. In congressional hearings, legal indictments, and public forums, he turned on the ideology that had sustained him for nearly two decades and slowly found the opposite worldview more to his liking. While not yet an anti-Communist ideologue, by the end of the decade Crouch was well on his way.

By the time Crouch lost his job in Texas and began his journey toward a new ideology, the Cold War had begun and the Second Red Scare was in utero. The Cold War, the ideological struggle between the Soviet Union and the United States, began just as World War II was winding down. During the Yalta Conference in February 1945, Stalin, Winston Churchill, and President Roosevelt had agreed to allow free and open elections in the Eastern European nations liberated from Nazi dominion. Instead, Stalin oversaw rigged elections that ensured the creation of puppet governments sympathetic to the Soviet Union. By 1947 Soviet domination over Eastern Europe was virtually complete and all the United States could do was announce the Truman Doctrine, by which the nation declared its determination to "support free peoples who are resisting attempted subjugation by armed minorities or by outside pressures," and implement the Marshall Plan, which ultimately provided $13 billion in economic recovery assistance to European nations under the assumption that strong economies would subvert the spread of Communism.[1]

In 1948 the Cold War threatened to turn hot. After Germany surrendered on May 8, 1945, the United States, England, France, and the USSR divided the nation and Berlin, the capital city, as a means of keeping Germany weak and preventing it from starting yet another world war. In early 1948 the United States, England, and France unified their sectors in an effort to stimulate the economic recovery of the land that now lay as a buffer between East and West. The Soviets responded by denying the Western powers ground access to West Berlin, which lay deep within Soviet occupied eastern Germany. The West countered with the Berlin Airlift and for eleven months supplied the needs of the citizens of western Berlin solely by plane, providing up to 13,000 tons of food, clothing, and coal a day. The Soviets eventually relented and reopened ground access to Berlin, but the divide between East and West was as severe as ever and each soon created their own Germany: the western-oriented Federal Republic of Germany and the Soviet-oriented German Democratic Republic.

As the United States and Soviet Union began to square off globally, at home the nation began to attack Communists, leftists, and anyone deemed a threat to the American way of life. Known as the Second Red Scare, the first coming after World War I, this search for internal enemies would dominate domestic affairs for nearly a decade after World War II, although to be fair, it had a long gestation. In May 1938 the Roosevelt administration created the House Committee on Un-American Activities, also referred to as the Dies Committee or HUAC. Whatever its name, its purpose was to investigate Nazis, Fascists, and Communists. So fearful of enemy infiltration was the nation that by 1940 Massachusetts, California, and Oklahoma had set up their own "little Dies" committees. Despite that fear, the committees were nearly dead when World War II ended. The growing threat of the Soviet Union and domestic Communism in the years after the war, however, resurrected both the state and federal HUACs, and in 1948 the Republican Congress increased the federal committee's funding from $50,000 to $200,000.[2]

The nation, however, needed more than an investigative organization to protect it from the growing Communist threat: it also needed legislation. To address that, in 1939 the Hatch Act forbid federal employment to any person who belonged to a group "which advocates the overthrow of our constitutional form of government" and in 1940 defined the CPUSA as just such a group. The Smith Act, properly known as the Alien

Registration Act of 1940, went even further and banned the advocacy of acts of force and violence designed to overthrow the government. According to the act itself, "any society, group or assembly of persons who teach, advocate, or encourage . . . the overthrow of the government of the United States" was liable to ten years in prison and a $10,000 fine. Anyone who joined, supported, or simply endorsed such measures also was in violation of the law.[3] As Peter Steinberg notes, "It would not be necessary to prove that the Communist Party or its officers actually had taken steps to overthrow the government or had even advocated the use of force and violence. Under section 11 it would be necessary simply to prove that communists had conspired—criminally joined 'knowingly or willfully to advocate, aid, abet, or teach the duty, necessity, desirability or propriety of overthrowing or destroying the Government of the United States by force or violence' or published literature to that effect, or had organized a group to accomplish this result."[4]

The same year the Smith Act took effect so too did the Voorhis Act, which required all organizations "whose aim or purpose is . . . seizure or overthrow of a government . . . by use of force, violence, military measures, or threats of any of the foregoing" to register with the government.[5] It also required organizations that were subject to foreign control to register. The CPUSA denied it sought the overthrow of the government, disaffiliated itself from the Comintern, and refused to register. Despite that refusal, as early as 1946 J. Edgar Hoover was alleging the CPUSA was a conspiratorial organization and on April 14, 1947, ordered the FBI to compile lists and investigate all party leaders. Indeed, Hoover ultimately developed a "Security index" and a separate "Communist index" in which he gathered "information on all known Communist Party members." Hoover justified such efforts with testimony before Congress, during which he said, "I do not think for one moment that we are going to have a revolution in this country tomorrow, but I do know that the Communists have penetrated every field of activity in this country."[6]

Fearful that congressional Republicans would use such assertions to attack him as soft on Communism, President Harry Truman determined to get into the act as well. On November 25, 1946, he issued Executive Order 9806, which established the Temporary Commission on Employee Loyalty. The purpose of the commission was to make recommendations about federal loyalty programs. It delivered its suggestions on February 20, 1947, and in response Truman instituted Executive Order 9835, which required every department and agency in the federal government to create some form of loyalty oversight program to examine every current and future employee. It also required the Attorney General to draw up a list of subversive organizations, membership in which would preclude federal employment.[7]

The attack on Communists continued with 1947's Taft Hartley Act, which required labor union leaders to sign an affidavit affirming they were not Communists. As Peter Steinberg notes, section 9(h) of the act even "required that the National Labor Relations Board not certify a labor union if any of its officers was or ever had been a member of the Communist Party or 'believed in' or was in any way associated with any organization teaching the forcible overthrow of the government."[8] In 1950, the Supreme Court upheld the constitutionality of the act, although Justice Hugo Black dissented and argued that the whole purpose of the First Amendment was to protect the rights of those whose ideas we did not like.

Many historians, including M. J. Heale, view such laws, and indeed the entire era, as having as much to do with domestic politics as with the growing geopolitical struggle with the Soviets. Indeed, Heale contends that after the 1948 election and Truman's miraculous reelection,

> Republican party leaders, seething at their defeat, were concluding that if the Democrats could win advantage by adopting an anticommunist stance, so could they. Some Republicans, of course, had regularly used the communist issue against the administration, but after 1948 their party embraced it with a vehemence hitherto exhibited by no major party in American politics. For the next four years the most powerful and sustained impulse behind the anticommunist cause was the Republican party's determination to end its prolonged exile.

Heale goes further and states that the American public was in a mood for the Red Scare:

> Economic growth, a great religious awakening, a revived white racism, and archaic electoral arrangements contributed in different ways to a red scare culture, as did the veterans' groups and other patriotic organizations, reinvigorated by World War II and

> the Korean War. A public mood broadly if not actively hostile to the Soviet Union and its ideology was being exploited by energetic pressure groups and insecure political elites. What gave the anti-communist cause its force was the incessant and complex interplay between popular opinion, private interest groups, and public officials.[9]

Heale has a point, but to be fair there did appear to be a Communist threat emergent in the nation in the immediate postwar era. The first major threat arose in 1945 after it was discovered that journalists for *Amerasia* magazine had access to hundreds of top secret government files. Worse, editor Philip Jaffe, a member of the CPUSA, met frequently with Earl Browder and other Communist leaders. No evidence proved that Jaffe ever turned the files over to foreign powers or provided Browder and the CPUSA with secret information, but he was charged nonetheless with unauthorized possession of government documents. Emmanuel Sigurd Larsen, a China expert for the State Department, was accused of supplying those documents. Both men pled guilty. More important, the case created a sense that the State Department, if not the entire government, could be swarming with Communists. That same year, long time CPUSA member Elizabeth Bentley went to the FBI and revealed the names of 150 Americans who were spying for the Soviets. In 1947 she went public with her testimony.

The year Bentley went public, HUAC began to investigate Hollywood as conservative politicians pushed the idea that the movie industry was overrun by Communists whose propaganda was making its way into the nation's theaters. Ten Hollywood writers, directors, and actors were dragged before the Committee and questioned about their Communist affiliations. When they refused to answer, or claimed immunity under the First Amendment, Congress charged them with contempt. As that travesty moved forth, the Alger Hiss case emerged when Whittaker Chambers produced the "pumpkin papers" proving that while a State Department employee, Hiss had spied for the Soviets and lied about his activity in previous testimony. All of these cases gave credence to the idea that the threat of domestic Communism was real and required executive, legislative, and judicial efforts to kill it.

And then came 1949. On August 29, 1949, the Soviets detonated their first atomic bomb, years earlier than American experts predicted possible. The result was two-fold. First, the nation lamented its lost nuclear monopoly and feared what having a nuclear Soviet Union meant for the future. Second, a widespread belief emerged that the only way the Soviets had been able to achieve the bomb so quickly was espionage. The fear of Communist infiltration thus expanded beyond the government to the military and scientific communities. Then, on October 1, 1949, Mao Tse-tung proclaimed the People's Republic of China, and the United States lamented the "fall" of China. The "fall," like the Soviet bomb, led to a search for scapegoats and yet again facilitated the search for Communists nationwide.

In the wake of such events, it is not surprising that the government instituted the aforementioned laws. Nor indeed was the government the only group fearing the Communist presence. In 1948 the Civil Rights organization CORE (the Congress of Racial Equality) expelled Communist members, as did the National Education Association in 1949, the NAACP in 1950, and the ACLU in 1951.

This emergent Red Scare also had a major impact on the life of Paul Crouch. Indeed, Crouch believed that one reason he lost his job with Pan Am was his Communist past—a past that was no longer acceptable for an employee in the airline industry. Unemployed and without prospects, and notably without an ideology to which to cling, Crouch lamented his life in early 1947. In February, however, he got a break when he received a letter from "Charlie" of the TWUA. "Charlie" informed Crouch that he had made arrangements to get him hired as a part-time organizer for the Florida State CIO. "Charlie" also related that he was making arrangements to get Crouch work as editor of a new CIO paper called the *Union Record*. He admitted to having trouble finding Crouch a place to live but hoped he would move to Miami and take advantage of the job opportunities. The letter ended, "You see, Paul, we *do* love you, and do want you with us if it's at all possible."[10]

Crouch took "Charlie" up on the offer and moved the family to Miami where he took the job as editor. Once again, however, he had trouble escaping his past. Not long after he moved the family to Miami and began work on the *Union Record*, Irving Gold, a CPUSA branch organizer, began to pressure him to return to the Communist Party. When he stubbornly refused, Gold sent a letter reading: "This is your last chance."[11] Crouch ignored the threat but was depressed when the recruitment did not end.

Florida state party leader Charles Smolikoff soon took up the cause and pressured him to join. He again rebuffed the efforts but came to believe that Smolikoff was trying to destroy the *Union Record* in retaliation. Crouch responded to Smolikoff's harassment by writing a letter to the office of Florida State Attorney George Brautigam alleging that Smolikoff and the Communists were trying to infiltrate the CIO in Miami.[12]

Nothing came of the letter, or Smolikoff's efforts, but the incidents caused Crouch to ponder how his life had gone so wrong. He began to think about his past and decided to write down his experiences and knowledge of the CPUSA. Crouch was unsure of what use he could put these remembrances, but he believed they might serve some future purpose, and his growing ire toward the party's treatment of him encouraged this project. He spent much of 1947 putting his thoughts and knowledge on paper and deciding what to do with the information. Ultimately he decided the material was ripe for a newspaper exposé and sent a letter to the editor of the *Miami Daily News* informing him of what he had. As he waited for a response, he was fired as editor of the *Union Record*. Crouch always assumed the CPUSA was behind the firing because of his refusal to rejoin, but he had little time to wallow as he soon found new work with the *Miami Herald*. Although the job required him to cross a picket line of *Herald* printers who were on strike for better wages and a shorter work week, he accepted the position as night supervisor of the teletypesetter department.[13]

Despite being newly employed, Crouch remained frustrated with the lack of a response from the *Miami Daily News*. While trying to determine his next step, he read newspaper accounts about Elizabeth Bentley, whom the federal government was beginning to employ in public hearings and trials. On December 18, 1947, following Bentley's example, Crouch contacted the FBI office in Miami and offered himself to the anti-Communist cause.[14] It seems that a variety of motives decided Crouch on this first move. It was, in part, retaliation for the Communist Party's alleged role in his several firings and retribution for the continual harassment he had faced since he quit. At the same time, he realized he could make money and supplement his otherwise meager income. Finally, it seems that he was coming to sense that he had wronged the nation and that testifying was a way to make things right. He was not yet an ideologue, but his decision to contact the FBI marks the beginning of his conversion to the anti-Communist cause. He was about to find a new ideology. As with many who are born again, he would become passionately devout.

The FBI, who knew Crouch well, was interested in his information but determined that he "should be handled in a most discreet and careful manner." The bureau set up a meeting in January 1948 but decided not to push him and to let Crouch do all the talking. During the meeting Crouch not only assured the agents that he had a wealth of information but also let them know he had been thinking about it and organizing it for months. Specifically, he told them that he had written an autobiography tentatively titled "Southern Radical" and was working on another book about the entire Communist movement in America. He also volunteered that he could be trusted, because he had had no contact with the CPUSA since November 1942 and that he was a true believer in American democracy. After assuring the agents that he had material and was loyal, he concluded this first meeting by describing the various Communist efforts to woo him back, naming six people he believed were leading Communists in Miami and offering his further services to the FBI.[15]

Although bureau sources labeled Crouch a member of the "No. 2 Club of the Communist Party" in Dade County, thus seeming to call into question his claims to loyalty, a few weeks after his initial meeting agents contacted him again. It is not clear if the FBI did not believe its own report or if it hoped to use him as an informant, but in either case Crouch agreed to the second meeting. He traveled to New York City where agents interrogated him and delved deeper into his claims. Satisfied with his answers, the bureau asked if he would be willing to testify against the Communist Party. Despite his earlier efforts to publish his knowledge, the request concerned him. Jan Masaryk, the Czech foreign minister, had died under mysterious circumstances on March 10, 1948, with many at the time believing Czech Communists had killed him. Crouch feared his testimony would put him in similar crosshairs. He met with the family to talk it over, and they eventually decided it was worth the risk. Crouch thus affirmed to the FBI that he would testify for the government. This agreement reached, he then returned to Miami where almost immediately he was fired from the *Miami Herald*. Crouch claimed the Communist Party, most notably Smolikoff, yet again was behind the firing, this time for his dalliances with the FBI. He eventually found work at a rival paper when he accepted a position with the *Miami Daily News* and then eagerly awaited the opportunity to serve the nation as an informant.[16]

While awaiting the opportunity to testify, Crouch had additional meetings with the local FBI. On March 20, 1948, he gave agents chapter 25 of his book about American Communism, which covered labor activism in California. He also explained to the agents the circumstances behind his exit from the Communist Party and described for them the Communist Political Association (CPA), which Earl Browder formed in 1944 after dissolving the CPUSA in the expectation that the United States and USSR would continue their wartime alliance into the peace. Crouch described the CPA as "neither Communist, political, nor an association but just a bureaucratic machine which was of no value to the workers and people of the country."[17] The Communists, in other words, were more interested in their own needs than in those of the proletariat.

In June 1948 Crouch met again with the Miami FBI and offered them a newly written three-page paper on the current state of Communism in the world. In it, he argued that Henry Wallace's opposition to the Truman Doctrine and support for a closer relationship with the Soviet Union were part of a Communist plot. Crouch ignored the fact that Wallace sincerely held those beliefs. He also ignored the possibility that Wallace might have had personal reasons for opposing the president. Truman had replaced Wallace as Roosevelt's vice president and then as president had fired Wallace from his job as secretary of commerce.[18]

In a sign of things to come, Crouch was beginning to see the world as divided between good and evil—American and Soviet. Anything that opposed the American worldview was inherently evil and undoubtedly hatched from within the nefarious Soviet empire. Further evidence of this new perspective can be seen by the fact that he informed the FBI that Soviet support for Israel was an attempt to stir up trouble in the Middle East and that any Soviet effort toward improved relations with the West was simply an effort to create a Trojan Horse.[19] The anti-Communist ideologue, in other words was developing apace. Just as he had once accepted Communism, so now he was embracing its antithetical ideology: anti-Communism.

That the federal government took at least this Trojan Horse theory seriously was evidenced in July 1948 when twelve Communist Party leaders (William Z. Foster, Eugene Denis, Robert Thompson, John Williamson, Ben Davis, Henry Winston, John Gates, Irving Potash, Jacob Satchel, Gilbert Green, Carl Winter, and Gus Hall) were arrested and charged with violating the Smith Act. Crouch hoped to be called to testify, but when the trial began in April 1949 the government informed him that he would not be needed. The reason was that it already had two former Communists willing to serve as informants. The first was the aforementioned Louis Budenz. During the trial, Budenz explained Communist ideology to the court but eventually was faced with a section of the CPUSA constitution that authorized the expulsion of any member who advocated the use of violence. Budenz explained this away by claiming that Communists used "Aesopian language," which, he argued, meant that they really supported the use of violence but said they opposed it for public consumption. As a result, the court was able to accept any element of Communist rhetoric or writing that suited its purpose and then argue away as Aesopian any element that undermined its case.[20] This would become common throughout the rest of the Red Scare era.

The second informant was Herbert Philbrick, who would later become famous for his book *I Led 3 Lives* about his time as an FBI agent in the CPUSA. During the trial, Philbrick admitted to reading FBI files in preparation for his testimony. The defense demanded the right to see the files, but Judge Harold Medina refused citing national security. This too would become common throughout the rest of the Red Scare era. Faced with that limitation, as well as the prosecution's "Aesopian language" tactic, the hamstrung defense could do little more than claim there was no inherent danger in people joining or leading the CPUSA and that there was no reason to limit their free speech and assembly. When giving instructions to the jury, however, Judge Medina specifically rejected the First Amendment argument, and it was little surprise that all twelve were convicted. Eleven received five-year sentences and $10,000 fines, while Thompson got three years due to his service record in World War II. In 1951 the Supreme Court upheld the conviction 6–2, with justices Hugo Black and William O. Douglas dissenting.[21]

According to Cedric Belfrage, the trial had an even more insidious outcome, albeit one that helped Crouch: since the "Aesopian Language" thesis meant the Communists never said what they meant, ex-Communists were needed to translate Communist tracts and explain what they actually meant. This gave birth to the informant model and provided

Crouch with ample opportunities to testify. The General Services and Administration Act of 1939 allowed the federal government to employ specialists part-time to take advantage of their knowledge. Although created to benefit the government from a scientific and technical standpoint, it was used during the Red Scare to bring in former Communists as witnesses. These part-time employees received $25 per day plus a $9 per diem. The usual pay for the testimony before a congressional committee was $4 per day.

It was not just their pay that was different. As Arthur Sabin notes, the informants during the Red Scare were different in that "these people held themselves out as experts on Communism and the Party, moving from trial to trial, from committee to committee, using their 'expertise' and naming names on behalf of the U.S. and state governments. They are distinguishable because they were not part of only a single trial and did not give information on one occasion of alleged criminal conduct."[22] Informing became their job. Richard Rovere agrees and notes that "American history offers no precedent for it."[23]

There was a further irony in the new informer model, to which Sabin also turned: the way to become a respected informant was for an individual first to convince the government "of their complete devotion to the Communist cause, which had resulted in their being trusted with Party secrets, Party policy, and exposure to Party members. Then came the conversion." Party members needed to be as important as possible in order to justify their testimony and then justify their conversion and testimony against their former comrades as some sort of effort toward forgiveness. As Bernard DeVoto writes, the informant tried to explain that "I am right now because I was wrong then. Only the ex-Communist can understand Communism. Trust me to lead you aright because I tried to lead you astray. My intelligence has been vindicated in that it made an all-out commitment to error." Richard Hofstader concurs with this description and asserts that the government relied on these individuals because they had "been in the secret world of the enemy" and were able to bring forth "the final verification of suspicions which might otherwise have been doubted by a skeptical world."[24] Crouch clearly fit the model, and as an astute student he quickly became aware of the dance that potential informants needed to perform.

In March 1949, therefore, he publicly broke with the CPUSA in *Plain Talk Magazine*. He did so in an essay ostensibly about the SCHW

(Southern Conference for Human Welfare), which he alleged was Communist controlled. More important than the specific allegations, however, was that Crouch took this first opportunity to demonstrate his former importance within the Communist Party and his newfound devotion to the anti-Communist cause. For instance, Crouch began the article with his Communist biography, noting that "I was a member of the District Buro of the Communist Party and was on all the party's steering committees and conferences before and during the Southern Conference." After laying out additional Communist credentials and implying that he had a wealth of information to share with the nation, Crouch then explained that he left the party as a result of being "sharply called to account by national leaders of the CP for his" failure to expose the demagogic character of President Roosevelt while in Utah.[25] He thus did well to make himself an important part of the Communist conspiracy and then to humanize himself by asserting that he broke from the Communist Party as a result of his bosses' unjust criticisms.

Crouch continued his public exposure by building up the Communist threat to the nation. He asserted that Communists were masters at infiltration who "try to get into strategic positions in all kinds of organizations—even churches." The SCHW, he asserted, was evidence of what happened to those organizations into which Communist infiltration was successful. He claimed the SCHW "might have achieved real progress for the South's welfare in the last ten years [but] has gone the way of all worthy ideas when their purpose is perverted to serve the ends of the Communist Party." He then finished by explaining that he had decided to testify against the party because "Moscow, the source of all decisions, has no real interest in public welfare in the South or in anything which does not contribute to Stalin's relentless drive for world power."[26] He thus hoped to teach the nation the lessons it had taken him seventeen years to learn.

Crouch played the anti-Communist game well from the very beginning. He offered himself as an insider with real knowledge of the party, provided his mea culpa, and then sought to scare the nation into calling him for service against his former master. Despite being a classic example of how informants earned their jobs, Crouch's public exposure did not immediately win for him the opportunity to testify in criminal or congressional proceedings. In an effort to improve his odds, and undoubtedly to get his hands on some of the money being paid to informants, he contacted HUAC and offered his services. In May 1949 HUAC officials responded positively and invited him to testify. According to Sarah Brown, HUAC was the perfect forum for Crouch as the committee's "rules were arbitrary and the decision of the chairman sacrosanct, with no statement or objection allowed. Investigatory reports could not be examined or verified, and witnesses, often unknown until they appeared to testify, faced almost no chance of cross-examination by unfriendly counsel."[27] Crouch, and any informant for that matter, could testify unimpugned and free from the fear of cross-examination. Crouch took advantage of those factors better than nearly any other informant.

On Friday May 6, 1949, Crouch offered his first paid testimony when he appeared before HUAC in Washington, D.C. He told his life story, described his experiences in the Communist Party, and named names. As he provided his biography, he made sure to list the many and varied Communist organizations for which he had worked. This included work on the national executive committee, the secretariat, and as the national education director of the YCL, as editor of the *Young Worker*, head of the antimilitarist department of a joint committee of the CPUSA and YCL, representative of the YCL at the YCL International in Moscow, representative of the YCL to the Red Army on its 10th Anniversary, honorary member of the Red Army, member of the editorial staff of the *Daily Worker* (where, he noted, he was an associate of Whittaker Chambers), national secretary of the Anti-Imperialist League, organizer in Gastonia and Norfolk, Utah State organizer (1933–1934), Carolina district organizer (1934–1937), editor of the *New South* and district organizer in Alabama (1938 to September 1939), district organizer in Tennessee (September 1939 to March 1941), and county organizer in Alameda County, California (May 1941 to January 1942). Crouch also explained that he had been "selected by the Communist Party to be the head of the apparatus in case the known Communists of the party should be outlawed and the known Communists arrested."[28] All of this, of course, was part of the game. By laying out his many positions, he made clear to HUAC, and future committees as well, his importance in the Communist Party and, theoretically at least, his knowledge base.

Crouch then moved to his time in the party, specifically his trip to Russia. He discussed a book called *The Struggle against Imperialist War and the Tasks of the Communists*, which was prepared by the World

Congress of Soviets. Crouch claimed to have helped write the book, and those sections were included in the record. Among the topics discussed in the portions Crouch wrote were the Communist desire to infiltrate war industries and the military; the desire to turn a future war into a revolutionary, proletarian struggle, or as the book put it: to "transform the imperialist war into a civil war"; the support for general and mass strikes during wartime; and the efforts required to undermine capitalist countries and strengthen the USSR.[29]

Crouch then began to name names. Among those he named as fellow travelers, that is, those who were not members but followed the party line, was Virginia Durr. Crouch claimed she was a subscriber to the *New South* from its inception and that she met frequently with known Communist officials. Crouch also named James Dombrowski as a fellow traveler. He claimed Dombrowski was "in closest consultation with Charles Smolikoff at Miami, and took no steps without consulting Smolikoff, the party leader in Miami." He also reiterated his charge that the SCHW, of which both Durr and Dombrowski were members, was Communist-dominated, and further asserted that Joseph Gelders, a Communist, actually ran the conference. Crouch finally claimed that after the formation of the SCHW, Gelders "succeeded in meeting President and Mrs. Roosevelt, and succeeded in getting an invitation to Hyde Park, where he posed as a New Dealer, and the President and Mrs. Roosevelt had no knowledge he was acting for the Communist Party."[30] Thus, in his very first opportunity to testify, Crouch publicly accused the Communists of infiltrating White House circles.

Crouch then mysteriously asserted that he had the name of a person who "has held very high positions in the Government prior to entering—not simultaneous with but prior to entering—the Communist Party." Crouch went on: "He has many friends among Government officials from whom, if he is still in the party, he might be able to obtain information of importance to national defense."[31] Crouch suggested that he could offer the name only in a private hearing but did note that the individual was a member of the SCHW, lived in Chattanooga, Tennessee, and had served in the military during World War II.

After so titillating the congressmen, Crouch next discussed Communist Party leader J. Peters, who oversaw espionage activities for the Soviets in the United States. Crouch said that throughout his time in the party, Peters gave him

> specific instructions regarding communications; the use of codes under which confidential messages were to be sent; private addresses; details as to receipts; instructions as to the selection of parallel underground apparatus ready at all times to take over; alternate party organizers; the selection of the place in the country where the district organizer could hide out until contact was established with him if he was not picked up; instructions as to the storing of both large mimeographs and a small collapsible affair which could be carried in a brief case; instructions as to how to make gelatin duplicating devices in case of emergency; and similar measures; also plans for the division of the party into groups of five, the groups being prepared to act as branches if the party was outlawed.[32]

Crouch thus encouraged the committee to focus on Peters. That focus quickly led to a subpoena, and on May 8, only two days after Crouch's testimony, Peters fled the United States for his native Hungary, where he remained until his death in 1990. In a sense, Peters was the first victim of Crouch's anti-Communist conversion.

The congressmen eventually began to ask Crouch questions and confronted him with a series of names. Crouch affirmed that dozens of those named were Communists. Among those who struck the committee's fascination was a group in northern California. Crouch alleged that he and Communist Party leader Steve Nelson were "active in trying to infiltrate all scientific research at the University of California" with the purpose of passing on information to the Soviets. Crouch claimed they were successful in their efforts, although he could not name the specific individuals engaged in such espionage because they were organized in a separate, secret group under the leadership of Kenneth May. He explained further that May was the son of Dr. Samuel May, a dean at the university, and was well known as an active and leading Communist, thus implying that the university tolerated a Communist presence on campus.[33]

Further inquiries from the committee elicited little additional information about the allegations, and the questions turned to Crouch's time in Florida. Of that state, Crouch asserted that Communists remained in important positions in the Transport Workers Union. Indeed, he warned that "I can say without reservation that the Communist Party still has sufficient strength to ground every plane of Pan American Airways within a matter of a few hours if it saw fit." Crouch further warned that Communists also had their hands in the Food and Tobacco Workers Union and the Cigar Makers Union. Worse still, he asserted that "the Communist Party of Florida maintains very close liaison with the Communist Party of Cuba." He alleged that Cuban Communists frequently met with Florida leaders and that they provided Spanish-language radio broadcasts into Florida. He then argued that "Miami is of the greatest importance from a general military point of view because of the role aviation plays, and the Pan American lines all have their hub in Miami. Miami offers the ideal place for Communists to direct operations in Latin America."[34]

Sensing that the congressmen were growing weary of such stories, Crouch once again spiced things up with the tale of a 1929 meeting with "Jimmy," the American head of the Joint State Political Directorate (OGPU), the Soviet secret police agency. Crouch said they met "in a fashionable West Side apartment near Central Park," and that "Jimmy" was "a tall Russian who spoke broken English" and was interested to know if the party had any members in the State Department or other federal offices. When told no, he urged Crouch to find Communist Party members who might be able to get such jobs and have them apply. Crouch also asserted that "Jimmy" requested blank passports, and when informed that the party did not have any he urged Crouch to contact him should they gain access.[35] Crouch thus played up the threat of Communist infiltration of the federal government and put himself center stage of the intrigue.

The testimony concluded when the committee asked Crouch why he left the party. He replied, "I left the Communist Party because of the gradual accumulation, which I could not avoid, of a tremendous amount of evidence showing that I and other Communists were victims of a gigantic fraud; that the international Communist movement existed for the purpose of bringing about Russian domination of the world; that instead of providing a paradise or improving the conditions of the Russian people, it had brought about a system of forced labor in which millions of Russians are imprisoned under unbearable conditions." He continued, arguing that he finally came to realize that he "was in fact working for a movement which, should it be successful, would wipe out civilization as we know it from the face of the earth." The refusal of Governor

Roosevelt to turn him over to Massachusetts, criticisms he faced while in Utah, and the refusal of the Communists in California to abide by his ideas, he explained, were additional and more personal events that pushed him from the Communist Party.[36]

Before Crouch left the witness stand, he provided the committee with fourteen exhibits to demonstrate both his standing within the party and the dangers Communism held for the nation. Those exhibits included a portion of the preamble to the CPUSA constitution, which, after invoking Jefferson, Jackson, and Lincoln and declaring that the party sought to defend "the United States Constitution against its reactionary enemies who would destroy democracy and all popular liberties," called for the nationalization of all industries, the end of segregation, and the creation of "a world without oppression and war." The exhibits also included Crouch's membership book from 1943, which he had saved after Nelson gave it to him in hopes of luring him back, a copy of the *New South*, with Crouch clearly denoted as editor, a copy of *The Struggle against Imperialist War and the Tasks of the Communists*, and several additional photos and newspaper clippings.[37] That done, he stepped down.

The general consensus was that Crouch had done his job well. He offered clear evidence of the Communist threat, tied American Communists to the Soviets, named names, and made himself out to be a man of importance in the party. He also kept the congressmen intrigued, offering titillating stories that fit in well with the nation's growing anti-Communist paranoia and presenting himself as both knowledgeable and willing to talk. Of even greater import, however, was his ability to sense what HUAC wanted and where it wanted him to go. Just as he had proved willing to bend with the ever changing policy shifts of the Comintern, so too did he prove able to shift with the political winds. In his very first appearance as an anti-Communist informant, Crouch demonstrated that he had all the tools needed to be useful.

Although a useful success, Crouch had originally agreed to the testimony on the grounds that it would be secret, but news of it soon leaked. Dubbed "the best-informed witness ever to appear before the House Committee" by his hometown newspaper the *Journal Patriot*, Crouch soon was hounded by calls from reporters. Initially he feared what the publicity would mean for his life and his future ability to testify, but he came to enjoy the notoriety and largely obliged interview requests, especially since the interviews provided him the opportunity to inflate his own importance. For instance, he gave an interview to the *St. Louis Post Dispatch* in which he reported, "I was able to lead the Gastonia strike," despite the fact that he spent little time in the city during the strike and was tangential to the main effort while present.[38]

He also used his notoriety to hone his answer to why he left the Communist Party. He informed the *Fort Worth Star Telegram*, "Communism is depicted throughout the world as a movement to help the worker, when actually it is a movement which is calculatingly exploiting the workers in the interests of the party." Crouch explained to the *Miles City Star* (Miles City, Montana) that "the rank and file party members were to have no voice in determining policy matters. Such decision was up to the leaders. . . . I objected to such a policy. Rank and file members were being allowed to vote only in the affirmative and those wishing to cast negative votes automatically were expelled except in rare instances. My objections led to a final break with the party." To the *Honolulu Star Bulletin* he asserted that he spoke with Fred Beal upon his return to the United States after spending several years in the Soviet Union to avoid his prison sentence resulting from the murder of Sheriff Orville Aderholt in Gastonia. Crouch said Beal described declining living standards, heavy industry being pushed to the detriment of consumer production, and an overall harshness of Soviet life. This differed from his memories of just a few years earlier, and he told the paper that he began to wonder if Communism was the cause of this collapse.[39]

Despite those varied answers, Crouch proved to be good copy, sold papers, and remained a hot topic for the remainder of the year. Determined to take full advantage of his notoriety, Crouch quickly provided the *Miami Daily News* his previously written essays about the CPUSA and the alleged Communist conspiracy in the United States. The first story appeared on May 8, 1949; it began with his biography and laid out the general outline of the upcoming series. The paper assured readers that it would name names and explain the importance of Miami to the world Communist movement. As a way of teasing that importance, the paper noted that Miami was the key link between Moscow and Latin America and was the linchpin in the Communist plot to take over the Western Hemisphere. The article continued by assuring readers that all they would learn was true because it was based on information Crouch gave under oath; information of which the paper asserted: "An official of the House un-American Activities Committee [*sic*] described Crouch's testimony as a break bigger than the Whittaker Chambers and Liz Bentley cases combined." The same day the paper carried another headline reading "Crouch, Wife will testify at Red Probe on May 24." The article explained that both Crouches were to appear before HUAC from May 24–27 and that their testimony "may develop another sensational chapter in the committee's unfolding of international intrigue just prior to and during World War II."[40]

With the hype machine set in motion, the series began in earnest on May 9 when Crouch explained that there were one hundred Communists in Miami, another one hundred in Tampa, fifty in Jacksonville, and another fifty scattered throughout the state. Although Communists were well established statewide, Crouch focused on Miami, which he asserted was central to the international Communist conspiracy. Crouch related that during his first trip to Moscow he was told of the need to expand Communist efforts in Miami in order to open access to the Caribbean and Latin America. Crouch claimed those efforts had paid off, and "The party apparatus has been built and is a highly organized machine today. And Miami has become, and is today, the base from which international Communism is going to spread over South and Central America and all the major islands of the Caribbean Sea." Should trouble arise in Latin America, he explained, Moscow would make an order that would be sent to Miami where it would be forwarded to be carried out. Miami was thus a key link in the Communist chain, as the Communists in Latin America were not allowed to act without word from Moscow, via Miami. Consequently, if the Communist group in Miami could be disrupted, the entire Communist effort in Latin America would suffer.[41]

As evidence of the importance of this link, Crouch noted that on January 14, 1948, Alexander Bittelman was arrested in an apartment in Surfside, Florida. Bittelman was "the chief advisor in the CI [Communist International] on Latin American affairs" and was not in Miami on vacation but rather was organizing the Communist effort. Further evidence of the Communist threat, he claimed, was Smolikoff's power in the TWUA Local 500, which, while containing many upstanding members, "is the core of the party machine in Miami." According to historian Alex Lichtenstein, Communists had once controlled the leadership positions of the TWUA, but by early 1949 national union president Michael Quill broke with the CPUSA, purged the union of Communists, and moved away from the radical left toward the political center, thus calling into question at least this element of Crouch's assertion.[42]

On May 10 the series returned to recount murder most vile. Crouch alleged that he was a close friend of Juliet Poyntz, a native of Omaha, Nebraska, a graduate of and former history professor at Barnard College, a 1928 Communist Party candidate for New York State attorney general, and a leading figure in the CPUSA. On June 3, 1937, Poyntz disappeared from her New York City home, never again to be seen. Crouch claimed that she had been murdered by an American citizen in the pay of Russian agents and that her dead body was thrown in New York City's East River. The murder was the consequence, he contended, of her effort to leave the Communist Party as a result of her growing unhappiness with its lack of autonomy vis-à-vis Moscow. Of the murder, Crouch said, "it is typical of the Communist tactics employed against those, such as I and such as Julia, who are about to expose the movement." Crouch said while he was still in the party he had inquired about her and was told by leading officials that she was a "traitor" and that he should leave the case alone. This was not the only murder of an American citizen for such an offense, Crouch alleged, and he assured the paper's readers that he would tell more, including the name of Poyntz's murderer, at an appropriate later date.[43]

The editors of the *Miami Daily News* could not let such an explosive article stand alone, and in the same issue they included an editorial in support of Crouch, his claims, and his anti-Communist efforts. The editors informed the readers that the CPUSA was not a political party but rather a foreign organization working solely in the interests of Russia. As such, "The Daily News is proud of the privilege of being able to present to its readers this information which is of such importance to the nation's security. It is proud to be able to offer this public service because by doing so, it is helping its readers to a knowledge which will help to keep them free."[44]

On May 13 the *Miami Daily News* continued the series, this time exposing Poyntz's assassin. Crouch named George Mink, his former traveling companion, as the man who killed Poyntz. Of the assassin Crouch relates, "I knew Mink received several thousand dollars in cash from Soviet Russia and that he was known as the most powerful and dangerous of all the GPU [State Political Directorate—the predecessor to the OGPU] agents—at least in this country." He further described Mink as a drunk, a man of low character, and a felon who once served time in a Danish jail for rape. Of the actual murder, Crouch said that in early 1948, more than six years after he left the party, he met with several Communist leaders and they discussed Poyntz's death. These leaders told him that she was lured from her home by a man named Epstein (allegedly another GPU agent) and a woman. Once they had her out of her house they kidnapped her and took her to an undisclosed location near Yonkers, New York, where Mink shot her. They told him that she was buried nearby, only to be dug up later and thrown in the East River. Crouch further alleged that the woman who helped kill Poyntz also played a role in the assassination of Trotsky in August 1940. According to Ellen Schrecker, Gerhardt Eisler, the German born liaison between the Communist International and the CPUSA, was the one who set up Poyntz.[45] The truth of Poyntz's murder remains unclear, but Crouch took advantage of the mystery to further prove his knowledge of the inner workings of the CPUSA.

For those paying attention, however, this article should have called his knowledge into question. Crouch asserted that Communist leaders had refused to tell him the truth about the murder while he was still in the party—but years later told him the truth even though he had quit. While he had not made public his break from the Communist Party in 1948, surely those with enough rank to know about the murder of Poyntz would have known of Crouch's dismissal. And even if they did not, why were they so willing to admit to murder? No one questioned Crouch about these issues at the time, and his standing as an informant only grew with each new *Miami Daily News* article.

The series continued with Crouch alleging that the Soviets completely dominated the American Party. He explained that even American leaders were not consulted about policy decisions or changes and that Soviet "leaders talk to America Communists like a school teacher talks to her children. The orders are not debatable. They are final as given and objectors are expelled from the party."[46] Indeed, Crouch argued that most Americans who left the CPUSA did so because of the lack of freedom and the rigid control of Moscow.

The paper turned next to the domestic military threat posed by the Communists. Crouch asserted that there were thousands of Communists in the military, implying a potential fifth column. Despite this dire scenario, he asserted that American Communists would not take up arms against the United States in the event of a war but would be more subtle by relying on sabotage. Among the most dangerous types of sabotage, he argued, would be the efforts of Southern Communists to create a "Negro revolt." The leading role in creating this revolt would come from the SCHW. In fact, Crouch asserted that the primary reason for creating the SCHW was to foment racial unrest. He followed this threat of a fifth column with the next article in which he alleged that since 1928 the Russians had been planning for a war with "the imperialists." Despite this plan, Crouch claimed the United States actually was in a good position in relation to the Soviets. He explained that some Soviet leaders feared that in a war with the United States many Russian people, whom he described as little better than slaves, would revolt. As such, he suggested that the United States do in the Soviet Union what he alleged the Russians were doing in America—create an organization to stimulate rebellion should war break out.[47]

On May 17 the serial continued when Crouch returned to his own biography and once again explained the reasons he quit the Communist Party. He noted that the decision to quit was hard and came only after much contemplation. He claimed he first thought about quitting in Utah when Pat Toohey criticized him and explained that the reason he did not denounce President Roosevelt, which was the basis of Toohey's attack, was because FDR had been nice to him. His fellow Communists had no such soft spot for the president and hated him because the New Deal gave people jobs, making them less likely to rebel and making their job as Communists harder. This, he asserted, led him to realize that the Communists did not care about the workers, only about themselves. He further argued that the Soviet purges turned him off because he knew many of the men affected and knew they would never have committed the crimes of which they were accused. He concluded with a litany of other complaints including the lack of democracy and freedom and his hatred for the spying and threats of sabotage that occurred during World War II. These factors, he explained, convinced him to go public and expose his story to the world.[48]

Crouch concluded his series in the *Miami Daily News* on May 20 when he offered his solution to the Communist threat facing the nation. He argued that most American Communists were not allowed into the inner workings and bedrock beliefs of the CPUSA. Once they were, however, they learned that the party's claims to be fighting for the working class were bogus and simply masked its drive for power. This realization led most members to quit in disgust. Crouch thus determined that the best way to kill Communism was to expose its core beliefs to the light of day. He then assured his readers that while it took him far too long to see the light, he too had come to see the reality and was determined to spend the rest of his life fighting to protect the United States, expose Communism, and ensure the survival of American democracy.[49]

Crouch and the *Miami Daily News* were pleased with the series, but the response was not entirely positive. The competing *Miami Herald* called the work a publicity stunt that offered no real insight or benefit to the readers. The *Daily News* responded with an editorial entitled "Sour Grapes" in which it criticized the *Herald* for its attacks and claimed the assault was simply due to its unhappiness at being scooped on such an important story. More significant than such newspaper squabbles, however, was that many in the FBI were unhappy. As early as May 26, 1949, the FBI had questions about Crouch's testimony and his articles; indeed one agent wrote: "much of the material appears fabricated . . . and written for public consumption."[50]

The FBI was not the only organization that was less than impressed with Crouch. In mid-May the federal grand jury that indicted Alger Hiss and the twelve top Communists called Crouch. According to news reports, the grand jury was unhappy with HUAC and had been investigating several of its informants. The unhappiness was based on the jury's belief that HUAC "made the grand jury's work more difficult by their off-hand statements criticizing this arm of the law." According to news reports, "the grand jury . . . snatched Mr. Crouch from the House Un-American Activities Committee [*sic*] just as his name was going up on the billboards as a star witness in public sessions of the committee." The same reports alleged that the reason the grand jury wanted Crouch was because it was time "people who claim to know about the inner workings of communism in the United States . . . put up or shut up." The grand jury questioned Crouch about his newspaper articles and previous testimony but was little impressed with the "evidence" he had to offer. The New York City police, who interrogated Crouch for forty-five minutes at about the same time, were similarly displeased. When asked what new they learned from him, Captain Daniel Mahoney responded "Not a thing."[51]

Despites those attacks on his veracity, Crouch got what he wanted:

notoriety and more jobs as a paid informant. With his name now well known, and his previous achievements on the witness stand slowly making their way through the halls of Congress, he became a man in demand. On May 16 he testified before the Senate Judiciary Subcommittee, which was then investigating ways to tighten immigration laws. Crouch alleged that the aforementioned Gerhart Eisler, who had been sentenced to three years in prison for refusing to address HUAC and lying on his immigration application, had been ordered by Moscow to jump bail and flee the United States. According to Crouch, "Such a far-reaching decision as that of forfeiting bail and fleeing the country certainly was not made by Eisler alone. He would never have dared to do so without the approval and instructions from the highest circles in Moscow. The effort to save Eisler from even a short term in an American jail is striking indication of how important he is to the Russian Politburo."[52]

When asked how he could be so certain the orders came from the Soviet Union, Crouch replied that during his seventeen years in the CPUSA he would not have dared to move from city to city without approval. As such, he was certain that Eisler would not have taken such a big step as fleeing the country on his own. Had he, Crouch told the subcommittee, he would have been "imprisoned and probably shot." Crouch then went a step further and asserted that Eisler and other foreign agents were "the real heads of the Communist party in this country." Therefore, Crouch firmly supported tightening immigration laws to keep out such dangerous foes.[53] And, indeed, in 1952 Congress passed the Immigration and Nationality Act that allowed the government to deport aliens and naturalized citizens who were engaged in subversive activities and allowed the government to bar suspected subversives from entering the country.[54]

On May 24 Crouch returned to the witness stand when he testified in the HUAC hearing of Dr. Clarence Hiskey. In 1949 Hiskey was a professor at the Brooklyn Polytechnic Institute, but during World War II he had worked on the Manhattan Project. He stood accused of providing nuclear secrets to the Soviets during his time on the project. Hiskey took the stand and testified to his present employment and acknowledged that his birth name was Clarence Szezechowski. Louis Russell, the "senior investigator" for the committee, then offered some additional background: he noted that in 1948 Hiskey had refused to answer questions about actions he allegedly undertook while working "on the SAM project which had to do with the development of the atomic bomb." According to testimony at this 1948 hearing, when Hiskey was called for active duty military service in 1944 he took with him "a personal notebook which contained notes on the atomic-bomb project in Chicago." Worse, additional testimony alleged that while in Chicago he met with Arthur Adams, a Soviet agent, and then traveled to Cleveland where he met with John Hitchcock Chapin, a chemical engineer who also worked on the atomic bomb program. The implication was that Hiskey had been supplying information to Adams, but upon entering the army he would no longer be able to do so. To continue the flow of nuclear information, Hiskey allegedly set up the Soviets with Chapin as their new source.[55]

According to Ellen Schrecker, the military had their eye on Hiskey from the very beginning. Military intelligence reports stated that he was "active in Communist movements while attending graduate school at the university [of Wisconsin]. Hiskey reportedly urged radical-minded young men to take ROTC training to provide for 'possible penetration of the Communist party in the armed forces of the United States.'"[56] His "radicalism initially kept him from getting a security clearance, but his superior, Dr. Harold Urey, appreciated the importance of Hiskey's research on the separation of heavy water and managed to get him approved." Despite that, "The military intelligence officers who had been watching him concluded that 'Hiskey's attitude was un-American and his discretion and integrity' questionable; he was 'Communistic in his beliefs.'" As a result, Hiskey's time on the Manhattan Project was cut short, his deferment was revoked, and he was drafted, spending the war in Canada.[57] Hiskey remained in the military until 1946.

During the 1949 hearing Hiskey refused to confirm or deny the allegations and then faced a series of questions about his biography, work experience, and associates. While he answered questions about his employment, he pointedly refused to answer questions about whether or not he knew people associated with the Communist Party, including Paul Crouch. The committee then produced Crouch and asked Hiskey if he recognized him. Hiskey refused to testify, whereupon Crouch was called to the stand. Crouch claimed to know Hiskey, asserting that the two met in Knoxville in 1939 when Hiskey was employed at the University of Tennessee. Crouch said the two met at numerous Communist Party meetings held in various members' homes throughout the Knoxville area. When asked flat out if Hiskey was a Communist, Crouch tentatively replied, "Mr. Hiskey was known to me as an active member of the Communist Party." Hiskey returned to the stand and refused to confirm or deny Crouch's charges.[58] Realizing they would get nothing more from Hiskey, the committee excused him and recalled Crouch.

Upon his return, Crouch suddenly was full of specific information. He claimed that he and Hiskey had attended several meetings at the home of Francis Martin and one at the home of David Martin. He remembered this last one, and Hiskey's appearance there especially, because it was at that meeting that ten former members who had been working in the TVA were encouraged to rejoin the Communist Party. According to Crouch, "Mr. Hiskey was present and joined me in an effort to persuade them to become active in the party again, but without success." Crouch then moved on and asserted that he had witnessed Hiskey pay his party dues directly to former Knoxville section organizer Francis Martin "on several occasions," and explained that he was "carried on the books as a member at large, not attached to a branch, as were two or three other professors at the University of Tennessee." He further asserted that Hiskey worked with a party unit at Fisk College in Nashville and had accompanied Crouch on a trip to New York City where they attended a central committee meeting. Crouch admitted that he did not know what else Hiskey did there, since they attended different meetings, but stated, "His contacts and his work apparently had been entirely in connection with . . . scientific work."[59]

When asked about other information he could provide about Hiskey, Crouch admitted that he did not talk to Hiskey much about science, not knowing about the field. He did tell the committee, however, that Hiskey did his job as a Communist fairly well and that "he furnished names from time to time" to whom Crouch then sent party material. When asked to produce specific evidence in support of his assertions, Crouch had little to say and explained that he actually gave Hiskey great leeway to work among his fellow scientists. When asked the last time he saw Hiskey, Crouch claimed it was at the home of Kenneth May in Berkeley, California, in July 1941.[60] The committee was pleased with Crouch's testimony, and his efforts demonstrate clearly that he had mastered the role of the former Communist informant.

As a result of Crouch's testimony, Hiskey was forced from Brooklyn Tech in 1952 and never again returned to teaching. He took a job as an industrial consultant, started his own company, and eventually worked for DuPont.[61] Crouch had thus succeeded in exposing yet another Communist, the first being Peters, and he certainly believed he was playing a key role in undermining the Communist conspiracy. This success only deepened his faith in his new anti-Communist ideology, and he sought ever so desperately to return to the stand and take down yet another American enemy. He would get the chance when confronted with Steve Nelson.

In June 1949, a month after taking down Hiskey, Crouch's name arose during the Steve Nelson hearings. According to government documents, "Steve Nelson, with aliases of Louis Evans, Joseph Fleischinger, and 'Hugo,' was born Steve Mesarosh on January 1, 1903, at Chaglich, Yugoslavia." He immigrated to the United States in 1920 with his mother and two sisters, but the family did so by falsely claiming to be the wife and children of Joseph Fleischinger. In 1922 arrest warrants were issued for the entire family for illegal entry, but after a hearing by an immigration inspector they were allowed to remain. Nelson gained citizenship in 1928 despite having already joined the Communist Party.[62]

Other federal documents note that he "received special training in the Lenin School in Moscow in 1931, and in 1933 acted as an operative for the Communist International in Shanghai, China."[63] When the Spanish Civil War broke out he volunteered for the Lincoln Brigade, a collection of American Communists who organized to fight with the Spanish Republic against the forces of Francisco Franco. The CPUSA initially opposed Nelson's service and claimed he was too important to the cause at home but eventually allowed him to enlist. He arrived in Spain in late April 1937 and quickly worked to improve both the brigade's morale and fighting ability. He was wounded in August but survived, and he was transferred back to the United States to raise money and awareness by speaking about the efforts in Spain.[64]

By the 1940s Nelson had moved on, and according to federal documents he was "active as a Communist Party organizer in California and Pennsylvania and as a member of the Communist Party National Committee." His most important work, however, was his effort "to recruit a Communist cell at the Radiation Laboratory of the University of California which was engaged in research work relating to the development of the atomic bomb."[65] It was this last component of Nelson's biography that most interested authorities, who believed he sought to do more than simply organize among these scientists. The committee believed he set out to spy on the atomic bomb project for the Soviets.[66]

At the June 1949 hearing, Nelson described his childhood and openly admitted to the committee that he was a Communist, but he refused to address questions related directly to his writings, efforts, and activities as a party member. He specifically refused to answer questions when congressmen read to him from the May 6 transcripts in which Crouch named him as a Communist and related their efforts in California. He did, however, take several jabs at Crouch saying, "if I may comment on the statement by a person who apparently got a job on a paper down in Florida operating one of those scab vari-type machines, you can about guess what I think of a person that would come in that category. I think it is about the lowest thing on earth, a fellow that would go out and scab on union members as he does." The congressmen were outraged by the accusation, although it was true, and demanded to know Nelson's evidence for making such a charge. When Emanuel Bloch, Nelson's lawyer, tried to protect him, the hearings got testy. Richard Nixon took the lead in the attack and complained, "Although he will not say the testimony is false, he proceeds to leave an implication in the record that Mr. Crouch is a liar. I would like to see the witness back it up." He went on, "it is apparent he is trying to leave an implication concerning Mr. Crouch's testimony, and certainly his veracity." When Bloch tried to intervene, Nixon snapped "Don't interrupt me" and once again demanded Nelson provide evidence that Crouch was lying. Nelson refused to answer further, and he refused to answer several subsequent questions about his specific Communist activities.[67]

The hearings proved of little interest beyond that, but they set the stage for Nelson's future troubles. On August 31, 1950, he was arrested and charged with sedition against the state of Pennsylvania. While contesting that arrest he was charged with violating the Smith Act.[68] During the sedition trial, Crouch testified for the prosecution. In his book *The 13th Juror*, Nelson described Crouch as he entered the courtroom: he was "a tall man with a small head, tiny ears, and a fool's grin. He walked with long shuffling steps, his ape-like arms hanging loosely, swinging at his sides." He further described him as having a "turtle-like neck" and being "sallow faced."[69] Although Nelson mocked Crouch's appearance, he was a formidable witness who spent most of his time on the stand explaining the importance of various Communist texts that he claimed Nelson taught to party members in California. Crouch also asserted that Nelson had violent tendencies, and he refused to give his current address, explaining that if he provided it, either Nelson or someone from the party would assassinate him.[70]

Nelson later asserted that during the trial he had "somewhat unnerved him [Crouch] by addressing him as 'Mr. Stoolpigeon.'"[71] Nelson derided Crouch for being expelled from the Communist Party and asserted that he was drunk during most of his service in California. He further mocked Crouch by noting that while he claimed to have read Marx and Engels at a young age he demonstrated no real depth or breadth of knowledge during theoretical discussions at party meetings. He further made fun of Crouch for alleging that the party handed out badges during "secret meetings" in New York City. Nelson could mock all he wanted, but Crouch ended up getting the better of the deal. Nelson was convicted on both the sedition and Smith Act charges and received a combined twenty-five-year sentence.[72] However, in January 1953 the Pennsylvania Supreme Court overturned his sedition conviction and in 1956 the U.S. Supreme Court overturned his Smith Act conviction. Those developments were far in the future, and Crouch clearly won the immediate contest with Nelson.

Indeed, Crouch was doing very well in his new incarnation as an anti-Communist informant. As he gained more experience on the witness stand he became ever more confident. His early successes also encouraged other government agencies, as well as prosecutors, to see him as a useful figure. He would become one of the most widely used and well paid informants of the 1950s, and with every successful speech, testimonial, and prosecution he found himself ever more in demand. But that does not mean he had become an ideologue who truly believed in the anti-Communist ideology. Crouch clearly was trying to understand for himself why he had left the Communist Party and what motivated him to begin testifying against it. He had a whole litany of complaints and legitimate reasons for abandoning Communism that ranged from the personal (Pat Toohey's criticism of him for coddling President Roosevelt), to the ideological (the ever changing party line), to the practical (the lack of democracy and freedom within the party).

He also had a sizeable list of reasons for testifying against the Communist Party including his belief that the Soviets had enslaved the people of Russia, his fear that the USSR had set out to dominate the globe, and his disgust with the purges. That list expanded to include wealth and fame when he realized how much he enjoyed the pay and notoriety that came with his public testimony. This combination of factors finally convinced Crouch that anti-Communism was the way and, as the new decade dawned, he threw off any qualms he may have had and adopted the anti-Communist ideology wholeheartedly. Whereas he occasionally had wondered if his actions in the CPUSA were righteous, he had no such reservations about serving the government. During the 1950s Crouch the ideologue thus returned, but this time he was an anti-Communist.

7 PROFESSIONAL INFORMANT, 1950–1951

Despite the occasional hiccup and a fleeting sense by some that he was not totally to be trusted, Crouch clearly was a rising star among the ranks of former Communist informants. The ever deepening Cold War only provided him with greater opportunities, and in 1950 and 1951 he continued to testify in court cases and before Congress as well as publish his insights about the Communist threat. Those successes deepened his faith in anti-Communism and made him more determined than ever to destroy his former ideology.

That Communism needed to be destroyed became ever more apparent to Crouch as yet more threats to the nation emerged in the new decade. In January 1950 German-born physicist Klaus Fuchs was arrested in England and charged with supplying the Soviets atomic information he collected while working on the Manhattan Project at Columbia University and Los Alamos, New Mexico. Fuchs confessed to the spying, named names, and was convicted and sentenced to fourteen years in a British prison. He served nine years and after his release moved to East Germany where he lived until his death in 1988. Among the names Fuchs named was Harry Gold, who acted as a courier for stolen secrets. Through Gold, the FBI began to investigate David Greenglass, who also had worked on the Manhattan Project.

Greenglass was arrested in June 1950, and while under interrogation he named names including Julius Rosenberg and his wife Ethel, Greenglass' sister. During the war Julius worked at the Army Signal Corps Engineering Lab in Fort Monmouth, New Jersey. While there, he provided thousands of pages of information to the Soviets, including material on the proximity fuse, and had encouraged Greenglass, his brother-in-law, to provide atomic secrets. In August 1950 Julius and Ethel were arrested and charged with espionage. They were convicted on March 29, 1951, and although Greenglass got a fifteen-year sentence and Gold got thirty years, the court sentenced the Rosenbergs to death. Despite worldwide protests, they were executed on June 19, 1953.

Faced with such clear evidence of the continuing Communist threat, Congress had to respond. On September 23, 1950, it passed the McCarran Internal Security Act, which required all Communist organizations to register with the federal government, authorized the Subversive Activities Control Board (SACB) to investigate individuals suspected of subversive activity, and gave the Immigration and Naturalization Service (INS) the right to restrict the travel of those accused of being subversive.

The most famous response of all, however, began on February 9, 1950, when the Republican senator from Wisconsin Joseph McCarthy announced in Wheeling, West Virginia, that he had a list of 205 members of the State Department who were Communists. Although the number would change, and the accusation was far from new, McCarthy's assertions sparked the public's fascination and began him on a four-year journey in search of domestic Communism, producing McCarthyism—a particularly virulent strain of Red Scare ideology—which asserted that the Communist conspiracy threatening the nation was so vast and vile that any means were acceptable to find and destroy the Communist menace.

McCarthy's rhetoric blamed all the nation's ills, and all the successes of the Soviets, on a conspiracy of Communists in the American government and military. He laid out his underlying beliefs in his books (*McCarthyism: The Fight for America* and *America's Retreat from Victory*), in countless speeches, and on the floor of the Senate. In each instance, he asserted that the nation's relative global power had declined since 1945 and blamed the "present situation" on "men high in this government [who] are concerting to deliver us to disaster." Put more clearly, he alleged that there existed "a great conspiracy, a conspiracy on a scale so immense as to dwarf any previous such venture in the history of man. A conspiracy of infamy so black that, when it is finally exposed, its principals shall be forever deserving of the maledictions of all honest men."[1]

He placed within this conspiracy George Marshall, Dean Acheson, and John Foster Dulles, among others, and asserted that their conspiratorial goal was to hamstring the nation so that it might "finally fall victim to Soviet intrigue from within and Russian military might from without."[2] Richard Hofstader sums up McCarthyism nicely: "the country [was] infused with a network of Communist agents . . . so that the whole apparatus of education, religion, the press, and the mass media [were] engaged in a common effort to paralyze the resistance of loyal Americans."[3] The nation was swarming with spies, traitors, and enemies, and only the most zealous efforts on the part of good, loyal Americans could save the nation. That those efforts included lies, slander, and deception was irrelevant as it all was done in the name of security. While McCarthyism would stretch the Constitution and terrify the nation in the name of anti-Communism, it failed to find any Communists. Despite that failure, some people benefitted from the era of McCarthyite fear. Republicans, to be sure, long appreciated McCarthy's effort for the political benefits it provided the party. Paul Crouch also appreciated the effort.

That Crouch benefitted from McCarthyism is evident by the sheer volume of testimony he provided—some eighty hours before HUAC alone in 1949. As 1949 turned to 1950, his star shone ever more brightly, the number of hours he logged on the witness stand only increased, and the importance of the people he took on rose exponentially. Among those people of import he challenged was Harry Bridges, who had long been the bane of the federal government. Bridges gained fame during the 1934 West Coast longshoreman's strike when he acted as chief spokesman for the International Longshoremen's Association, which in 1937 would become the International Longshoremen's and Warehousemen's Union (ILWU). The strike infuriated businessmen and politicians nationwide, and the fact that Bridges was an Australian immigrant did not help.

Indeed, by 1938 the Labor Department inaugurated an effort to deport Bridges, who by then had become president of the union. The charges were based on the 1917 Espionage Act that allowed for the deportation of aliens who attempted to overthrow the government or who belonged to groups that supported the overthrow. The case against Bridges was thrown out after the special examiner, Harvard Law School Dean James M. Landis, argued that the thirty-two government witnesses included "self confessed liars," "pathological" types, and people whose "evasions are truly labyrinthine in nature." Despite that defeat the federal government reopened the case in 1940, but with the Justice Department in charge. In 1941 the government tried Bridges again and brought forth thirty-one witnesses. This time the evidence was enough to support deportation, but a Board of Immigration Appeals reversed the finding. In 1942, however, Attorney General Francis Biddle reversed the reversal and ordered the deportation. Bridges appealed to the Supreme Court, which in June 1945, in a 5–3 decision, reversed Biddle's order.[4] Bridges remained in the country and became a naturalized citizen.

Amid the Cold War the government could not let the case go, and in 1949 the Department of Justice brought forth perjury charges, claiming Bridges had lied on his application for citizenship when he denied being a member of the Communist Party. The perjury trial began in December 1949, and among the witnesses was Paul Crouch, who took the stand on December 15. During his testimony he claimed he was at a meeting in New York City in 1936 during which Bridges was elected to the Communist Party's central committee. He claimed that when the announcement of Bridges' election was made to the full convention "the California delegation rose to its feet, applauding more enthusiastically than ever." More important, at least for the case at hand, Crouch also alleged seeing Bridges at the convention.[5] Crouch further claimed Bridges was reelected to the central committee in 1938, although under the alias "Dorgan." Crouch asserted that CPUSA leader Earl Browder personally encouraged the reelection and that when "Dorgan" was elected "the entire convention burst into stormy applause."[6]

As the hearing continued, Crouch testified that he had numerous conversations with American party leaders who often expressed their fear that Bridges would be exposed as a Communist and deported, thus doing great damage to the Communist cause in the United States. Despite that fear, by 1941 the CPUSA was growing wary of Bridges. Party leaders, it seems, believed he was lacking loyalty and had not supported the Soviets enough in the aftermath of the Nazi invasion. There was, Crouch claimed, even talk of expelling him: "We already had gone to work to expel Mr. Bridges if necessary. We had worked out details for removing him from positions he held in the CIO."[7] According to Crouch, as a test of Bridges' loyalty he wrote and gave to the union leader a document calling for all-out war against Germany, which he was to distribute at union meetings. Crouch testified that during a California CIO meeting in 1941 Bridges did as he was ordered and proffered a resolution in favor of "all-out support of Russia." Crouch attended the convention to make sure Bridges presented the proposal and then reported this act of loyalty back to party leaders. That act, according to the prosecution, proved Bridges was a Communist. Bridges' lawyer stipulated the document but claimed it was consistent with Bridges' own beliefs and was not proof of Communist control.[8]

On December 16 Crouch continued his testimony when he alleged that as early as spring 1934 CPUSA leaders viewed Bridges as "a future leader of the Party" but also desired to protect his position in the union and his mainstream appeal. When asked how he learned these facts, and indeed how he first learned Bridges was a Communist, Crouch said that it occurred in April 1934 as he was driving from Denver to Cleveland: "I was in a car driven by John Harvey, a seaman and former member of the Politbureau. He stated that after discussing the value of Mr. Bridges as a leader in California, the party would not be able to bring him forward as a party member. He would have to be kept in the background."[9]

Crouch concluded his direct testimony by asserting that while Bridges could be stubborn, he usually accepted the party line. Indeed, Crouch testified that in 1941 Bridges opposed the Communist Party's no strike pledge made in the aftermath of Pearl Harbor. Demonstrating that Bridges was more beholden to the party than to labor, however, Crouch explained that he eventually accepted the change even though it hurt the working class.

All of this testimony seemed damning, but for the first time as a witness Crouch faced cross-examination. The cross turned into a brutal five-day affair that called into question much of his testimony. On December 19, Bridges' lawyer Vincent Hallinan presented to the court a list of forty-two members of the CPUSA national central committee, as elected by party members in 1938. When questioned why Bridges' name did not appear as a member of the committee, Crouch claimed that Bridges had been elected "under the name of Durken or Dorgan." Hallinan noted, however, that those names did not appear on the list either, nor did "Rossi," which, according to Crouch, was Bridges' secret party name. Crouch tried again and argued that he heard Browder often used aliases known only to himself for such lists as a means of protecting important party members. Hallinan did not buy that assertion and asked for any evidence other than Crouch's own assertion that Bridges had been elected. Crouch tried again and explained that Bridges was such an important figure that all his information was maintained in secret files administered by the Soviets in Moscow. He assured Hallinan and the court, "I have no doubt that the list reached Moscow within 30 days of the election and today they are in the files of the NKVD [the People's Commissariat of Internal Affairs, the Soviet secret police force that replaced the OPGU]." The judge eventually rescued Crouch, and the prosecution, when he refused to admit the list of central committee members into evidence, claiming, ironically, that there was no way to verify its authenticity.[10]

Hallinan then introduced evidence to prove Bridges could not have been in New York for the 1936 convention as Crouch claimed. He offered the minutes of a union meeting from June 22, 1936, which noted Bridges' presence; a newspaper report from the *Stockton Record* (California) about a union meeting on June 27, 1936, at which Bridges was present; a signed affidavit by a William H. Christensen who reported driving Bridges to breakfast in Albany, California, on the morning of June 28, 1936; and a signed affidavit from five members of a local union who reported hearing Bridges make a speech. Hallinan then argued that it was impossible for Bridges to have been in California on those dates and in New York for the Communist Party convention. Just to make the point clear, he noted that in 1936 the party convention took place from June 24–28. Crouch maintained a stoic façade when confronted with this exculpatory evidence but responded with evasive language using "to the best of my recollection" countless times as Hallinan pressed him to admit his error.[11] Crouch never conceded the point.

On December 20, Hallinan made the cross-examination personal when he called Crouch "a perpetrator of smirking murder . . . a man with a silly smile on his face." He further labeled both Crouch and Manning Johnson, who previously had testified against Bridges, as "pet cobras trained in the East to run around the country and testify in these cases." He then turned to Judge George Harris and said, "These men come in and commit black, bold, brazen, perjury. . . . We ask you, we beseech you to take some action to see that these people are stopped here and are not allowed to go on to destroy some other victims."[12] He concluded his appeal: "We ask that these men Johnson and Crouch, be placed in custody of the marshal and turned over to the grand jury for investigation."[13] Despite the evidence that Bridges could not have been in New York when Crouch placed him there, Judge Harris refused to address the issue at the moment, but he warned Crouch and Johnson to "hold themselves in readiness for the process of this court until the conclusion of the trial, for any or all purposes."[14]

The interactions between Crouch and Hallinan remained frosty and, if possible, only got worse on December 21 when the lawyer asked if Crouch had ever been confined to an asylum. Crouch complained about the insinuation, but Hallinan brilliantly responded by saying, "I claim to be an expert on insanity. I have testified as such in court. I think I can recognize an insane person when I see one." The prosecuting attorneys objected, the matter passed, and Crouch was formally excused, but Hallinan had made an important point. Although it would take years, others eventually would join him in questioning not only Crouch's veracity but also the very foundation upon which the government relied on Crouch and other former Communist informants. Crouch simply asserted to be an expert and was given free rein to testify. Worse, whatever he said was accepted as the truth because of his position as a former Communist. He was, in a sense, in a no-lose situation: if he testified before the government he faced a crowd who wanted to hear, and believe, what he had to say for their own political and personal reasons, and if he testified in court and faced cross-examination he was protected from charges of perjury by the generally accepted belief that as a former Communist he knew more than anyone else and what he said was true. Challenges to such assumptions would only break the surface in later years, but Hallinan deserves credit for planting some fertile seeds.

The destruction of Crouch on the witness stand proved a pyrrhic victory, however, as the jury convicted Bridges and Judge Harris sentenced him to five years in prison. Although the Supreme Court would overturn the verdict in 1953, claiming the prosecution had not taken place in a timely fashion and violated Bridges' constitutional right to a speedy trial, the federal government would continue to try to deport him until 1954 when it finally gave up. Through it all, Bridges remained the head of the ILWU, a position he held until his retirement in 1977. Despite those results, Crouch never took back his claims against Bridges. Indeed in his own later writings he asserted that "after serving on that buro (California) and hearing the day to day reports on how he [Bridges] was executing CP directives, there could be no doubt in my mind that he remained as active a member of the Communist Party as William Z. Foster, Eugene Denis, or William Schneiderman."[15] He further asserted that California party leader William Schneiderman often met with Bridges "regarding policies, tactics, and organization steps to be carried through. Schneiderman conveyed to Bridges the decisions of the district bureau, and reported to us Bridges' reactions to them."[16] Crouch, in other words, remained firmly convinced that he had done his best to save the nation from a true Communist threat.

More important, it seems that the contest with Bridges' lawyer may have been the point at which Crouch the anti-Communist ideologue emerged. Heretofore, he had testified before sympathetic audiences and without any real challenges to his claims. He also had been reactive, offering testimony or writing pieces for the newspapers. After Hallinan's unsympathetic challenge to his veracity and sanity, however, he became much more proactive. While he continued to testify in trials and before congressional panels, he also wrote and spoke much more vociferously about the Communist threat. He no longer needed to be prodded to make his case, and with each new instance he made ever more damning charges, foresaw an ever more dangerous future should the Communist menace survive, and willingly told ever larger lies to try to prevent that future. In the process, he became ever more famous and wealthy and became ever more beholden to this new ideology. Crouch thus became the very definition of McCarthyism in the 1950s: a man who would do anything to destroy Communism.

To be fair, there were other events that deepened the Cold War and seemed to offer Crouch, and all Americans, further evidence that the Communist menace needed to be destroyed. On June 25, 1950, the American public learned that Communist North Korean forces had streamed across the 38th Parallel and invaded the South. The United States, of course, would join with the United Nations to fight back the incursion—but at the cost of some 36,000 American soldiers. The outbreak of the Korean War may have shocked the nation, but Crouch claimed the only real surprise for him was how unprepared the United States was. Just days after the war erupted he published his immediate impressions in a work called "Observations on the Present International Situation and Role of American Communists in the Event of War," in which he argued that the war "brings us face to face with the *possibility* of a new Pearl Harbor and another world war at any time."[17] As such, he argued that the situation demanded a renewed study of Communism and the threat the Soviets posed. As a part of that renewed study, Crouch graciously offered his expertise (undoubtedly for a fee) regarding general Communist strategy and the appropriate American response to it.

As befitting the more proactive ideologue he had become, rather than await the invitation to testify, Crouch simply laid out his argument. He asserted that Communists never believed in the continuation of peace and had been preparing for war for a long time. He alleged that there were a few minor differences among the top Soviet military and political leaders, but those differences were about when and under what conditions the Soviet Union would be most able to destroy the United States. All agreed, however, that the USSR needed to attack first. Crouch then theorized that the Soviets would not attack the United States without first creating a diversion and that Korea may well be that diversion. Even if it was not the planned prelude to a larger war, he argued, Korea was important because it "PROVES that the Politburo feels the Soviet Union is READY for war."[18]

Whenever that war began, the Soviets would attempt to inflict "several Pearl Harbors" in an effort to destroy the nation's war making abilities at the outset. Crouch theorized that Hawaii might again be a target, this time of an atomic bomb, but noted that San Francisco, Los Angeles, Seattle, New York City, and Boston also were potential targets. He further opined that he expected an invasion of Alaska within twenty-four hours of the first attacks and that the Soviets would order their bomber pilots to attack the continental United States even though they would not be able to get home. These suicide attackers, he alleged, would have been told that their families would be tortured if they refused, so they would carry out the task. Crouch concluded his bleak assessment by asking why there were no civil defense efforts to fight back against such threats. He argued that civilian efforts from the previous war were outdated and would not help, so new plans were needed to address the problems he had laid out. Fearful of Communist infiltration and sabotage, however, he demanded careful examination of those chosen to oversee such programs.[19]

Crouch continued to write and fret about America's preparedness to take on the USSR throughout the Korean War. He especially complained about the nation's failure to take the war and the Soviet threat seriously. He criticized the nation's unwillingness to mobilize fully for the war effort and was appalled at the continued production of consumer goods. As he wrote years later, "The last half of 1950 seemed like a nightmare.

The United States seemed to be walking to its doom almost as unconcerned as cattle in a slaughterhouse."[20] In an effort to address those concerns, Crouch traveled 50,000 miles nationwide to speak to VFW groups, American Legion halls, schools, and conferences. He explained to his audiences that the nation was heading in the wrong direction and that the best way to turn it around was to take advantage of former Communists like himself who could guide government policy with their deep knowledge of the Communist agenda.

During these travels Crouch also returned to the family home in Hays, North Carolina. His father Isaac died on November 15, 1942, after which his mother Emma moved in with family, where she lived until her death on May 21, 1952. Their abandoned home remained untouched until family members began to go through it and discovered a trove of Communist material Crouch had left behind. He gathered the material, organized it, and offered it to the FBI hoping the bureau could use it to fight the Communist threat. Of this action Crouch less than modestly asserted, "This event is typical of many. Again and again I have gone to personal expense to cooperate with official agencies and to make every possible contribution to the fight against Soviet Communism. And the total financial loss has been no small amount." He was thus willing to sacrifice, even if the nation was not. In keeping with his growing anti-Communism ideology, and yet again evidencing his place within McCarthyism, he truly believed that the government's effort had come up short: "I will continue doing everything in my power to help the United States and the civilized world, regardless of personal loss, sacrifices and physical danger. The personal sacrifices the other former Communist leaders and I have made would be of even less relative importance if the information we have been able to provide had been used more intelligently and effectively by government agencies. Most of the personnel I have met in the FBI and other intelligence services have been men of character, sincerity and personal ability. But they are cogs in a machine, restricted by legislative and executive branches of the government."[21]

After promoting himself and criticizing the government for its failure to utilize him better, Crouch then turned on Secretary of State Dean Acheson, whom he held responsible for the current ill state of American foreign policy. In "The Case against Dean Acheson" Crouch blamed the secretary directly, as did McCarthy, for losing China, and more important, for allowing the United States to lose its position of global dominance after winning World War II. He wrote, "It is only as a result of his [Acheson's] pro-Soviet policies that our boys are dying in Korea." He explained his assertion by alleging that Acheson was guilty of "collaboration with and protection of Communists and fellow travelers in the State Department," and he then proceeded to list those individuals as: Lauchlin Currie, Alger Hiss, E. C. Acheson, Gustave Duran, Hamilton Robinson, Michael Greenberg, Harold Glasser, and Harding Bancroft. He went on, without any real evidence, to claim Acheson had supported the Communists against Franco in Spain, to attack him for criticizing General Douglas MacArthur, and to blame him for allowing the Soviets to get atomic secrets. Crouch then concluded by asserting that "on August 16, 1945, when Mr. Acheson was appointed Under Secretary of State to succeed Joseph Grew, a celebration of the event was held in the headquarters of the CP."[22]

Although little came of the assault on Acheson, excepting that it provided McCarthy additional ammunition against the State Department, it demonstrated well Crouch's bona fides as an ideologue and an expert on Communism. By 1951 his standing as an anti-Communist informant was well developed, and according to Sarah Brown not only was he well renowned for his services, he was also being well compensated. He made $4,840 as an informant in 1951, was living rent free in Hawaii in a home provided by the Chinese National Archbishop, and regularly stayed at the home of the Most Reverend Pane Yu-pin, National Archbishop of Nanking, while he was in Washington, D.C.[23]

While Crouch enjoyed his professional successes, life on the home front was decidedly mixed. Good news came with the arrival of his first grandchild, Karen Faye Hartley, born on July 23, 1951, to Crouch's daughter Tanya and her husband Stephen Hartley. The couple also adopted a daughter named Deborah. All was not well in this paradise, however, as on March 4, 1951, Crouch's son Carl died. He had been critically ill with internal bleeding, exacerbated by his hemophilia, and passed away at the age of nineteen. He was buried in the Oak Ridge Baptist Church Cemetery in Hays, North Carolina, not far from his grandparents.[24] Devastated by the loss of his son, but determined to save the nation, Crouch carried on.

The person who first bore the brunt of this determination was former Commerce Department economist William Remington. In 1948, when Crouch was first trying to break into the informant game, he had told the FBI that Remington associated with Communists in Tennessee. In 1949 he offered more information when he testified that Remington "may have belonged to the CP." When the FBI ignored his testimony, Crouch went to HUAC and demanded they investigate. The committee did. Remington denied ever being a member of the CPUSA and subsequently was indicted for perjury. In January 1951 Crouch testified in Remington's perjury case, and despite his previous rather circumspect assertions claimed with absolute certainty that Remington had been a member of the Communist Party in Tennessee.[25]

Led through the testimony by Assistant U.S. Attorney Roy Cohn, Crouch claimed that when Remington was nineteen he began to subscribe to Communist publications the *New South* and *Southern Worker*. Crouch dated that membership to 1937 when Remington took a year off from Dartmouth College to work as a messenger with the TVA in Knoxville. He produced a file and held up the card listing "Bill Remington" as a subscriber to the *New South* from June 1937 through March 1939 and claimed that Box 1692, to which the material was sent, was an "official box" for the Knox County Communist Party, thus proving that Remington was tied to the Communists.[26]

Despite such specifics, Crouch spent most of his time on the stand describing his organizing techniques and explaining the inner workings of the Communist Party. Key to his testimony was his explanation that party discipline in the South was so lax, especially in Tennessee under his predecessor Ted Wellman, that rarely were dues collected or people's names entered as official members. This was key, according to the *Washington Post*, because "Remington is charged with having lied that he was not a Communist Party member. The government has refused to define exactly what constitutes being a member of the Communist Party. The defense has taken the position that being a party member meant holding a party card as prescribed by the party constitution and otherwise following those rules and regulations." Crouch's testimony seemed to undermine even this element of the defense's position. He further undermined the defense when he asserted that even if Remington had been a card-carrying party member, he, Crouch, had burned all the Communist Party records in 1940 when he feared the government might confiscate them.[27]

The *New York Journal-American* reported that "so damaging was Crouch's testimony that Joseph L. Rauh, Jr., Remington's lawyer for the

Figure 5. Photograph of Paul Crouch at the time of the William Remington hearings, January 1951. Licensed from Corbis.

past two years, ceased his giggling and clowning at the defense table."[28] Rauh may have ceased mocking the prosecution, but he did not abandon his duties, and after the day's testimony he moved to have Crouch's words stricken from the record on the grounds that he was not in Tennessee during Remington's tenure and the two had never met. Judge Gregory Noonan denied the motion and Crouch's testimony remained in the record. On February 7, 1951, the jury convicted Remington of perjury, and the court sentenced him to five years in prison and a $5,000 fine.[29] An appeals court overturned the verdict, however, charging that Judge Noonan had poorly instructed the jury as to what constituted guilt or innocence.

That was not the end of the case for Remington, as he again was indicted for perjury. The second case began on January 23, 1953, and after only ten days a jury convicted him and the court sentenced him to three years in prison. His appeals failed, and in April 1953 Remington went to jail. He would not serve out his time, as fellow inmates murdered him in November 1954. Although Crouch did not take part in this second trial, his testimony in the first trial facilitated the second and thus puts some of Remington's blood on his hands.[30]

In early February 1951, as Paul was busy testifying in the Remington case, Sylvia Crouch testified in the Foley Square trial in New York State. Sylvia made the conversion from Communist to former Communist to anti-Communist along with Paul and, while never as active or as highly placed within the party as her husband, she had seen and done plenty and the government was more than willing to use her as an informant. The Foley Square case pitted the International Workers Order (IWO) against the State of New York's Department of Insurance, which sought to destroy the organization because it did not like the politics of the IWO's leaders. During direct examination, Sylvia testified that the Communist Party ordered her to join the IWO in Virginia in 1932 and then again for a few months in California in 1941. In both instances, she testified, she was only a "social member" and her dues were paid by others. Sylvia also testified that party leader Max Bedacht spoke to the Norfolk IWO lodge during a campaign to raise money in 1932 and again in 1933. When asked if anyone protested such Communist influence, she said they did not because all order members were at least sympathetic to the Communist cause.[31]

Defense attorney Raphael Weissman took up the cross-examination of Sylvia and worked to show that her seventh grade education made it hard for her to understand basic concepts, let alone the intricacies of Communist ideology, thus making her incapable of judging who was or was not a Communist. He also used IWO proceedings to prove that she could not have been a "social member" in 1932, since that category did not exist until 1940. Weissman then noted that when Sylvia rejoined the

IWO in 1941 there was a question on the application that asked if she previously had been a member. He asked how she answered that question, and when she claimed she could not remember he wondered how she could remember some things so specifically but others so poorly. She responded, "I don't remember the exact words I answered. I know what was said, the text of what I said. I know what I remember. Maybe I don't remember at this moment just exactly the same thing I remembered at that moment." After breaking her down and getting her to admit that her memory was faulty, Weissman also got her to admit that she and her husband made their livelihood as paid informants.[32]

Defense attorney Milton Freidman then took over the cross of the clearly flustered witness. He got Sylvia to admit that she was not an expert on the IWO despite her presence on the stand and the fact that the INS had hired her as such. He then carried on Weissman's line of questioning by noting that many of the events about which she testified took place eighteen years prior. He wondered how she possibly could remember every little detail. He also focused on the fact that she could not remember anything, even vaguely, which did not have to do with the order's relationship with the Communist Party. Freidman even introduced dozens of documents noting all the various activities the IWO was involved in and demonstrated that Sylvia could remember only one event (a folk festival) that did not tie directly to Communism.

In fact, Friedman explicitly questioned Sylvia about only remembering things that helped the prosecution, specifically her remembrance that Communist materials appeared in the IWO meeting halls: "Is it possible that the reason you don't remember . . . [other] publications is that you are being paid to testify that you saw Communist publications and you are not being paid to say that you saw IWO publications; is that the reason?" After the judge overruled an objection, she replied, "No." He asked her again, "That could have nothing to do with the case?" She again answered, "Nothing what so ever."[33] Freidman clearly did not believe her but pushed forward, getting her to admit that some of the meetings she testified about were held in languages other than English, languages she did not understand. He then excused her from the stand.

Historian Arthur Sabin calls Sylvia Crouch "the least effective, least credible, and least knowledgeable [witness] about the IWO." He also notes that on February 8 the IWO, for the first time during the trial, issued a press release specifically attacking a witness—Sylvia Crouch. They did no such thing for the other witnesses. The release read:

> Mrs. Sylvia Crouch, mother of two children, who in deportation hearings has helped send mothers to jail and tear fathers from their families, is the state's current witness in the liquidization trial of the International Workers Order.
>
> This marks the fifth time Mrs. Crouch has appeared as a paid government witness against working men and women. After a lifetime of trying to raise a family on ten or twelve dollars a week, Mrs. Crouch now earns twenty-five dollars a day plus nine dollars in expenses as an "expert" informer. With her husband, Paul Crouch, she is part of a husband-and-wife team testifying jointly before Un-American Activities committees and in deportation trials. Their joint income, then, becomes fifty dollars a day plus expenses. This is the kind of money the Crouches use to put meat on their table and clothes on their backs.
>
> But for all her willingness, the lady proved a poor witness for the prosecution. A fellow informer in the trial, George E. Powers, had "identified" from a page of photographs, Max Bedacht, former IWO official, as a Communist. Shown the same page of photographs, Mrs. Crouch fingered a photo of Powers and said, "This is Max Bedacht."
>
> A shocking thing about her attack on the Order is her admission that when she and her family were destitute in Norfolk, Virginia, in 1932, IWO members gave them bread, shoes, clothes and money. She offered no explanation for turning against the Order except to voluntarily testify that her present career as informer "pays her way."
>
> Mrs. Crouch who sells her testimony with a Southern accent, left the stand today and will undoubtedly make other appearances in the witch hunting world.[34]

Despite Sylvia's shortcomings, or maybe because of them, at the end of March, Paul sent a letter to the prosecution inquiring how the case was progressing and offering his services. He also included an itinerary, so the lawyers would know when he would be in the vicinity, as well as Communist publications, including several of which had the

IWO meeting hall listed on the return address. Finally, he passed along his wife's regrets at being a poor witness. James Henry responded for the prosecution and assured Crouch that his testimony would not be needed and that they were happy with Sylvia's efforts on the stand. Although this assessment of Sylvia's effort may have been more kind than truthful, the trial indeed was going well. West Virginia, Indiana, and Pennsylvania already were in the process of decertifying the IWO, and since a number of IWO leaders had taken the Fifth Amendment the prosecution was convinced that in this, a civil case, the judge would have no problem assuming that meant they were Communists. The prosecution thus was a bit taken aback when on April 30 the federal government removed the IWO from its list of subversive organizations. Despite that, on June 21, 1951, Judge Henry Clay Greenberg ruled that the IWO was Communist controlled and ordered it dissolved. After two appellate courts upheld the ruling and the Supreme Court refused to hear the case, in 1953 the IWO was liquidated.[35]

As Sylvia floundered on the stand, Crouch returned to his journalistic roots and published an article in the *Freeman* magazine, the successor journal to *Plain Talk* in which he made his first public exposure. In it, Crouch explained the greatest danger then facing the United States: the CPUSA underground. In 1951, after its success in prosecuting the twelve Communist Party leaders with the Smith Act, the federal government arrested 134 "second string" Communist leaders. Those party officials who remained free believed the arrests marked the beginning of an all-out assault on the Communist Party and determined to go underground. Crouch went into great detail explaining how the underground units would be organized and how they would emerge and carry on should the United States and the Soviet Union go to war or should the United States declare the CPUSA an illegal organization.

Claiming the underground would be led by "at least one reserve Central Committee, and probably a second one or even a third," Crouch explained that below this group were reserve district committees, and "the lowest and the basic unit in the underground plan is the *group* of three to five members." Crouch further described "confidential mail channels and codes for communication" as well as stockpiled mimeograph machines, paper, and money, all of which were organized "to cripple and weaken the American war potential. Communists will turn out leaflets and stickers, of course. But far more important and dangerous will be specific acts of military and economic sabotage" that the *groups* would engineer.[36]

Crouch concluded his fear-mongering essay with advice on how to undermine this great threat. He argued that the CPUSA and its underground apparatus had an Achilles heel: "the growing disillusionment of many Communists and the ever-increasing number of former party members." He contended that "collectively these ex-Communists could identify practically all party units in the country and most of the reserve officials and personnel in the underground apparatus. Not all of those still in the party are completely loyal to Stalin. Some now hesitate at the final step of becoming traitors to their country in time of war." Crouch urged the federal government to use former and current members of the Communist Party to identify the potential fifth columnists and to win away those party members whose loyalty was still up for grabs.[37]

While this clearly was an effort to justify his own standing, Crouch made what seems to be a slip that most likely went unnoticed by many who read the article. Early in the essay Crouch explained, "A dozen or more national leaders and scores of local party officials have broken with the Communist movement since 1930. They have lifted the curtain of secrecy from many inside operations of the party, yet little has been told about the special underground apparatus. *This is true because Communist officials are given only such information as may be necessary to carry out work assigned to them*" [italics added]. Although Crouch continually pawned himself off as an expert on all things Communist, here he admitted that by design no one knew everything about the CPUSA.[38] At the time no one appreciated the reality of this statement, and Crouch continued on as a well-paid informant who could and would testify about anything having to do with the Communist Party.

Indeed, on May 8 and 9, 1951, Crouch testified before the Senate Internal Security Subcommittee (SISS). The SISS, which was formed in January 1951, offered senators the opportunity to submit their bona fides as anti-Communists, as HUAC did for congressmen. As M. J. Heale writes, it was formed "so that senators too could win some Communist scalps."[39] For whatever reason it was created, the senators were interested to hear what Crouch had to say. He testified first about Gilbert Parks, who was then up for federal employment. Crouch asserted that

Parks should not be given a government job because he continued to deny his Communist membership. Crouch claimed they had worked together in the Communist Party for three years in North Carolina and that he and Sylvia were friends with Gilbert and his wife Gertrude. Crouch warned the subcommittee that Parks likely was trying to infiltrate the government and from that position offer information to the CPUSA and the Soviets. In an aside, Crouch also complained that his previous testimony had unleashed a "smear" campaign against him and demanded that the government investigate Parks so as to exonerate him and the entire informer system.[40]

The senators seemed uninterested in Parks' standing, but they did take interest when Crouch turned to atomic espionage. He alleged that he knew many of the leading scientists working for UC Berkeley, the Radiation Laboratory, the Shell Development Project, and the War Manpower Commission of Northern California. Not only did he know these people, he claimed to have attended Communist Party meetings with them as well. He went even further and named names. He alleged that the leaders of the Communistic scientists were Kenneth May and Rudy Lambert. Crouch also named Joseph Weinberg, Frank Oppenhiemer, David Bohn, Klaus Fuchs, Allan May, David Greenglass, Bruno Pentecerve, Irving Fox, Giovanni Lomanitz, Robert Oppenheimer, Max Freidman, Robert Leevinger, David Hawkins, David Adelson, and Harry Gold as members of the Communist Party. The result, Crouch asserted, was that "the United States has never had any atomic secrets not known to the Soviet Government."[41] All told, he estimated that about fifty Communists had been part of the atomic bomb effort, between those in California and Los Alamos, while the Communists had a majority of the positions in the War Manpower Commission. These scientists/Communists were directed by Marcel Scherer, whom Crouch claimed was "a Moscow trained national head of the department for work among scientists" who arrived in San Francisco in the early 1940s and took control of the group. As a result of Scherer's control, Crouch had little direct knowledge of what the group was up to, but he testified that others informed him that the group was providing the Soviet Union a great deal of useful scientific information. Although Crouch had testified to much of this before, the senators were outraged by what they perceived as new information. Crouch, sensing an opportunity, followed up this testimony with a letter to Senator McCarthy in which he urged his testimony, specifically that about Robert Oppenheimer, be distributed throughout the government to facilitate an investigation of the nation's scientists.[42]

That investigation would come, but in the meantime the senators were duly impressed with Crouch's testimony and invited him back on September 1, 1951. That day Crouch offered the Internal Security Subcommittee testimony about Paul R. Porter, the acting director of the Economic Cooperation Administration (ECA). Crouch claimed Porter's wife and brother were members of the Communist Party. While he had no evidence to prove Porter was a Communist, he noted that Porter previously had worked on a magazine entitled *Revolt* that denounced the American government and capitalism "in more violent and abusive language than I ever employed when I was a Communist leader." Crouch also noted that in 1937 Porter published a book entitled *Which Way for the Socialist Party* in which he attacked capitalism and supported Marx. Additionally, Crouch alleged, the book was sold by the CPUSA to raise money. As a result of these issues, Crouch urged the committee not to make Porter the permanent head of the ECA.[43] In the end, Porter did not get the job, as the ECA became the Mutual Security Administration (MSA) under the leadership of William Averell Harriman. Porter would go on to serve in the MSA, however, as Deputy U.S. Special Representative in Europe.

In June and July 1951, Crouch continued to testify for the government when he appeared before the Subversive Activities Control Board, which was investigating the CPUSA to determine whether or not it was foreign dominated and supported the violent overthrow of the government. His testimony consumed some 387 pages. On June 26 and 27 Crouch rehashed stories about his time in Hawaii, his incarceration in Alcatraz, the subsequent speaking tour, and his work as a CPUSA functionary. He also explained how the CPUSA hierarchy was organized and the functions of the various party organs. He concluded by describing his trip to Moscow.[44]

On July 7 and 10 he focused on the CPUSA's relationship with the Comintern, labor, and various Communist front organizations. He then addressed the essence of Marxism-Leninism and asserted that "the attitude of the CP . . . toward the United States government was that the

United States government was a capitalist government opposed to the interest of the workers and the people, that no allegiance was owed by the people of this capitalist government, and that it had to be destroyed in order to provide freedom for the people of this country."[45]

Crouch then turned to the Communist Party's policy shifts that resulted from the changing international situation of the late 1930s and early 1940s. He explained that after the Nazi-Soviet Non-Aggression Pact the party opposed American intervention in the war but that after the Nazi invasion of the USSR the party came out in support of intervention. He thus made clear that the Communist Party was more interested in protecting the Soviet Union than it was defending the American working class. As further proof that the party had a foreign focus, he spent a large portion of his testimony addressing Communist efforts to infiltrate the U.S. military and the party's use of codes and other secretive measures.[46] Although little of this information was new, the board was pleased with Crouch's testimony.

That changed beginning on July 10 when he faced an extended and withering cross-examination. For eight days (July 10–12, 16–19, and 23) Crouch demonstrated both his mastery of judicial procedure as well as a remarkable difficulty remembering his testimony from previous cases, including testimony offered only days earlier before the same body. His mastery of the process is evident from his consistent refusal to answer simple yes or no questions. For instance, when asked about specific statements from his first HUAC hearing in May 1949, he replied, "If the record says I made it, I did so. I don't recall." He was similarly evasive throughout, using phrases such as "My best recollection is . . ." and "I have no recollection" when confronted with questions about his prior testimony, assertions, and allegations. Even when lawyers for the CPUSA actually read to him his prior testimony he managed to turn things around. "Q: 'Do you recall the language that I read to you from your testimony?' A: 'I don't know what you mean by recall. Do you mean do I recall you just read it or do you mean that I recall having given that testimony?"[47]

Although such evasions succeeded in frustrating the cross-examination, the Communist Party's lawyers continued to hound him and succeeded in tripping him up on several occasions. On July 16 Crouch explained that William Z. Foster was chairman of the CPUSA in 1928.

Crouch clung to that assertion despite the introduction of numerous documents and statements that demonstrated that Foster was not chairman until 1930 and that no such position existed in 1928. Even more damning was his inability to remember his own testimony. While the party lawyers made a big deal over his inability to remember to what he had testified in 1949, the fact that that testimony occurred two years and several hearings prior offers some understanding. What is harder to understand is his inability to remember his testimony from the very same SACB hearing. On July 23 Crouch was asked about his testimony from July 17 regarding Clarence Hiskey. Crouch did not recall the testimony, and even after lawyers read his statement into the record Crouch asserted that he did not recall it. When an incredulous lawyer asked, "You don't recall giving that testimony here?" Crouch replied, "No, I probably did. I don't happen to recall it now."[48] Although Crouch remembered decades-old events with precision under direct examination, once faced with an unfriendly lawyer he turned vague, uncooperative, and so forgetful that a week sufficed to cloud his memory.

Despite this shaky cross-examination, the SACB relied heavily on Crouch's testimony and ruled that the CPUSA was foreign dominated and dedicated to the violent overthrow of the government. The CPUSA appealed the SACB findings and asserted that three witnesses, Crouch, Manning Johnson, and Harvey Matusow, "committed perjury, are completely untrustworthy, and should be accorded no credence." The appeal also labeled them "professional perjurors [*sic*]" and noted that despite questions of veracity, the board's final report referenced Crouch and his testimony thirty-six times.[49] The board rejected the call for new hearings and asserted that the findings of the three men in question were supported by evidence from nineteen additional witnesses. The CPUSA appealed the decision in a federal appeals court in 1953. The court rejected the claim, noting that Crouch was cross-examined during the hearing, during which the majority of the questions sought to impugn his integrity. The Communist Party thus had had its chance to debunk his assertions in the courtroom.

Undaunted, the Communists appealed to the Supreme Court, which heard the case on November 17, 1955. The high court eventually ruled on the *CPUSA v. SACB* case in 1956 and ordered it reheard in light of Crouch's (as well as Matusow and Johnson's) questionable testimony.

The SACB subsequently scrubbed the questionable testimony, reexamined the findings, and again determined that the CPUSA was foreign dominated. The party again appealed, but in 1961 the Supreme Court upheld the decision. The Communist Party refused to abide by the decision and in December 1961 was cited for not registering as a foreign controlled organization. The party appealed the citation and in 1965 the Supreme Court overturned the verdict.[50]

All of that was in the future, and for the moment Crouch remained an unimpeached source. Thus, in August 1951 he offered Congress some additional advice on how to deal with the threats his testimony disclosed. First, he provided a list of several expectations on which the CPUSA was functioning. He asserted that members believed in the inevitability of military conflict between the United States and USSR; believed that legislative action against the party and the arrest of leaders would occur prior to the outbreak of war; that all party members would be arrested within twenty four hours of the outbreak of war; that the party needed several reserve central committees to survive those assaults; and that the party would continue to function through the operation of "legal" fronts and the use of "illegal press operations."[51]

Since the CPUSA was so well prepared for the coming war, Crouch offered some suggestions on how to disrupt those efforts. He first asserted that the Smith Act was the most efficient and effective method for defeating the Communist Party. He then supported new legislation, including a law that would prevent the firing of people who testified against the CPUSA and one that would prevent unions from expelling those who testified. He also supported the creation of a private foundation to help those who testified and lost their jobs anyway. Other new legislative ideas included the requirement that the names of all the officers of political parties and lobbying groups be made public and the requirement that all groups that required dues, membership cards, or in any other way restricted membership be forced to publish the names of all members and make their financial records public.[52]

Crouch then offered several suggestions to safeguard the nation, including calls to make it a felony "with drastic penalties" for anyone convicted of convincing another to join the military "for the purpose of subversive and revolutionary activities" and for the revocation of military commissions for anyone who refused to answer questions raised by congressional committees. Finally, he called for an increase in the use of ex-Communists such as himself. He specifically supported the use of ex-Communists over FBI agents for the rather unconvincing argument that FBI agents who infiltrated the party would only be able to testify once, whereas ex-Communists could testify repeatedly. More realistically, he claimed there were thousands of ex-Communists who were willing and able to testify against the party and urged that they be used as the prime source of information to help destroy domestic Communism.[53]

Crouch followed up these suggestions by writing an essay entitled "The Role of Ex-Communists in National Defense." In it he argued that there were 200,000 former Communists in America who could do a great deal to help fight domestic Communism. Many were afraid to come forward, however, so he urged the federal government to do more to make clear that those who testified would be safe. Crouch also offered a ten-point plan for how the government could use those ex-Communists including having them send letters to current Communists, having them work with the American Legion, and sending them out as public speakers.[54]

In October 1951 Crouch got the opportunity to put some of these ideas into practice when he returned to the witness chair and testified about the alleged infiltration of Memphis Local 19 of the Distributive, Processing, and Office Workers of America (Independent) Union. Chaired by Republican senator from Mississippi James Eastland, the investigation heard Crouch testify that leading union officials, including Ed McCrea and Simon Kaset, were Communists, and that as far as he knew all the union leaders were party members. To further inflame the situation, at least from Eastland's perspective, Crouch reiterated earlier allegations that several professors and students from Fisk College, the historically black college in Nashville, were Communist Party members. He also explained that African Americans were encouraged to join the party because leaders hoped they would foment racial strife that would weaken the nation and facilitate the Communist takeover. When traditional efforts to get them to join failed, Crouch explained that the party worked to get African Americans to join Communist-controlled unions, like the one under investigation, in which they could "be fed propaganda until they join[ed] the Party."[55]

The *Memphis Appeal* covered the hearing and further inflamed the racial issue when it asserted that the union had "enrolled thousands of

Negro industrial workers in Memphis and the mid-South." As a result of these racially tinged charges, all eyes were on Lee Lashley "Negro president of Local 19" when he testified before the Committee. After Lashley refused to answer several questions, Senator Eastland asked, "Boy, what have you got to hide?" Such taunting, and a long and grueling time on the stand, eventually overwhelmed Lashley who "broke down under a second day of merciless questioning and admitted that he was a former member of the Communist Party, though he denied present membership."[56] As a result of Lashley's admission, Local 19 disaffiliated itself from the Distributive, Processing, and Office Workers Union and instead aligned with the more conservative Retail, Wholesale, and Department Store Union.[57] The hearing thus proved a success for Eastland, who demonstrated his opposition to Civil Rights and Communism, and for Crouch, who won yet another Communist scalp. More important than the destruction of this union or these personal gains, however, was that Eastland took a liking to Crouch the informant and would recall him in later hearings, albeit with much less success.

Crouch rounded out his busy year by giving additional speeches on the Communist threat. On December 17, 1951, he spoke to the American Legion Cheverly Post 108 in Cheverly, Maryland. The title of his speech was "Communism—Infiltration of the Armed Forces and What it Means in the Korean Situation." Days later he spoke to the Los Angeles Kiwanis Club. Stealing the title from Sinclair Lewis, Crouch called his speech, "It can't happen here," and warned about the general threat of Communist infiltration into all elements of American society. He also appeared on television and espoused similar concerns. Freedom Clubs, Inc., a conservative political organization, sponsored the appearances and James Newman, national director of the clubs, sent Crouch a thank you letter noting, "The response to this program has been extremely enthusiastic, and your comments were especially well received." Sylvia did her part as well, penning an article entitled "The Communist Use of Women" in which she warned that "Communists have never hesitated to exploit sex for their objectives. Girls will be assigned to become sweethearts of as many soldiers as possible, obtaining any bit of information from them."[58] She urged the military to recognize this danger and to train soldiers to avoid this potential security breach.

The late 1940s and early 1950s thus proved good years for Crouch. He was earning a living and protecting the nation by speaking out and testifying against the Communist menace. He was fully confirmed in his ideology and despite the occasional error was well regarded by politicians and law enforcement agencies. He had handled himself well on the witness stand, proactively spread the anti-Communist message, and was relatively successful in winning convictions. That was all politicians and prosecutors could demand, and in ensuing years Crouch remained both ideologically driven and highly employable. Although the future also included his first public criticisms, they proved but minor concerns and he remained fully enthralled with his anti-Communist faith.

8 LIMELIGHT, 1952–1953

The death of Stalin in March 1953 and the end of the Korean War four months later in July did little to ease the Cold War. McCarthy continued on his search for domestic Communists and the nation at large remained petrified by the Soviet menace. As such, Crouch continued to be a popular figure in court proceedings and congressional investigations throughout the era. Indeed, in 1952 and 1953 he testified in three major state trials of alleged Communists, charged a federal employee and a Hollywood icon with being party members, and proffered a significant amount of testimony regarding the dangers of Communist infiltration from Hawaii and Latin America. He also got a raise. At the same time, however, he faced his first organized opposition and his first major judicial defeat. Despite those negatives, Crouch remained confirmed in his ideology and adamant in his anti-Communist activism.

On August 7, 1951, George Meyers, Leroy Wood, Maurice Braverman, Philip Frankfeld, Regina Frankfeld, and Dorothy Rose Blumberg were arrested during a roundup of Communists in Baltimore. All six were charged with violating the Smith Act, which made it illegal to conspire to teach or advocate the overthrow of the government or even to belong to an organization that did so. Indeed, as Judge W. Calvin Chestnut III directed the jury, "It is not alleged in this instance that the defendants have actually committed violations of the act, but only that they have agreed or conspired to do so."[1]

Their trial began in March 1952. Crouch testified on background issues and Communist ideology, part of which included reading from Communist pamphlets and books to demonstrate that Communists sought the overthrow of the government. Crouch specifically testified that Communists viewed the United States as an enemy that needed to be destroyed, and as proof he asserted that in the 1920s Moscow had directed Communists to infiltrate the U.S. military. Crouch went even further and alleged, "Throughout the period of my membership the attitude of the Communist Party toward the United States Government was that it was an enemy government which must be overthrown by armed insurrection within and with the aid of the Red Army of the Soviet Union with its defeat, its destruction, annihilation, and replacement by a Soviet America."[2] Crouch also used the opportunity to advertise his manuscript when he mentioned his unpublished autobiography "Broken Chains." When asked about it he replied, "The theme is how a native of the South was lured into a vast and evil conspiracy without realizing just what was involved, and how he called upon the people of the nation to become aware of the peril before it was too late."[3]

These generalizations aside, the only elements of his testimony that had a direct impact on the case came when he claimed to have met the Frankfelds in New York City, where they worked on plans to infiltrate the army. He concluded his testimony with the warning that the "stolen" atomic secrets were a direct threat to Baltimore, although he failed to explain how. The jury deliberated for less than three hours before finding all defendants guilty. On April 4, 1952, they received two to five years in prison.[4] Yet again Crouch had helped weaken the Red menace.

On August 28, 1951, the FBI arrested Charles Fujimoto, Eileen Fujimoto, James Freeman, Koji Ariyoshi, Jack Kimoto, Jack Hall, and John Reinecke, and charged the seven leaders of the Communist Party in Hawaii with violating the Smith Act. The trial of the seven began on November 5, 1952. Crouch was the first witness and testified for five days during which time he again provided background information on Communism. Despite defense protests that his testimony had nothing to do with the specifics in the case, Judge Jon Wiig allowed it claiming it demonstrated the inner workings of the CPUSA. Among the background issues Crouch addressed was Communist ideology. In so doing, he enabled the prosecuting attorneys to introduce Communist literature into the record, which Crouch then explained. Even more important, he claimed that the goal of the CPUSA was to overthrow the government, which was key in a Smith Act prosecution.

The only specific testimony he provided in this case was his assertion that James Freeman was ordered to Hawaii in 1941 as a Communist organizer. Crouch said he recommended Freeman for the job, knew him well, visited his house several times, and gave him quantities of

Communist literature. When Crouch admitted that he did most of the talking at the meetings, the defense protested and argued that listening to a spiel about Communism did not prove that Freeman was a Communist. Judge Wiig rejected the defense motion and allowed Crouch's testimony to continue. That continuation allowed him to name Koji Ariyoshi as a Communist Party member as well. Crouch alleged that Ariyoshi once wrote an article for *Doho*, the Japanese language newspaper for the CPUSA in which only party members could publish.[5]

Once Crouch finished with his testimony, defense lawyers Richard Gladstein, A. Wirin, Myer Symonds, and Harriet Bouslog got the opportunity to cross-examine him. During cross-examination, Gladstein asked Crouch if he had ever denied the CPUSA would use violence to seize power. As Crouch pondered the question, Gladstein reminded him that when he was trying to get the Communist Party on the Tennessee ballot he, indeed, had done so. Crouch admitted that was the case but said he made such a statement simply to dupe the capitalists. Having set the trap, Gladstein then presented to the court evidence that in other trials Crouch had testified that Communists did not seek the use of violence to overthrow the government. When asked if the testimony was perjured, Crouch stammered, which was exactly what the defense wanted. Their object was to undermine Crouch as a witness. The prosecution stepped in, however, and objected that the questions were "touching on confidential information that touches on the security of the nation." Judge Wiig overruled the objection and allowed the line of questioning to continue. Despite that judgment, as Gladstein pressed Crouch about force and violence the prosecution objected continuously, ultimately doing so seventy-five times.[6]

Crouch eventually escaped the stand, but during the final defense summary Gladstein criticized the prosecution witnesses, including Crouch by name, for their "inherently improbable, self-contradictory . . . false . . . and suspicious testimony." He claimed they were motivated by money and that their desire to be paid was what drove them to invent the stories they told. The *Honolulu Record* agreed and reported that "He [defense lawyer Richard Gladstein] showed Crouch up as a liar who said he remembered details of a Marxist study outline he saw 11 years ago in someone's office, but never had it himself. He talked for days . . . but did not remember the simple facts of his court martial in Hawaii in the '20s, a kind of experience one ordinarily remembers."[7]

Despite those problems, all seven were convicted. ILWU workers protested the conviction—as Jack Hall was head of ILWU—but most Hawaiians were relieved. The men received five-year sentences and $5,000 fines, while Eileen Fujimoto got three years and $2,000 in fines. All appealed, and the case slowly made its way through the courts. In 1957 the Supreme Court overturned a similar decision, ruling that action to overthrow the government had to take place before people could be arrested. As a result, in 1958 all seven were exonerated. They had only spent a few weeks in jail prior to their trial, and the court decision meant they did not have to return.[8]

This trial was not the only time that Crouch the informant focused on the islands. He also testified on several occasions about the continuing presence of Communists in Hawaii, as well as what he perceived to be the dangers of Hawaiian statehood. On October 22, 1951, Crouch sent a memo to the District of Columbia field office of the INS in which he complained that a year earlier he had sent the office a list of one-hundred names of "known Communists" in Hawaii, but as far as he knew no action had been forthcoming. Crouch explained his fear that Communists were fighting for Hawaiian statehood so as to gain easy access to the United States, and he demanded the federal government do something to tamp down the Communist threat on the islands before it had the chance to spread to the mainland.[9]

More dramatically, he argued that Communists had long desired Hawaii become a state because there were so many of them on the islands that they would be able to elect a representative to Congress and from there begin the takeover of the nation. He went on to contend, "Today I am seriously alarmed by the American public's failure to understand the importance of Hawaii in Stalin's blueprint for world conquest and the significance of current developments in the islands. For 20 years Moscow has regarded Hawaii as a place of the greatest importance. . . . Today the Communist strength in Hawaii is not due to the number of Communists, probably not more than 200. It is due to the strategic positions certain Communists have been able to establish for themselves, with the help of the mainland."[10] Crouch also offered specific numbers to demonstrate this influence. He listed 152 known Communists on the islands and broke down those numbers by race, ethnicity, and gender. He alleged that 78 percent were men, 52 percent Japanese, 20 percent white, with smaller numbers of Filipinos, Chinese, Korean, and African.[11]

In July 1953 Crouch continued his focus on Hawaii when he testified before the Senate Interior and Insular Affairs Committee. He remained opposed to statehood and asserted that while there were fewer than 100 Communists in Hawaii, they controlled "all employment in the basic industries" and the attitudes of 30,000 workers through the ILWU. Crouch even asserted that it was impossible to get a union job without the approval of the Communist Party. When asked why, if the ILWU was Communist-controlled it was not on the federal list of subversive organizations, he asserted that the government was still trying to determine if unions belonged on the list and noted that HUAC had called it a Communist-dominated union.[12] Crouch also told the senators that he supported the expansion of the Taft-Hartley Act to cover Hawaii and the ILWU and its amendment to allow the government to remove the bargaining rights from all unions under Communist control.

He went on to suggest other changes to prevent the spread of Communism in Hawaii. He suggested large scale public works projects to create better irrigation on the islands. So doing, he argued, would make Hawaii self-sufficient and reduce the need to import food, which would diminish the size, power, and influence of the ILWU. He argued further that the economic benefits of irrigation projects would decrease unemployment and increase home ownership, both of which would create a more stable social order as employed homeowners would support the status quo. Crouch concluded by calling for increased funding of the Hawaiian Residents Association in its fight against Communism, increased funding for the territorial HUAC, and greater support for and use of ex-Communists in government investigations of the territorial party.[13]

When nothing came from his testimony, and it appeared that Hawaii was on the path to statehood, Crouch penned a letter to President Dwight D. Eisenhower. In the letter he lamented that both parties were either ignoring or actively hiding the Communist threat in Hawaii in their desire to absorb it into the union. He then provided Eisenhower with a list of Communists and Communist efforts in the territory and asked for the president's help in keeping it out of the union.[14]

When this letter failed to elicit a response, Crouch sent two letters to INS official Robert Woytych, in which he labeled himself "Consultant, Washington, D.C." In the first letter he offered his analysis of Communism in Hawaii. He explained that while some twenty-five members recently had left, no efforts had been made to use them to learn more about the group. If they resisted testifying, he suggested offering them jobs to make them feel more open to talking. Of the Communist Party that remained, he said it still controlled the ILWU and that its control "over island industrial life and especially its power to halt shipping between the mainland and Hawaii constitutes a serious threat to the national security of the United States."[15] Crouch further claimed there were many more Communists in Hawaii than the number of card-carrying members, and once again he lamented the almost total lack of anti-Communist efforts on the islands.

In the second letter to Woytych, Crouch suggested the use of *Revolutionary Struggle against War vs. Pacifism* by Alexander Bittelman as a good book to understand the aims of the CPUSA. He claimed that the INS had not used the book in any of its prosecutions, "yet I know of no party document that presents the objectives of overthrowing the American government by armed force and insurrection in a more clear, simple and unmistakable language than this document." He even offered a few quotations from it in order to prove his point. That done, Crouch suggested buying enough copies so the INS could distribute it to all offices involved in Communist prosecutions. Finally, he noted that the fact that Bittelman was still alive and was well known as a prominent member of the CPUSA would do a great deal to demonstrate the validity of the document.[16]

When these letters also failed to elicit a response, Crouch returned to addressing the president directly and mailed him four letters regarding Hawaii. In the first, a letter of some thirty pages, Crouch suggested commonwealth status, rather than statehood, for both Hawaii and Alaska. He then offered five reasons he supported such a move, two of which are worthy of note. Reason number three asserted that a commonwealth government would have greater local control than would a state government, but at the same time if the Communist threat arose, the federal government could step in and help a commonwealth more easily than it could a state. Reason number four asserted that if the territories became states, people would be able to move from them to the mainland without any oversight, which would make it easier for Communists to infiltrate the nation. If the lands were commonwealths, however, the INS would have more control to decide who got into the United States and who did not. Crouch claimed this was an especially important tool as 25 percent "of the aliens of Hawaii are members of

Communist controlled organizations, subject to daily Red anti-American propaganda and influence." He then summarized his standing as follows: "I submit, Mr. President, that anyone who votes for statehood is voting to open the gates so hundreds of subversives in Hawaii could pour into the mainland, and also would enable alien Communist leaders on the mainland to travel to Hawaii."[17]

After this litany of general reasons Hawaii should not become a state, Crouch then turned to specific threats in Hawaii. He first addressed his nemesis Robert McElrath, a Hawaiian radio broadcaster who recently had described Crouch as an "ex-Communist who is trying to go to Heaven by sending his ex-friends to hell."[18] Crouch called him "Hawaii's leading Communist radio commentator" and informed the president that "McElrath's daily Communist broadcasts on the Honolulu radio are filled with the most vitriolic and vicious attacks on our government and our way of life. He is an enemy of America and his every effort is devoted to the cause of destroying our nation and replacing the Stars and Stripes with the Red Flag of atheistic Communism." Crouch eventually moved away from this personal squabble to warn the president that both the Republican and Democratic parties of Hawaii had been infiltrated by Communists, that the public schools had been taken over by Communists, and that the county of Kauai was in danger of immediately falling under Communist rule. "The situation there," he frantically wrote, "may call for the drastic action of separating the County from the rest of Hawaii and placing it under military government until the Red menace is brought under control to the extent that it can be handled by civil authorities."[19]

Crouch concluded by returning to the original issue in the letter: Hawaiian statehood. He warned the president, "But above all it [Hawaiian statehood] would give the international conspracy [*sic*] the opportunity it has been waiting for so long—and so eagerly. . . . I tremble at the prospect of having to set back and watch the present Red control over the County of Kauai extend its tentacles until all of Hawaii is crushed by the Red octopus. The balance of power in the world struggle today is balanced so delicately that the loss of Hawaii to Communism might well mean the destruction of civilization under the Red tide of atheistic Communism."[20]

In three additional letters—of three, forty-eight, and eighty-eight pages—Crouch continued to warn the president of his fears. In the longest letter, he claimed, "the Communist Party controls the economic life of Hawaii," and warned that "Communist power in Hawaii does not end in the economic field. It is powerful in the political field and if statehood is granted to Hawaii or this Communist menace remains so great, there is a great danger indeed that we may see Communist Party members sitting in our Senate, our House of Representatives." He expanded on the claims in his previous letters and alleged that the Democratic Party in Hawaii was so badly infiltrated with Communists that it "no longer deserves to be called the Democratic Party." It was not simply the Democrats, however, who had been taken over. He informed the president that the ILWU remained the center of Communist control in Hawaii and that the mainstream papers the *Honolulu Record* and the *Honolulu Star* followed the lead of the *Daily Worker*. The only group working to defend the islands from this threat, he told the president, was the Hawaiian Residents Association, and he urged the federal government to help the group save the islands and the nation from the Communist scourge.[21]

Hawaii was not the only region concerning Crouch. When not badgering the president and the INS about the islands, he returned to his continuing fear of the Communist infiltration of Latin America. In an essay entitled "Communism in Latin America," Crouch offered a detailed analysis of the Communist presence there and warned that while America's military tended to defend the nation from a potential assault from the east and west, the growing presence of Communists to our south was an even greater threat. In fact, Crouch alleged that the Soviets already had a plan for world conquest. Their goal was to conquer Asia first, followed by Europe and Africa. Once the eastern hemisphere was under their control, he explained, the Communists would move into Latin American from which they would engage in their final assault on the United States—the last bastion of democratic capitalism.[22]

Crouch began his formal assessment of this threat with an overview. He claimed there were twenty-one Communist parties in twenty Latin American countries, including Puerto Rico. Of Puerto Rico, Crouch admitted that the Communist presence was small but argued that while it could never seize power it was large enough to stir up other, larger Latin American parties. Of the rest of Latin America, Crouch offered a brief history. He said early efforts in the region had fallen short, and Communism remained weak until the formation of the All-America

Anti-Imperialist League, of which he had once been the head. Centered in New York City, Crouch argued that the league was one factor in unifying, organizing, and spreading the movement throughout the region. A second factor was American intervention in Nicaragua. Crouch alleged that the league had used the intervention as a propaganda tool but also supported as best it could General Sandino in his opposition to the United States. Crouch further explained that in the 1930s the league headquarters moved to Montevideo, Uruguay, to be closer to the heart of Latin America and that Montevideo, along with Mexico City and Havana, remained the key centers of Communist activism. Thanks to these efforts, Crouch asserted, the Communist presence grew throughout the 1930s and 1940s to the point that Communists were being elected to Congress in Chile, won 25 percent of the vote in Brazil, were the main opposition force to Fulgencio Batista in Cuba, and that Mexican president Lazaro Cardenas "was surrounded by Communists and many of them held leading government posts."[23]

From these generalizations, many of them untrue, Crouch moved to specifics, many of which also were false. He claimed the Communists in Cuba earned 200,000 votes in the previous election. The Mexican Party, by contrast, had been diminished after the Nazi-Soviet Non-Aggression Pact but was reemergent as evidenced by its getting 420,000 signatures on the Stockholm Petition, a favorite among the Communists with its call for an international prohibition on atomic weapons. He explained that the party in Mexico would continue to grow as many Mexicans traveled to the United States for training, while many Mexican-Americans returned to Mexico with their Communist agenda intact.[24]

The parties in Central America, he claimed, were small but dangerous beyond their numbers. As evidence, he asserted that the group in Nicaragua was working with the government and the group in Panama was a threat simply due to the presence of the canal. Of South America, he asserted with no real evidence that First Lady Eva Peron had ties to the Argentinean Communist Party, that Bolivia "has a very active Communist movement and is one of the danger spots in Latin America," and that Brazil had the largest party in all of South America with strength comparable to the parties in France and Italy. Of Brazil Crouch also wrote, "The Communist movement in Brazil may be in a position to cause more serious danger to the democratic world than any of the other Soviet controlled parties in Latin America." Should a Communist power emerge there, he warned, the United States would be in grave danger.[25]

Crouch concluded his study with another warning and a suggestion that the nation needed to pay attention to its southern neighbors lest Communism make a sneak attack from the south. He wrote, "The potential strength of Stalin's fifth column in Brazil, and in the nineteen other Latin American nations, should cause us to watch for storm clouds on the Southern horizon while we are facing the rising tide of Communism in Asia and Europe."[26]

Crouch continued to raise his concerns about Latin America in February 1952 when he produced another affidavit specifically about Cuba. He explained that he met many Cuban Communists during his trip to Russia in 1927–1928 and that by 1929 the CPUSA had a relationship with the Cuban Communist Party. He claimed to have met "Blas Roca," who was a leading Cuban Communist and asserted that they worked together often. He then claimed that Jack Strong, a CPUSA organizer in Florida, had been in close touch with Cuban Communists in 1936 and 1937 through the Cigar Makers Union in Tampa.[27] The trouble in Latin America, in other words, was an American problem that needed to be addressed before it was too late.

Although Crouch achieved little with his screeds against Communism in Hawaii and Latin America, he did enough to keep his name relevant, and in 1952 Senator McCarthy turned to him during his investigation of Mary and Leon Keyserling. The two already had been investigated thoroughly in 1948 when the Commerce Department loyalty board requested that Mary, director of the Commerce Department's International Economic Analysis Division, respond to allegations of disloyalty. Specifically, the board charged her with signing the "Open Letter to American Liberals," which was then published in *Soviet Russia Today*, "receiving Communist mail from Mexico, joining or associating with four groups the attorney general listed as subversive, lending a Commerce Department document to a member of a known subversive group, and associating with known and former communists." Keyserling, aided by her defense counsel and future Supreme Court Justice Abe Fortas, defended herself vigorously. She denied associating with Communists, and while she admitted to signing the open letter, she expressed regret with so doing. She was cleared of the charges, but in 1951 the same loyalty board made eleven new allegations of disloyalty against her, with the new charges focusing on the claim that she had been a member of the CPUSA or the YCL. In August 1952 the board ruled against her, although in 1953 the ruling was reversed, mere days before she and her husband resigned with the arrival of the Eisenhower administration.[28]

Dissatisfied with the loyalty board's investigation, McCarthy determined to investigate for himself. Crouch happily accepted the senator's request for him to testify and proceeded to claim that in 1928 and 1929 he knew Mary Keyserling as a Communist and that he met with her a dozen times in Yonkers, New York. He informed the committee that she told him her father was wealthy and an anti-Communist and, because of this, she asked not to be assigned to party work that would involve publicity.[29] The *Washington Post* reported, however, that "after confronting Mrs. Keyserling . . . Crouch was unable to testify that she was the person he knew."[30] Leon Keyserling, Truman's chief economic advisor, responded to the testimony with a statement that called Crouch's allegations a "monstrosity, based on false testimony by an ex-convict (Alcatraz), ex-Communist, informer."[31] By this point Keyserling had left the government and McCarthy was moving on to bigger fish, so the allegations and Crouch's inability to affirm Keyserling's identity dissipated.

Despite the relative failure of the Keyserling investigation, and despite some of its own concerns, in October 1952 FBI agents requested authority to extend Crouch's time on the payroll noting that he had offered information on seven cases and had been interviewed four times over the last several months. Crouch, realizing his importance, used the opportunity to request the FBI support his application to carry a gun. He claimed that as a result of his testimony the CPUSA would try to kill him to prevent him from testifying further and he needed to be able to defend himself. The FBI refused the request. The bureau did decide, however, to alter his remuneration. For his previous service he had been paid $25 per eight hours. A payment voucher from the Justice Department dated November 25, 1952, for instance, listed Crouch as having been a consultant for the department for seventeen days and as testifying for eight days between October 29 and November 25, 1952, for a total payment of $625. The bureau now decided to offer him $100 per session.[32]

Now with even more financial incentive to testify, Crouch willingly met with the INS on October 2, 1952. Crouch testified about a central committee meeting in 1935 in New York City during which members discussed the possible recruitment of Hollywood writers, directors, and actors "for the purpose of using the names of these well-known people in Communist front activities . . . [of obtaining] financial contributions for the Party . . . and [of] attempting to influence the content of moving pictures." Crouch further explained that Communist Party leader Jack Johnstone told the group that Charlie Chaplin "was a devoted and loyal member of the Party," but that the party had decided to keep that fact secret to better employ him. When asked by a seemingly incredulous interviewer why Johnstone had raised Chaplin's name in the first place, Crouch explained that "Chaplin was one of the best known actors in the United States and the question of how he should be used by the Communist Party was a very important question to determine. It was particularly important in connection with the fact that a large apparatus was being set up in Hollywood and the relationship of nationally prominent people like CHAPLIN to the local organization was a very important policy question."[33]

When asked if Chaplin's name came up during any other meetings, Crouch remembered another discussion with party leader V. J. Jerome in Chapel Hill, North Carolina, in 1937. Crouch claimed Jerome had just returned from a trip to Hollywood and informed him that Chaplin remained "a member at large directly responsible to the Central Committee and that he had no organizational connections with the local Party organization in Hollywood." Crouch further asserted that Jerome informed him that Chaplin was absolutely loyal to the Communist Party and that he had evidence that Chaplin had been unswayed when other Hollywood types left the party. Jerome allegedly went further and said that "Chaplin was pained by desertions from the Party of people he had believed to be loyal Communists, but that nothing could shake his own faith in Communism." As a result of that loyalty, and because Chaplin was British and subject to deportation, Jerome told Crouch that it was absolutely necessary to protect him from public exposure.[34]

Despite Crouch's testimony, which historian Kenneth Lynn notes means Chaplin was "not only a member of the party . . . but unshakably loyal to it," the FBI never uncovered corroborating evidence. Even Lynn's search "in archives in Moscow came up dry."[35] Although only Crouch ever linked Chaplin to the Communist Party, when the actor left the country in 1952 to premier the film *Limelight* in London, J. Edgar Hoover, who had been tailing Chaplin for years, convinced the INS to prevent him from reentering the United States. Chaplin would only return once before his death in 1976; he spent the last twenty years of his life in Switzerland.

With such star power now behind him, as the man who had taken on Harry Bridges and Charlie Chaplin, and despite a few slipups along the way, Crouch was a man in demand. In May 1953 that demand led him to testify in the trial of seven leading Washington State Communists. Henry Huff, Terry Pettus, William Pennock, John Daschbach, Paul Bowen, Karly Larsen, and Barbara Hartle were accused of leading the Washington State Communist Party. Crouch testified for four days regarding Communist ideology and goals but had little to say about the specific individuals. About the Communist Party and ideology, he asserted that Communists had no interest in helping the workers and used them as pawns in their own struggle for world domination. As a part of that struggle, he alleged, Communists willingly used force and violence to overthrow governments. Crouch further testified about the methods the Communists used to win over new adherents. He claimed that "the Communists have infiltrated the educational system of America consistently, and have smuggled the teachings of Karl Marx into our universities."[36]

Finally, he asserted that Laura Law, the wife of alleged Communist Party member Richard Law, had been killed by party members in 1940 to prevent her from speaking out against Communism. Defense attorney John Caughlan objected that Crouch was not testifying about anything pertinent to the immediate case and the specific individuals and that his testimony was about events prior to the dates focused on in the indictment. He moved that Crouch's testimony be stricken from the record, but the judge refused, although he agreed to consider telling the jury to ignore some elements of it.[37]

On the second day of Crouch's testimony he talked about Communist plans to sabotage and destroy all capitalist governments. The formula for such destruction, he claimed, was written down in *The Struggle against the Imperialist War and Tasks of the Communist*, which the *Seattle Post Intelligencer* called "a blueprint for Communist action throughout the world." Crouch claimed the document was created by the 9th World Congress of the Comintern and that he was there during its creation. Portions of it were read into the court record, including sections that claimed capitalism was the cause of war and the only way to prevent future wars was to replace it with socialism. Other sections called for Communists to carry out efforts in the military to weaken the capitalist defenses. Defense attorney Caughlan again objected throughout, calling it "the rankest hearsay" that had nothing to do with his defendants, but the judge again rejected all the defense motions to quash Crouch's testimony, as well as their motions for a mistrial.[38] Despite the best defense efforts, Crouch's testimony helped convict five of the seven defendants. William Pennock died during the trial and Karly Larsen, the only one of the defendants who refused to admit she was a Communist, was acquitted. The five who were convicted received five-year terms, which eventually were overturned on appeal.

In September 1953 Crouch continued his hot streak when he met with FBI agents and claimed that it was Charles Dirba who in 1938 gave him the task of identifying the Georgia Communist who spoke out against the CPUSA. He described for agents the effort of two Soviet officials to kill the author—and his efforts to protect the man. The FBI appreciated the new intelligence but was concerned that Crouch had not told them about this sooner. Crouch assured the FBI that he had told them about the murder plot, but he could not remember where or when. As a result, the FBI determined that he had given so much information to so many different people that it was time to roundup all the reports and create a "Crouch File." The bureau ultimately decided creating such a file was not worth the time, however, and dropped the issue.[39] One wonders if the bureau, which already had expressed concerns about the veracity of Crouch's testimony, realized that creating such a file might simply provide evidence of Crouch's difficulty with the truth and decided not to venture down that avenue for fear of what they might find.

Whatever the case, Crouch remained on the federal payroll and continued to testify against alleged Communists. But questions about him would continue to arise as 1953 waned. In 1949 Crouch had claimed that Armand Scala, a Pan Am employee in Miami, was a Communist and a courier between the United States and Latin America. The Hearst Corporation published Crouch's claims in several of its outlets, and Scala sued for libel. In 1953 a jury found Hearst liable and awarded Scala $5,000. Although Crouch had been able to get away with his claims before HUAC, where he did not face cross-examination, his assertion against Scala did not hold up in court. Despite this outcome, the *Nation* magazine noted that "Scala's legal victory did nothing to lessen the fear and intimidation which by this time had engulfed a sizable portion of Miami's permanent community. Liberal organizations purged their membership of 'radical' suspects; liberals themselves retired from organizations which they thought might be vulnerable; many persons left the community altogether."[40]

In other words, Crouch was part of a larger assault on the American left—an assault the magazine labeled the "Miami formula," in which anti-Communists used "witch hunt propaganda—the irresponsible listing of individuals prominent in liberal movements as Reds or subversives, and . . . hair-raising account[s] of espionage and sabotage," combined with constant demands that the guilty repent and inform on others.[41] Anti-Communism had become so strong, and the "formula" so potent, that it was powerful enough to terrify the nation even when it failed in an individual case.

Evidence of this was apparent as Crouch proffered his final testimony for the year in the case against Jacob Burck. In 1953 the Immigration and Naturalization Service moved to deport the Polish-born Burck under the newly enacted Immigration and Nationality Act, which allowed the government to deport aliens and naturalized citizens who were engaged in subversive activities.[42] Burck fit the parameters, as he had moved to the United States with his family at the age of ten, and during the Depression made money selling cartoons, including several to the *Daily Worker*. In 1934 or 1935, after numerous offers, he accepted a CPUSA membership card and remained in the Communist Party until 1936. He quit after realizing he was losing his artistic freedom, and he went to work for the *St. Louis Post Dispatch* and later the *Chicago Times*. He eventually won a Pulitzer Prize for his work.

Burck claimed he never attended Communist Party meetings and joined more for expediency (to sell cartoons) than for ideological reasons. By the 1940s he was openly anti-Communist and publicly admitted shame for having worked for the *Daily Worker*. As embarrassing as was this association, Burck's real problem was that in 1936 he visited the Soviet Union and returned to the United States illegally. Despite an admission by the INS that since he left the party Burck had been an upstanding and loyal citizen, his past membership and illegal reentry attracted the attention of Senator McCarthy and led to an investigation by the Justice Department. During the hearing, Burck was asked about Crouch and reported that he had never met him. Burck also denied ever having attended a Communist Party meeting.

Crouch then took the stand and named Burck as a Communist. When asked to point out Burck, however, Crouch's veracity collapsed. According to the *Chicago Sun Times*, Crouch and Burck had been in the same hearing room for hours without Crouch making any kind of identification. Then when Crouch was asked to point out Burck, he pointed to *Chicago Tribune* photographer Max Arthur, who looked nothing like the cartoonist. As a result, the defense demanded Judge Jerome T. McGowan throw out the case. McGowan refused and Crouch concluded his testimony. After stepping down, Crouch wrote a letter to INS official Robert Woytych assuring him that despite the error the two had met and that Burck's claims were false. He also said he could produce evidence to support his claims. The next day Crouch wrote Woytych another letter in which he offered a list of potential witnesses who could support his assertions and demonstrate that Burck had committed perjury.[43]

In the atmosphere of Cold War America, with the "Miami formula" holding sway, Crouch's mistake proved irrelevant and Burck was convicted. In June 1954 his lawyers, Joseph Fanelli, Harry Rand, William King, Jr., and John Forrester, filed nineteen affidavits questioning Crouch's veracity and submitted them as part of the effort to spare Burck deportation. The affidavits included evidence that Crouch claimed to have discussed Communism with Judge Oscar Dancy in Brownsville, Texas in 1946. Dancy certified that he had never met Crouch. They also included evidence that Crouch lied about his jobs in the Florida newspaper industry. Specifically, Crouch claimed to have been the editor of the *Dade County News*, which the lawyers claimed never existed, and that he worked as a copy supervisor for the *Miami Daily News*, while fellow employees asserted that he was a tape cutter in the teletype room. Crouch also was accused of lying as to why he was fired from Pan Am. Crouch claimed to have been fired as a result of pressure from the CIO after his refusal to participate in a strike, while Pan Am officials claimed he was fired for lying on his job application. The lawyers concluded their filing with a statement that read, "Here is a man whose long experience in the Communist conspiracy (1925–1942) has bred in him a disrespect for the truth. Falsehoods, contradictions, and evasions are his pabulum.

Extensive training in deception and falsehood received as a Communist, and blatant disregard for the truth then inculcated in him, have become for him a very discipline of living."[44] Crouch sent a letter to Thomas Finucane, chair of the U.S. Department of Justice Board of Immigration, asking to be allowed to testify under oath about the allegations, but as evidence that his merit as a witness might be on the decline, the board denied the request without explanation.[45]

Journalists Joseph and Stewart Alsop also commented on the appeal in the *Washington Post* and all but begged the Justice Department to investigate Crouch. The brothers noted that some of the people Crouch had testified against probably were Communists and needed to be deported or jailed. With Crouch tainting the perception of the government's cases, however, they feared those guilty individuals might be able to win acquittals or appeals. They demanded that Justice investigate so as to assure the public that its informers were trustworthy and that no guilty person would go free because of Crouch's perjury.[46]

Despite the litany of affidavits against Crouch, and the burgeoning opposition among at least some journalists, Burck's deportation stood. In 1957, however, Congress overruled the decision and allowed him to stay in the United States.

As the Burck case proceeded apace, and despite questions about his veracity, Crouch continued his anti-Communist efforts when he told a group of supporters that Communists remained active at the University of Chicago and other Midwest campuses. He asserted, "It is my belief that at least one Communist cell still exists at the University of Chicago, one at Roosevelt College, [and] one at state universities in Minnesota and Wisconsin," although he admitted that the Communist Party had reached its peak in the region in the early 1940s and only the "diehards" remained active. He also claimed there were cells at Harvard and that at future hearings he would "show that at a recent Communist conference in Columbia, S.C., several dozen southern universities were represented by faculty as well as student delegates."[47]

In other words, even as the luster was coming off of his standing as an informant, Crouch continued to preach the anti-Communist agenda. He was fully enmeshed in the ideology and was unwilling to pull back even a little from his objectives. He was preaching the word, true or not, wherever he could find an audience. And like all good speakers, he molded the message to the crowd. Unfortunately, that message often had significant legal ramifications for the people he attacked. That would be true in two additional cases with which Crouch became involved in 1953 and 1954. What made these cases even more significant was that they involved atomic secrets and some of the most important scientists in the nation. For Crouch this was the perfect opportunity to use his powers to destroy the Communist menace. For the nation and the scientists involved, that determination ruined lives and demonstrated the dangers of the unchecked ideologue.

9 ATOMIC SECRETS, 1953–1954

In 1953 and 1954 Crouch was a part of two trials that had to do with allegations of spying, or at least misconduct, by leading scientists in the Manhattan Project. The first centered on Dr. Joseph Weinberg; the second on Dr. J. Robert Oppenheimer. As important as these cases are in and of themselves, they also demonstrate the continued willingness of the U.S. government to use former Communist informants in significant court cases and the continued willingness of Crouch to participate. Most important, these trials demonstrate the growing realization by some in power that Crouch, despite his adamant opposition to Communism, might not be the most useful, or truthful, of informants.

Both cases began in the late 1930s with the outbreak of World War II and the subsequent research into the potential of atomic weapons. The University of Chicago; Columbia University; Oak Ridge, Tennessee; Los Alamos, New Mexico; and the University of California, Berkeley, were key centers of the American research effort, but three factors set UC Berkeley apart from the other locations. The first was the presence of Dr. J. Robert Oppenheimer, the man who would lead the scientific and engineering effort to build the bomb. The second was the presence of the Radiation Laboratory on the UC Berkeley campus, with its array of brilliant scientists and technicians who would play key roles in the creation of the bomb. The third was the presence of Communists in and around the UC Berkeley campus and Radiation Lab. While the first two factors were fundamental to the creation of the atomic bomb, it was this final factor that became the focal point in the years after the war.

The presence of Communists on the UC Berkeley campus was known from early in the war. In 1940 the University of California Board of Regents fired Kenneth May, a teaching assistant in the mathematics department and son of the dean, for his open and avowed Communism.

The firing did not stop May from continuing his association with Communism or those who were still working at Berkeley. Indeed, according to Ellen Schrecker, the meetings of the Communists in the Berkeley area, including those still working at the Radiation Lab, "were open to party members and outsiders alike. They were no secret. Certainly the security men on the Manhattan Project must have known that they were taking place, for [Steve] Nelson, as well as the Radiation Lab scientists, was under surveillance."[1] Even the effort of scientists and lab technicians to form a local of the Federation of Architects, Engineers, Chemists, and Technicians union (FACET), raised the attention of the security forces, so oversight certainly was not lacking. Little came of the surveillance during the war, but as the Red Scare and McCarthy era emerged, HUAC and other groups decided to revisit Berkeley and the whole Manhattan Project. Dr. Joseph Weinberg was the first one to feel the pressure.

Weinberg was the son of Polish immigrants who had settled on the lower east side of Manhattan in the early 1900s. Weinberg attended City College and then went on to the University of Wisconsin for graduate studies in physics. He was dismissed from Wisconsin by his professor Gregory Breit "who told him that Berkeley was one of the few places in the world where 'a person as crazy as you could be acceptable.'" Weinberg protested that he did not want to study at UC Berkeley because there he would have to work with Oppenheimer, whose scientific papers he did not understand.[2] Breit assured him that he would do fine and, despite his fear, by 1941 Weinberg was at UC Berkeley studying for his PhD. He even had impressed Oppenheimer enough to be made teaching assistant for his physics class.[3]

Weinberg did not spend all his time in the lab or the classroom, however. He also was an active and open Communist. He had joined the party in 1938 and quickly found a thriving group of Communists on and around the Berkeley campus. Those Communists did more than just talk: several actively were engaged in espionage. Indeed, in 1943 an illegal FBI bug on Steve Nelson's house in Berkeley recorded the known Communist talking with someone new—at least new to the FBI. The individual was named Joe, who arrived at the Nelson home late on the evening of March 29, 1943. Nelson was not in, and his wife informed Joe that he would only return early in the morning. Joe waited, and the FBI frantically sent agents to Nelson's house in hopes of getting a picture of this mysterious new man. As the agents traveled, Nelson returned home, and he and Joe talked while agents listened in.

It quickly became apparent that the two had met previously as they referenced events not part of the immediate discussion. More important, during the conversation Nelson informed Joe that he was "looking for a Comrade who was absolutely trustworthy." Joe assured him that he was the man and that he "believed in it [the Communist Party] and the fact that it was right." Joe also informed Nelson that the project he was working on soon was going to be relocated to a remote location, thus hinting that he would be able to deliver important information. When Nelson asked what the project was, however, Joe demurred. He clearly wanted the job Nelson had mentioned but feared disclosing information about his work, knowing full well it was important to the war effort and secretive. Joe tried to brush aside the question and told Nelson that most of what he was working on already was common knowledge among physicists. Nelson did not buy the story and pushed Joe for more information. Joe then expressed his fear that as a well-known Communist he quickly would become a target should evidence emerge of a leak or security breach. Nelson backed off the hard sell, and the two continued to talk about other issues.[4]

According to the FBI, which failed to get a picture of that evening but continued to listen in on the conversation, eventually Joe agreed to talk about his research. Bureau records indicate that Joe spoke so softly that only bits and pieces were recorded. Those morsels included: "Separation method is preferably that of the magnetic spectrograph with electrical and magnetic focusing, or less preferably, that of a velocity selector . . . sphere 5 centimeters in diameter with material . . . deuterium . . . this design is tentative and is being experimented upon."[5] Joe then told Nelson about a separation plant in Tennessee that already was employing 2,000–3,000 people. Based on the twenty-seven pages of recordings taken from the illegal wiretap, it became clear that Joe told Nelson of the atomic bomb project and that he believed the program would be ready with a workable device within a year.[6]

During the conversation the two also discussed "the professor," obviously a reference to Oppenheimer. They first lamented that "the professor" had decided to keep Joe from becoming too intimate with the project. Joe explained to Nelson that Oppenheimer "kept me off the project because he's afraid of two things. First of all, that my being there will attract more attention. . . . The other is, he fears that I will propagandize." In other words, Oppenheimer knew that Joe was a Communist. The two also lamented the fact that "the professor," whom they believed was a friend of the party, seemed to be unwilling to provide it scientific material and was becoming ever more security conscious. They agreed that Oppenheimer's wife was to blame for these changes but could think of nothing to win him back, and eventually the two parted for the evening.[7]

With Oppenheimer linked to the Communists on the Berkeley campus and within the atomic bomb program, the FBI continued to stake out Nelson and began the search for Joe. The focus on Nelson paid dividends as on April 6 he was spotted meeting with the third secretary of the Soviet consulate, Pyotr Ivanov, and on the 10th he met in Washington, D.C., with the third secretary of the Soviet embassy, Vassili Zublin. The FBI eavesdropped on both conversations and heard the men discuss Soviet espionage in America.[8] Connecting the dots, the FBI put its focus on scientific espionage on the front burner and, as a part of that, ratcheted up its search for Joe.

That search took two months but eventually paid off. While spying on Giovanni Rossi Lomanitz, a well-known CPUSA member, the FBI saw Lomanitz and a group of friends get their picture taken in front of the Sather Gate on the UC Berkeley campus. An agent quickly purchased the negative from the cameraman after the group left. The FBI used the photograph to tail the men in it and learn who they were. They eventually realized one of them was Joe Weinberg and began to investigate his background and current status. The bureau learned that Weinberg had a long history with the Communist Party and that he was working with Oppenheimer. Worse, they discovered that he already had filled out a security questionnaire and had requested, in a handwritten note to Oppenheimer, that he be allowed to participate in the atomic bomb project. Despite Oppenheimer's previously mentioned reservations about Weinberg, he desperately needed help and eventually hired the young scientist to work on magnetic field calculations in the Berkeley lab.[9]

The FBI and military intelligence began to tail Weinberg, and after several weeks they hatched a plan to abduct him, take him to a San Francisco hotel or possibly onto the Bay, and "convince" him to become a double agent. That plan was quashed, and instead the bureau determined to continue watching him. Weinberg remained at Berkeley teaching physics, doing research for the bomb project, and meeting with his fellow Communists, including Nelson, throughout the war years. The FBI also remained active and gathered mountains of evidence.

Five days after the Japanese surrendered, formally ending World War II, the FBI laid plans to charge Weinberg with espionage. Those plans, however, were put on hold by two concerns. One was the fact that much of the material gathered against him was from illegal wiretaps and surveillance, which would not be admissible in court. The other problem was that the military feared that going after Weinberg would drag in Oppenheimer, by then a national hero.[10] The charges thus remained unfiled.

Weinberg blithely continued on with his career and took a teaching job at the University of Minnesota. As he taught, however, the Red Scare and Cold War caused many in the government and the developing security apparatus to question why an alleged spy was allowed to roam free, regardless of who his prosecution might harm. This opinion only spread when, in September 1948, HUAC authored a "Report on Soviet Espionage Activities in Connection with the Atom Bomb," in which it detailed the espionage efforts of Clarence Hiskey and an unknown "Scientist X." According to Ellen Schrecker, HUAC never found any substantive evidence of espionage. And the evidence it did find was laughable. According to Schrecker, "One story involved . . . ["Scientist X"] dictating a secret formula to [Steve] Nelson in the middle of the night. Government agents claimed that they had climbed a tree near Nelson's house and watched the whole transaction." According to HUAC, this formula was of "importance in the development of the atom bomb," but for many the very notion of transcribing a set of mathematical equations while perched in a tree was absurd.[11]

Despite the absurdity, the belief that spies had infiltrated the Manhattan Project piqued the public's attention, and the search for "Scientist X" proceeded apace. It took until 1949, but eventually HUAC put all the pieces together and realized "Scientist X" was Joseph Weinberg. Thus, the story that HUAC told of a scientist giving Nelson a formula was a bit off base, but the generalities were correct: Weinberg told Nelson of the bomb project and some of the generic issues associated with it. Determined to learn more, HUAC subpoenaed Weinberg. He appeared on May 25, 1949, and while he admitted to attending one Communist

Party meeting, he denied being a Communist, denied giving material or information of any kind to Steve Nelson, and then refused to answer additional questions, taking the Fifth Amendment. When confronted with Nelson, Weinberg simply denied knowing him. According to Ellen Schrecker, "from HUAC's perspective he was a far more interesting character as 'Scientist X' than he was as Joe Weinberg. For Weinberg, as Weinberg, was a disappointing witness."[12]

Although disappointed, HUAC pushed forth and continued the investigation. James Sterling Murray, who worked in the military's Counter Intelligence Corps during the war, testified in August 1949. He told the committee that in his position as head of security and intelligence he was informed by "a highly confidential informant" that Weinberg had provided atomic secrets to the Soviets. Murray also asserted that Weinberg turned a considerable amount of material over to Steve Nelson and that he personally had seen Weinberg do so on one such occasion, August 12, 1943.[13] What made Murray's testimony even more powerful was that it occurred a week after the Soviets detonated their first atomic bomb, thus giving ample evidence of the damage espionage could do.

Despite that, Weinberg remained free, although the investigations continued and would soon involve the Crouches. On May 9, 1950, Sylvia testified before the California State Un-American Committee. She asserted that Robert Oppenheimer and Joseph Weinberg had attended Communist Party meetings in Berkeley in 1941. Sylvia also picked Weinberg out of a lineup. Paul did his part, as noted earlier, when on May 8, 1951, he testified before the Senate Subcommittee on Internal Security. He reiterated Sylvia's story and alleged that many of the leading scientists working for UC Berkeley, the Radiation Lab, the Shell Development Project, and the War Manpower Commission of Northern California were Communists. Among them were Weinberg and Oppenheimer. Crouch also named Marcel Scherer as the mediator "between the Communist Party and certain scientists at the Radiation Laboratory."[14]

The Crouch allegations seemed to speed up the investigation, and Weinberg was called before a federal grand jury. Once again, he refused to answer questions about his actions during the war. As a result, on May 11, 1951, the jury held him in contempt. Five days later, on May 16, the University of Minnesota suspended Weinberg, and on June 16 the institution fired him, albeit with a year's severance. Judge Alexander Holtzoff eventually overturned the contempt citation, stating that

Weinberg was within his constitutional rights not to testify before the grand jury, but the University of Minnesota stood by the firing. University President Dr. J. L. Mitchell explained: "Whatever his legal rights or the outcome of the pending litigation, it is my held belief that his judgment in this refusal to cooperate with Federal authorities is incompatible with common sense and with a proper appreciation of his duty and obligation as a member of the university staff."[15]

After all these years, and despite losing his job, Weinberg still had not been prosecuted for the alleged espionage. The Justice Department knew that the wiretaps were illegal and, of the twenty witnesses called in all the years of hearings, only the Crouches tied him directly to the CPUSA. Despite that, by late 1952 the Justice Department believed it had enough circumstantial evidence to make the case against him on charges greater than contempt. Weinberg was charged with lying to HUAC when he denied being a member of the Communist Party, lying when he said he had attended only one Communist meeting, and lying when he said he did not know Steve Nelson was a high-ranking Communist. As court proceedings slowly moved forth, the charge relating to Nelson was dropped—most likely because of the questionable evidence.

When the trial began in February 1953 Weinberg faced two charges and a public enraptured by the case. Not only did it involve atomic espionage but also there was a widespread assumption that Oppenheimer would testify. Indeed, during the opening arguments Weinberg's lawyer told the jury that "this case can be cut down to whether they believe the word of a criminal [Crouch] or the word of a distinguished scientist and outstanding American."[16] Gordon Dean, head of the Atomic Energy Commission (AEC), begged President Truman to intercede with the Justice Department to keep Oppenheimer's name out of the trial despite the potentially important role he could play in the outcome. According to historian Priscilla McMillan, Dean warned that such testimony would "mean that Dr. Oppenheimer must take the stand and contradict the testimony of Crouch, the only government witness. It will be Oppenheimer's word against Crouch's. . . . Such a conflict in the atmosphere of a criminal court, involving two such colorful figures will attract great attention." Dean feared that the attention would ruin Oppenheimer's name and damage the nation.[17] Truman agreed but feared getting involved and offering more "proof" of Republican charges that Democrats were soft on Communism. The president thus breathed a sigh of relief when the trial did not begin until after the 1952 election cycle.[18] Dean was not so relieved and only relaxed when the Justice Department dropped a second charge: that Weinberg had lied about attending only one Communist Party meeting. That meant Oppenheimer did not have to testify—and pleased everyone. Everyone, that is, except Crouch, who was not among the five prosecution witnesses ultimately called.

Of those who did take the stand, UC Berkeley statistician Joseph Biskind was potentially the most damaging to the defense when he testified to having attended twenty Communist meetings with Weinberg. The defense, however, was able to prove that Biskind once lied to the FBI when he said he had never been a Communist. It also demonstrated that he once received psychiatric care. The other four witnesses were equally dismal, and according to the *Washington Post* "Judge Alexander Holtzoff expressed doubts as to the strength of the evidence."[19] Indeed, he was later reported having told the prosecution, "The court is troubled very much by the doubt as to whether there is evidence in the case from which the jury would be justified in finding that the defendant's membership in the Communist Party was proven beyond a reasonable doubt."[20] The jury also seemed perplexed by the weak case and went to the judge three times saying it was unable to reach a verdict. Each time, however, he sent them back. Finally on March 5, 1953, after eight hours of deliberation, the jury reached a verdict and found Weinberg not guilty. Despite his previous statements, Judge Holtzoff was shocked and said "the court does not approve of your verdict," although he told the jury he respected the decision.[21] In spite of the legal victory, Weinberg was unable to return to work in his chosen field, but he did not remain unemployed forever. He eventually turned to optics and took work at the Spero House of Vision in Rochester, New York. There he would play a role in the creation of lineless bifocals.[22]

Not long after the trial, Crouch offered a sworn statement before the Senate Subcommittee on Internal Security in which he testified that the reason Weinberg had not been convicted was that the prosecution willingly withheld the most damning evidence, evidence he would have supplied. He claimed they did this because if he had testified he would have brought up issues surrounding Oppenheimer, and the government was determined to protect the scientist. Therefore, they allowed Weinberg to go free for fear of stirring up more trouble around an even bigger scientist.[23] While that was part of the issue, so too was the fact that the government knew Crouch was lying. It, along with Weinberg's lawyers, had evidence that neither Weinberg nor Oppenheimer could have been in Berkeley in 1941 when the Crouches claimed to have seen them there. The government had bypassed him not solely to protect Oppenheimer, but because it feared he might actually destroy the case against Weinberg. Crouch was unaware of this, at least for the moment, and was outraged.

Sylvia was similarly outraged and penned her own letter of complaint.

> During that trial [of Weinberg] in Washington I was kept under subpena [*sic*], ready to take the stand at any time. But I was not called—because the closed Communist Party meeting I attended with him was in the home of Dr. J. Robert Oppenheimer, with Dr. Oppenheimer present. The lobby was so powerful that Dr. Weinberg—identified as Scientist X by the House Committee, was acquitted for lack of sufficient evidence rather than permit identification of Dr. Oppenheimer as a party member. I hope the public does not permit . . . the Oppenheimer lobby to pull a curtain of secrecy over the investigations. The future of our nation and the future of the world is involved. Let us have the truth, the full truth and a determination to bring out the facts regardless of powerful lobbies.[24]

Senator McCarthy soon got wind of these assertions and believed he smelled more evidence of Communist subversion. As a result, on September 15, 1953, he called Crouch into executive session to talk about Weinberg, Oppenheimer, and all he knew about the proceedings in Berkeley. The transcripts of the meeting, which were released in 2003 by the Senate Permanent Subcommittee on Investigations, show that Crouch spent the first part of his testimony, as he often did, recounting his past within the CPUSA. He also claimed that the United Nations was a tool for spreading Communist propaganda and then named a few names. The committee was not particularly interested in much of this, so Crouch quickly moved to more pertinent matters and reiterated his allegation that the government refused to call him to testify in the Weinberg case because it knew that if he did so he would have implicated Oppenheimer. McCarthy feigned outrage at such a cover up and supported Crouch's allegation that Weinberg had been acquitted "because of a lack of evidence."[25]

Crouch then explained his absolute certainty that Oppenheimer was a Communist, although other than his assertions that he saw him at party meetings in California, his only other proof was that Oppenheimer's opposition to the Hydrogen bomb corresponded to that of the party. Crouch testified: "His position, in substance, his efforts have corresponded with the efforts of the Communist press throughout this period. The Communist press has sought to prevent the development of the H-bomb. They have sought to obtain a U.S. pledge not to use the atomic bomb, first in time of war, and their policy has coincided with the public statements of Dr. J. Robert Oppenheimer and the authoritative press accounts of J. Robert Oppenheimer's position as appeared recently in *Fortune* magazine, *Life*, and others."[26] Apparently anyone who agreed with anything the Soviets believed was a Communist.

As much as McCarthy thrived on such ludicrous allegations and innuendos, Crouch tried to provide more substantive evidence. He turned next to his previous testimony in California. Crouch claimed that "in my work with the California Un-American Activities Committee I learned that military intelligence has a vast amount of evidence regarding his [Oppenheimer's] membership in the Communist party and his Communist activities, and that the California Un-American Activities Committee has a great deal of information which, of course, would be at the disposal of this committee." McCarthy then directed Crouch back to the Manhattan Project and asked if Oppenheimer, as a Communist, would have turned over atomic information to the Soviets. Crouch replied that he would have and explained that he might have been ordered to turn over material directly to the Soviets or to appoint Communists to leading positions in the project so they too could supply data.[27]

As proof of this later possibility, he asserted that Lloyd Lehman, who was recommended for a job on the bomb project by Oppenheimer, went on to become an open Communist in Northern California. He also claimed that a "Dr. Hawkins" was made historian of the project and, despite his Communist past, was given access to an array of top secret documents. (In this case Crouch was correct. Dr. David Hawkins indeed was the official government historian of the Manhattan Project, but allegations that he was a Communist were not new. In 1950 he had been called before HUAC where he admitted to being a member of the party from 1938 through 1943.) Crouch finally asserted that there were plenty of other examples and even alleged that Marcel Scherer, whom he already had accused of being the conduit between the Radiation Lab and the Soviets, had been trained at the Moscow School of Espionage and Sabotage.[28]

McCarthy loved the testimony and used it to demand a formal investigation of Oppenheimer. None was forthcoming, however. But that did not mean Oppenheimer was going to get off unscathed. Indeed, as Weinberg's legal problems were coming to an end, Oppenheimer's problems were just beginning. While he did not face the possibility of jail, he did face the embarrassing possibility of losing his security clearance and his ability to do research. Crouch, who had helped push the case this far, was more than ready to help push it along further.

J. Robert Oppenheimer was born in 1904 to German immigrants living in New York City. The family was rather well to do and nurtured Robert's obvious intellect from a young age. He enrolled at Harvard in 1922, studied chemistry, and graduated in three years summa cum laude. He then headed to Cambridge to study physics at the world-renowned Cavendish Laboratory. After a year there he moved to Georgia Augusta University in Göttingen, Germany, where he earned his PhD in 1927.

Oppenheimer eventually returned to the United States and settled in as a professor of physics at the University of California, Berkeley. While there he also found time for some political activities: he gave money to a Spanish Civil War fund, was a member of the Friends of the Chinese People and the American Committee for Democracy and Intellectual Freedom (both of which later would be deemed Communist front groups), attended CPUSA meetings, and donated money to the Communist Party. Although the Venona transcripts, which include intercepted Soviet diplomatic and intelligence communications between 1942 and 1945, hint that he might have joined the Communist Party, there is neither solid evidence nor historical agreement on his membership.

There is evidence, however, that Oppenheimer felt comfortable around Communists. Beginning in 1931 he rented a house from Mary Ellen Washburn who was "an active member of the Communist Party in Alameda County." Oppenheimer's girlfriend of the time, Jean Tatlock, also was a Communist, although not an ideologue, and she introduced him to her Communist friends. Oppenheimer eventually broke up with Tatlock and in 1940 married Kathryn (Kitty) Puening, the widow of Joe Dallet, a Communist and member of the Lincoln Brigade who died in 1937 fighting in the Spanish Civil War. Kitty also was a party member, and it was Steve Nelson who informed her of her husband's death and stayed with her for several days as she dealt with the shock. According to Oppenheimer biographers Kai Bird and Martin Sherwin, "without question, Robert was surrounded by relatives, friends, and colleagues who at some point or other were members of the Communist Party." But these same people always insisted that he was never a member. Again according to the authors, "In short, he was a classic fellow-travelling New Deal progressive who admired the Communist Party's opposition to fascism in Europe, and its championing of labor rights at home. It is neither surprising nor revealing that he worked with Party members in support of those goals."[29]

By 1939, however, his "fellow traveling enthusiasm had cooled," and by most accounts he began to turn away from radical politics.[30] The timing of that turn was crucial, as Oppenheimer soon was asked to head the Manhattan Project. He filled out security clearance information honestly and admitted his radical associations, as well as those of his wife, but made clear that those associations were in the past. The military had some concern about granting the clearance as a result of this history, but General Leslie Groves, who was in charge of the entire project, read Oppenheimer's FBI file and encouraged the clearance be granted. It was, and Oppenheimer set off for Los Alamos. According to biographer Gregg Herken, among the last people Oppenheimer met before heading to New Mexico were Steve Nelson and Haakon Chevalier. Those meetings would change Oppenheimer's life.

Nelson's role, as both an Oppenheimer acquaintance and a Communist, is already evident, but Chevalier's is not. Chevalier was born in 1901 in Lakewood, New Jersey. His father was French and his mother Norwegian, and he spent time in each country as a child, becoming fluent in both languages. He earned a doctorate in Romance languages from UC Berkeley in 1929 and taught French there. By 1937 Chevalier was a committed Communist, and at about the same time he met Oppenheimer. In 1942 George Eltenton, a British-born Cambridge-educated physicist then working for Shell Oil, approached Chevalier with a plan to have Oppenheimer provide scientific data that could then be forwarded to the Soviets. When Chevalier broached the topic, Oppenheimer responded by calling it treason and refused to have anything to do with the plan.[31]

Oppenheimer told no one of the request, fearing to implicate his friend Chevalier. At about the same time, however, the FBI was beginning to unearth the information about Weinberg thanks to the wiretaps on Nelson's home. As a result, the FBI began to watch Oppenheimer ever more closely and eventually tapped his phones. General Groves was informed of the FBI's fears and began to tighten security at the Radiation Lab. When Oppenheimer became aware of the increased security, he informally mentioned that if people were worried about leaks they should investigate George Eltenton. Lieutenant Colonel Boris Pash, who was the head of the military security over the Manhattan Project, quickly set up an interview with Oppenheimer to find out what he knew about Eltenton.

In that interview, Oppenheimer admitted that he had been approached by "intermediaries" for Eltenton who were interested in passing along atomic secrets to the Soviets. He assured Pash that he had rebuffed the effort but then stated that three others had been approached as well. He refused, however, to give any names. Pash then informed General Groves, who met with Oppenheimer and ordered him to provide the names. Oppenheimer named Chevalier as the one who had approached him but refused to name the other three who had been approached. Groves was adamant, but Oppenheimer refused unless the general promised not to divulge the information to the FBI. Groves agreed, even though he knew he was obstructing justice, and Oppenheimer told him that in reality only one other person had been approached—his younger brother Frank. Oppenheimer assured Groves that Frank had not participated in the scheme.[32]

Groves was good to his word: the case remained hushed up during the war, and Oppenheimer emerged a hero for overseeing the successful creation of the atomic bomb. Despite that, the FBI remained interested in Oppenheimer, even as he moved east in 1947 and took a job as director of the Institute for Advanced Study at Princeton. As a part of the move, the AEC had to reexamine Oppenheimer's security clearance. Despite concerns, the AEC granted him clearance.

In 1949 HUAC called Oppenheimer to testify, in executive session, about the growing revelations of spying and Communism at the Radiation Lab at Berkeley. As a part of the testimony, Oppenheimer admitted to the Chevalier incident, although he refused to talk about his brother. The committee members, including Richard Nixon, thanked Oppenheimer for his testimony and it appeared that the turmoil was over. A week later, however, he was called before the Joint Committee on Atomic Energy. The committee had little interest in the issue of spying and instead asked about prior testimony by AEC chairman Lewis Strauss who had argued that the United States should not export radioactive iron for fear of it being misused. Oppenheimer laughed at the idea and suggested that exporting radioactive iron was about as dangerous as exporting "bottled beer, a shovel, or vitamins."[33] Although the two were old friends, and it was Strauss who got Oppenheimer the job at Princeton, the chairman was outraged at being publicly mocked, and he was determined to get back at Oppenheimer.

It just so happened that the Crouches would make Strauss' goal much easier. In April 1950 Paul took California Un-American Activities investigators around Berkeley until he pointed out a house in which he claimed to have attended Communist Party meetings. He described the interior of the house accurately and told the investigators of a specific meeting he remembered having attended there in 1941. Investigations eventually discovered that the house, 10 Kenilworth Court, had been owned by Oppenheimer in 1941. Intrigued, the California Un-American Activities Committee called both Crouches to testify. On May 9, 1950, both picked Oppenheimer's picture out of a lineup and stated that they attended a closed Communist Party meeting at Oppenheimer's home in July 1941. After again describing the inside of the home, they claimed that Kenneth May drove them to the meeting, which consisted of twenty-five leading state party figures, none of whom the Crouches were introduced to for security reasons.

Paul told investigators that he updated the individuals on the new Communist Party line resulting from the Nazi invasion of the USSR and oversaw group discussions. He further testified that Oppenheimer asked several questions during the meeting and that he and Oppenheimer talked privately for ten minutes after its conclusion. Crouch did not realize who Oppenheimer was at the time, but on the ride home Kenneth May informed him that he had been talking to "one of the nation's leading scientists."[34] He later learned that George Eltenton and Joseph Weinberg were present at the meeting as well. The Crouches claimed to have seen Oppenheimer at several additional Communist Party functions but never again at a closed meeting. On May 10, a day after the Crouches testified, former party member Alfred Barbosa confirmed their claims and added that he remembered seeing Oppenheimer at a house warming for Kenneth May at which between fifty and seventy-five people were present, all Communists.[35]

The *Washington Post* reported these allegations as a "bombshell" and referred to Crouch as the West Coast Whittaker Chambers, which Crouch must have enjoyed greatly. According to the newspaper, "The testimony caused an immediate stir in scientific circles, where Dr. Oppenheimer's standing is high. His name never before has been publicly connected with possible Communist Party membership, although his brother . . . has admitted having been a party member."[36] The *New York Times*, meanwhile, described the meeting at which the Crouches claimed to have seen Oppenheimer as consisting of "a top-drawer Communist group known as the special section, a group so important that its make-up was kept secret from ordinary Communists."[37]

Not every paper was as enthralled. The *Honolulu Record* ran a multipart series on the event and noted that General Groves had been well informed of Oppenheimer's left-leaning background but was comfortable enough to put him in charge of the Manhattan Project. The paper also rightfully noted that the project succeeded in creating the atomic bomb, thus demonstrating Oppenheimer's patriotism. Of the specific allegations Crouch made, the paper explained away the fact that Steve Nelson often visited the Oppenheimer home by noting his previous relationship with Kitty Oppenheimer. The paper also noted that it seemed oddly suspicious that Crouch had held his tongue about the meetings with Oppenheimer for more than a decade. Crouch later claimed that the reason for his reticence was that he did not realize who Oppenheimer was and explained that it was only after seeing him in *The March of Time* movie reels that his memory of their meetings years earlier was revived. The paper was skeptical of such vivid recall of old memories.[38]

Oppenheimer did not leave his defense in the hands of others and issued an immediate denial, stating "I have never been a member of the Communist Party. I never assembled any such group of people for any such purpose in my home or anywhere else." He denied knowing Crouch and, while he admitted to having left-leaning ideas, noted that he had made his politics known to the government years earlier.[39] Better yet, Oppenheimer presented an alibi. He and Kitty were more than 1,000 miles away at their New Mexican ranch, *Perro Caliente*, when Crouch claimed to be meeting with them in Berkeley. Oppenheimer even had medical records to prove the point. On July 24, 1941, he was kicked by a horse and the next day received an x-ray at a hospital in Santa Fe. He also had a witness: world-famous physicist and future Nobel Prize laureate Hans Bethe was at the ranch and corroborated the story. In the end, the Oppenheimers had evidence that they were in New Mexico from July 12 to August 11 and therefore could not have attended the meeting. It should also be noted that Weinberg had similar evidence regarding the alleged July 1941 meeting. His lawyers had gathered evidence to prove that he was with his ill wife in Banning, California, some 500 miles from the alleged meeting site.[40] It was the government's awareness of these alibis that played a role in the prosecution's determination not to call Crouch during Weinberg's trial.

Despite the evidence, investigations of Oppenheimer continued, and on May 20, 1952, he appeared before the Justice Department in Washington, D.C. Oppenheimer again denied knowing the Crouches or holding any Communist meetings in his home. Justice Department lawyers then asked if Oppenheimer would mind confronting his accuser. He agreed. "The door then opened and Crouch walked up to Oppenheimer, shook his hand and said, 'How do you do, Dr. Oppenheimer?' He then turned melodramatically to the lawyers and said that the man with whom he had just shaken hands was the same person who had been his host at a meeting in July 1941 at 10 Kenilworth Court. Crouch reiterated that he had given a talk on the 'Communist Party propaganda line to be followed after the invasion of Russia by Hitler'" and asserted that Oppenheimer had asked several questions.[41]

Oppenheimer asked Crouch exactly what questions he was supposed to have raised. Crouch responded that "Oppenheimer's questions involved a philosophical analysis of Russia's involvement in the war 'based upon Marxist doctrine.' Crouch said, 'Dr. Oppenheimer stated that he could see why we should give aid to Russia but asked why we should aid Britain, who might double-cross us.' Crouch claimed Oppenheimer also asked whether or not the German invasion of Russia had now created two wars: a 'British-German imperialist war' and a 'Russian-German people's war.'" Oppenheimer derided this assertion claiming that "he had never at any time thought or advanced the suggestion of two wars."[42] Despite this scoffing denial, and the fact that Crouch failed to remember that Oppenheimer wore his hair much longer in 1941 than he did in 1952, Crouch's testimony seemed legitimate. In spite of that, nothing came of the hearing.

But questions about the scientist lingered, and in May 1953 Crouch wrote a letter to McCarthy aide Roy Cohn. Crouch claimed the impetus for the letter was a *Fortune* magazine article entitled "The Hidden Struggle for the 'H-Bomb': The Story of Dr. Oppenheimer's Persistent Campaign to Reverse U.S. Military Strategy." The article noted that Oppenheimer opposed the creation of the H-bomb, worked to get the United States to promise not to use it against the Soviets, and argued that the only reason the Soviets were pursuing the bomb was for defensive purposes. In his letter to Cohn, Crouch called the article significant and encouraged Cohn and others to read it because it demonstrated all the reasons Oppenheimer was dangerous to national security.

> I have no doubt whatever—not the slightest doubt—after a study of this material, that Dr. Oppenheimer is at the present time using his position, ability and energy to bring about a complete physical military defeat of the United States and the victory of the Soviet Union and conquest of the entire world. . . . It is my opinion . . . that he is today the most powerful force in the United States working in behalf of the Soviet Union. It is my opinion that if he is permitted to continue to do so . . . that the outcome will be the destruction of our nation and the reduction of the entire human race to slavery.[43]

He further informed Cohn that prior to his trip to Washington, D.C., in 1949 to testify before HUAC, he talked with William Baggs of the *Miami Daily News*. Crouch claimed Baggs had "conversations with people in Washington" who urged him not to name Oppenheimer in his testimony because of the service he had rendered the country. Crouch thus implied that there was a conspiracy of sorts to protect Oppenheimer. He then concluded: "Through my work as a staff member of the California State Committee and other work with government agencies, I am familiar with the general nature of military intelligence files and information regarding Dr. J. Robert Oppenheimer's membership and activities in the Communist Party. They show that J. Robert Oppenheimer was very active in the Communist Movement over many years, roughly from 1937 until 1943, that he was a close friend of Steve Nelson, who often visited him at his Berkeley home."[44]

The letter, and Crouch's history, clearly struck a nerve, as both he and Sylvia soon appeared in a confidential document entitled "Suggested Witnesses Regarding Dr. J. Robert Oppenheimer and Background of Communist Party Activities Facilitating Soviet Atomic Espionage." The document included both Crouches as potentially friendly witnesses for the government. Of Sylvia it noted that she would be able to testify that she, Paul, and Kenneth May went to a "closed party meeting of 'special section'" at which she saw Oppenheimer. The document explained that only Communist Party members participated in closed meetings, thereby implicating Oppenheimer as a member. The document further asserted that Sylvia saw Oppenheimer at a housewarming party for CPUSA leader Kenneth May, saw him in conversation with party members May, Steve Nelson, and William Schneiderman, and saw him at several other social events designed to raise money for the party.[45]

Of Paul the document revealed that he could testify that the goal of Communism was to seize power violently. More specifically, he would be able to explain that the Communist Party sought scientific information for passage on to Russia and that Marcel Scherer had used FACET to gather information for the Soviets. Regarding Oppenheimer, the document asserted that in July and August 1941 Crouch met with Oppenheimer and asked him many technical questions. The two met additional times at the home of Kenneth May and at various fund-raising efforts. The document also noted that in 1952 Oppenheimer denied ever meeting or knowing Crouch, thus setting up the possibility that he could be charged with perjury.[46]

Despite all this, Oppenheimer kept working and maintained his security clearance. Weinberg's acquittal seemed to offer hope that it all might end, but the forces against Oppenheimer were building. Those forces included Crouch's testimony, the Red Scare, the breaking news of the spy ring at Los Alamos, Strauss' continuing hatred, and Oppenheimer's continued opposition to the H-bomb. This final factor took on even greater significance when William Borden, the executive director of the Joint Committee on Atomic Energy, came to believe that such opposition could only result from Oppenheimer's ties to the CPUSA. Indeed, on November 7, 1953, Borden penned J. Edgar Hoover a three-and-a-half-page, single-spaced list of "factors" that led him to believe that "more probably than not [Oppenheimer] acted under a Soviet directive influencing United States military, atomic energy, intelligence, and diplomatic policy." Borden also charged Oppenheimer with espionage. Although he could present no real evidence to support the charges, he alleged simply that Oppenheimer was guilty because he was, in Borden's opinion, a Communist and all Communists wanted to destroy the government.[47]

Borden's letter, for some reason, seemed to be the magic bullet. Hoover accepted the allegations and passed his concerns on to President Eisenhower. Eisenhower ordered a "blank wall" put between Oppenheimer and atomic secrets, but he wanted it done quietly so as not to embarrass the scientist. His real hope was that Oppenheimer would resign. Oppenheimer refused to do so, and in 1954 the AEC went public and attacked Oppenheimer for "substantive defects of personal character," accused him of three lies in his previous security clearance testimony, and removed his security clearance.[48] A formal hearing was set for May. Historian Richard Polenberg contends that the AEC board already had made up its mind about Oppenheimer even before the hearing, and there was little surprise when on May 27 the three-person board found Oppenheimer loyal but voted 2–1 against returning his security clearance. On June 29, 1954, the full AEC board agreed in a 4–1 vote.[49] Without the clearance Oppenheimer could no longer do real research, so he left Princeton and spent the rest of his life traveling the world and writing and talking about science. In 1963 President Lyndon Johnson presented Oppenheimer with the Enrico Fermi Award for contributions to physics. He died of cancer on February 18, 1967.

The response to the AEC vote was immediate. The Alsops raged at the decision and wrote *We Accuse!* in which they pointed fingers of blame at those they charged with engineering Oppenheimer's downfall. The diatribe began, "We accuse the Atomic Energy Commission in particular, and the American government in general, of a shocking miscarriage of justice in the case of Dr. J. Robert Oppenheimer." They then focused specifically on Lewis Strauss, whom they noted supported Oppenheimer's security clearance in 1947 but opposed it in 1949 after Oppenheimer challenged his theory about the export of radioactive iron. Indeed, the brothers contended that it was Strauss' grudge that was key to Oppenheimer's defeat. They also pointed their finger at the security clearance machinery of the McCarthy era, which they contended was never designed to find the truth but to serve the political needs of the moment. The combination of Strauss' grudge and an unfeeling political machine doomed Oppenheimer. In "Is Paul Crouch a Reliable Witness against Oppenheimer?" the Alsops added Crouch to the list of those who were to blame. After reiterating the facts that Crouch's charges against Oppenheimer and Weinberg had little basis in reality and were easily proven false by their lawyers, they defined Crouch as part of that unfeeling security clearance machinery that sought not the truth but political vengeance.[50]

The *Bulletin of Atomic Scientists* came out with a similarly vocal defense of Oppenheimer. The journal alleged that the charges against him were "much ado about nothing," and joined the Alsops in criticizing Strauss, whom it claimed had "manipulated the press to secure a favorable hearing . . . and who is said to be preparing another campaign . . . to stifle any hostile criticism." The *Bulletin*, however, broke with the Alsops over their contention that Oppenheimer was the victim of a conspiracy. Instead, the journal claimed he was "actually the victim of a national obsession."[51]

While journalists lamented the outcome, the scientific community suffered from it. According to Oppenheimer biographers Bird and Sherwin, "The scientific community remained traumatized for years. . . . All scientists were now on notice that there could be serious consequences for those who challenged state policies." They further note, "For a few years after World War II, scientists had been regarded as a new class of intellectuals, members of a public policy priesthood who might legitimately offer expertise not only as scientists but as public philosophers. With Oppenheimer's defrocking, scientists knew that in the future they could serve the state only as experts on narrow scientific grounds."[52]

Historians largely agree that Oppenheimer was not a threat and that the case against him had more to do with the times than an actual threat. Ellen Schrecker calls Oppenheimer "completely loyal," while John Earl Haynes and Harvey Klehr rightfully assert that if Oppenheimer had been a spy the Soviets would have developed the atomic bomb even faster than they did. Oppenheimer, they note, knew everything about the bomb. The fact that it took the Soviets so long proves that he did not provide them information. Jerrold and Leona Schecter, however, claim that Oppenheimer was a Communist, and while they admit he never personally handed over documents to the Soviets, they allege that he "knowingly facilitated the 'sharing' of atomic secrets."[53]

Whatever historians have to say, the fact is that Crouch played a role in both the Weinberg and the Oppenheimer cases. Although a tangential figure, especially in the Weinberg case, he continued to be of service to the government in the cause of anti-Communism. What is notable, however, is that while he was good theater he did not make a good witness, as evidenced by the fact that he was ignored for the Weinberg case and his testimony served no real part in the events that ultimately brought down Oppenheimer. In other words, yet more people were beginning to learn that Crouch the anti-Communist might be Crouch the liar. Indeed, by this point Crouch was so wrapped up in his hatred for Communism that he would say and do nearly anything to further the cause. Despite all that, he emerged from the atomic espionage cases relatively untainted in the public eye. Indeed, he was untainted enough to be used in two major legal cases in 1954.

10 "LET ME AT HIM!" 1954

In early 1954 Crouch took part in two hearings that would prove to be the end of his career. The first occurred in New Orleans and focused on the Southern Conference Education Fund (SCEF). The second was the trial of nine Communists from Philadelphia who were indicted under the Smith Act. In each case Crouch came off so poorly that his opportunities to testify dried up and he faced a new life as an ideologue from whom no one wanted to hear. Despite remaining firm in his beliefs, enough people had come to question his veracity that even his fervor could not spare him.

In 1954 Senator James Eastland was in a tough reelection campaign and determined that the best way to demonstrate to the people of his state that he served their interests was to focus on two issues that remained bugaboos in Mississippi: Communism and race. Even before the *Brown v. Board of Education* decision, which was announced in May 1954, many Mississippians, and indeed many Americans, had come to link Civil Rights and Communism. The CPUSA openly supported integration as a part of its struggle to free the working class. Relying on Marx's statement in *Das Kapital* that "Labor cannot emancipate itself in the white skin where in the black it is branded," the Communist Party initially proposed the aforementioned theory of self-determination as a means of benefitting the African American community. Eventually it created a more formidable Civil Rights agenda.[1]

In 1925 the CPUSA organized the American Negro Labor Congress (ANLC), which later became the League of Struggle for Negro Rights (LSNR), to demand an end to segregation and lynching and to support the full enfranchisement of African Americans. That same year the Communist Party backed the Dyer Anti-Lynching bill, which would have made lynching a federal felony. Although neither the ANLC nor the LSNR nor the anti-lynching bill achieved much, the CPUSA won some support from the African American community for being one of the few national organizations willing to address needs specific to the community. The CPUSA won even more support when in 1931 it funded the drawn out struggle to save the Scottsboro Boys from a legal lynching in Alabama. That campaign succeeded, and the Communists took credit for saving the lives of nine young African American men.

Communists also took credit for promoting African Americans within the party. The CPUSA had several African Americans in positions of power, including James Ford, who ran as the Communist Party's vice-presidential candidate in 1932, 1936, and 1940; Otto Huiswoud, who became the first black member of the Central Executive Committee in 1927; and Harry Haywood, who served on the CPUSA Central Committee from 1927–1938 and in the Politburo from 1931–1938. All of these factors demonstrated to African Americans that the Communist Party not only supported Civil Rights but also was willing to fight for those rights and actually live up to its rhetoric. Many white Americans, however, saw such support and activism as foreign and dangerous.

It was not simply the Communist Party's support for Civil Rights, however, that caused concern. What worried many were the international implications of the struggle. In 1946 the Communists formed the Civil Rights Congress (CRC). Although, like the ANLC and the LSNR, it advocated for Civil Rights and, like the ILD, staged legal campaigns to assist African American defendants, it went one step further and worked to expose American racism to the world. Those efforts culminated with the publication of *We Charge Genocide*, which claimed that under the United Nations Genocide Convention, Article 2, the U.S. government was guilty of genocide for its failure to prevent lynching. The Soviets quickly made use of the CRC's campaign and raised Civil Rights issues throughout the Cold War. The Soviets publicly noted again and again that the "land of the free" was not so free for African Americans and used every incident of racial violence or bias as a tool to attack the United States, both at home and abroad. Indeed, in 1947 the president's Committee on Civil Rights issued *To Secure These Rights*, in which it asserted that the nation needed to solve Civil Rights issues in part due to the damage the struggle had on our international standing. Massachusetts Senator Henry Cabot Lodge went a step further and in 1950 dubbed segregation and racism as America's Achilles heel in its fight with the Soviets.[2]

Faced with such open support by the Communists for African American rights, and the growing awareness of the dangers that the Civil Rights campaign had in the Cold War setting, many politicians quickly linked the two in their drive for votes and power. In 1947 Mississippi Congressman John Rankin declared that all Civil Rights activism was part of a Communist conspiracy, and in 1949 HUAC held "Hearings Regarding Communist Influence of Minority Groups" in an effort to further ferret out the alleged links between Communism and Civil Rights. James Eastland supported such efforts and engaged in similar rhetorical and investigative campaigns. For those previous efforts, Eastland received several awards during a ceremony on March 8, 1954, in Memphis, Tennessee. Among the awards were an engraved scroll from the American Coalition of Patriotic Societies, a medal of merit from the Daughters of the American Revolution, an "Americanism award" from the VFW, and a medal from the Sons of the American Revolution. Determined to carry on with such award-worthy and electorally beneficial efforts, he turned his focus on the Southern Conference Education Fund (SCEF), the successor to the SCHW.

Eastland claimed the fund was Communist-controlled, and as a part of his inquiry into that claim he subpoenaed Aubrey Williams, James Dombrowski, Alva Taylor, Myles Horton, Leo Sheiner, Max Shlafrock, and Virginia Durr to hearings in New Orleans. Williams was an Alabama native, former deputy administrator in the Works Progress Administration, and head of the Rural Electrification Administration. He also had been active in the SCHW and formerly was president of the SCEF. At the time of the subpoena he was publisher of a liberal journal called *Southern Farmer*. Dombrowski was a graduate of Union Theological Seminary and was the current executive director of the SCEF; Taylor was a professor at the University of Tennessee Divinity School; Horton was the director of the Highlander Folk School in Monteagle, Tennessee; Sheiner was a Miami attorney; Shlafrock was a Miami contractor; and Durr was a member of the SCHW and SCEF, sister-in-law to Supreme Court Justice Hugo Black, and the wife of Washington lawyer Clifford Durr.[3]

Despite the subpoenas and Eastland's claims of Communist control, there did not appear to be much to investigate. The SCHW was formed in 1938 and its first meeting took place on November 20, 1938, in Birmingham. As noted earlier, six avowed Communists, including Crouch, and another twelve covert members or fellow travelers took part in the first meeting, during which the conference called for shorter hours, worker compensation laws, state level Wagner Acts, desegregation, abolition of the poll tax, anti-lynching legislation, aid to farmers, uniform federal voter registration laws, and state level graduated income taxes.[4] Despite the presence of a few Communists, the SCHW was simply a liberal organization determined to help the working class that was still struggling through the Great Depression. In 1945 the Southern Conference Education Fund was formed as the educational wing of the SCHW. In 1946 it became its own distinct entity focused solely on integration and Civil Rights, and in 1948 it replaced the SCHW, which then disbanded.

Despite the lack of an obvious target, Eastland pushed forth. When Virginia Durr learned the hearings would proceed, she was outraged. Years later in her autobiography she wrote, "The idea of Jim Eastland, just as common as pig tracks as they used to say, trying to call me to account—it made me so angry my adrenaline began to rise. I wasn't scared. I was just as mad as hops."[5] Durr used her political connections prior to the hearing, and on March 10 she called Lyndon Johnson hoping that he could pressure Eastland to call them off, or at least tone them down. Johnson told Durr he could do little to halt Eastland, but he did make calls and appeals to subcommittee members Senator John McClellan, a Democrat from Arkansas, and Senator Pat McCarran, a Democrat from Nevada.[6] Both Senators stayed away, but Paul Crouch, whom Eastland remembered from the 1951 hearings on Local 19 in Memphis, agreed to attend.

Eastland pushed forward, and he used his powers enthusiastically if randomly and awkwardly. At the same time, he understood the dangers of such hearings and promised, as did chief counsel Richard Arens, to use "extreme caution" in order to prevent "innocent individuals" from being harmed. But Eastland could not control himself, and as the hearings opened the New Orleans *Times Picayune* asked the Senator about people taking the Fifth Amendment. He said he did not want to prejudice the case but then replied, "I think they're Fifth Amendment Communists. It seems to me with the conditions that exist in the world today any man would be glad to say that he is not a Communist and not guilty of treason."[7] The hearings, like Eastland's reply, often would be schizophrenic, disorganized, and chaotic.

When the hearings finally began on March 18, 1954, Leo Sheiner was the first of those subpoenaed to testify. After answering questions about his biography and stating that he was not currently a member of the Communist Party, he took the Fifth when asked if he ever had been a member. After Eastland and Arens badgered Sheiner about the Fifth Amendment and other issues associated with the Communist Party, Eastland called in Paul Crouch. When asked his "occupation," Crouch testified that he was a "consultant of the United States Immigration and Naturalization Services, Department of Justice," and he proudly admitted being one of the key witnesses in the Harry Bridges trial.[8] He then proffered his Communist credentials and stated that he had served as "head of the Communist Party's department for infiltration of the US armed forces, CPUSA representative to the Executive Committee of the Communist International in Moscow, honorary regimental commander of the Red Army, [and as a] member of a commission in Moscow to draft plans to infiltrate and subvert all the armed forces of the world."[9]

His qualifications established, Crouch turned to Sheiner and his ties to the SCHW. He asserted that in 1947 and 1948 he worked with the FBI to investigate subversive organizations and, through those investigations, came to learn that Sheiner was not only a member of the conference but also "an important undercover member in the Communist party." When asked if he knew for sure Sheiner was a Communist, Crouch stated: "He told me personally in his office in the Pacific Building that he was an important undercover member in the Communist Party. He told me that he was the reserve head of the Communist Party for the State of Florida, if the Communist Party was to go underground that he was to head the organization. He stated further that he had been directed by Fred Brown, the national head of the organization department of the party . . . when he came to Florida that only a few leading people were to know his membership."[10] Crouch never explained why a secret agent would gossip about his status but assured the committee that Sheiner had.

Crouch next turned to the SCHW, which he claimed to have played a key role in forming. He asserted that he, along with Communist Party leaders Rob Hall and Joseph Gelders, created the SCHW, and he further maintained that the conference was set up with funds from the national CPUSA, funds that numbered several thousand dollars and often were given to the SCHW directly by Earl Browder. When asked about the objectives of the SCHW, Crouch stated, "The purpose of the Communist Party in setting up the Southern Organization [*sic*] for Human Welfare was to have a mass organization through which the Communist line could extend all over the South, through intellectuals, professionals, even ministers, could be brought within the scope of the Communist Party influence to enable the Communists to gain entry in to the Government." He continued, "It was a vehicle to promote communism. It was intended to lead to class hatred, to race hatred, dividing class against class and race against race as its real objectives in spite of the words that were put on paper, some of them by myself."[11]

When asked about the SCEF, Crouch assured the committee that it was the same organization, with the same goals as the SCHW, but with a new name. Of the leading figures in the formation of the SCHW, Crouch alleged that Joseph Gelders' job was "to visit the White House and Hyde Park to which he had access because of the fact that the president and Mrs. Roosevelt did not suspect him of being a Communist, to gain their friendship, and one of his major jobs was to report secret information obtained from Hyde Park and the White House to J. Peters for transmission to the Soviet Union."[12] As he had done during his earliest testimony, Crouch charged the Communists with infiltrating the highest reaches of American government.

Turning back to Sheiner, Crouch claimed to have met him personally at the home of Charles Smolikoff, whom he described as "the real boss of the Communist Party for Florida" as well as an agent for the CIO and the Transport Workers Union. Crouch claimed he met Sheiner in Smolikoff's home in Miami on Easter Sunday 1947. Although he admitted it was not a formal party meeting, he explained it was open only to those Smolikoff believed would "carry out Communist objectives." Crouch claimed that he was such a good spy that Smolikoff believed he was of that ilk even though he had been out of the party for more than five years.[13] Finally tying Sheiner back to the purpose of the hearings, Crouch asserted that he was the head of the fourth congressional district committee of the SCHW in Miami.

When Crouch finished, Sheiner took the stand once again, and Eastland asked him to comment. When Sheiner refused, Eastland replied:

> I think that if a man accused me in an open hearing of being a Communist, unless I were guilty I would be glad to answer it. I

> think any patriotic American, any loyal American, any man who loved his country, if accused of belonging to an organization that is traitorous to his country, an organization that affiliated with a power abroad [which] has killed and maimed thousands and thousands of American boys, if I were accused of belonging to that organization, and I were not guilty I certainly would not slink behind the fifth amendment.

Eastland was obviously doing two things here. First, he was playing to the crowd back home, which was a key reason for holding the hearing in the first place. Second, he was hoping to infuriate Sheiner into saying something he would regret. The effort to antagonize Sheiner initially failed, although he did take exception to the idea of "slinking" behind the Fifth Amendment. He reminded Eastland that "a witness who uses the Fifth Amendment is clothed with just as much innocence as he is with guilt," and continued, "and I resent the interpretation you place upon those patriotic Americans who have used the Fifth Amendment." Not about to give up the fight, Eastland and Arens continued to badger Sheiner until he finally exploded and said, "this committee has no right to subject me to these questions and these indignities . . . you have no right to inquire into my political thoughts and beliefs, and if I must say just one word to the people in this courtroom, they ought to see that these rights are preserved." Having instigated the reaction he wanted, Eastland responded, "you are a disgrace to the United States. Take him out, Marshal."[14]

As Sheiner was unceremoniously escorted from the room, Max Shlafrock took the stand. A general contractor from Miami, Shlafrock was a native of Poland who migrated to the United States with his family in 1921 when he was twelve. When asked if he had ever met Charles Smolikoff, Elizabeth Gurley Flynn, Paul Crouch, and others, and if he had joined the SCHW, or if he had committed espionage, he took the Fifth Amendment.[15] Eastland had little interest in the contractor, and he quickly excused him.

The committee moved on to James Dombrowski, who was born in Tampa in 1897, served in World War I, graduated from Emory University in 1923, and took a PhD from Columbia University in 1933. Dombrowski acknowledged being the executive director of the SCEF and holding the same position previously with the SCHW. He provided the names of the other directors of the SCEF but was not able to provide the committee with a list of all the members of the fund. When pushed about membership, Dombrowski eventually took the Fifth. When asked about his alleged membership in the Communist Party, Dombrowski protested about the committee inquiring into his political beliefs, as did his lawyer Benjamin Smith who said he was "profoundly shocked by this procedure." Eastland was not concerned with such protests, nor did he care about Smith's surprise and retorted, "I am not interested in what you are shocked about. I care nothing at all about it. . . . I know these kinds of tactics. I know the sources from which they come and you are not going to take this hearing over."[16] Eastland believed such arguments were a common Communist tactic used to sidetrack a hearing from its intended purpose. Not about to let that happen, Eastland let everyone know he was in charge and would not allow it in his hearing room.

After asserting his power, Eastland allowed Arens again to ask if Dombrowski was or ever had been a Communist or ever was under Communist discipline. Dombrowski denied all the charges, which led the committee to call John Butler. Butler claimed to have been a Communist and to have known Dombrowski as one as well. Butler specifically charged that in 1942 Dombrowski was the secretary-treasurer of the Alabama Communist Party. As Eastland was finishing up with Butler, Benjamin Smith again interjected and demanded the right to cross-examine. He complained, "I can see where if a person attempts to answer the questions truthfully, then evidence is given to the contrary to his answer; . . . there should be a thorough investigation into who is telling the truth, and I respectfully request the right to cross-examine this man."[17] Eastland rejected the request out of hand, and he called Crouch to the stand.

Early in Crouch's testimony, Smith, along with fellow defense attorney John Kohn, again asked for the right to cross-examine the witnesses. Eastland said, "Mr. Kohn, you're supposed to be a lawyer. You should know that never in history has the right of cross examination been permitted before a Congressional committee. Sit down."[18] Following Eastland's refusal, Smith carped about not knowing the rules of the hearing. He complained, "We can't find out what the rules for a Senate committee are. We've written to Washington and we can't find them. We wish you'd let us know what the rules are so we can behave accordingly." Eastland responded: "Sit down. I know dilatory tactics when I see them. I'll let you know what the rules are as we go along."[19] Another version had Eastland saying, "I will announce them when I desire."[20]

Once Crouch got to testify, he claimed to have met Dombrowski on several occasions dating back to 1937, asserted that the Communist Party chose Dombrowski to lead the SCHW, and charged that Dombrowski accepted party discipline. He also maintained that Dombrowski assiduously carried out Communist Party orders within the SCHW and had demonstrated his ties to the party by singing the popular socialist anthem *The Internationale*. Crouch further asserted that Sheiner and Dombrowski once met and "discussed . . . the hideouts for Communist leaders." After this last assertion Dombrowski shouted, "That is a lie, sir." Crouch continued, unshaken, and alleged that Dombrowski and Charles Smolikoff were friends and that Smolikoff "spoke to me in the highest terms of Dr. Dombrowski as one who is carrying through the party line and party activities in the Southern Conference for Human Welfare." Outraged, Dombrowski yet again interjected, "Is he accusing me of being a Communist? Is that the burden of what he said?"[21]

That is what Crouch said, and Dombrowski was afforded the opportunity to reply. While Sheiner had refused to do so, Dombrowski fervently rebutted Crouch's charges. He admitted to meeting Crouch and knowing him slightly, but he rejected the idea that he was under Communist discipline, that he sang *The Internationale*, or that the SCHW used access to the president to gather secret information for the Soviets, as had been asserted previously. Dombrowski then faced questioning about Leo Sheiner, Ted Wellman, and others, and whether or not he knew they were Communists. Dombrowski said he knew them but did not know their political affiliations.[22]

He also noted that while there might have been some Communists in the SCHW, the organization itself consisted of thousands of members and none of the Communists were in positions of leadership. When challenged on this assertion by Arens, who noted that HUAC found that "key posts are in most instances controlled by persons whose record is faithful to the line of the Communist Party and Soviet Union," Dombrowski attacked the HUAC reports as "suspect," and alleged that "they are so careless about fact, that a careful and intelligent person can't make up his mind as to the truthfulness about anybody or anything that the committee has reported on." When Eastland snidely asked Dombrowski whether that outburst was his own or "the inspiration of some other people," clearly implying that Communists had encouraged him to question HUAC, Dombrowski responded, "Mr. Chairman, apparently you refuse to believe that anybody or any person before you has any integrity."[23]

After that exchange things settled down and the questioning returned to the SCHW. Dombrowski denied that Communists played any role in the formation of the group and called Crouch's charges "perfectly absurd." He also rejected the idea that Communists ever led the SCHW and stated that it did not take money from the CPUSA.[24] Eastland eventually excused Dombrowski from the witness stand and gaveled the hearings to a close for the evening. In the end, he was probably happy with the course of the day's testimony. His mood would soon change.

Virginia Durr took the stand Friday Morning, March 19. Before she said a word, her attorney, John Kohn, objected to the whole hearing.

> We object, first, to the proceedings on the ground that in view of what has happened since we have been before this hearing, that the subpoena does not follow the authority of the resolution creating this committee and delegated to this committee, in that as the language of the subpoena is so broad that it amounts to a fishing expedition and puts my client in a position to have her brain probed by an instrumentality of government which she contends is against the First Amendment of the Constitution of the United States and that part of it, sir, relative to her personal liberty. Second, she objects to this hearing on the grounds that this subcommittee does not consist of a quorum of the committee of the Senate delegated to conduct this hearing. . . . She does not and is not in any way, shape, or form claiming benefits of the Fifth Amendment to the Constitution of the United States. However, sir, she does invoke every other provision in the Bill of Rights to the Constitution of the United States and the Constitution of the United States, and at this time I ask you as her counsel to give her permission to read a short statement to this committee.[25]

Eastland simply overruled the objection, rejected her request to read a statement, and began the questioning.

When asked her name and several similar questions she said not a word. After several more questions she conferred with Kohn, and when again asked if she was Virginia Durr stated "yes." She replied the same when asked if she were Clifford Durr's wife. When next asked about the SCEF, she replied, "I am not answering. I stand mute." When asked if she were under Communist discipline, she said, "No," but proceeded to state simply "I stand mute" or else not reply to all subsequent questions.[26] Her husband Clifford Durr, who was in attendance, described her time on the stand thus: she simply sat there and refused to say a word, but "every now and then she'd take out a compact and powder her nose. It drove them into a rage." In her autobiography, Durr explained why she behaved as she had. She wrote: "I refused to admit I was a witness. I was being persecuted. I took the attitude that I was a victim, not a witness, so I wouldn't even take the witness fee they paid."[27]

Frustrated, Eastland quickly held Durr in contempt and called in Crouch who brought some order to the hearing and provided Eastland with the red meat he desired. Eastland began the questioning of Crouch by reviewing his biography. Eastland first asked if Crouch was an ex-con. Crouch responded, "I am not an ex-convict in the legal sense of the term. I have never in my life been convicted of any felony and legally I cannot be described by anyone as an ex-convict. I was court-martialed under the 96th Article of War for organizing a Communist organization in the United States Army which legally is a misdemeanor and does not reflect the term ex-convict." Crouch then noted that he had been employed by the INS for more than two years and had testified in the Harry Bridges and William Remington cases as well as four Smith Act trials. That biography established, Eastland explained what it meant: "The Attorney General for the United States has vouched for your veracity. That is what that means."[28]

The questioning then turned to Virginia Durr. Crouch claimed that when he moved to Alabama and took over the *New South* he found Virginia Durr listed as a subscriber to and financial supporter of the paper. Between 1938 and 1939, he claimed, she sent in various contributions to the paper ranging from five to twenty dollars. Evidence of these financial ties, he told the hearing, was then in the custody of the FBI. He next asserted that during the same period he "received frequent reports in Communist Party meetings with reference to Mrs. Durr," and that the Durr home was used frequently as a "meeting place for the people connected with top Soviet espionage and infiltration of the United States Government."[29]

While Crouch admitted he had no evidence that she ever joined the party and doubted she had done so, he did assert that she accepted Communist discipline and "went beyond that; she plotted with the Communist leaders to exploit her relationship as sister-in-law of a Justice of the Supreme Court in the interests of the World Communist conspiracy and interest of overthrowing our government."[30] Specifically, he testified that Durr was a key figure in getting Justice Hugo Black to address the first meeting of the SCHW.[31] More important, Crouch claimed that during the New Deal, Durr had used her relationship with Black and her friendship with Eleanor Roosevelt to introduce the president, his wife, and his advisors to Communists. As John Salmond so aptly puts it, Crouch claimed Durr "made the Roosevelts the unwitting accomplices to Soviet espionage activity."[32]

Crouch then turned back to the SCHW and explained that when they were organizing the committee, he, Gelders, and Hall, with the approval of Earl Browder, had decided specifically to get Black and Roosevelt as public supporters. The idea, he claimed, was "to deceive the public and lure in intellectuals, professionals, and ministers, and people of that category." As a part of that effort, he continued, Gelders went to Hyde Park, met with Mrs. Roosevelt, and got her to agree to speak at the foundational meeting. He also claimed that Gelders met with the president and got him to agree to write a letter of greeting to the assembly. That achieved, Gelders then traveled to the District of Columbia where he met with Durr who agreed to set up a meeting for him with Justice Black. At that meeting, he convinced Black to speak at the conference opening. "Then armed with the magic of names like Mrs. Roosevelt, a letter from the President that had been promised, and a scheduled address by a Justice of the Supreme Court, the Communists were able to send out its organizers throughout the South . . . to bring highly respected university professors in, ministers, loyal Americans did not suspect that the conference that they attended in 1938 was planned and conceived with the aim of getting a wedge in the South and leading to the overthrow by violence and force, an insurrection ultimately, of the Government of this great nation."[33] After this seemingly impressive description, Crouch admitted that he was told all of this by others but asserted that he once spoke with Durr for ten or fifteen minutes and that she remained active in the SCHW for years, thus somehow vaguely supporting his point.

The weakness of these outrageous claims led Kohn, Durr's lawyer, to request that Eastland exclude Crouch's testimony. Eastland refused because Durr had refused to testify. So doing, he claimed, had led her to forfeit her rights. "If your client will answer questions that are propounded, I will be glad to let her make a statement," said Eastland. When Kohn tried to press further, Eastland told him to sit down, excused Crouch, and called John Butler to the stand.[34] Butler offered similarly vague assertions that Durr was not a Communist but somehow was associated with them and supported the Communist Party. When Butler stepped down, Durr also was excused.

As interesting as the first four witnesses had been, Friday's afternoon session with Aubrey Williams proved to be the key to the whole hearings. Williams was born in Springville, Alabama, in 1890. Raised poor, he worked his way through the University of Cincinnati after serving in World War I, and then moved to Wisconsin where he became a social worker. During the New Deal he worked for the Federal Emergency Relief Administration and the Civil Works Administration and played a role in the formation of the National Youth Administration. He also attended the first meeting of the SCHW. In 1938 he was accused, for the first time, of being a Communist, but made it clear that he did not like Communists nor did he trust them. Indeed, when those working for him were accused of being Communist he had them investigated. When the SCHW and later the SCEF were accused of being Communist-affiliated, Williams did all he could to fight the allegations. He even went so far as to oppose a SCHW-sponsored concert by African American singer Paul Robeson fearing his Communist ties would further taint the group.[35] Such a history interested Eastland and he dragged Williams to New Orleans.

On March 6, 1954, Williams received the subpoena to appear before Eastland's committee. He responded by releasing a blistering letter to local newspapers in which he called the hearings "dishonest" and "contemptible." He went on to criticize the committee for fear-mongering, and then challenged it: "if you have any charges against me, I suggest you refer them to a grand jury in order that the truth of the matter may be arrived at in the American way by trial in an impartial court . . . on the basis of evidence and not of gossip, and with the right to be confronted by my accusers. . . . The only activity in which the SCEF has been engaged has been its fight for the abolition of discrimination. . . . You may regard this as Un-American, but it is unthinkable that an American jury will agree with you."[36]

As if Williams' public rebuke of the hearings was not enough drama, he was represented by Clifford Durr, Virginia's husband. Durr opened Williams' time on the stand by objecting to the manner in which the subpoena was registered and then to the entire proceedings themselves, following the same line as his wife. Eastland referred to the objections as "trivial" and "utterly without merit" and attempted to proceed. That process was halted briefly when Sheiner interjected that he too wanted to be part of such objections. After Sheiner again was escorted from the room, the investigation began as Arens asked Williams about the SCEF. Williams admitted being the president of the fund and to having served in that capacity for several years. He further acknowledged being the publisher of *Southern Farmer* magazine and to having ties with the Highlander Folk School, which by 1954 had changed its focus from labor organizing to Civil Rights activism. That background out of the way, Eastland asked about the purpose of the SCEF. Williams informed the Senator that it "has to do with fighting racial discrimination of all kinds," in all areas of society, against any group, and through scientific studies.[37] When asked if he knew Hall, Gelders, or Crouch, he acknowledged knowing them all vaguely but denied being a Communist or ever being under Communist control.

John Butler then took the stand and claimed that he had attended a closed Communist Party meeting with Williams in Nashville. Williams immediately responded, "I feel a personal privilege to say that I challenge this man to go out in the hall and make that statement in the presence of newspapermen." Butler replied, "I'll make it in the presence of anybody in the world." Eastland attempted to maintain order and told the two to settle it at "recess." Butler then turned the screw deeper, called Williams "Comrade Williams," and further alleged that they had attended Communist meetings together in Bessemer, Alabama. Williams could not restrain himself and yelled: "That's a lie and the other's a lie. . . . If you got anything you are going to pay for this." Durr interjected at this point and said, "We have a case of conflicting testimony under oath, two diametrical opposite stories from two witnesses, and I would like to inquire if there will be any action taken to determine that." Eastland assured Durr that that was what he was there for, but the lawyer then tweaked the senator by asking, "Might we have a little recess now so that Mr. Williams and Mr. Butler can go outside?" Eastland was not amused and instead called Crouch to the stand.[38]

Crouch first described meeting Williams in 1935 in Washington, D.C., during which he explained his work with unemployment councils in North Carolina and Virginia. Crouch said, "I do not recall Mr. Williams' exact remarks, but as nearly as I can recall they were in the nature of expressing pleasure at the way things were going locally and nationally." Crouch claimed to have met Williams again in 1938 or 1939 and testified that during their conversation they discussed Communist activities in Alabama and that Williams had again expressed support for the effort. When asked if Williams was a Communist, Crouch responded that his "activities always coincided with the work and the interests of the Communist Party" and then alleged that Rob Hall told him personally that Williams was "a secret member of the Communist Party." When Durr objected that this was hearsay testimony, Eastland quieted him by saying, "Just a minute, now. Mr. Williams, I am going to give you an opportunity." Durr was stunned by what he thought he had just heard and asked for clarification. "Will we have the opportunity to cross-examine?" Eastland assured him, "Yes, sir. Just let me handle it."[39]

True to his word, and despite his previous statement that cross-examinations were never a part of such hearings, Eastland then said, "Mr. Williams has answered all the questions and I think his attorney should be given the right of cross-examination as he requested." He then turned the hearings over to Durr to cross-examine Crouch; and things got really interesting. Durr first led Crouch through his biography, drawing out Crouch to tell all the stories and important events of his Communist experience. He then moved to why Crouch left the Communist Party. Crouch explained that his decision was the result of a number of factors including the early refusal of Governor Roosevelt to extradite him to Massachusetts in 1929, the criticisms of him by party members while he was in Utah, and his growing sense that "the Communists were leading to a slave society, to labor camps in which millions would be imprisoned in America as in Russia . . . and that due to mistaken idealism I had become part of the most dangerous conspiracy in history, that I had helped build a Frankenstein that threatened my children and the children of all Americans, and that it was my duty to get out of this conspiracy." Durr then asked why, in light of this great fear, it took him five years to go to the government to offer what he knew. Crouch, rightfully it seems, claimed that he needed time to "free myself from all the ideological chains of Communist ideology. I still regarded the American Government as a bad government, a cruel government."[40] He then noted that by 1947 he believed the Soviets were on the way to conquering the planet and finally went to the FBI.

Although the testimony so far seemed to be going well, Crouch suddenly lost control of the situation when Durr asked him to prove he was no longer a Communist. "What evidence can you present," Durr asked, rightly pointing out the predicament into which Crouch placed others of trying to prove a negative. Richard Arens, trying to spare Crouch, interjected: "Mr. Crouch, is Mr. Durr a Communist?" Crouch responded, "I don't know whether he still is a Communist or not." Durr asked, "You say I was a Communist at one time?" Crouch: "Yes, sir." Eastland, realizing too late that things had gotten out of control, moved to strike Crouch's assertion. Durr refused to allow that, however, noting that it was made under oath. Eastland allowed the testimony to remain in the record but tried to get the hearing back to the issue at hand—the SCEF. Durr played along, sort of, and asked whether or not Crouch took notes at all these meetings where he remembered seeing people. Crouch admitted that he did not and also admitted to not knowing a few key dates of various events. He further acknowledged that he had no direct evidence that Williams was a Communist. Durr then dismissed Crouch, and Williams returned to the stand to rebut Crouch's testimony.[41] That done, things got even more interesting.

Durr demanded the right to rebut Crouch's charges against him. Durr had long faced attacks as a Communist: he had been labeled a Communist as a result of his ties to the National Lawyers Guild, which would later play a role in the Army-McCarthy hearings, and for advising his clients to take the Fifth Amendment should they be asked about Communism. He also was included in *Red Channels: The Report of Communist Influence in Radio and Television* as one of 151 people named "Red Fascists and their sympathizers." He was expert at defending himself and, granted the right to do so in this case, he re-called Crouch to the stand. He pressed Crouch to give the exact dates and places where he saw Durr in Communist meetings. Crouch provided some vague assertions that he had seen Durr between 1938 and 1941 but could offer nothing specific. When Durr asked what he did in those meetings, Crouch claimed that he simply sat back and never spoke. Over and over Durr repeated these questions and Crouch provided the same vague answers, although eventually he claimed that in 1938 he and Durr met in Miami, where he saw Rob Hall suggest that Durr be given secret party information so that he could pass it along to Hugo Black. He also asserted that the two met between two and five additional times. Despite the rarity of their meetings, Crouch claimed that when Durr appeared at HUAC hearings in 1949 he immediately recognized the lawyer because of his "distinctive personality."[42] Unimpressed, Durr dismissed Crouch.

Durr then took the stand in his own defense. His first words were: "The statement that Mr. Crouch saw me in Communist Party meetings in New York during the years 1938 to 1941 or at any other time is a complete and absolute falsehood. I have never been a member of the Communist Party. I am not now a member of the Communist Party. I have no intention of being a member of the Communist Party. I have never taken the Communist discipline and this statement is completely and absolutely false. One or the other of us should be jailed for perjury." Neither Eastland nor Arens moved to determine who was the perjurer and instead asked Durr about his political associations with the National Lawyers Guild, of which he was president in 1949 and 1950, the SCHW, and the World Congress of Intellectuals for Peace.[43] Durr explained his relationship with each group, and the hearing ended for the day.

The committee reconvened on Saturday March 20, with Durr briefly retaking the stand, followed equally briefly by Miles Horton. The main focus of the day, however, once again was Crouch. Recovered from the previous day's brutal testimony, and undoubtedly assured that no similar cross-examination would happen again, Crouch proceeded to assert that the CPUSA tasked five people with gathering information from the White House. Those five, he claimed, were Joseph Gelders; Reverend Malcolm Cotton Dobbs, head of the youth section of the SCHW whom Crouch claimed, "boasted to me that his position as a minister helped prevent any possibility of any suspicion by either the President or Mrs. Roosevelt of the fact that he was a top Communist leader"; Howard Lee, a lawyer for the SCHW; Joseph Lash, a *New York Post* columnist; and Gilbert Parks, former business manager of Eleanor Roosevelt's magazine *Babies-Just Babies* whom Crouch previously had labeled a Communist. He claimed all five provided important information to the CPUSA.[44]

Crouch then turned back to Virginia Durr and her connection with

Hugo Black. More important, he asserted specifically that she was a member of the Communist Party. He concluded his testimony with this statement: "Justice Black had no knowledge of the work of the conspirators—but Mrs. Durr, his sister-in-law, had full knowledge of the conspiratorial nature of the work."[45]

Clifford Durr later described what happened next:

> Virginia was out when this happened. Crouch was put on the stand again. He began to tell about Virginia, how Mrs. Roosevelt would pass cabinet secrets to Virginia and Virginia would pass them on to the Communist spy ring. I get angry very slowly and very seldom, but when I do, I sort of blow up. I found myself tensing up during the testimony. Jennings Perry was sitting behind me and I must have given evidence of this, because he patted me on the shoulder as if to say, "Don't let him get your goat. Don't get worked up about this idiot. Nobody's going to take him seriously." I thought I'd relaxed, but something happened to me when he got up to leave the witness stand. For a while I blacked out. What I know is what I read in the papers later. I guess my hands were white and I was gripping the jury rail, and as he got up to leave I vaulted over the jury rail and blurted: "You goddamn son of a bitch, lying about my wife that way—I'm going to kill you!" Maybe I did say it, but I don't remember. I do remember a couple of marshals grabbing me. I didn't get within ten feet of Crouch. The marshals were holding me firmly, but I have a feeling, rather gently as if to say, "Look here, we don't blame you, but we can't let this kind of thing go on in the federal courtroom." They escorted me out.[46]

The *New Orleans States Item* put the story thus: "Suddenly, Durr lunged forward at Crouch, shouting: 'Let me at him!—I'll kill the . . . for talking about my wife like that." The paper further reported that dozens of spectators grabbed the two men and separated them while Durr continued to yell "Let me at him!" The *Washington Post* and the *New York Times* recorded Durr shouting, "You dirty dog. I'll kill you for lying about my wife."[47] Whatever Durr said, the two nearly came to blows. Durr "suffered a nervous, twitching attack after the encounter," while "Crouch at his own request was given a police guard."[48]

After the encounter, Clifford and Virginia Durr and Aubrey Williams left the courthouse and took a walk. Upon returning they saw an ambulance and wondered what had happened in their absence. When they returned to the third floor where the hearing was taking place, two doctors approached. A young doctor examined Durr, pronounced him fit, but suggested a prescription for a sedative. The older doctor chastised the younger one for allowing a man with a history of heart trouble to go on his way after such an outburst with only a prescription and informed Durr that the ambulance was for him and that he had to go to the hospital. Durr rejected the idea, claiming later that he wanted to walk back into the courtroom to "let them know they haven't gotten me down." The doctor refused, fearing another explosion, but agreed to allow Durr to take a taxi to the hospital rather than the ambulance.[49] He was examined and released soon thereafter.

The Durrs later discussed the day's events extensively, especially their impression of Crouch. Clifford explained:

> During my cross-examination, I didn't know what to do except to let the press see this guy with all of his paranoia—not paranoia; he was a psychopath. So I just asked him questions to let him brag about his Communist activities. He began to brag that he was a greater menace to the country in its heyday than Russia and the hydrogen bomb combined. He told how he was trained to blow up planes. I said, "You were trained to lie too." "Oh yes," he said, "we were trained to lie."

Virginia wrote, "He was crazy as a bat. He said that the Russian Navy was going to land at Miami Beach because there were so many Jews there. Can you imagine anything crazier than that?"[50] She even noted that his very life story seemed unbelievable:

> Here's a guy who had one year in the U.S. Army as a private and the Russians had him lecturing at their military college which was the equivalent of our West Point. And they let him in on their plans against the Panama Canal. These were the yarns Crouch would spin. That was all I knew about him. He said he spent five thousand hours telling the FBI what he knew about Communist activities and he wasn't through yet. You asked him a question and it was like putting a dime in a jukebox. He just played a record. With all the other witnesses, he was well rehearsed. He had met Aubrey

Williams after a speech. . . . He referred to Aubrey as "Comrade Williams" and gave all the dates, times, and so on.[51]

In 1969 Virginia offered some additional insight. She compared Crouch to "a dirty piece of Kleenex about to disintegrate" but went on to say that he was "such a wretch of a man that even while he was destroying you anyone would feel sorry for him."[52] Of the hearings, she later said:

> They had a paid informer named Paul Crouch, and he just told a string of lies. He said he'd seen my husband and J. Robert Oppenheimer together at Communist meetings, all of which was totally a lie. He said I had close connections with my brother-in-law, Hugo Black, and he intimated, he didn't actually say it, but he intimated I had influenced the Supreme Court. He accused me of subverting the White House and being a friend of Mrs. Roosevelt's—well, I really was a friend of hers but not an intimate, personal friend, but I was in meetings with her a lot. When he accused me of subverting the White House, my husband got furious and tried to hit him, and the marshals rushed in and separated them.
>
> It was just the most fantastic, mad sort of absurdity you can imagine, but he was paid by the United States government to inform. It was just the most ridiculous thing you've ever seen, and the purpose of it was to try to implicate my brother-in-law Hugo Black as tinged with Red.
>
> The whole thing was such a lie, I just refused to testify. My husband refused as well, and Jim Eastland said he was going to send us all to jail for contempt of the committee, and I certainly was in contempt of it. But we never went to jail. Lyndon Johnson was one of the main friends we had in the Senate. And Lyndon I think struck a deal with him.
>
> Eastland trying us for being Red was one of the dirtiest things that happened that I know of in the whole long [Civil Rights] struggle. Because he did it to influence people's opinion about the *Brown* decision. He didn't think he could scare Hugo, but he thought he could make other people think there was something wrong about the decision. He was a very nasty man, no doubt about that.[53]

The contemporary press, which not surprisingly had a field day with the hearings, offered similar assessments of Crouch and the proceedings. The *Daily Worker* accused Eastland, although a Democrat, of following McCarthyite techniques and attacked him for allowing "the loathsome Paul Crouch [to] spread on the record tall tales attacking Aubrey Williams . . . Clifford Durr . . . and Mrs. Durr." The *New Orleans States Item* described the hearing as a "wild and wooly session," while the *Nation* labeled it the "Battle of New Orleans." The *Nation* also attacked Eastland for staging the event for political purposes and then offering poor leadership throughout but saved most of its bile for Crouch. The magazine reported that "Crouch billed himself to the press as one who helped convict Harry Bridges (the conviction has since been reversed). He did not mention his spectacularly unsuccessful attempt to smear Mrs. Leon Keyserling, wife of the noted economist." As journalists wrote their stories and wallowed in the spectacle, Fred Anderson of the *Montgomery Advertiser* polled nine of his fellow reporters one evening with the question: "'From what you have heard here who do you think represents the greatest threat to the American way of life?' Eastland received four votes, Crouch two, Arens one, and Dombrowski one."[54]

Several of those who were smeared during Crouch's testimony also took the opportunity to speak out. Joseph Lash responded as a journalist and as one named by Crouch as a Communist. Lash, at the time a *New York Post* correspondent, denied serving as a conduit for information between the White House and the Soviets. In a letter to the subcommittee, Lash wrote, "Paul Crouch lied in his statement about me." He went on to enumerate the lies.

> 1. My only access to the White House came at the end of 1939 when I was fighting the Communists following the disillusioning experience of Nazi-Soviet Pact. At that time a common interest in combating Communist and isolationist ideas among young people brought me together with Mrs. Roosevelt. 2. Although I accept full responsibility for having cooperated closely with the Communists from 1937 to 1939 in the era of the Popular Front, which preceded the Nazi-Soviet Pact, I did not become a member of either the Communist party or the Young Communist League. 3. My writings and activities, public and private since September, 1939, when the Nazi-Soviet Pact exposed the Communist party as a willing total

> instrument of Soviet interests, will testify to my uncompromising opposition to the Communists since that time.[55]

Eleanor Roosevelt also responded with a note in her "My Day" column. She informed readers that the Durrs were her good friends, were not Communists, and never would have had the opportunity to get information from the White House or to alter policy.

As all this hand-wringing took place, the real-life implications of Crouch's testimony began to be felt. Leo Sheiner was disbarred by the Florida Bar for taking the Fifth Amendment. Judge Vincent Giblin, who ordered the disbarment, asserted that Sheiner had demonstrated "manifest evasiveness, duplicity, and insufficiency of the answer justified." He rejected the idea that Sheiner was being robbed of his Fifth Amendment rights and asserted, "He entered the courtroom possessed of a right, the right to protect himself from self-incrimination, and a privilege, the privilege to practice law. The right was not denied him. He was not required to give evidence against himself. He emerged from the courtroom with the right accorded him by the Fifth Amendment unimpaired. But he left divested of the privilege to practice law." He then explained himself further: the law license "was taken from him because his conduct—particularly his silence when, in his presence and hearing, a witness testified as to his disloyalty and perfidy—demonstrated his unwillingness to dispel the aura of suspicion and doubt in which he stands and in which he has chosen to remain."[56] Despite such a damning report, in 1959 the Florida Bar readmitted Sheiner.

Others suffered, if not as severely. Clifford Durr found it hard to get clients when he returned to Washington, D.C., and Max Shlafrock found it nearly impossible to get construction work. James Dombrowski suffered minor business setbacks but fared relatively well. Aubrey Williams saw many of his friends distance themselves, resigned from the SCEF in 1961 for health reasons, and died of cancer in 1965. Even Eastland suffered from the circus he had wrought. He quickly called an end to the hearings after the tussle, and on May 9, 1954, called off planned hearings in Birmingham. He later admitted that Crouch had not convinced him that either Durr or Williams were Communists, although he remained convinced that the SCEF was a Communist front for the Civil Rights Movement.[57] Eastland also won his reelection bid and remained a U.S. senator until 1978.

The SCEF may have suffered more than any individual, however, as Eastland's subcommittee issued its final report in September 1955. The subcommittee concluded that the SCHW had been "conceived, financed, and set up by the Communist Party in 1938 as a mass organization to promote communism throughout the Southern States."[58] In other words, the committee believed Crouch and based much of its finding on his testimony. The findings also determined that the SCEF "is operating with substantially the same leadership and purposes as its predecessor organizations, the Southern Conference for Human Welfare," and posed a threat to the nation.[59] As such, the committee recommended a formal investigation of the SCEF by the Subversive Activities Control Board. Although none was forthcoming, the SCEF was hurt by the report. In the immediate aftermath of the hearings contributions tripled, but, with the issuance of the report, finances dried up, and mainstream Civil Rights groups wanted nothing to do with the Fund.[60] In spite of that trauma, the SCEF survived until 1985.

According to Thomas Krueger's authoritative study of the SCHW *And Promises to Keep*, Eastland and his committee got it all wrong. Krueger notes that the SCHW "was not a Communist front but a popular front, a conglomeration of individuals from organizations as diverse as the Baptist Church and the Communist party united about a minimum program on which all of the constituent factions could agree." He further asserts that "the available evidence fails to sustain the charge of Communist domination no matter how it is spelled out: whether that interpretation claims Communist origins and domination or liberal origins and subsequent Communist capture." He also notes that even when the Communists did succeed in affecting policy, they did so along moderate lines: "Paul Crouch, then a known member of the Communist party, introduced a resolution on education which the convention unanimously adopted. . . . The ease with which Crouch's resolution passed indicated the widespread agreement among Southerners on the need for federal aid to Southern education to correct its manifest deficiencies, not Communist manipulation." In the end, he concludes that the Communist presence in the SCHW and the SCEF was "dormant" and at worst "innocuous."[61]

Of Crouch, Krueger writes that he

> was an interested, not disinterested, party; the most important events of the last years of his life, the ones from which he

> presumably drew the greatest personal satisfaction, were those involved in the hearings where he bore witness. By dramatizing, not to say exaggerating, the importance and power of the Communist party, he dramatized, not to say exaggerated, his own importance and power: this involved naming a large number of real and imaginary members of the Communist party. Crouch's interest in his charges may have been as great—if such things are comparable—as the interest of those whom he accused in denying them.[62]

This can be said not only of Crouch's testimony about the SCHW and the SCEF but of all his testimony. He truly believed what he was saying but also benefitted financially and emotionally from being the center of attention. For the first time in an important public setting, however, that attention was not all positive.

Amazingly, less than a month after the travesty in New Orleans, Crouch again was on the witness stand. In April 1954 he testified against nine alleged Communists in Philadelphia. In July 1953 David Davis, Walter Lowenfels, Irvin Katz, Robert Klonsky, Joseph Kuzma, Sherman Labovitz, Thomas Nabried, Joseph Roberts, and Benjamin Weiss were arrested and indicted for being "in violation of the Smith Act by unlawfully, willfully and knowingly advocating and teaching the duty and necessity of overthrowing and destroying the Government of the United States by force and violence."[63] Bail was set at $25,000 for all except Kuzma, who was fingered as the leader of the local group, and his bail was set at $50,000.

The trial began on April 12, 1954. Crouch was the first witness, and the *Philadelphia Evening Bulletin* described him as "a six-footer, lank in build with thinning grey hair." He was on the stand for three weeks and produced 423 pages of testimony. Much of that testimony was his life story, including his assertion that he had been made a colonel in the Red Army during his trip to Russia. He also described how the Communist Party functioned. He had presented this material dozens of times, knew it well, and knew how to mold it to the needs of each individual case. As defendant Sherman Labovitz wrote years later,

> Paul Crouch gave all of his fanciful testimony in previous trials and Congressional hearings, always having it especially tailored for the occasion and this case would be no exception. At our trial, Crouch testified that he returned to the United States with secret plans

> for "communist infiltration" of America's armed forces and that he discussed those plans at meetings, in 1928 and 1929, where one of my co-defendants, David Davis, was present. In considerable detail, Crouch called this task of infiltration "his most important activity" as a member of the Communist Party. This testimony contradicted what he said at an earlier trial involving the Farmers' Union, where it was much more expedient to claim that his most important work was his position on the Agricultural Commission of the Communist Party's Central Committee.[64]

Labovitz's assessment aside, Crouch's generic testimony allowed the prosecution to read or present into evidence twenty-two books on or by the Communist Party and several articles written by Lenin between 1905 and 1917. When the defense objected and asked why such old documents written in a foreign land should be allowed into evidence, Judge Cullen Ganey stepped in to help the prosecution. He asked Crouch to elaborate on how the articles were "made applicable" to developments in the United States decades later. According to Labovitz, "The experienced professional witness got the message: 'Lenin would draw a basic conclusion from a situation existing then and party leaders using that book would apply it to the situation that they were considering.'"[65] With that in the record, Judge Ganey allowed the books into evidence.

It was not just with his rulings that the judge aided the prosecution; according to Labovitz, the judge actually assisted the state's lawyers. At one point, the prosecution moved to introduce an article from the October 1939 edition of the *Communist*. As they began to read it to the court, Labovitz claims, Ganey realized it was contradicting the prosecution's case and suggested that "it is a matter which would be certainly not favorable to the position you assume."[66] Prosecuting attorney W. Wilson White promptly withdrew the document.

Crouch, of course, also helped the prosecution and spent much of his time on the stand addressing the issue of force and violence. He claimed that one Communist Party objective was to infiltrate the military so as to weaken its ability to defend the nation from the Soviets. More important, he claimed that in this weakened state it would be easier to turn an "imperialist war into a civil war and at an opportune time during the course of the war, of utilizing the war to organize the armed insurrection for the overthrow of the American government."[67]

As useful as this generic testimony was, it was not nearly as important, for everyone involved, as one brief moment when Crouch got specific. The specific focus had to do with David Davis. Crouch identified Davis as a Communist and claimed that they had worked together as delegates at a YCL convention in Cleveland. He also said he met Davis at a meeting in Manhattan during which they discussed the infiltration of the military. Indeed, he claimed that it was Davis who arranged his trip to Moscow and that Davis was key to the overall effort to infiltrate the U.S. military. Defense counsel Thomas McBride objected several times during Crouch's testimony, complaining that all the material had to do with events that took place long before the dates noted in the indictment. Labovitz took it a step further and noted that all the material in Crouch's testimony related to "purported events some 13 years before the passage of the Smith Act, 18 years before our indictment stated any conspiracy took place and 26 years before the charges that led to our trial." Judge Ganey rejected the objections and allowed Crouch to proceed. As he did so, Crouch named Davis as a Communist no less than twenty-nine additional times.[68]

As the prosecution case continued apace and the defense prepared for cross-examination, defense lawyers Thomas McBride and Joseph Lord studied the several informants, including Crouch. Ben Read, one of the team of junior lawyers assisting McBride and Lord, was given the task of learning about Crouch. Years later he reflected, "I wrote to attorneys all over the country who had defendants in cases where Crouch testified, asking them if they would send me transcripts of his testimony. I was amazed at the response. Not just a few, but everyone I wrote to responded and everybody included transcripts together with comments like 'Nail the S.O.B. He lies through his teeth.'" Labovitz writes that when he asked the lawyers who worked on his case about Read's efforts they praised him to a man, noting his "laborious examination of the scores of transcripts of Crouch testimony," his work "indexing . . . every word of more than 40 Crouch appearances," and his "meticulous research."[69]

The background information Read gathered gave McBride a great deal to work with when he began to cross-examine Crouch on April 21, 1954. He began by getting Crouch to admit that he wrote letters to imaginary people. After laughing at that, McBride asked how he had communicated with the Soviet soldiers he met during his 1927 trip to Moscow when he did not speak Russian. When Crouch responded that he talked to them in Esperanto, McBride sarcastically wondered aloud in which language the soldiers listened. Although scolded by the judge, McBride carried on in a similar vein and scoffed at Crouch's alleged meetings with Soviet leaders and his claims to have been made a colonel in the Red Army. As well as McBride did in calling Crouch's general truthfulness into question, however, he had not been able to challenge the specific facts about which Crouch had testified.[70]

The evening after this first cross, McBride became ill and was rushed to the hospital. Fortunately, the defense had the weekend to prepare for his absence. In the midst of that preparation, late Sunday night, Read found the smoking gun he was looking for to challenge Crouch's testimony. He discovered that on pages 2585 and 2586 of the *United States v. Harry Renton Bridges, et al* trial transcript, Crouch had testified that he did not know David Davis. Read informed Lord, who visited McBride in the hospital Monday morning and gave him the news. McBride urged Lord to use it to destroy Crouch.

According to Labovitz, that day in court "Joe Lord was at his absolute best, continuing McBride's tactics of getting Crouch to repeat his exaggerations while feeding what seemed like an insatiable ego." Lord then moved from Crouch to the defendants and asked Crouch to identify Davis. After Crouch did, Lord asked several times if he was sure of the identification. Crouch assured the defense lawyer that he was. When asked if Davis had changed over the years, Crouch responded, "Surprisingly little." Lord then asked one more time if Crouch was sure he did not have this Davis mixed up with another. Crouch alleged that he had seen Davis at twelve different Communist meetings and assured Lord that he was not confusing him with anyone else. Then, despite several prosecution objections, Lord introduced into evidence the Bridges testimony, during which Crouch, on five separate occasions, had said that he did not know David Davis. Lord even read from the trial transcript, in which Crouch clearly asserted that he had "no knowledge of the existence of David Davis." When confronted with this apparent contradiction, Crouch stammered and then simply replied that he did not recall such testimony, but "If it is an authentic record, I so testified."[71] The destruction complete, Lord was finished with Crouch.

Although done with Crouch, the defense was not done destroying his testimony. John Lautner took the stand next and testified that in 1929, at the age of twenty-nine, he had joined the CPUSA and had remained a member until 1950 when he was expelled. He further testified that during his membership in the party, he, like Crouch, had been made a member of the Red Army. When asked his rank, Lautner asserted that the Red Army had no ranks. Lawyer Joe Lord responded, "What! You didn't know Colonel Crouch!"[72]

Despite the shenanigans and the clear evidence of Crouch's perjury, all nine were convicted. Four, Kuzma, Nabried, Davis, and Roberts, were sentenced to terms of three years while the remaining five got two-year terms. On September 7, 1957, after the Supreme Court ruled that the Smith Act was flawed, defense lawyers for the nine filed an appeal. On November 13, 1957, the Third Circuit Appeals Court acquitted Weiss, Katz, Lowenfels, and Labovitz, but allowed the government to proceed if it wanted to retry Klonsky, Kuzma, Nabried, Davis, and Roberts. On May 16, 1958, the government dropped the case against the other five.[73]

That outcome was in the future, and while Crouch could feel good about being on the winning side in both cases—in that Eastland's committee found the SCEF subversive and the Philadelphia nine were convicted—serious doubt had crept into the minds of many about his testimony. Although he still believed in his anti-Communist ideology, not everyone still believed in him. Indeed, the number of his opponents grew wildly in the aftermath of the two hearings, and while he still had his supporters, 1954 and 1955 would be difficult years. He faced an unprecedented backlash and saw his income dry up amidst concerns about his honesty. Crouch did not meet these challenges well and began to flail out in all directions, attacking anyone and everyone who questioned him.

11 "IS PAUL CROUCH RELIABLE?" 1954

That Crouch received a great deal of negative publicity as a result of his testimony in New Orleans and Philadelphia should come as little surprise. Despite that, during the ensuing months he defended himself and gathered around him a small group of supporters. More important, he never lost his faith and remained adamant that Communism threatened the nation and that those who were attacking him either were Communists or unwitting dupes. In spite of this faith, the criticism began to take a toll, and as McCarthy fell from the heights in 1954 so too did Crouch.

The attack from the left was brutal, though expected. The Trotskyite journal the *Militant*, no friend of either McCarthyism or the CPUSA, responded to Crouch's anti-Communist agenda:

> And what about Paul Crouch, another informer who makes his living supplying "evidence" against anybody the witch hunters are out to indict and convict, and who will apparently swear to anything just as long as he gets paid for it. . . . There are scores of these professional stool pigeons—human vermin who will "remember" anything if the price is right. Decent people don't touch them with a ten-mile pole. But the U.S. government regards them as front-line defenders and exponents of "the American way of life," pays them well out of taxpayers' money and protects them when they get caught committing perjury and other crimes. . . . The people who ought to be jailed or fired from their jobs are not radicals, liberals and others who have exercised their rights of free speech and association, but these stoolpigeons and the "respectable" people who hire and protect them.

The *Daily Worker* joined the assault. The Communist paper briefly assailed his testimony in Philadelphia and asserted that the federal government was losing faith in him as a witness. The paper then mocked Crouch's alleged history, specifically his claims to have met Tukhachevsky, Krupskaya, and other Soviet leaders, and sneered, "He, then 24 years old, with eight months of service in the American Army, was a big shot abroad! The important Communists from all over the world listened with awe to him, Crouch!" It also laughed at his recent claim to have met with Georgi Malenkov while in Moscow. Crouch had never before mentioned meeting Malenkov, but when he became Soviet premier in 1953 Crouch suddenly remembered his presence at several events in 1928.[1] Such a useful recovered memory encouraged many a Communist journalist to attack.

The Communist press did not stop at attacking Crouch, and like the Trotskyites they too went after the politicians who exploited Crouch's testimony. The *Daily Worker* asserted that it knew how Crouch would respond to the attacks against him—he would dare the government to expose and fire him. The paper noted that if the government did so it would be admitting that many of the people in jail or under assault were there based on questionable testimony. Those individuals would then have ample justification for appeals and the cost would be exorbitant. Worse, the paper alleged that politicians on both sides of the aisle knew all along Crouch was a fraud but used him nonetheless for their own personal, political gains.[2]

It was not simply the radical left that attacked Crouch, however, so too did mainstream papers. The *Honolulu Record* joined the chorus when it published an article focused on Crouch's apparent precarious hold on the truth. The paper reported, "Paul Crouch, 'expert witness of prosecutors in Smith Act cases and employee of the Bureau of Investigation,' has been called a liar more often even than most of the stoolpigeons used in such cases. How often is he telling the truth when he speaks of himself under oath? No more than 50 per cent of the time, if a check of his own statements on his education . . . are an indication." The paper then noted that at various points in his life Crouch claimed he had attended or taken correspondence classes from the University of California, Brownsville College, the University of Texas, and the University of North Carolina. The paper found, however, that Crouch only took one noncredit Spanish class from Brownsville College and that while in Alcatraz he took some Russian courses from the University of California. He never completed any of the classes. This was important, the paper indicated, because if he lied about his education he likely lied about the rest.[3]

The *Nation* magazine also joined the fray and in April 1954 offered an assessment of Crouch's life and testimony in an article entitled "The Informer on the Stand." In it the magazine reminded readers that as far back as his 1924 arrest in Hawaii, Crouch had admitted to being a liar and making up stories for his own entertainment. The magazine argued he had made good use of storytelling abilities throughout his testimony and specifically cited as examples his depiction of himself as a "Marxist *Wunderkind*" who read Communist literature as a young teen and met with Soviet leaders at the age of twenty-four.[4]

The article then addressed more recent incidents, focusing especially on Armanda Scala. The magazine followed Crouch's testimony about Scala chronologically and noted that when he testified before HUAC on May 6, 1949, and was asked whether Scala was a party member, he said "I do not know. I do not know of my own knowledge what his party affiliations are." The magazine then noted that on May 11 a *Miami News* editor entered into evidence in a HUAC executive session Crouch's soon to be published series of articles, as well as several affidavits offered by Crouch, in which he wrote more about Scala—this time charging him with being the "chief Communist courier to Latin America." The magazine explained that even here Crouch had not directly accused Scala of being a Communist, simply a courier, and it was only on May 16 when he testified before the Senate Subcommittee on Immigration and Naturalization that he said he had "every reason" to believe that Scala was a "very active Communist." But, as the paper noted, he claimed this knowledge came only from "many references which I have heard around the office." The paper then explained that it was not until September 20, 1949, that "Crouch's memory had jelled sufficiently to enable him to designate Scala unequivocally as a Communist Party member."[5] Such evolving testimony, the magazine asserted, showed every evidence of falsehood. And it was not just the magazine making that allegation, as a jury had ordered the Hearst Press to pay Armand Scala $5,000 in a libel lawsuit after the press printed allegations made by Crouch.

The furor over Crouch soon expanded to include the whole practice of using informers. The *Washington Post* questioned Crouch's veracity on the stand but went deeper and questioned why ex-Communists always were believed—a point that Harry Bridges' lawyer Vincent Hallinan had made five years earlier. The *Post* wrote: "It appears to be a canon of contemporary conduct that the fidelity of 'former Communists' must never be questioned—once they have embarked on witnessing as a career; but let us at least, in the name of common sense, retain a little healthy skepticism as to the myth of 'former communist' infallibility."[6]

This critique was similarly espoused by Charles Walker of Cheyney, Pennsylvania, who complained in a letter to the editor that, "In addition to the idea of guilt by association, we see developing the idea of 'guilt by opposition' also. In this latter theory, if a person makes a statement opposing Communism, it is to be interpreted as a cover-up for his real status as a concealed Communist." Walker admitted that Communists did exist and were a threat, "But to spread the idea that public acts and statements are all misleading means that . . . the professional informer is the only final authority." He went on to lament that, "Only a certificate of political purity from Louis Budenz or Paul Crouch, or some other Commissar of Ideological and Political Rectitude, apparently means anything. This means death to the wellsprings of democratic and responsible society. Democracy cannot function in such an atmosphere of suspicion."[7] Clearly there was a small but growing fount of opposition against Crouch, the use of informants, and indeed the entire Red Scare era.

In May 1954 the *Washington Daily News* added to the hubbub when it broke the story that Crouch had authored a seven-page memo for Roy Cohn in March 1953 entitled "Communist Infiltration in the American Armed Forces." In it, Crouch largely reiterated previous claims about infiltrating the military and National Guard, spying on and sabotaging the military in the event of war, and spreading Communism in Latin America and Hawaii. These efforts, he explained to Cohn, were the result of the work he and Tukhachevsky had begun back in 1927.[8]

When confronted with the paper's claim, Cohn admitted that he had received "specific details about what the Communist conspiracy had done to infiltrate the United States Army, and to place Communists in key places, sensitive places, in the Army," but initially refused to tell who had provided the memo. He eventually acknowledged that it was Crouch but alleged that there was "nothing of earth-shaking significance" in the memo. Cohn's claim clearly was belied by the very first line of the document, which reads: "There are more than a thousand Communists in the armed forces of the United States today, prepared to carry on espionage, sabotage, and any kind of disruptive activities during all-out war between the Soviet Union and this country. Additional hundreds are in the National Guard and at least several hundred hold commissions as reserve officers."[9] To most, those assertions would seem to be of some significance.

More notably, and again to belie Cohn's claim, just a month prior to the news report, in April 1954, Cohn had introduced the memo into the Army-McCarthy hearings. The infamous televised hearings had less to do with the search for Communists in the military and more to do with McCarthy's outrage when Cohn's assistant David Schine was refused special treatment by the military. Schine was drafted in 1953 and, at Cohn's insistence, received relief from various duties as well as extended leave to search for Communists. Eventually military officials became fed up with the continuing demands and accused Cohn and McCarthy of improperly attempting to influence the armed forces. Cohn and McCarthy fired back that the charges and the refusal to help Schine were clear indicators that the military either was attempting to thwart the search for Communists or already was overrun by Communists. With Crouch's accusation as all the evidence he needed of this second possibility, McCarthy determined to investigate. Indeed, according to historian Cedric Belfrage, "The immediate impulse for his [McCarthy's] fatal army probe came, according to the record, from . . . Crouch who could vouch for the presence of 'over 1000' Communists waiting in the armed forces to disrupt any war against Russia."[10] Crouch, in other words, was the source that led McCarthy to investigate the military.

ABC television decided to air the investigations, not so much out of any real interest but because they needed programming to fill the day. That decision changed history. As the television cameras broadcast the hearings, the public got its first live sense of McCarthy. What they saw was a rude, blustery senator who interrupted or ignored witnesses and seemed more interested in his own self-aggrandizement than in finding the truth. All these factors became evident when McCarthy charged the law firm defending the military with employing a Communist named Fred Fischer. As McCarthy blustered away, defense lawyer Joseph Welch gathered himself before defending Fischer and then delivering the coup de grâce on McCarthy's career when he asked the senator: "Have you no sense of decency sir, at long last? Have you left no sense of decency?" The gallery erupted in applause and McCarthy was on the road to censure.

Not only did the hearings destroy McCarthy and fail to find any Communists in the military, they did serious harm to Crouch's reputation by linking him ever more closely with McCarthy, just as the senator was falling from public favor.

Indeed, Crouch had few opportunities to testify in the first half of 1954. He reported $8,000 in earnings from his testimony in 1953 and claimed to have a deal with the government by which it would employ him at least eighteen days per month. He argued that the government had reneged on the offer in 1954 and owed him $788 for June, despite the fact that he had not performed any work. He blamed the lack of opportunity to testify on the growing chorus of attacks and on his specific association with the Army-McCarthy hearings. He went so far as to state: "I wish the FBI to note this fact carefully, for in this case the attempted starvation of a Government consultant as punishment and retaliation for accidental aid to Sen. McCarthy . . . affects national security."[11] Raymond Ferrell of the INS denied any deal or retaliation and claimed the government owed him nothing. Showing that despite his bravado the pressures might be getting to him, for the first time in years Crouch also began to complain of health problems. Indeed, in May 1954 he informed U.S. Attorney Thomas Daily that due to "complete physical breakdown" he would not be able to testify in Philadelphia at the trial of several veterans of the Lincoln Brigade.[12]

While Crouch's association with McCarthy and all the attacks on him in early 1954 took a toll, the criticism that came from Stewart and Joseph Alsop may have been the most important. Not only were they among the earliest and most consistent critics of Crouch and the whole informer system, they did real research and uncovered ever more examples of failure or ineptitude. On April 19, 1954, they published a round of attacks on Crouch in the *New York Herald Tribune*. Entitled "The Powerful Imaginer," the Alsops labeled Crouch a full-time informant since "being an informer seems to be his main source of income." They then laughed at his claims that by the age of twelve he was reading Marx and Engels: "He was clearly an infant prodigy, with access to a library without parallel in the rustic South of that simple and remote period." The brothers then turned to more serious issues and noted that Crouch claimed to have broken with the CPUSA in 1942 but in testimony claimed that in 1946 he discussed Communism with Judge Oscar Dancy in Brownsville, Texas. Not only was the date wrong, but they noted that

Dancy had since denied being present at such a discussion and claimed never in his life to have met Crouch.[13]

The Alsops then argued that these discrepancies were not unique and that nearly all his stories varied wildly. They related, for instance, that he gave "six quite different and conflicting accounts of the attendance at meetings of the Communist Party Central Committee." They also pointed out that on two occasions he claimed to have played a major role in the effort to infiltrate the military and even quoted him as saying one time that he was building "a vast apparatus in the armed forces of the United States" and again as supervising another group "for the purpose of supplying the Soviet Union with information regarding scientific experiments at the University of California." They did note, though, that on a third occasion he claimed that such ideas were mere "barroom talk" and that he "did not obtain any military secrets from this country." In conclusion, they argued that "no man in his sense can read Crouch's multitudinous, widely various and often highly peculiar accounts of his own past and conclude that this man is a witness to be relied on."[14]

The Alsops took another swipe at Crouch in an article entitled "Is Paul Crouch Reliable?" They rehashed his prior failings in the Oppenheimer and Weinberg cases, with particular interest on the fact that the federal government failed to call him in the Weinberg case after lawyers unearthed evidence that much of his testimony was false. Of this decision the brothers wrote, "But the failure to call Crouch to testify on the supposed Communist meetings suggests that the Justice Department itself harbors occasional doubts about the reliability of its 'expert' witness." Indeed, they noted that the judge who heard the Weinberg case, Judge Holtzoff, said, "I am amazed that [the Justice Department] should employ him as a member of its staff." They also pointed out that "Crouch himself has boasted about his 'imaginative powers,' and there is much to suggest that he has frequently given these powers free rein."[15]

The article further asserted that if Crouch was telling the truth, then Oppenheimer was the "liar" since he denied meeting Crouch in a Communist meeting in Berkeley in 1941. "What is more," they wrote, "if Paul Crouch was telling the truth, Dr. Oppenheimer was a secret Communist throughout the whole wartime period, with implications too hair-raising to think about." Because of this, they wanted to be sure of Crouch's truthfulness. Indeed, Stewart and Joseph Alsop intimated that similar questions abounded with other informants and demanded that the government make sure its informants were honest or else the whole struggle against Communism was doomed. In the end, they argued that they were not defending Weinberg, Oppenheimer, or anyone accused of being a Communist but instead spoke out "in defense of the eccentric notion that the word of the ordinary American citizen should be given equal weight, at least, with that of the professional ex-Communist."[16]

As a result of these attacks, specifically the ones by the Alsops, Crouch finally decided to defend himself publicly and penned a letter of complaint to the *New York Herald Tribune*. In it he wrote, "In this story ['Is Paul Crouch Reliable?'] I find . . . libelous, malicious and false statements in reference to myself—statements causing me great and lasting injury and clearly written with malice intent." He further complained about being called "an ex convict," arguing that he was never convicted of a felony but only a misdemeanor. He concluded by noting that he had been employed by the federal government for three years, which he believed spoke to his integrity, and demanded a public retraction or else he would file a $1 million libel suit.[17] Everette Walker, the managing editor of the *New York Herald Tribune* which ran the Alsop articles, responded to Crouch's letter with one of his own. He explained that what the Alsops did was legal and as such the paper would not retract the article. Crouch quickly replied to Walker's letter and addressed nine points in various articles about which he remained mad. Among the points that infuriated him were the claim that he offered conflicting testimony about the infiltration of Communists into the U.S. military and the claim that he had made varying statements regarding his attendance at central committee meetings. He then argued, "The very language employed by the Alsop brothers drips with venom, is more libelous of our government than of me personally, and sounds like a quotation from the *Daily Worker*."[18]

Stewart and Joseph Alsop were not put off by Crouch's threats and indeed were invigorated when they learned that the federal government had determined to investigate Crouch. As a result of the uproar his testimony had created, in May 1954, U.S. Attorney General Herbert Brownell began to investigate the entire informer system. According to the *Washington Post*, "NUMBER ONE is Paul Crouch. Crouch is being investigated because of sharp conflicts in his own sworn testimony in Government trials. In the last two years, Crouch has received $9,675 from the Justice Department, an average of just under $420 per month."[19] Of specific focus for the attorney general was the case of the Philadelphia Communists during which Crouch was caught lying about David Davis. The Alsop brothers saw this investigation as an important development; and if they ever considered settling with Crouch, were stiffened in their resolve by the attorney general's decision.[20]

They would have been ever more firm in their resolve had they known that the FBI was investigating Crouch as well. The bureau was upset with Crouch's propensity for going public with his attacks; indeed it learned that he had sent information to conservative radio commentator Fulton Lewis, gossip columnist Walter Winchell, ABC, *Life* magazine, and dozens of other media outlets. The FBI demanded that he tell them before he did any future press. The bureau was even more concerned about his previous testimony in New Orleans. In May 1954, the FBI interviewed Crouch in Philadelphia about the revelations regarding Durr, Dombrowski, and Williams. Specifically, agents wanted to know why he had not informed them first. Crouch assured them it was all true and that oftentimes something simply happened to jog his memory about someone being a Communist, so he was not withholding information nor was he making it up. He reminded them that he had been in the Communist Party for seventeen years and argued that it should not be a surprise if he did not remember everyone or everything all at once. Agents feigned acceptance of this explanation but privately determined not to meet with him in the near future for fear that he would publicize such meetings to claim that the government still trusted him. While the FBI, or at least some of its agents, had long been suspicious of Crouch, the bureau had been willing to use him for its own benefit. With doubts about him ever rising, however, the bureau clearly was seeking to distance itself.[21]

In June the *Washington Post* cheered the newly announced decision to investigate Crouch. In an article entitled "The Cult of the Informer," the paper supported the investigation because some of the people he fingered probably were Communists, and they needed to be deported or imprisoned. The paper feared that his failures could endanger the nation by allowing real Communists to go free. Crouch read the editorial in a different manner, however, and responded days later. He claimed that the editorial did a disservice to the nation because it would "cause thousands of former Communists to think twice before they come out as I have done . . . [to] provide information our government needs." Crouch called for the government to investigate the *Post*, the Alsops, and any news service that derided him or his fellow ex-Communist informants.[22] Only such an investigation, he asserted, would halt the attacks and ensure that future informants would feel free to testify about the Communist threat.

When the investigation he called for was not forthcoming, Crouch followed through with his earlier threat and sued the *New York Herald Tribune*, president of the company Whitelaw Reid, and the Alsops. In court documents he accused the paper and the brothers of "wickedly contriving and intending to cause it to be believed that plaintiff now is and long has been a liar, a perjurer, a professionally mendacious witness and unreliable informer." He went on to contend that the paper "falsely and maliciously published . . . false and defamatory matter," and that several articles "were published by defendant without investigation and carelessly, wantonly and recklessly, in disregard of rights of plaintiff; and out of spite and malice toward plaintiff as an alleged 'informer,' in the pejorative sense of the world [*sic*] informer." The suit then listed thirty-seven untruths the Alsops had written or implied about Crouch, including that he lied about attending a meeting with Oppenheimer, that he had no real expertise and testified only to make money, that he was a habitual liar, that he committed perjury, that he "has frequently given his imaginative powers free rein, disregarding responsibility for the truth," and that he was so unreliable that the government had dropped him as a witness. The suit alleged that "all of the aforementioned statements and innuendos, maliciously published by defendants of and concerning plaintiffs, are false." Since these attacks cost him his income, he demanded $500,000 in compensation.[23] He also sued the *Daily Worker* for $150,000 for "seriously curtailing my earnings" as a result of the attacks in several of its articles.[24]

Crouch followed the lawsuit with a letter to Attorney General Brownell and another to J. Edgar Hoover. In the June 8 letter to Brownell he wrote, "I respectfully request that the entire investigation of all matters regarding me and the many derogatory allegations made by the Communist press and radio . . . since the Oppenheimer case be referred to the Federal Bureau of Investigation. I respectfully request further that the Federal Bureau of Investigation be directed to deal with this matter with the utmost speed consistent with thorough and complete investigation of every detail of the derogatory allegations." After listing the various attacks he faced, he concluded, "I respectfully request an immediate and thorough investigation by the Federal Bureau of Investigation, with public hearings and open and public findings as early as possible. It is my humble opinion that prompt and public investigation is essential to national security in view of developments."[25]

When Brownell refused to respond, Crouch wrote a fourteen-page letter to J. Edgar Hoover complaining that the efforts of Stewart and Joseph Alsop and others amounted to "the most audacious and gigantic character assassination plot ever conceived." He requested that in his next testimony he be allowed to use a lie detector to prove his veracity and argued that once he proved his sincerity and defeated the conspiracy, thousands of other ex-Communists would come forward to testify.[26]

He also laid out the fourteen allegations he believed the Alsops and others were making against him and provided the bureau chief with a refutation of each and every point. Charge one was that he was still a Communist. His reply merely was to point out his anti-Communist efforts. Charge two was that he had claimed California Representative Robert Condon was a Communist. He simply denied doing so. Charge three was that he was a professional witness. Again, he simply denied it. Charge four was that he lied about Oppenheimer. He ignored the specific charge and referred to years of testimony with the FBI, thus asserting that the agency would not use a liar. Charge five was that Judge Holtzoff said, "I am amazed that [the Justice Department] should employ him." Crouch asserted that Holtzoff later said he was taken out of context and did not oppose Crouch's service as an informant. Charge six was the Alsop's claim that he was a liar and that they had a "competent witness" who could prove it. He claimed the "witness" was Gilbert Parks, and he challenged to meet him in open court. Charge seven was that the Department of Justice had no confidence in him. He said a government attorney told him, "At no time during the Weinberg trial was there any lack of confidence by the Department in Crouch." Charge eight was that he made conflicting statements about knowing Sam Donchin. Crouch said he knew him under a different name (Sam Don). Charge nine was that he made conflicting statements about knowing David Davis. Crouch said he knew him only as D. Davis. Charge ten was that he had picked out the wrong person when pointing out Jacob Burck. Crouch said he lacked time to make a good reply but told the director that it had been a long time since he had seen Burck and his memory was unclear. Charge eleven was that he lied about his early Socialist education. He asserted that there were several socialist newspapers near his home and that he had been a scholar of the left from an early age. Charge twelve was that he claimed to have met with Judge Dancy, but Dancy denied the meeting. Crouch said they did meet, but only casually. Charge thirteen was that he gave conflicting testimony about his role leading Communist efforts to infiltrate the military. He said there was plenty of evidence to back up his claims. Finally, there were questions about much of the material gathered during his arrest in Hawaii. Crouch said he left behind fake minutes and correspondence to impede the military's investigation, so any questionable material was actually a ploy to protect himself and his fellow La Homaro members.[27] While Crouch provided no tangible evidence to support his claims, he believed he had given Hoover and the FBI enough to defend him and go after his enemies.

When Hoover proved unmoved, Crouch tried a different tact. A week after his lengthy critique of the charges against him, he wrote another letter to Hoover complaining about his financial straits. He told the director that he had not been paid since May 28 and that his family faced real starvation. He denied recent editorials in the *Washington Daily News* and the *New York Times*, which asserted that he had made fabulous sums as an informant, and instead claimed to have netted only $1,500 from the government in 1953, not the $8,000 to $9,000 others claimed, with the vast majority of the money going toward expenses. He then begged the director for help in getting him assignments or at least clearing his name so others would hire him.[28]

Undaunted when this note also went unanswered, Crouch wrote another letter to the FBI director on June 29:

> I am requesting . . . the Senate Judiciary Committee, the Senate Committee on Government Operations and the President of the United States to see that the FBI is directed and authorized (1) to make a full and complete investigation of all charges against me since April 11, and also of my counter charges; (2) to gather all evidence relating to possible perjury by any and all persons for presentation to Federal grand juries; (3) to prepare a report for the President and Congress on Communist exploitation of the 25

> charges against me, and responsibility of any and all people in the Government for the extent and success of such propaganda that has been prejudicial to national security.[29]

He also complained that recently he sent the FBI a thirty-four page document that would help the bureau rebut the charges being made against him. Thus far, he lamented, "I have seen no indication that such investigation is even contemplated before 1999." He went on to call the charges against him "complete and deliberate falsehoods, sometimes supported by perjured affidavits," sometimes the result of taking statements out of context, and other times the result of "finding contradictions between statements where it is clear and obvious that there is no contradiction." He concluded by reminding the director of all his service to the federal government's assault on Communism and said he expected more from the government in return. In his own words: "As you know, I have been a witness in some sixty proceedings and hearings involving exposure of Communist activities. . . . One would logically expect the full forces of the government to be used in cooperation with me in bringing out the full facts about the character assassination plot and alleged charges."[30] Finally, he warned that "if my reputation could be destroyed 31 Communist leaders could get new trials, 20 investigative proceedings would be reopened, [and] the registration order against the CP would be reversed, with a cost to the government of millions."[31]

Outraged when action still was not forthcoming, in the summer of 1954 Crouch publicly accused Attorney General Herbert Brownell and Deputy Attorney General William Rogers with violating their oaths of office by failing to defend him from "slander." In fact, he offered to testify against the two Justice officials, undoubtedly for a fee, should they be called before Congress to defend themselves for their alleged crimes. Indeed, in July 1954 he sent a letter to William Langer, Republican senator from North Dakota, in which he asserted that both men were guilty of giving "considerable aid and comfort to enemies of the United States" by investigating him and impugning his integrity. He also alleged that the two men had put partisan politics ahead of national defense in allowing him to be so poorly treated.[32] Langer turned over the letter to the chair of the Internal Security subcommittee, Republican senator from Indiana William Jenner. When asked for a response, Jenner said, "That sort of thing is absurd. We don't act on charges like that. I'll have to call a meeting of the subcommittee on it, but I don't anticipate anything will be done on that kind of request."[33] The *New York Times*, in reporting Crouch's attacks on Brownell, took a similar tone and noted that "Mr. Crouch, whose credibility is now under investigation by the Justice Department" was a less than believable witness who probably was getting what he deserved. It concluded, "There was a touch of irony in Mr. Crouch's situation. Faced with possible punitive action by the Justice Department, he has appealed to the American Civil Liberties Union for assistance."[34]

The appeals to Hoover and attack on Brownell amounted to little, but the lawsuit against the Alsops continued apace. Crouch, meanwhile, upped the ante and authored an article entitled "Stewart Alsop was an Ex-Marxist." In it, he alleged that Alsop once believed in Marxism and thus was as responsible as anyone for the Communist threat the nation faced. Crouch pointed to a May 1941 article in the *Atlantic Monthly* entitled "Wanted: A Faith to Fight For," in which Alsop wrote, "I was, like many thousands of my years and bent, that curious hybrid, a Marxian liberal." Alsop explained that the type of Marxism that "filters down through liberal education . . . dominated my political thinking." He continued, "It was the supreme logic of Marxism, even the diluted Marxism which characterizes the thinking of the Marxist liberal. For it is a magic touchstone, a bright and lovely mirror which reflects the truth, the whole truth and nothing but the truth. It does your thinking for you. . . . Indeed, the real cowardice and un-Americanism still seems to me to be those who could look upon the America of 1933 and fail to look for an alternative."[35] From this decades-old article Crouch alleged that Alsop remained a Communist and that that was the reason for his attacks. As he put it, "The Alsop brothers are the most prominent and influential of those who display venomous hatred of ex-Communists who are trying to fight the Frankenstein they once helped create."[36]

For once, Crouch got some support. George Sokolsky, the son of Russian émigrés, a longtime supporter of Senator McCarthy, an ABC news commentator, and a syndicated columnist, agreed with Crouch. On July 15, 1954, he wrote an essay in the *Washington Post and Times Herald* in which he asserted that most of the good and reliable information on Communism in America came from former Communists and that should attacks on Crouch continue potential witnesses would be scared to step forward. He defended Crouch and other former Communists as "sincere fighters against communism and in spite of the fact that some of them accept a per diem fee, they all serve at a sacrifice and receive less than they would earn at other work." He then defended Crouch's errors in testimony by asserting that the mistakes were minor, resulted from testifying to things he had heard rather than witnessed himself, and asserted that "we are dealing with a conspiracy and conspirators do not make it easy to uncover themselves." He concluded by calling for a continuation of the informer system and defending Crouch and other informants as "serving this country and . . . not deserving of the calumny currently being heaped on him."[37]

Crouch also received some support from Ellis Rubin, the Florida state chairman of the Un-American Activities Committee of the American Legion. He wrote a letter to the *Miami Daily Herald* in which he addressed the recently completed Oppenheimer security clearance hearings. He noted that of the two men, Crouch and Oppenheimer, only Oppenheimer had been proven a liar, as evidenced by the AEC vote to strip him of his clearance. By contrast, he asserted, Crouch had never been proven a liar. In summary he wrote, "I think that this attempt to discredit Paul Crouch and his wife by making it appear that they were in part responsible for 'loyal' Dr. Oppenheimer's removal from security clearance . . . is misleading, beclouding the facts, and is aimed at all former Communists who have come forward . . . to help other Americans see the dangers of international subversion."[38]

In June 1954 the *National Republic* magazine joined the pro-Crouch effort when it returned to the link between Communism and Civil Rights. As a result of the recently ruled *Brown v. Board of Education* decision and the growing determination on the part of many Southerners to oppose integration, as witnessed by the Southern Manifesto and massive resistance, this link now became an even more important tool for segregationists to justify their opposition. The magazine argued that 1,000 to 1,200 Communists remained in the South and had ties to the Civil Rights Movement through the SCEF. The paper argued that most of the leading figures in the fund were respectable people who no one would think were Communists, and that was exactly the way the party wanted it. That secrecy was what made them so insidious, the paper explained, and why people needed to listen to Crouch and destroy the fund. The magazine asserted that the Communist Party was especially active in Birmingham, New Orleans, and Miami, but existed in every southern state, and it demanded more investigations of Communist activity in the South.[39]

Crouch got even more help when J. Gerald Brennan penned a letter to Attorney General Brownell. In the letter Brennan listed the various attacks on Crouch and demanded to know when the attorney general would take them up and defend him. He quoted Assistant Attorney General Warren Olney III from a speech he gave in Michigan on July 23, 1954, as saying that "the DOJ makes no apology for the former Communists that it has produced as witnesses for the government in the smith act and other Communist prosecutions. In advance in every case their testimony has been carefully checked and evaluated. . . . We have been satisfied they have in all instances testified truthfully and accurately." Brennan asked that since these things surely applied to Crouch, why had Justice not fought back and defended him? He concluded, "I do not question your technical power to drop without notice a man who had worked as a full time per diem consultant for about three years. But under these circumstances, is it not both unwise and extremely unjust?"[40]

The VFW also announced its support of Crouch and indeed of all informants who were helping the federal government fend off the Communist threat. In a "Fact Sheet on Un-American Activities," the VFW attacked those who criticized the Justice Department for using former Communists in prosecutions. It named specifically a *Washington Daily News* article by Anthony Lewis entitled "Justice Paid the Fees 87 Ex-Reds Got $75,000 for Talking." The group claimed that those, like Lewis and the *News*, who criticized the government's use of informants, were helping Moscow by creating "the impression in the minds of many Americans that any former Communist who helps the Government expose spies and traitors of the operations of Red Fascists is a loathsome creature who has adopted a 'dirty business' as his profession." Instead, the group countered,

> Communists who have broken completely with Moscow's conspiracy and who testify for the US Government are not "informers." They are not buying immunity from prosecution nor are they giving testimony to collect a monetary reward. Furthermore, they are not betraying to oppressors good people who are fighting for

> a worthy cause. In the great majority of cases, they are persons who are trying to make amends for wrongs they freely admit having committed in the past and who are trying to protect you, your family and your country from what they know is a grave danger.[41]

Crouch thus had a small and unorganized group of supporters who saw him as the victim in this larger struggle against the Communist threat. In an effort to bring together this diverse group, Crouch allies created the "National Committee for the Vindication of Paul Crouch." The committee's specific agenda was "to present the facts about the smears on Crouch to the country, showing the attacks to be not a personal issue, but one involving the entire security of the nation. Paul Crouch has been selected from among the ex-Communists in America as a target for concentrated attack by open and secret Communists, [and] left-wing forces. If his credibility were to be destroyed, the efforts of all federal agencies and congressional committees would be strangled by cutting off their sources of information from disillusioned former Communists." The defense of Crouch continued:

> Since early April, 1954, Crouch . . . has been the victim of an unprecedented smear campaign by the Alsop brothers, Drew Pearson, THE NATION, NEW REPUBLIC, and many newspapers like the WASHINTGON POST, NEW YORK HEARLD TRIBUNE and even THE NEW YORK TIMES. A total of some twenty-five charges have been published against Crouch, and it can easily be proven that all of those charges in their entirety are false. Most of them were Communist fabrications, and were then circulated by the Alsops and others. Some of the charges are supported by affidavits that can be proven to be perjured by documentation alone. Some are so fantastic as to deny the existence of a weekly newspaper Crouch edited, and to deny that he did any writing for the MIAMI DAILY NEWS, although a dozen articles appeared under his byline in that paper and were syndicated and reprinted in more than thirty newspapers throughout the country.

The committee planned to publicize these facts and indeed all that Crouch had done to save the nation despite the vicious lies he faced. It also raised funds to pay his lawyer fees, which were estimated at $16,500.[42]

Crouch clearly faced serious attacks in early 1954, but he had a group of defenders who supported him throughout the ordeal. Despite such defense, the attacks continued into the summer. In July Stewart and Joseph Alsop were back when they noted that three of the federal government's fifty informants were under investigation for possible perjury. Of those fifty, only twelve, including Crouch, were "professional" informants who had received more than $1,500 for their services. At that rate, they argued, 25 percent of the informants were under investigation, not a very good ratio. Worse, they noted that informants had a financial incentive to be used as much as possible, giving them an incentive to lie to keep themselves employable. The *Nation* magazine also took on Crouch that summer. The magazine focused on his testimony in Philadelphia and opened its piece noting that, "Crouch clashed so strongly with defense lawyers that the reverberations have been felt nationally." It then praised defense lawyer Thomas McBride who "exposed" Crouch and "demolished Crouch's recital of his career as a Communist Party member from the 1920's to 1942."[43]

The *New Republic* took its swipe in an article entitled, "Paul Crouch, Informer." Of his current efforts, it wrote, "Paul Crouch, best-paid of all government career informants . . . is a mild-mannered but fiercely determined man with a sense of mission, a long and still-continuing affinity for secret-lodge operations, and a persecution complex." The magazine explained that this complex was evident from the fact that he saw enemies everywhere, including in the Justice Department. It then scoffed at Crouch's claim that the reason journalists hated him was because Senator McCarthy liked and trusted him and concluded by offering one of the best psychological insights of the man:

> A key to Crouch's character—the world within him, the pattern of his thoughts—may be revealed by a fragment of his testimony in the old Army court-marital. Testifying on a letter addressed to his parents, in which he named one of the other people helping Communists infiltrate the forces, he denied the authenticity of some of his letters in these terms: I am in the habit of writing letters, both to my friends and to imaginary persons, sometimes to Kings and foreign rulers, and in this work, in writing these letters, I place myself in all kinds of imaginary positions. I do this for the purpose of developing my imaginary powers.[44]

Crouch clearly continued to use those imaginative powers, the magazine implied, and he was doing so for his own benefit and to the detriment of the nation.

The *Miami Daily Herald*, meanwhile, ran an essay by Jack Kofoed in which he wrote, "Crouch, like Chambers, Budenz, and others of their ilk, spent years trying to tear down America. They recanted and told what they knew about the Great Conspiracy. Suddenly they became tremendously patriotic. Many years ago Samuel Johnson said, 'Patriotism is the last refuge of the scoundrel.' That typifies these poor little lambs who went astray in Red fields and came bleating back to beg forgiveness." While he admitted that people like Crouch may have been of use to the FBI and others fighting Communism, he rejected the idea that since that was so we had to accept everything they said. He argued that it was clear Crouch lied, and lied many times, and asserted that the public needed to acknowledge that fact. He concluded, "I don't like Communists, and my regard for those who fled back to the protection of the country they betrayed is no higher. This includes the intellectual aristocrat, Whittaker Chambers, as well as the mental plebian Paul Crouch. They were traitors."[45]

As if these many and varied attacks on Crouch were not enough, on June 22, 1954, the Crouch Appendix appeared. The document brought together, in one place, all the documented instances of Crouch's fabrications and exaggerations. The appendix began with a brief biography and then proceeded to address the numerous instances of "evasion or exaggeration" in Crouch's various public testimony. The appendix noted that Crouch claimed to have recruited dozens of soldiers into the Communist Party but only provided one specific name (Taylor), which was a generic name the Communist press often used. The appendix noted that he initially took credit for placing soldiers on the *USS Oklahoma* but later said Trumbull did it. It also noted that he initially said he left the Communist Party for ideological reasons, later added that he quit due to the party's spying, and even later added that he quit after the party expelled all the Japanese members following Pearl Harbor.[46]

The appendix also offered the insight of those who knew Crouch and could corroborate the opinion of him as a liar. In a letter dated July 20, 1953, union leader Charles Cowl argued that Crouch was never the director of the CIO in Florida as he had once claimed. He further alleged that the *Union Record* was not a newspaper but simply a "sheet" printed by a renegade group from the CIO, and that Crouch had never been editor of the *Dade County News*. Extant copies of the *Union Record* from 1947, however, show it to be a small newsletter of eight pages or so, much smaller in size and length than a traditional paper, but a paper nonetheless. Similarly, a copy of the *Dade County News* from December 1947 shows Crouch listed as the editor, thus calling at least this part of the appendix into question.[47]

The Crouch Appendix additionally quoted Herb McCusker, editor of the *Miami Labor Press*. McCusker called Crouch "a faker and an obvious one. He doubtless had illusions of grandeur and tried to impress strangers with his importance." George Beebe, managing editor of the *Miami Herald*, offered further criticism when he noted that while Crouch did work for the paper, his claim to have been editor was false. Bill Baggs, meanwhile, noted that he conferred with Crouch on several occasions about Communism for a series of articles he was writing for the *Miami Daily News*. Of those meetings Baggs said, "Paul Crouch was a rich treasury of information on the Communist Party. He had a good memory of his spiritual expedition with the Communist Party. Now and then, however, he got the facts confused." Numerous similar letters noted Crouch's penchant for lying and exaggeration from those who knew him and worked with him.[48]

As a result of these findings, the appendix offered its assessment of Crouch: "Here is a man quick to brand acquaintances and associates as fellow-Communists; an inveterate 'name dropper' prepared to meet the exigencies of any situation with a conveniently pat story; a witness himself who confesses that he does not recall 99 out of every 100 names he speaks as he moves from hearing to hearing." It also quoted the assessment of Jacob Burck's lawyers who in their appeal of Burck's deportation had said of Crouch: "Here is a man whose experience in the Communist conspiracy has bred in him a disrespect for the truth. Falsehoods, contradictions, and evasions are his pabulum."[49] The Crouch Appendix supported such an assessment and damned Crouch, his testimony, and all those who used his testimony in open court.

When Crouch learned of the appendix he wrote to J. Edgar Hoover to denounce it: "I brand every alleged charge false in so far as it attempts to show either untrue or contradictory testimony." He went on to try to prove that any errors in his testimony were minor and irrelevant and that his accusers made many errors as well.[50]

Crouch also turned to a new ally in his struggle against the appendix—the church. Although raised in the Baptist tradition, Crouch had left the church at a young age and as a Communist had nothing but distain for organized religion—the "opium of the masses" according to Marx. Once out of the Communist Party, however, and when faced with the stresses and strains of his anti-Communist testimony, he found solace in the Church. The Church was more than happy to embrace him and his new found anti-Communism. Under the leadership of Billy Graham and others, American Christians were among the most ardent anti-Communists of the era. As early as 1947, Graham was warning his flock that Communism threatened the world and needed to be destroyed. A year later he made the threats Communism beheld clearer when he thundered, "Communism . . . has decided against God, against Christ, against the Bible, and against all religion. Communism . . . is a religion that is inspired, directed, and motivated by the Devil himself who has declared war against Almighty god." Indeed, Graham even came to support Senator McCarthy. In a 1953 sermon he said, "I thank God for men who, in the face of public denouncement and ridicule, go loyally on in their work of exposing the pinks, the lavenders, and the reds who have sought refuge beneath the wings of the American eagle and from that vantage point, try in every subtle, undercover way to bring comfort, aid, and help to the greatest enemy we have ever known—Communism."[51]

In an effort to bring those loyalists together, several anti-Communist Christian groups emerged in the 1950s. One, Circuit Riders, Inc., formed in 1928 with the simple goal of spreading the gospel. By 1952 it had expanded its focus to include anti-Communism and counted among its allies Paul and Sylvia Crouch. Both spoke to churches under its auspices and provided the group information on the Communist menace. A second group, Christianform, was created by ministers and rabbis from across the nation as "an incorporated non-profit religious and educational organization for the defense of Christian form and civilization, founded . . . to work for the defeat of atheistic Communism." Named so as a counter to the Cominform, the Communist Information Bureau that succeeded the Comintern in 1947, the new organization arose in 1949 and, according to Crouch, who served on the board of advisors, attacked Communism on the basis of "Christian love and charity rather than hate." That love, he argued, won countless Communists away from the party and rehabilitated numerous former Communists struggling to overcome years of radical propaganda.[52] The group frequently compared those who joined the fight against Communism to David fighting Goliath, and various Christianform pamphlets and fliers depicted the globe with a cross, emblazoned with the phrase "In Hoc Signo Vinces" (by this sign you shall conquer), crushing and shattering a hammer and sickle.[53]

The June 1, 1954, volume of *For God and Freedom*, the organization's main publication, was dedicated entirely to defending Crouch and taking on his critics. In an article entitled "My Reply to the Alsops," Crouch attacked the Alsops, among others, for simply repeating the lies fed to them by the Communist press. He then repudiated everything he did as a Communist and argued that anything he said decades ago that contradicted his current testimony should be ignored. In his own words, "I leave it to the American people to decide whether it is Christian, decent and fair to attack the Paul Crouch of 1954 for what I did when my mind was enslaved by an ideology that gave me a completely false view of life and the world." Crouch continued by rejecting the "proof" that Oppenheimer was not at the meeting Crouch said he was at by claiming, wrongly, that the "proof" was a power bill. By that logic, he rationalized, he could prove he was in several different places at any one time thanks to his farm in North Carolina and his home in Hawaii. He also attacked those who wondered why he did not testify against Weinberg by saying, "I know of highly important confidential national security reasons why I do not believe it would have been in the best interests of the country to have presented the full testimony that I and other witnesses knew." He said he could not explain his reasons fully and would do so "publicly only if given unconditional authorization by the President of the United States." Crouch concluded his article by asserting that "the record shows that the campaign [against me] was planned with great care and daring imagination, that almost unlimited finances and political influences were employed in the conspiracy; and that the object was nothing less than the utter destruction of my good name and my place in society. Those who have been delivering one carefully planned blow after another in coordinated activities from coast to coast and in Hawaii, are soulless men using ruthless methods." Fortunately, he argued, "With the aid of my fellow members of The Christianform and 'Davids' everywhere fighting the Goliath of Communism, I do not stand alone."[54]

Crouch did not reserve this Christian rhetoric and symbolism for Christianform literature. He frequently invoked his faith while defending himself against the Crouch Appendix and various other attacks. Even more frequently he attacked the irreligion of Communism.

> Communism is a religion—an atheistic religion. It has an emotional grip on its followers, blinding them to reason and common sense. Outwardly, Communists usually look like other people, indistinguishable in dress and appearance from their neighbors. But they live in a mental world far removed from an average American as though they were people from Mars. They violently refuse to accept facts that conflict with their dogma. Like true fanatics, they refuse to believe any of the evidence about the realities of slave labor in the Soviet Union and the low standards of living there.[55]

The ideologue finally realized what he had been but failed to appreciate that he had traded one dogma for another.

Crouch went on to assert:

> The Communist religion holds out a Utopian promise of a better world in the future—after the world revolution. The followers of this strange atheistic religion are told that after world Soviet power is established there will be no more war, hunger, unemployment or any other evils of life. They even believe in the ultimate withering away of the state—believing that under Communism people will become so good and selfless that government will no longer be needed and that all courts and jails will be abolished. This has always been the core of Communism, based on its theories of the class struggle, armed insurrection, civil war and dictatorship. There is only one answer to the HATE of Communism. It is LOVE, the heart and foundation of all true religion.[56]

Crouch thus argued that the reason Communism had been successful was because people had failed to live their lives according to Christian faith. Man had become selfish and refused to help others, with the result that Communism found inroads.

To cure this ill, not only did he encourage people to turn to Jesus, he also tried to create the Federation of Former Communists to help people free themselves from Communist hate and to get them to appreciate Christian love. The group also sought to study totalitarian regimes and determine democratic answers to them, to focus attention on the struggle between totalitarian regimes and democracy, and to support those citizens who had joined the CPUSA but wanted out. In Crouch's words, its goal was "to promote and sponsor the study of political, social and economic problems arising out of ideological conflicts in the world and to develop and affect solutions to these problems, in cooperation with other patriotic citizens and organizations, based on loyalty to the American government and to our democratic institution."[57] Put another way, he hoped to institutionalize his new ideology as a means of overcoming his previous one. The effort failed, however, and the federation never came into being.[58]

Although the federation failed, Crouch never wavered in his defense of himself. He even took to television, and on July 22, 1954, appeared on the NBC *Today Show*. Political commentator Richard Harkness began by asking him to explain the apparent contradictions between his testimony in the Philadelphia Smith Act trials and the Harry Bridges trial. Crouch replied that the major charge against him was easily explained. He said it related to a man named Davis, whom he named as a Communist Party member in the Philadelphia trials. Crouch claimed that when he was first asked about Davis during the Bridges trial, he was given a vague description and as a result could not place him nor could he appreciate to whom the prosecution was referring. When he saw Davis at the trial in Philadelphia, he immediately recognized him, as he would have done had the Bridges' prosecution provided a picture. This instance of alleged fraud, he claimed, was nothing more than poor legal work.[59]

Harkness next asked Crouch about being a paid informant. Crouch took exception to the label and said while he was proud of helping the government protect the nation, he was not an informer or informant. He explained that he was simply a consultant like any other outside expert the government employed. He also asserted that he did not make much money from his employment and placed his pay at a mere $500 per month plus expenses.[60]

Harkness then moved to an obvious question when he asked, "You left the Communist Party in 1942 and went to the FBI in 1947. Does there not come a time when you have exhausted your knowledge of the Communist conspiracy?" "No indeed," Crouch responded. He explained that he had been in the Communist Party for seventeen years and had served as a "full time leading official" for fifteen years. During that time he had recruited hundreds of members and had attended thousands of meetings. He thus had a great deal of information, but some of it was buried amid his various experiences and was jogged free only when new people came forward. As with most people, he argued that he had a great deal of knowledge that was not always easily accessed but which events might recall. He followed up by alleging that he still had plenty of new information to offer the nation and would be busy for years naming names. He also vigorously defended his actions, again, and ended by saying he was proud of having convinced other former Communists to join the anti-Communist cause.[61]

Pleased with his appearance on television, Crouch continued to defend himself publicly and penned a lengthy article answering twenty-four specific charges against him. Entitled "Paul Crouch Replies to the Smear Attacks by Communists, Fellow Travelers, and others: The Facts about the charges against him and the reasons for these accusations," the article appeared in several major papers, including the *Washington Post*. Crouch also sent a copy to Attorney General Brownell. About the charges that he lied about Oppenheimer, Crouch explained that what he testified was true as evidenced by the corroborating testimony of his wife as well as others who knew what he said was true but did not testify. That he lied about the Keyserling case, Crouch replied that what he said was true and that Gilbert Parks (whose testimony contradicted his) was the liar. That he smeared Clifford and Virginia Durr in New Orleans, Crouch asserted that the testimony was true and they did subscribe to a Communist magazine. (He conveniently forgot, of course, that he also had accused them of being Communists.) Of the charges that he remained a Communist, Crouch wrote, "This is too absurd for serious consideration." After this extensive defense of his testimony, Crouch concluded that the smear attacks on him had cost $100,000 or more and asked, "Who is <u>behind</u> this character assassination conspiracy and put up the money for it? <u>This extraordinary conspiracy should be thoroughly exposed.</u>"[62]

Always there to support and defend her husband, Sylvia aided the effort when she participated in a "March to the Mike" radio program in which participants explained why they loved America. With no hint of irony, she explained that she was happy to live in a country where she could admit her past without fear. "I was once fooled by the party line. I said that in the Communist Party in the United States you are never really free. You cannot state your own thoughts. You always have to do what the party tells you to do." She went on to hope those behind the Iron Curtain would hear her voice "and would someday know freedom."[63]

As useful as were these media appearances, Crouch wanted a more concrete means of defending himself for posterity. Plus, he was low on money. To defend himself profitably he decided to sell his autobiography. Crouch knew of the other books by former Communists, including *I Led Three Lives* by Herbert Philbrick, *Witness*, by Whittaker Chambers, Louis Budenz's *This Is My Story*, *Men Without Faces: The Communist Conspiracy in the USA*, and *The Techniques of Communism*, as well as the serialized essays by Matthew Cvetic that were published in the *Saturday Evening Post* and later made into the radio series and movie *I Was A Communist for the FBI*. All of these works sold well, and Crouch desperately wanted the money, notoriety, and permanence that went with publishing a book. The bonus was that he had begun work on his life story years earlier.

In its final form of thirty-one chapters, "Broken Chains" laid out Crouch's life both inside and outside the Communist Party. He explained the book's agenda:

> For more than thirty years Soviet Communism has prepared for the eventual armed conflict with the democratic world—with the earth as the prize. That moment is now here, and the next ten years will determine the fate of humanity for centuries. From a military point of view the odds definitely are on the side of the Soviets. But that does not necessarily mean that they will win—not if we are ready for greater sacrifices than our ancestors at Valley Forge and if we understand the real character of our enemy.
>
> The military power of the Soviet world is tremendous. It has a hard shell, but a weak core. The millions of oppressed people in the satellite countries and above all the slave laborers in Russia itself are the greatest sources of danger to Stalin and his henchmen. The Soviet Union has built a fifth column inside every democratic country by clever ideological appeals and the strange emotional power of the world's first atheistic religion. And we cannot expect to deal effectively with those fifth columns unless we understand not only their methods of work but also study the invisible

> ideological chains through which the Kremlin holds it foreign agents in intellectual bondage.
>
> My own life story of how I became a Communist, my life in the Party for 17 years, and my eventual success in freeing myself from Moscow's grim fetters should provide many valuable lessons to those who seek to understand the true nature of the Soviet enemy. Such an understanding is absolutely essential if a free America and the democracy and personal freedoms it represents are to endure.[64]

Despite that purpose, Crouch had little success selling the manuscript, which now sits in the Hoover Institution for War and Peace archives at Stanford University. T. O'Conor Sloane III, editor of the Devin-Adir Company Publishers, wrote Crouch that the company wanted to publish his book but "the market for books by former Communists is simply finished, and unless a perfectly staggering piece of revelation were to come along there just won't be any sale. Your book has some tremendous things in it—but I am not quite staggered." Crouch received similar bad news from Duquesne University Press when it rejected his book for publication. The press informed him that they did not think it would sell well without much revision and they could not offer him a contract before such revision.[65]

Undaunted by this literary failure, as well as the attacks on him and the disappearance of his revenue stream, Crouch remained devoted to the anti-Communist cause as 1954 came to a close. He even created a list of people he claimed to know as Communist Party members. The "Names of Members of the Communist Party" listed some 400 people "limited exclusively to those I have personally known as members of the Communist party. I can identify all as having been members of the Communist party under strict rules of evidence. I have seen all of them in closed party meetings or they have told me that they belonged to the party." He added, "However, this is not a complete list of such personal acquaintances and will be supplimented [*sic*] from time to time. . . . In this list I have not included hundreds of others I knew to have been party members through their correspondence with me, through reports at party committees, from party minutes and other authentic sources, as such information might be questioned under strict application of rules of evidence in court proceedings."[66]

Despite that effort, and indeed all he did in 1954 to try to maintain his standing as an informant, the government was done with him. Although Attorney General Brownell announced in February 1955 that he "had no reason to believe that Paul Crouch . . . ever gave false testimony," William Tompkins, the chief of the Justice Department's Internal Security Division, recommended that Brownell no longer use Crouch "unless his testimony is essential to successful prosecution and your prior approval has been obtained."[67] Crouch's career as an informant was thus over. He refused to concede the point, however, and throughout 1955 fought to recover his good name, to convince the nation that the Communist threat remained, and to prove that he and the other former Communist informants were the only ones who could save the nation. The ideologue, in other words, remained.

12 "A LONELY AND DESPISED MAN," 1955 AND BEYOND

As 1955 dawned and the attacks on him continued, Crouch fought back as best as he could. Refusing to admit that he was wrong, and with his lawsuits against the Alsops and the *Daily Worker* dragging through the courts, he continued his public relations efforts to defend himself and his beliefs. Despite those efforts, he physically disappeared from the scene, moving, ironically enough, to Hawaii where his career as a Communist began. As the year wore on and the Red Scare began to dissipate, however, his defenses floundered. So too did his health, and he would not live out the year. Despite that, Crouch never once publicly questioned his ideology, and he remained an ardent anti-Communist to the bitter end.

As Crouch continued to defend himself from personal attacks, he also took the opportunity to defend his fellow informants as the new year dawned. As a part of that, on February 7, 1955, he weighed in on the Matusow affair. Harvey Matusow joined the U.S. Army at age eighteen in 1944 and the CPUSA in 1947 at the age of twenty. Commonly regarded within the Communist Party as a liar and a thief, he remained an active if not influential member until 1949.[1] Disillusioned, he considered simply quitting, but instead went to the FBI. Under bureau guidance, he remained in the party for two more years as an active undercover agent.

Eventually Matusow was expelled from the Communist Party, but in 1952 he gained his revenge when he made his first public appearance to testify at the federal trial of thirteen party leaders charged with Smith Act violations. The thirteen were convicted, in part thanks to his 700 pages of testimony, and that success enabled him to live for the next two years as a paid informant. According to his own recollections he testified in twenty-five trials and hearings and named 180 people as active or former Communists.[2] He supplemented his income by speaking and writing about the Communist menace.

As a result of his efforts, Matusow, like Crouch, was the subject of journalistic attacks and charges of perjury. Crouch was outraged at these attacks, and in 1955 he came out swinging, as much to defend himself and the entire informer system as to defend Matusow. He began by claiming the attacks on Matusow were "the culmination of a well planned and highly organized character assassination against ex-Communist government witnesses for almost one year, in which I was selected as the first and major individual target." He then defended himself from the various charges and asserted that by continually using him in judicial proceedings the FBI had intimated that the charges against him were false, even if it never formally came out in his defense. He then lamented that the FBI had not done more to defend him and warned that such a weak effort undermined the bureau and threatened its ability to fight Communism. (Crouch, of course, remained unaware that the FBI and the Justice Department already had determined to cease using him.) He concluded by warning Congress that the same dangers arose from the attack on Matusow and asserted, "The bizarre Matusow affair certainly should show the need of presenting the facts about ex-Communists and their testimony to the country. If the facts and all the facts are not presented our country will be made safe for future Alger Hisses, and for future Rosenbergs—through sealing the lips of potential witnesses."[3]

Unfortunately for Crouch the facts about Matusow soon came out, and they were not good for him, the government, or the informer system. On February 28, 1955, Matusow testified before the Senate Subcommittee to Investigate the Administration of the Internal Security Act and Other Internal Security Laws. During his testimony he claimed to know Crouch "quite well" through their shared efforts to create the Federation of Former Communists. When asked what he thought about Crouch, Matusow said, "I know Paul Crouch. I know he is a liar." When challenged, Matusow reiterated, "I know him well enough. I have talked to him enough. I know he is a liar."[4]

In March things got even worse when Matusow published *False Witness*, a memoir in which he claimed to have given perjured testimony throughout his time as a government witness. More damningly, he claimed that Senator McCarthy knew he had lied and actively encouraged him to do so. In a subsequent statement either meant to exonerate himself or publicly rebuke Crouch, Matusow also explained that he become an informant because he wanted to be a hero and labeled among the heroic types he envied—Paul Crouch. As a result of his admission to perjury, Matusow was arrested, convicted, and sentenced to five years in prison.[5] Crouch faced no jail time for his alleged lies, at least not yet, but Matusow's admission and his inclusion of Crouch in that confession did not bode well.

Frustrated by Matusow's admissions, and confronted by the continued attacks on his own merit, Crouch became ever more determined to defend himself. After television host Drew Pearson spoke on KULA (ABC) radio in March 1955 and accused Crouch of lying twenty-eight times, Crouch demanded an apology. When none was forthcoming, he informed Pearson that he was willing to participate in a joint television presentation as long as Pearson provided him the opportunity to give a fair accounting. He informed Pearson that he had no plans to be in the east any time soon, but he would get there when he could and would willingly go on the air. Despite demanding an apology and air time, Crouch also took a swipe at the media personality whom he criticized for presenting a biased and one-sided examination of the anti-Communist forces.[6]

Pearson ignored the criticism and accepted the offer, but Crouch proved unable to comply. In May he wrote to explain that illness prevented him from traveling. His doctors, he stated, had warned him from flying, but he assured Pearson that as soon as he was healthy he would fly east and meet the challenge. At the same time, Crouch demonstrated that the attacks on him were continuing to take a toll, as he asked Pearson to provide him a list of the specific charges against him so he could prepare for the talk.[7] Never before had Crouch made such a request, and usually he was well aware of the charges. Illness, however, was beginning to sap his mental and physical powers.

Ailing, stuck in Hawaii, and unable to defend himself, Crouch was open season, and the attacks continued. In May 1955 *Harper's Magazine* writer Richard Rovere published a scathing article on "professional witnesses," including Crouch. Rovere noted that Crouch and the other eighty-two "kept informants" of the INS, all of whom were self-identified Communists, were employed as "expert consultants" to name names, identify people as Communists, describe Communist activity, and interpret Communist doctrines.[8] He went on, "Fortunately relieved of any accountability for . . . their past, they play a crucial role in determining who is and who is not of sufficient uprightness to work for the United States government." Specifically, he labeled them "the key figures in the field of loyalty and security clearance." What made all of this truly dangerous was that these "men and women . . . are themselves—almost alone in the whole teeming structure of the federal bureaucracy—exempt from the need for clearance. More than that, they compose a group whose individual members would have almost no chance of getting clearance if it were required of them."[9]

Rovere then used Crouch, and his "convenient memory," to serve as a specific example of the type of people on whom the government was relying. He noted the countless hearings during which Crouch never mentioned Jacob Burck, only to remember him after Burck found himself at a deportation hearing. He related the well-known stories of Crouch's flip-flop on David Davis, his evolving memory of Armand Scala, and his sudden recollection of meeting Georgi Malenkov. Rovere offered Crouch some sympathy, noting that "the memory is notoriously the most vagrant of human facilities," although he added that "there are few cases on record of a bent for mnemonic topicality as powerful as that revealed by Paul Crouch." He further conceded that "it may well be that Crouch was, as he presently insists, testifying to the best of his recollection on each specific case," but he concluded that Crouch was a liar who had tainted all former Communist informants.[10]

Rovere ultimately called on the federal government to cease using paid informants, asserting, "In the Department of Justice . . . success is quantitatively measured. It has been customary in this country to take what steps we can to prevent quantitative measurement of truth. The use of professional witnesses, though it may be warranted by many present needs, should at least be recognized as a step in the other direction." Worse, paid informants had affected federal policy, "not through appeals to public opinion but through direct appeals to the governing powers." The result, he concluded, was that "the kept witnesses have been given an opportunity to foul American due process and quite a bit else besides." The perfect example of this fouling was the Army-McCarthy hearing which "uncovered not a single Communist but did incredible harm not only to government research but to the government's relationship with the whole scientific community."[11]

By the time Rovere's diatribe was published, the combined failures of Crouch, Matusow and other former Communist informants, as well as the mounting journalistic critiques, had convinced the Justice Department that the informer system was problematic. On April 15, 1955, Attorney General Brownell announced that the government would no longer employ full-time Communist "consultants." Instead, individuals would be hired as "experts" and employed only as needed. Brownell claimed the new system would help avoid the appearance that the "consultant" was a government employee, a confusion Crouch had tried very hard to foster.[12]

Rovere's attack and the Justice Department's decision had only a minimal impact on Crouch, and by this point he was only a shell of his former self. On April 28, 1955, he informed Senator James Eastland that he was ill, required an extended stay in the hospital, and would be unavailable for testimony in the near future. He explained specifically that he had a spot on his lung and that "the current critical condition was unquestionably brought on by incredible and unbelievable hardships over a period of many months." Rather than accept some of the responsibility for those hardships, Crouch demonstrated that his ideology remained firm as he blamed "the powerful long arm of Soviet vengeance" for his illness and his recent failures and asserted that the Soviets had somehow "reach[ed] into our government and into the Justice Dept. itself to destroy and crush a much hated victim." He additionally blamed Harvey Matusow for exacerbating the situation with his "repeated false attacks and slanders" and assured the senator that before he became sick he had planned to rebut the charges by asking Congress to call him to the stand.[13] Apparently realizing the end was near, however, Crouch had no plans to make that request in the future.

Crouch's illness progressed rapidly, and on July 5, 1955, Sylvia informed the FBI that he was in the hospital and was about to undergo an operation on his lung that might result in its removal. She informed the bureau that he would not be able to offer his assistance in the near future. To make up for that loss, and probably in hopes of receiving some financial considerations, she offered the FBI information to help it fight "the current Communist and leftist smear attacks."[14] That information, however, turned out to be a simple chronology of Crouch's testimony and a list of the attacks on him for that testimony. She provided little new evidence to the bureau.

Two days later Sylvia reported back to the FBI that the surgery found cancer in Paul's bronchial tubes and windpipe. The disease was widespread and terminal, and the doctors had determined not to remove the lung. Crouch accepted his fate, she informed the FBI, but expressed as his last wish that his name be cleared. She lamented that "Paul has tried so hard to make amends for his communist past, and to help the country expose and fight the communists. . . . It will be a terrible crime for him to have to die feeling that the country has turned against him for his efforts."[15] She begged the FBI to do what it could to resuscitate his image.

Two weeks later Sylvia wrote a letter to James Larkin Pearson in which she further recounted Crouch's recent prognosis. She related that Crouch had a four-and-a-half-hour surgery on July 6, 1955, in the hospital in Hilo, Hawaii. Afterward, the doctors explained that he had only a few months to live, news which Paul "took . . . very calmly." She assured Pearson that Crouch was "determined not to accept defeat in advance" and offered a glimmer of hope noting that doctors suggested he go to the mainland for better treatment. She also reiterated Crouch's earlier assessment of his illness and claimed that "it was the past year of great stress due to the communist and leftist inspired vicious smear campaign that lead [*sic*] to the extremely rapid extension and spread of cancer. . . . The communists, Alsop brothers, Drew Pearson and their associates are fully responsible for Paul's present precarious condition."[16]

As Crouch moved to the University of California medical center for treatment, and news of his illness began to spread, some of his enemies took the opportunity to engage in some unfortunate schadenfreude. An unnamed letter writer from Portland, Oregon, penned this to Crouch in September 1955: "Your cancerous and ganghrened [*sic*] heart were [*sic*] abhorrent to all decent people. . . . It is a pleasure to know you are there in the condition you are in, knowing that Mr. Death is slowly drawing nearer. I have never believed there was a Hell as describing [*sic*] in the Bible but I really think there should be one for you. . . . Well Crouch, go ahead and die slowly and painfully."[17] Crouch wrote a return letter in which he called the person a coward and a Communist and defended all his testimony as truthful. He wrote that he had no regrets for serving his country, only for the time he spent as a Communist. He said he knew he had done a great deal of damage in his seventeen years as a party member and hoped his testimony made up for it. He then criticized the writer for preaching hate and concluded by urging him to seek love by reading the Bible and finding Jesus.[18]

Most correspondents responded with sympathy. In November 1955 longtime supporter Ellis Rubin sent a letter to Crouch's daughter Tanya Hartley, who was then living in San Francisco. He asked her for information to exonerate Crouch, which he hoped to put together for a story in the *Miami Herald*. Rubin specifically requested a copy of the Crouch Appendix, all the testimony given by Crouch (in order to refute the appendix), information on the lawsuits, and information on the Justice Department's investigation of Crouch's reliability. Rubin admitted, "I realize that the above request is a big order but it may be our only chance to . . . tell the whole truth. I must have answers immediately as the first article is tentivly [*sic*] scheduled for the end of next week." He further assured her, "If any money is realized I have given instructions that all checks are to be made out to Sylvia Crouch."[19]

Despite such support and the best efforts of his doctors, Paul Crouch died on November 18, 1955, at the University of California Hospital. On November 26 he was buried in the Oak Ridge Baptist Church cemetery in Hays, North Carolina, beside his parents and his son Carl, and only fifteen miles from where he was born. His passing marked the end of his lawsuits against the *Daily Worker* and the *New York Herald Tribune* and also relieved the FBI and Justice Department of having to go through another Matusow affair. As Cedric Belfrage notes, Crouch's death "eased the inquisition's task of tidying up after familiars [Belfrage's term for former Communist informants] who marred its image." Despite the family's despair, in other words, for many the passing of Crouch was a relief. Indeed, both the *Journal Patriot* and the *North Wilkesboro Hustler*, the newspapers from Crouch's hometown, buried the news of his death and offered simple obituaries that noted his biography but avoided detailed coverage of his controversial testimony.[20]

Few national media outlets bothered to cover Crouch's death, although the *Daily Worker* did. In a brief article buried deep in the paper, the Communist organ took a parting shot noting, "Paul Crouch, Justice Department stool-pigeon, died Friday." *I. F. Stone's Weekly* took a more thoughtful approach. Ironically, it was Clifford Durr who penned the obituary, in which he was rather kind. While taking a few shots at Crouch's lies and fabrications as an informant, Durr's real object was to take on the politicians who used Crouch for their own political gains. He asserted, "Because he served their purpose, they sheltered and guarded him and paid him in the taxpayer's money and in fame. They sanctified his words with their benediction of their own exalted positions and, lest the truth of his words be challenged, they wrapped him in the mantle of the Government's own immunity." As much as Durr clearly loathed Crouch, his animus for the politicians was even greater: "Crouch did just what he was hired to do, and whatever may be said about him, he gave his employers full value of what they wanted of him. . . . [Crouch was] not the source of the evil, but its mere conduit. Crouch did what he was hired to do. . . . He died a lonely and despised man by those who used him, but those who used him remain in respectable and powerful positions. They used him, and when he was no longer of any use to them, they threw him aside." That these politicians knew Crouch was lying Durr had no doubt, and he argued, as had others, that Crouch gave them a second gift by dying before he, and they, faced any real accounting for those lies.[21]

Sylvia, of course, was not interested in such accounting and was distraught by Paul's death. Not only did she lose her husband of thirty years, she also lost whatever earning potential he still had. Devastated, she settled in San Francisco, not far from her daughter Tanya and her family, and lamented her lot. She eventually roused herself, and in an effort to survive she carried on the family tradition and offered the occasional testimony to federal officials. On January 7, 1958, she was deposed by the Florida Legislative Investigation Committee about Communism. She offered a brief biographical background and then described her life with Paul in and out of the Communist Party. She also explained that the party remained a threat because members did not believe in the possibility of a peaceful revolution and accepted that violence would be necessary to bring about a Communist state. She reiterated Paul's earlier claims that the SCHW was simply a front for the CPUSA, that the Highlander Folk School was closely associated with Communists, and that the party had attempted to infiltrate groups such as the NAACP, ACLU, the League of Women Voters, various veterans groups, and countless other organizations. The insidious nature of the Communists, she hinted, was what made them so dangerous. She concluded her deposition by naming names.[22]

Such testimony was rare, however, and for all intents and purposes Sylvia was left penniless. In desperation she looked for money in odd places. According to Virginia Durr, she "wrote Aubrey Williams a letter from Hawaii, if you can believe this. Mrs. Crouch wrote Aubrey Williams a letter from Hawaii that her husband . . . had had nothing personal against Aubrey. She said he'd always admired Aubrey very much and thought he was a fine person and he was glad to have it cleared up that Aubrey had never been a Communist. She asked if Aubrey would send some money because . . . they need money. I think Aubrey sent twenty-five dollars or so. Aubrey's attitude was, the poor devil. He was a strange man, Aubrey was. Cliff got angry, but Aubrey just had tremendous pity for people."[23] Thanks to such funding, as well as the support of her family, Sylvia managed to eke out a living as the Red Scare faded and the memory of Paul's efforts dissipated. She settled into a decidedly apolitical existence and eventually moved to San Antonio, Texas, where she died on January 12, 1992.

History, of course, waits for no one, and as Sylvia floundered in a world without Paul, the national and international situations changed dramatically. One wonders what Crouch would have made of that future. The anti-Communist efforts, combined with the generally conservative attitude of the country in the 1950s, undermined the CPUSA's popularity and ability to operate. Infighting also hurt its efforts. As Los Angeles area Communist Party leader Dorothy Healey later explained: "We did almost as much damage to ourselves . . . as Joe McCarthy and J. Edgar Hoover and all the other witch-hunters combined."[24] From a peak of 75,000 to 85,000 members in 1945, the party collapsed to only 3,000 members by 1960. Although he facilitated its decline, Crouch did not live to see its relative disappearance. Neither did he live to see the end of McCarthyism. Although he saw McCarthy censured by the Senate on December 2, 1954, he did not live to see him die in relative obscurity on May 2, 1957, a victim of alcoholism. While McCarthy's name subsequently became synonymous with excess and political overreach, those who had supported or empowered him quietly distanced themselves from his legacy. Without McCarthy as its guiding force, and without the CPUSA as an enemy to attack, the Red Scare soon abated. Its end was yet one final domestic development Crouch did not live to see.

Crouch also failed to see Nikita Khrushchev's 1956 secret speech in which he admitted to Stalin's crimes, only to then invade Hungary to put down an anti-Communist rebellion. Crouch might well have felt vindicated by the Soviet invasion, as well as by Sputnik, Castro's 1959 seizure of power in Cuba, the erection of the Berlin Wall, or the Cuban Missile Crisis. The events in Cuba may have been especially heartening, considering his numerous assertions that Communists sought to infiltrate Latin America.

While Crouch very well may have seen these events as justification for his ideological conversion, much of what he warned against was the danger of domestic Communism and the threat posed by American Communists. It is hard to see any vindication here. While his track record in finding Communists was better than McCarthy's, the collateral damage was extreme. From the perspective of sixty years hence, many historians now view the entire era as a travesty. David Caute contends that, "There is no documentation in the public record of a direct connection between the American Communist Party and espionage during the entire post war period. Even during the Korean War, no evidence of Communist sabotage or attempted sabotage came to light." According to Theodore Draper, "Except for a tiny minority, the Communist membership . . . devoted its efforts to gaining mass influence with means that have been blatantly non-conspiratorial."[25]

Since the release of the Venona transcripts in 1995, the debate about the true nature of the Communist threat has become more balanced but no more clear. John Earl Haynes and Harvey Klehr contend that the Venona transcripts prove there were at least 349 Americans, immigrants, or permanent residents who "had a covert relationship with Soviet intelligence agencies." Victor Navasky rejects the argument that all 349 were spies and asserts, "The reader is left with the implication—unfair and unproven—that every name on the list was involved in espionage, and as a result, otherwise careful historians and mainstream journalists now routinely refer to VENONA as proof that many hundreds of Americans were part of the red spy network." Navasky also asserts that the few who were spies transferred little classified information to the Soviets and notes that some of the exchange was part of the normal flow of ideas between scientists, especially Allied scientists who were unified in their war with the Nazis. Ellen Schrecker agrees with Navasky that Venona, while a useful tool, does not prove espionage on the level that Haynes and Klehr assert.[26] Historians thus remain divided on the actual threat the CPUSA posed to the nation.

A look from the legal perspective proves a bit more illuminating. In 1955 Chief Justice of the Supreme Court Earl Warren weighed in on the Red Scare and asserted that in the current state of affairs the public probably would reject the Bill of Rights. Although merely opinion, his standing gives it some heft. More important, Warren would oversee a number of cases that sought to reclaim the Bill of Rights and turn back the worst abuses of the era. In 1957 the court ruled in the case of Clayton Jenkes. In 1954 Jenkes, an organizer for the International Union of Mine, Mill, and Smelter Workers, was accused of perjury for denying membership in the CPUSA. Matusow testified at his trial and claimed that the union planned to call a strike in the copper industry as a means of undermining the American effort in the Korean War. He also asserted that Jenkes was a member of the CPUSA and that he played a role in calling the strike. Jenkes' lawyers requested the right to review Matusow's FBI file as they prepared for cross-examination, but the court refused.

Unable to counter Matusow's claim or question his competency to make such claims, the defense had little to go on, and Jenkes was convicted and sentenced to five years in jail. His lawyers appealed, and the case slowly made its way through the federal court system. When the Supreme Court heard the case it upheld the appeal and, in a 7–1 decision, not only ordered Jenkes retried but asserted that his defense lawyers had the right to examine Matusow's FBI files. As Ellen Schrecker notes, "Although the decision actually opened few Bureau files, it was, nonetheless, a stunning reassertion of the rights of individual defendants in the face of the government's claim that national security would brook no restrictions on the FBI." This helped put an end to the informer system once and for all as the informants were now subject to real scrutiny.[27]

Then came Red Monday, June 17, 1957, when the Court handed down three separate rulings. In the *Watkins v. United States* case it dismissed a

HUAC contempt citation claiming the questions the defendant refused to answer were irrelevant; in *Sweezy v. New Hampshire* it did the same in a state case; and with the *Yates v. United States* case the court fundamentally voided the Smith Act. The Yates case dealt with fourteen California-based Communists who had been convicted under the Smith Act for advocating the overthrow of the government. The Supreme Court ruled that simple advocacy was not illegal. Justice John Marshall Harlan spoke for the majority and said that "those to whom the advocacy is addressed must be urged to do something, now or in the future, rather than merely to believe in something."[28] In other words, to be convicted under the Smith Act people had to urge others actively to overthrow the government or had to actively attempt to do so themselves; supporting such an overthrow or simply debating the merits of it was not illegal.

As a result of the decision, five of the Yates defendants were freed while the other nine had their cases sent back to lower courts where they were dismissed within the year. Although elements of the Smith Act remained, the court clearly took a major stand against the worst abuses of the Red Scare era. To be fair, the entire judicial system seemed to work as it should throughout the era. By 1957 there had been 145 indictments under the Smith Act with 108 convictions worth 418 years in jail and $435,500 in fines. After appeals, only twenty-eight of those so convicted ever spent any real time in jail.[29]

The numbers, of course, are deceptive as they do not count those charged with perjury or other crimes, as well as those whose lives were destroyed by the simple accusations of former Communist informants. Added to the personal costs are the financial costs. The *Cleveland Press* determined that 6,000 FBI agents (nearly half the entire force), 1,859 Justice Department agents, 22,059 military personnel, 16,000 treasury agents, and an additional 7,300 individuals from agencies such as the AEC, the Labor Department, and the General Accounting Office participated in the hunt for Communists. Yale Law School professor Ralph Brown claimed that in 1955 alone eighteen million individuals faced loyalty tests, at a cost of $37.4 million. Additionally, between 1952 and 1954 the Department of Justice had eighty-three ex-Communists on the payroll, of whom thirty were "regularly used as witnesses" and fifty-three were "occasionally used." Most were paid a minimum of $34 a day—$25 for their services and $9 "in lieu of expenses"—while others, like Crouch, received substantially more. Despite the expense of these informants, few of them, other than Bentley and Chambers, had any real information. Most of what they did was provide background information on Communists and Communism.[30]

While such figures boggle the mind, what we cannot account is the damage these individuals did to the nation. M. J. Heale writes, "Not only did such witnesses persuade the courts that the CP was a tightly organized criminal conspiracy, as they testified before congressional committees and television cameras an indelible impression was created in the public mind of an amoral and ruthless force single-mindedly bent on destroying American institutions." Any effort to challenge that image was overwhelmed because, as Ellen Schrecker contends, the former Communist informant "came to dominate the national debate about domestic Communism, shaping the ideas that . . . Americans, as well as politicians, held about Communism." These individuals, in other words, were key players in pushing forward the Red Scare paranoia. By their very words and actions they ensured public panic, which they and the politicians who supported them used for their own benefit. Worse, according to historians Robert Lichtman and Ronald Cohen, the Justice Department repeatedly used informants it knew were lying because of the political benefits of continuing the Red Scare.[31] The era thus benefitted the informants, the military industrial complex, the politicians and pundits, and the countless anti-Communist agencies, but it devastated those individuals caught in the wheels of the anti-Communist machine and otherwise petrified the innocent American public.

The impact of the era went beyond the paranoia and destruction of innocents. It also sidetracked the nation from other pressing domestic issues. The incipient Civil Rights Movement, the emergent Feminist struggle, the growing concerns about the youth culture, and the worries over conformity, poverty, and sexual liberation were at least partially ignored or undermined as the threat of Communism overrode nearly everything else. Foreign policy also suffered. As historians Thomas Laird, David Mayers, and others make clear, America's focus on domestic Communism fatefully colored the nation's understanding of developments in Korea and Vietnam, leading it to follow a flawed course with both countries. Similarly, instead of exploiting the differences between Chinese and Soviet Communism, American politicians lumped all Communists together as the enemy who needed to be destroyed.[32] Even Soviet expert George Kennan grew frustrated as the nation largely misunderstood his famous *Long Telegram* and "Mr. X" studies of why the Russians expanded and how best to prevent them from continuing to expand. In other words, our national myopia, made worse by the Red Scare and McCarthyism, only led us to fight the Cold War poorly.

So where did these informants come from and how were they able to affect national policy so forcefully? Thousands spent some time in the Communist Party, yet very few acted as witnesses, and even fewer reached the levels of importance, or infamy, of Crouch. In answer to the question "Whence come the fanatics?" Eric Hoffer explains:

> Whence come the fanatics? Mostly from the ranks of the non-creative men of words. The most significant division of men of words is between those who can find fulfillment in creative work and those who cannot. The creative man of words, no matter how bitterly he may criticize and deride the existing order is actually attached to the present. . . . The man who wants to write a great book, paint a great picture, create an architectural masterpiece, become a great scientist, and knows that never in all eternity will he be able to realize this, his innermost desire, can find no peace in a stable social order—old or new. He sees his life as irrevocably spoiled and the world perpetually out of joint. He feels at home only in a state of chaos.[33]

Herbert Packer agrees and contends that most informants were unstable personalities "with a tendency to go to extremes." He also calls them "true believers," which explains their ability to appear confident even when lying.[34]

According to David Caute, the informers achieved such importance because of their pretended "encyclopedic knowledge of the Communist movement across the face of a vast country." Equally important, they played the game well, and "on a nod from prosecutors, they sold hunches or guesses as inside knowledge, supporting their claims with bogus reports of conversations and encounters."[35] Ellen Schrecker agrees and contends that the informants were "disproportionately influential in shaping the political repression of the McCarthy period" because "they selected its targets and developed the mechanisms through which the repression operated. Even more importantly, because they were considered the nation's leading experts on the subject, they came to dominate the national debate about domestic Communism, shaping the ideas that most ordinary Americans, as well as politicians, held about Communism." She further asserts, as has been previously noted, that the nation accepted them as the final arbiters of who was a Communist and who was not because "only they could identify someone as a party member and only they could discuss the inner workings of the CP." She even quotes the chief counsel of the SISS who explained, "When civilization is in mortal danger, the ex-Communist is one of the most valuable members of society."[36] So fearful was the nation that it turned all responsibility for determining who the threat was to those who used to be part of that threat.

All of this describes Crouch, both the Communist and the anti-Communist. He certainly was a fanatic—an ideologue who thought himself a man of letters, but was unsuccessful, unfulfilled, and uncreative, except when describing the threat posed by either capitalism or Communism. His literary and journalistic efforts were mundane at best but fit in perfectly with what Communist Party leaders and the downtrodden, or politicians and juries, wanted to hear. To have seen his stories in the movies or to have read them in books would have been to consume the contrived and unbelievable. But the tales seemed perfectly acceptable when told to those workers who felt exploited by management or those citizens who feared that the American way of life was threatened by global Communism. According to Cedric Belfrage, the reason for that acceptance was that "Crouch's sense of melodrama rivaled that of [Elizabeth] Bentley."[37] As a Communist and an anti-Communist, Crouch knew how to play to the crowd, and he built on the fear of those who worried about their present and future.

Crouch also was a man of extremes, going from seventeen years as a devout Communist to seven years as a devout anti-Communist and capitalist. Similarly, he was extremely self-confident; one who, from all accounts, could tell his lies to workers, party members, judges, and politicians with a straight face and respond similarly when confronted with evidence of those lies. While some may call him an actor, it seems more likely that he simply believed so firmly in his immediate ideological incarnation that he did not believe he was lying. Whatever the truth, he exuded an authority that led people to believe him long after his lies should have become obvious. And finally, he was astute enough to perceive the body language or linguistic subtleties of Communist Party leaders, workers, politicians, and lawyers, and was shrewd enough to mold his rhetoric or testimony to what was required at the moment. He could shift his beliefs along with the needs of international Communism and shift his stories to meet the needs of domestic anti-Communism.

In other words, Crouch seems to be the perfect definition of an ideologue. The immediate facts or concepts were largely irrelevant to the larger cause. Whether it was Communism or anti-Communism, whatever he believed he believed to the depth of his heart and anyone or anything that opposed him was not simply wrong but evil and dangerous.

Despite all that, his true impact on the nation was minimal if by no other measure than that no one before has found him worthy of detailed study. But as a symbol of the era he certainly is exemplary. Like millions of Americans, he felt displaced by modernity and the industrialization of the early twentieth century. Buffeted by the social, economic, political, and international vagaries of the era, he joined thousands of others who turned to the Communist Party in hopes of finding themselves and solving the nation's ills. As a Communist, he, like most who joined, quickly learned the power the Soviets had over the American party and came to appreciate that foreign needs often dominated local and national concerns.

Unlike most members, Crouch put up with that reality, as well as the ever shifting Communist Party line, for seventeen years. Eventually, however, he followed most who had preceded him and quit the movement in disgust. Unfortunately, he then found himself amid a world of drastic change as the end of World War II saw massive population shifts, economic turmoil, and the onset of the Cold War. Adrift in this whirlwind of change, Crouch only found his rudder when he joined the growing ranks of ex-Communist informants. Relying on the government's insatiable need for information, the public's often irrational fear of Communism, and the morally questionable efforts of Senator McCarthy, Crouch entered the elite ranks of informants. He thus helped push forward this era of fear, and he even came to justify deceit as a legitimate tool in the struggle against domestic Communism. Ultimately discarded once that deceit became a liability, he died a broken and lonely man.

Throughout his life Paul Crouch was used by forces larger than himself; forces in which he believed, but over which he had little control and only a minimal understanding. He was not a dangerous man. He was a tool of dangerous men, however, and he serves as a clear warning of the dangers that ensue when ideology begets paranoia, paranoia begets fear, and fear leads individuals, organizations, and governments to dehumanize, attack, and destroy *them*.

NOTES

Introduction: The Most Dangerous Man in America

1. Wheen, *Strange Days Indeed*, 96.

2. Hofstader, *The Paranoid Style in American Politics and Other Essays*, 29–30.

3. Lerner quoted in Wheen, *Strange Days Indeed*, 299.

4. Ceplair, *Anti-Communism in Twentieth-Century America*, 132; Budenz, *This Is My Story*.

5. Kessler, *Clever Girl*; Olmsted, *Red Spy Queen*; Bentley, *Out of Bondage*.

6. Chambers, *Witness*, 191.

7. Lichtman and Cohen, *Deadly Farce*; Matusow, *False Witness*.

8. Brown, *Standing against Dragons*, 121; Fariello, *Red Scare*, 98n2; Schrecker, *No Ivory Tower*, 145; Caute, *The Great Fear*, 126; Lichtenstein, "Putting Labor's House in Order," 7.

Chapter 1. Childhood and Youth, 1903–1924

1. "The Carolina mountains are a long way back," Paul Crouch Papers, Box 1, Hoover Institution Archives. Walker and several dozen American mercenaries took control of the country, and Walker briefly declared himself president. They were forced from the country in 1857.

2. Gilmore, *Defying Dixie*, 72.

3. "The Carolina mountains are a long way back," Paul Crouch Papers, Box 1, Hoover Institution Archives.

4. Ibid.

5. "I learn realities from life," Paul Crouch Papers, Box 1, Hoover Institution Archives.

6. "The Carolina mountains are a long way back," Paul Crouch Papers, Box 1, Hoover Institution Archives.

7. The Anarchist Fighters, "Plain Words," June 2, 1919.

8. "I learn from experience," Paul Crouch Papers, Box 1, Hoover Institution Archives.

9. *Journal Patriot*, November 21, 1955; "I learn from experience," Paul Crouch Papers, Box 1, Hoover Institution Archives.

10. "The Enchanted Mountain," Paul Crouch Papers, James Larkin Pearson Library.

11. "I try my hand at textiles," Paul Crouch Papers, Box 1, Hoover Institution Archives.

12. Ibid; "Indians and Spanish blood and printer's ink," Paul Crouch Papers, Box 1, Hoover Institution Archives.

13. *Pearson's Paper*, March 1923.

14. Ibid., May 1923.

15. Ibid., June 1923.

16. Ibid.

17. Gilmore, *Defying Dixie*, 73.

18. "I try my hand at textiles," Paul Crouch Papers, Box 1, Hoover Institution Archives; *Testimony of Paul Crouch*, HUAC, May 6, 1949, 184.

19. "I join the army with the pacific isles in mind," Paul Crouch Papers, Box 1, Hoover Institution Archives; "Broken Chains," Paul Crouch Papers, Box 17, Hoover Institution Archives.

Chapter 2. The Hawaiian Communist League, 1924–1927

1. "Over many trails in paradise," Paul Crouch Papers, Box 1, Hoover Institution Archives.

2. U.S. Military Intelligence Reports, *Surveillance of Radicals in the United States, 1917–1941*, Reel 21; "Court martial—and an appalling sentence," Paul Crouch Papers, Box 1, Hoover Institution Archives.

3. Reinecke, *The Filipino Piecemeal Sugar Strike*, 4, 78, 83.

4. *Honolulu Advertiser*, March 24, 1925.

5. Ibid., March 27 and 29, 1925; *New York Times*, August 10, 1939. Van Gelder served part of his term in Alcatraz before being transferred to the Atlanta Penitentiary. In 1934, after he had served nearly ten years, President Franklin Roosevelt commuted the sentence. Although free, Van Gelder was unable to set his life straight. Two years after his release he was convicted of passing counterfeit money and served two years in the federal penitentiary in Lewisburg, Pennsylvania. This second stint in prison did nothing to rehabilitate Van Gelder who moved to New York City upon his release. On July 29, 1938, he confronted stationary store worker Edgar Loebl with what later turned out to be a toy gun. Van Gelder bound and gagged Loebl and robbed the store of forty dollars. The next day Loebl fingered Van Gelder, whom New York City police quickly rounded up. In 1939 he pled guilty to armed robbery and was sentenced to five to ten years in Sing Sing Prison.

6. *Honolulu Advertiser*, February 12 and 15, 1925.

7. Ibid., February 16, 1925.

8. Ibid., February 18, 1925.

9. "Letter from Fred Creque, March 5, 1925," Paul Crouch Letters, James Larkin Pearson Correspondence; *Daily Worker*, May 7, 1925.

10. *New York Times*, April 11, 1925.

11. *Honolulu Advertiser*, June 24, 1925.

12. *New York Times*, April 11, 1925; *Time*, April 20, 1925.

13. *Daily Worker*, March 28 and 30, 1925.

14. *Young Worker*, April 11 and 18, 1925.

15. *Honolulu Advertiser*, April 4, 1925.

16. Ibid., June 24, 1925.

17. U.S. Military Intelligence Reports, *Surveillance of Radicals in the United States, 1917–1941*, Reel 21.

18. *Honolulu Advertiser*, May 12, 1925.

19. *New York Times*, April 11, 1925.

20. Ibid.

21. *Daily Worker*, May 6, 1925.

22. Ibid., May 5 and 7, 1925.

23. Ibid.

24. Ibid., May 7, 1925.

25. Ibid., May 19, 1925.

26. Ibid., May 19 and 20, 1925.

27. Ibid., May 11, 1925.

28. Ibid., May 12, 1925.

29. Ibid.

30. Ibid.

31. Ibid., May 13, 1925.

32. Ibid., May 20 and 26, July 8, and August 20, 1925; *Young Worker*, May 23 and June 6, 1925.

33. *Honolulu Advertiser*, June 24, 1925.

34. *Daily Worker*, June 11 and 18, 1925; *Honolulu Advertiser*, June 24, 1925.

35. *Daily Worker*, June 27, 1925; *Honolulu Advertiser*, June 26, 1925.

36. *Daily Worker*, August 17, 1925; *Honolulu Advertiser*, July 17, 1925.

37. *Honolulu Advertiser*, July 17, 1925.

38. Ibid., July 18, 1925.

39. Ibid., July 21 and 31, 1925.

40. *Daily Worker*, July 6, 1925.

41. "Letter from Paul Crouch, July 11, 1925," Paul Crouch Letters, James Larkin Pearson Correspondence.

42. "Letter from IM Crouch, October 28, 1926," Paul Crouch Letters, James Larkin Pearson Correspondence.

43. "Letter to IM Crouch, November 8, 1926," Paul Crouch Letters, James Larkin Pearson Correspondence.

44. "Letter from IM Crouch, November 15, 1926," Paul Crouch Letters, James Larkin Pearson Correspondence.

45. *Daily Worker*, July 17 and August 12, 1925.

46. *Young Worker*, July 25, 1925; *Daily Worker*, July 30, 1925.

47. *Daily Worker*, August 17 and 21, 1925; *Young Worker*, December 12, 1925.

48. *Young Worker*, April 17, 1926.

49. Ibid., December 12, 1925, April 12 and July 31, 1926.

50. Ibid., June 30, 1926.

51. U.S. Military Intelligence Reports, *Surveillance of Radicals in the United States, 1917–1941*, Reel 21.

52. Ibid.

53. Ibid.

54. Salmond, *Gastonia*, 79, 94; Dilling, *The Red Network*, 328. Trumbull received only 103 votes out of more than 93,000 cast.

55. "Chapter XI (no title)," Paul Crouch Papers, Box 1, Hoover Institution Archives.

56. "Questions and answers with Paul Crouch," Paul Crouch Papers, Box 16, Hoover Institution Archives; "Letter from Paul Crouch on Alcatraz stationary, November 2, 1926," Paul Crouch Letters, James Larkin Pearson Correspondence.

57. *Young Worker*, August 1, 1928.

58. Ibid., January 1929.

59. Ibid., August 1, 1925.

Chapter 3. "Paul Crouch, Bolshevik," 1927–1932

1. Klehr, *The Heyday of American Communism*, 5; Klehr and Haynes, *The American Communist Movement*, 54, 56–57.

2. Jay Lovestone quoted in the *Communist*, October 21, 1921.

3. Klehr and Haynes, *The American Communist Movement*, 38.

4. "Paul Crouch, Bolshevik," Paul Crouch Papers, James Larkin Pearson Library.

5. "Letter to Paul Crouch, June 15, 1929," Paul Crouch Letters, James Larkin Pearson Correspondence.

6. "Flyer, July 18, 1927," Paul Crouch Papers, James Larkin Pearson Library.

7. *Young Worker*, November 1 and December 1, 1927, and August 1, 1928; "Bomb near home marks my speaking tour's end," Paul Crouch Papers, Box 1, Hoover Institution Archives.

8. "Letter from Paul Crouch, September 9, 1927," Paul Crouch Letters, James Larkin Pearson Correspondence.

9. "Letter from Paul Crouch, June 3, 1930," Paul Crouch Letters, James Larkin Pearson Correspondence.

10. "Letter from Paul Crouch, September 9, 1927," Paul Crouch Letters, James Larkin Pearson Correspondence.

11. "All America Anti Imperialist League speech in Chicago, October 1, 1927," Paul Crouch Papers, James Larkin Pearson Library.

12. "Flyer advertising October 14 speech in NYC," Paul Crouch Papers, James Larkin Pearson Library; U.S. Military Intelligence Reports, *Surveillance of Radicals in the United States, 1917–1941*, Reel 21.

13. U.S. Military Intelligence Reports, *Surveillance of Radicals in the United States, 1917–1941*, Reel 21.

14. *Young Worker*, June 1 and September 15, 1927.

15. "Letter from Paul Crouch, September 13, 1927," Paul Crouch Letters, James Larkin Pearson Correspondence.

16. *Wilkes-Journal Weekly*, September 22, 1927; *Wilkes Patriot*, September 22, 1927.

17. "Klux burns cross, fire bombs, but Crouch Speaks," Paul Crouch Papers, James Larkin Pearson Library.

18. *Wilkes Patriot*, October 13, 1927.

19. "Bomb near home marks my speaking tour's end," Paul Crouch Papers, Box 1, Hoover Institution Archives.

20. Taylor, *The History of the North Carolina Communist Party*, 14; "Report on the War Danger and Anti-Militarist Work," Paul Crouch Papers, James Larkin Pearson Library.

21. "Questions and Answers with Paul Crouch," Paul Crouch Papers, Box 16, Hoover Institution Archives; *Testimony of Paul Crouch*, HUAC, May 6, 1949, 183–84.

22. Taylor, *The History of the North Carolina Communist Party*, 14–15; "I visit Russia, land of ironic contrasts," Paul Crouch Papers, Box 1, Hoover Institution Archives.

23. Griggs, "McCarthy's Witches," 14; "FBI Files, July 10, 1941," Paul Crouch FBI Files, James Larkin Pearson Library; Taylor, *The History of the North Carolina Communist Party*, 15.

24. "Letter from Paul Crouch in Moscow, January 26, 1928," Paul Crouch Letters, James Larkin Pearson Correspondence; Taylor, *The History of the North Carolina Communist Party*, 15.

25. "I visit Russia, land of ironic contrasts," Paul Crouch Papers, Box 1, Hoover Institution Archives.

26. *Testimony of Paul Crouch*, HUAC, May 6, 1949, 185.

27. Ibid., 188; "Plans for World-Wide Revolution," Paul Crouch Papers, Box 1, Hoover Institution Archives.

28. "Plans for World-Wide Revolution," Paul Crouch Papers, Box 1, Hoover Institution Archives.

29. Ibid.

30. *The World Situation and Economic Struggle: Theses of the Tenth Plenum ECCI*, 3.

31. *XIth Plenum of the Executive Committee of the Communist International: Theses, Resolutions, and Decisions*, 7.

32. Ottanelli, *The Communist Party of the United States*, 19; Smith, *Subterranean Fire*, 101; Klehr, *The Heyday of American Communism*, 12–13.

33. "Plans for World-Wide Revolution," Paul Crouch Papers, Box 1, Hoover Institution Archives.

34. "Questions and Answers with Paul Crouch," Paul Crouch Papers, Box 16, Hoover Institution Archives.

35. *Testimony of Paul Crouch*, HUAC, May 6, 1949, 185.

36. "Eventful months in the Soviet Capitol," Paul Crouch Papers, Box 1, Hoover Institution Archives.

37. "Broken Chains," Paul Crouch Papers, Box 17, Hoover Institution Archives; Gilmore, *Defying Dixie*, 71; Allen, "The Black Belt: Area of Negro Majority," 586; Taylor, *The History of the North Carolina Communist Party*, 15.

38. Belfrage, *The American Inquisition*, 16.

39. "Eventful months in the Soviet Capitol," Paul Crouch Papers, Box 1, Hoover Institution Archives.

40."Letter to Paul Crouch, August 19, 1928," Paul Crouch Letters, James Larkin Pearson Correspondence.

41. "Letter from Paul Crouch, June 15, 1928," Paul Crouch Letters, James Larkin Pearson Correspondence.

42. "Infiltrating American Armed Forces," Paul Crouch Papers, Box 1, Hoover

Institution Archives; "FBI files, July 10, 1941," Paul Crouch FBI Files, James Larkin Pearson Library.

43. "Broken Chains," Paul Crouch Papers, Box 17, Hoover Institution Archives; *Testimony of Paul Crouch*, HUAC, May 6, 1949, 186; "Infiltrating American Armed Forces," Paul Crouch Papers, Box 1, Hoover Institution Archives.

44. "FBI files August 5 and 28, 1941," Paul Crouch FBI Files, James Larkin Pearson Library; U.S. Military Intelligence Reports, *Surveillance of Radicals in the United States, 1917–1941*, Reel 21.

45. U.S. Military Intelligence Reports, *Surveillance of Radicals in the United States, 1917–1941*, Reel 21.

46. Belfrage, *The American Inquisition*, 16.

47. "Conflict in Russia reflected in Party here," Paul Crouch Papers, Box 1, Hoover Institution Archives.

48. "Questions and Answers with Paul Crouch," Paul Crouch Papers, Box 1, Hoover Institution Archives.

49. "Conflict in Russia reflected in Party here," Paul Crouch Papers, Box 1, Hoover Institution Archives.

50. "Statement of the All-America Anti-Imperialist League on Hoover's visit to Latin America," Paul Crouch Papers, James Larkin Pearson Library.

51. "Letter from Paul Crouch, February 2, 1929," Paul Crouch Letters, James Larkin Pearson Correspondence.

52. "FBI files, August 5, 1941," Paul Crouch FBI Files, James Larkin Pearson Library; *New York Times*, March 9, 1929.

53. "Infiltrating American Armed Forces," Paul Crouch Papers, Box 1, Hoover Institution Archives.

54. "Unnamed, undated newspaper article," Paul Crouch Papers, James Larkin Pearson Library.

55. "Conflict in Russia reflected in Party here," Paul Crouch Papers, Box 1, Hoover Institution Archives; "A Brief History of the Communist Movement in North and South Carolina," Paul Crouch Papers, Box 1, Hoover Institution Archives; *Daily Worker*, August 9, 1928; "Draft Outline and Report on Situation in Textile Industry, September 22, 1928," Comintern Archives, Reel 114, Folder 1507, Numbers 37–39; "Report of Activities—Southern Tour, J. DiSanto, October 24-November 9, 1928," Comintern Archives, Reel 97, Folder 1292, Numbers 22–24; "Report on the Work of the NTWU, December 8, 1928," Comintern Archives, Reel 114, Folder 1509, Number 77; Taylor, *The History of the North Carolina Communist Party*, 18–19.

56. "Letter from Paul Crouch, December 1, 1928," Paul Crouch Letters, James Larkin Pearson Correspondence.

57. "Letter from Karl Reeve to Juliet Poyntz, May 21, 1929," Comintern Archives, Reel 128, Folder 1661, Numbers 44–46; Taylor, *The History of the North Carolina Communist Party*, 33.

58. "Guns Flare in Gastonia, Class Hatred Rife," Paul Crouch Papers, Box 1, Hoover Institution Archives; *Miami Daily News*, May 22, 1949.

59. "Letter from Paul Crouch June 12, 1929," Comintern Archives, Reel 128, Folder 1660, Numbers 28–29; Taylor, *The History of the North Carolina Communist Party*, 39.

60. Salmond, *Gastonia*.

61. "Guns Flare in Gastonia, Class Hatred Rife," Paul Crouch Papers, Box 1, Hoover Institution Archives; Taylor, *The History of the North Carolina Communist Party*, 54.

62. Ibid.

63. Annual Report of the Committee on Un-American Activities for the Year 1949, March 15, 1950, 4.

64. Klehr, *The Heyday of American Communism*, 32.

65. *Daily Worker*, July 25 and 26, 1930.

66. "Broken Chains," Paul Crouch Papers, Box 17, Hoover Institution Archives; "Letter from Paul Crouch, June 3, 1930," Paul Crouch Letters, James Larkin Pearson Correspondence.

67. Ibid.

68. "FBI files, July 10, 1941," Paul Crouch FBI Files, James Larkin Pearson Library.

Chapter 4. District Organizer, 1932–1937

1. Belfrage, *The American Inquisition*, 23.

2. "We Cut Down Segregation in Norfolk," Paul Crouch Papers, Box 1, Hoover Institution Archives; "Letter from Fred Allen to Secretariat, November 19, 1932," Comintern Archives, Reel 225, Folder 2924, Number 233; "Broken Chains," Paul Crouch Papers, Box 17, Hoover Institution Archives.

3. "We Cut Down Segregation in Norfolk," Paul Crouch Papers, Box 1, Hoover Institution Archives.

4. "Letter from Fred Allen (Paul Crouch) to J. Louis Engdahl, March 19, 1932," Comintern Archives, Reel 225, Folder 2924, Number 34.

5. U.S. Military Intelligence Reports, *Surveillance of Radicals in the United States, 1917–1941*, Reel 21.

6. "Letter from Fred Allen (Paul Crouch) to J. Louis Engdahl, March 19, 1932," Comintern Archives, Reel 225, Folder 2924, Number 34; "We Cut Down Segregation in Norfolk," Paul Crouch Papers, Box 1, Hoover Institution Archives.

7. "The Norfolk Worker," April 1932, Comintern Archives, Reel 225, Folder 2924, Number 44.

8. "Letter from Fred Allen (P. Crouch) to Clarence Hathaway, August 25, 1932," Comintern Archives, Reel 252, Folder 2924, Number 103; "Letter from Fred Allen (P. C.) to National Election Campaign Committee, September 30, 1932," Comintern Archives, Reel 225, Folder 2924, Number 145; "Letter from Fred Allen (P. C.) to Clarence Hathaway, September 14, 1932," Comintern Archives, Reel 225, Folder 2924, Number 119; "Letter from Fred Allen to National Election Campaign Committee, September 20, 1932," Comintern Archives, Reel 225, Folder 2924, Number 119.

9. "Letter from Fred Allen to National Election Campaign Committee, October 6, 1932," Comintern Archives, Reel 225, Folder 2924, Number 132.

10. Lewis, *In Their Own Interests*, 132.

11. "We Cut Down Segregation in Norfolk," Paul Crouch Papers, Box 1, Hoover Institution Archives.

12. "Letter from Fred Allen to National Election Campaign Committee, October 14, 1932," Comintern Archives, Reel 225, Folder 2924, Number 176; "Telegraph from Fred

Allen to National Campaign Committee, October 17, 1932," Comintern Archives, Reel 225, Folder 2924, Number 182; "Letter from Fred Allen (P. C.) to Secretariat, October 26, 1932," Comintern Archives, Reel 225, Folder 2924, Number 203.

13. "Letter from Fred Allen to Secretariat, November 9, 1932," Comintern Archives, Reel 225, Folder 2924, Numbers 216–22.

14. "FBI files, July 10, 1941," Paul Crouch FBI Files, James Larkin Pearson Library.

15. "We Cut Down Segregation in Norfolk," Paul Crouch Papers, Box 1, Hoover Institution Archives.

16. "Letter from Paul Crouch to Secretariat, February 12, 1933," Comintern Archives, Reel 255, Folder 3308, Number 29.

17. Papanikolas, "Unionism Communism and the Great Depression: The Carbon County Coal Strike," 260.

18. Ibid., 261, 262, 264.

19. Ibid., 267.

20. Ibid., 269–72.

21. Ibid., 274, 277.

22. Ibid., 280.

23. Ibid., 281, 284; "FBI files, July 19, 1941," Paul Crouch FBI Files, James Larkin Pearson Library.

24. Papanikolas, "Unionism Communism, and the Great Depression: The Carbon County Coal Strike," 287–88.

25. "FBI files, July 19, 1941," Paul Crouch FBI Files, James Larkin Pearson Library; Papanikolas, "Unionism Communism, and the Great Depression: The Carbon County Coal Strike," 293–94.

26. "Tumult in Utah Coal Fields," Paul Crouch Papers, Box 1, Hoover Institution Archives.

27. Ryan, *Earl Browder*, 82.

28. *Daily Worker*, July 8, 1933; Klehr and Haynes, *The American Communist Movement*, 69; Ottanelli, *The Communist Party of the United States*, 69.

29. "The Roosevelt Program—An Attack Upon the Toiling Masses," *Communist* (May 1933): 420–22; *Daily Worker*, July 8, 1933; Klehr, *The Heyday of American Communism*, 123.

30. "FBI files, July 10, 1941," Paul Crouch FBI Files, James Larkin Pearson Library.

31. Klehr, *The Heyday of American Communism*, 124.

32. "Letter from Paul Crouch to Org Com CC," Comintern Archives, Reel 281, Folder 3625, Numbers 55–57; *Washington Post*, July 31, 1934; *Miami Daily News*, May 22, 1949.

33. *Charlotte Observer*, September 28, 1934; Taylor, *The History of the North Carolina Communist Party*, 105.

34. Salmond, *General Textile Strike of 1934*, 53, 77–78; *Daily Worker*, September 12, 18, and 19, 1934; *New York Times*, September 22 and 23, 1934; *Charlotte Observer*, September 18 and 28, 1934. For a thorough analysis of this nationwide strike beyond the Communist influence, see Salmond, *The General Textile Strike of 1934*.

35. "CLOSE EVERY MILL! STOP THE SCABS!!!" (emphasis in original source), Comintern Archives, Reel 281, Folder 3266, Number 49.

36. "NATIONAL GUARDSMEN REFUSE TO BE STRIKEBREAKERS!" (emphasis in original source), Comintern Archives, Reel 281, Folder 3266, Number 50; Taylor, *The History of the North Carolina Communist Party*, 105.

37. *Daily Worker*, September 26, 1934; "National Textile Party Conference, October 6, 1934," Comintern Archives, Reel 265, Folder 3424, Number 7; "Resolution and Six Weeks Plan of Work for District 16, November 10 and 11, 1934," Comintern Archives, Reel 281, Folder 3623, Numbers 2–4; Taylor, *The History of the North Carolina Communist Party*, 112–13.

38. "Letter from Paul Crouch to Org. Com. CC, December 19, 1934," Comintern Archives, Reel 281, Folder 3625, Number 104; "General District Report, by Paul Crouch, November 25, 1934," Comintern Archives, Reel 281, Folder 3625, Numbers 95–98; "Letter from Paul Crouch to Org. Com. CC, November 25, 1934," Comintern Archives, Reel 281, Folder 3625, Numbers 95–97; "Letter from Paul Crouch to Comrade Satchel, November 25, 1934," Comintern Archives, Reel 281, Folder 3625, Number 98; "Letter from Jim to Paul, November 23, 1934," Comintern Archives, Reel 281, Folder 3625, Number 100; "Letter from Paul to Jim, November 24, 1934," Comintern Archives, Reel 281, Folder 3625, Numbers 101–2.

39. "Letter from Paul Crouch to Org. Com. CC, November 20, 1934," Comintern Archives, Reel 281, Folder 3625, Number 91.

40. "Letter from Paul Crouch to Org. Com. CC, November 25, 1934," Comintern Archives, Reel 281, Folder 3625, Numbers 95–97; "Letter from Paul Crouch to Comrade Satchel, November 25, 1934," Comintern Archives, Reel 281, Folder 3625, Number 98.

41. "Letter from Paul Crouch to CC-CPUSA, December 30, 1934," Comintern Archives, Reel 281, Folder 3625, Numbers 108–10.

42. "Letter from Paul Crouch to Org. Com. CC, February 21, 1935," Comintern Archives, Reel 298, Folder 3882, Numbers 1–2.

43. "Minutes of District Conference Held February 10, 1935 in Charlotte, NC," Comintern Archives, Reel 297, Folder 3881, Numbers 1–4; Taylor, *The History of the North Carolina Communist Party*, 113.

44. Ryan, *Earl Browder*, 86.

45. "The Advance of the United Front: A Documentary Account, Communist Party in Carolinas Asks Socialist Party for United Action in Strike through Letter to Thomas, September 21, 1934," Theodore Draper research files, Manuscript, Archives, and Rare Book Library, Emory University; "Draft of United Front Proposals to be Submitted to State Conference of SP," Comintern Archives, Reel 281, Folder 3624, Number 6; *Daily Worker*, September 28, 1934; "A Brief History of the Communist Movement in North and South Carolina," Paul Crouch Papers, Box 1, Hoover Institution Archives; Taylor, *The History of the North Carolina Communist Party*, 114–15.

46. Ibid.

47. *Daily Worker*, September 24, 1934; "A Brief History of the Communist Movement in North and South Carolina," Paul Crouch Papers, Box 1, Hoover Institution Archives; "Letter from Paul Crouch to Org Com CC, May 30, 1935," Comintern Archives, Reel 298, Folder 3882, Number 30; "Meeting of textile problems, April 20, 1935," Comintern Archives, Reel 300, Folder 3919, Number 1; "Broken Chains," Paul Crouch

Papers, Box 17, Hoover Institution Archives; Taylor, *The History of the North Carolina Communist Party*, 115–16.

48. "Letter from Fred Gray to Org Com, July 15," Comintern Archives, Reel 298, Folder 3882, Numbers 50–51; "Plan of Work for District 16–September 15 to November 15," Comintern Archives, Reel 298, Folder 3883, Numbers 10–11; "The Organizer," Volume 1 Number 8, December 18, 1935, Comintern Archives, Reel 298, Folder 3883, Numbers 12–15; Taylor, *The History of the North Carolina Communist Party*, 116.

49. "NO MORE Cuts on Relief Work!," Comintern Archives, Reel 298, Folder 3882, Number 5; "Program and plan of work for the Unemployment Council," Comintern Archives, Reel 190, Folder 2517, Numbers 55–56; Taylor, *The History of the North Carolina Communist Party*, 117–18.

50. "Letter from Paul Crouch to Org. Com. CC, May 30, 1935," Comintern Archives, Reel 298, Folder 3882, Number 30; "Letter from Jim Weaver to F. Brown, June 8, 1935," Comintern Archives, Reel 298, Folder 3882, Number 36.

51. "Letter to parents," Paul Crouch Papers, Box 10, Hoover Institution Archives; "Letter from Paul Crouch to Org Com CC, June 10, 1935" (emphasis in original source), Comintern Archives, Reel 298, Folder 3882, Number 37–39.

52. "Letter from Paul Crouch to Earl Browder," Comintern Archives, Reel 298, Folder 3882, Number 25.

53. "Letter from Paul Crouch to PolBuro, October 18, 1935," Comintern Archives, Reel 298, Folder 3882, Numbers 103–6.

54. "Letter from Fred Gray to F. Brown, November 11, 1935," Comintern Archives, Reel 298, Folder 3882, Numbers 110–13; Taylor, *The History of the North Carolina Communist Party*, 119.

55. "The Golden Trumpets," Junius Scales Papers 4879, Southern Historical Collection, Wilson Library, University of North Carolina at Chapel Hill; *Daily Worker*, September 30, and October 26, 1936; *Durham Morning Herald*, October 23 and 24, 1936.

56. *Afro-American*, October 31, 1936; *Durham Morning Herald*, October 26, 1936; *The Communist Party of the United States of America: What It Is, How It Works. A Handbook for Americans*, 37; Taylor, *The History of the North Carolina Communist Party*, 120–24.

57. "A Brief History of the Communist Movement in North and South Carolina," Paul Crouch Papers, Box 1, Hoover Institution Archives.

Chapter 5. Questioning Communism, 1938–1947

1. "Communists Exploit Southern Liberals," Paul Crouch Papers, Box 1, Hoover Institution Archives; *Testimony of Paul Crouch*, HUAC, May 6, 1949, 190; Krueger, *And Promises to Keep*, 29–31.

2. Brown, *Standing against Dragons*, 122; "Communists Exploit Southern Liberals," Paul Crouch Papers, Box 1, Hoover Institution Archives; *Testimony of Paul Crouch*, HUAC, May 6, 1949, 192.

3. Krueger, *And Promises to Keep*, 71.

4. *New South*, October 1938, 9–10.

5. "Questions and Answers with Paul Crouch," Paul Crouch Papers, Box 16, Hoover Institution Archives; "Stalin Upsets the Apple-Cart," Paul Crouch Papers, Box 1, Hoover Institution Archives.

6. *Daily Worker*, August 24, 1939; Klehr, *The Heyday of American Communism*, 388; Ryan, *Earl Browder*, 160; Isserman, *Which Side Were You On?*, 34.

7. *Daily Worker*, August 25, 1939.

8. Ryan, *Earl Browder*, 162, 182, 205; Klehr, *The Heyday of American Communism*, 390, 396–97; Ottanelli, *The Communist Party of the United States*, 191–92; Isserman, *Which Side Were You On?*, 47, 53, 85, 88. In September 1939, Browder testified before HUAC and admitted to using false names on passports in the 1920s. He received a four-year sentence and a $2,000 fine for his crimes. He was freed in 1942 as a gesture of goodwill to mark the arrival of Soviet Foreign Minister Vyacheslav Molotov.

9. Ottanelli, *The Communist Party of the United States*, 199.

10. Klehr, *The Heyday of American Communism*, 409.

11. Purcell, *White Collar Radicals*, 50–51.

12. *Chattanooga Daily News*, September 22, 1953; Bass, "Bolsheviks on the Bluff," 142.

13. *Chattanooga Daily News*, September 22, 1953.

14. *Testimony of Paul Crouch*, HUAC, May 6, 1949, 200; Korstad, *Civil Rights Unionism*, 146.

15. *Testimony of Paul Crouch*, HUAC, May 6, 1949, 199 and May 24, 1949, 403.

16. "FBI files, January 6, 1940," Paul Crouch FBI Files, James Larkin Pearson Library.

17. "FBI files, May 14, July 10, and August 5, 1941," Paul Crouch FBI Files, James Larkin Pearson Library.

18. *Testimony of Paul Crouch*, HUAC, May 6, 1949, 192.

19. "FBI files, March 25, 1941," Paul Crouch FBI Files, James Larkin Pearson Library; Bass, "Bolsheviks on the Bluff," 154–56; "Letter from Robert Minor, January 8, 1941," Paul Crouch Papers, Box 16, Hoover Institution Archives.

20. Bass, "Bolsheviks on the Bluff," 152–53; "List of District Committee, Tennessee, 1939–1940," Paul Crouch Papers, Box 16, Hoover Institution Archives; *Chattanooga Daily News*, September 22, 1953.

21. Ibid.

22. "Rise and Fall of the TVA Branch," Paul Crouch Papers, Box 1, Hoover Institution Archives.

23. Schrecker, *Many Are the Crimes*, 101.

24. "FBI files, August 5, 1941," Paul Crouch FBI Files, James Larkin Pearson Library.

25. "I break with the Communist Party," Paul Crouch Papers, Box 1, Hoover Institution Archives.

26. *Testimony of Paul Crouch*, HUAC, May 24, 1949, 406.

27. Ibid., 405; "Gladstein's Questioning of Crouch Relative to Subjects Taught at Alameda Co. School in 1941," Paul Crouch Papers, Box 1, Hoover Institution Archives; "Pueblo Espano, Amantes de la libertad, Paz y Justicia," Paul Crouch Papers, Box 1, Hoover Institution Archives; "FBI files, May 15, 1948," Paul Crouch FBI Files, James Larkin Pearson Library.

28. "Undated statement of Paul Crouch," Paul Crouch Papers, Box 16, Hoover Institution Archives.

29. Ibid; *Testimony of Paul Crouch*, HUAC, May 6, 1949, 201.

30. "I break with the Communist Party," Paul Crouch Papers, Box 1, Hoover Institution Archives.

31. "Prologue from Broken Chains," Paul Crouch Papers, Box 1, Hoover Institution Archives.

32. Belfrage, *The American Inquisition*, 45.

33. "Summary of Report by Paul Crouch on the Alameda County Committee, December 13, 1941," Paul Crouch Papers, Box 8, Hoover Institution Archives.

34. "I break with the Communist Party," Paul Crouch Papers, Box 1, Hoover Institution Archives.

35. *Testimony of Paul Crouch*, HUAC, May 24, 1949, 405.

36. "Letter from Paul Crouch, July 5, 1944," Paul Crouch Papers, Box 10, Hoover Institution Archives.

37. "FBI files, October 30, 1943 and September 1, 1945," Paul Crouch FBI Files, James Larkin Pearson Library.

38. "I break with the Communist Party," Paul Crouch Papers, Box 1, Hoover Institution Archives; "FBI files, August 5, 1946," Paul Crouch FBI Files, James Larkin Pearson Library; "Long Arm and Elephant Memory," Paul Crouch Papers, Box 1, Hoover Institution Archives.

39. "FBI files, January 13, 1947," Paul Crouch FBI Files, James Larkin Pearson Library.

40. "Long Arm and Elephant Memory," Paul Crouch Papers, Box 1, Hoover Institution Archives; "FBI files, May 14, 1947," Paul Crouch FBI Files, James Larkin Pearson Library; "Western Union Telegram from ML Edwards, January 4, 1947," Paul Crouch Papers, Box 5, Hoover Institution Archives.

Chapter 6. "Then Came the Conversion," 1947–1949

1. McCullough, *Truman*, 546, 562.

2. Heale, *American Anti-Communism*, 140.

3. Brown, *Standing against Dragons*, 5.

4. Steinberg, *The Great "Red Menace,"* 108.

5. Ibid.

6. Heale, *American Anti-Communism*, 126; Steinberg, *The Great "Red Menace,"* 7, 12, 59, 100; U.S. House of Reps, 80th Congress, 1st Session, Appropriations Committee, Department of Justice Appropriations Bill for 1948, 147.

7. Steinberg, *The Great "Red Menace,"* 24, 27.

8. Ibid., 44.

9. Heale, *American Anti-Communism*, 123, 145–46, 168.

10. "Letter From Charlie, February 8, 1947," Paul Crouch Papers, Box 11, Hoover Institution Archives.

11. *Testimony of Paul Crouch*, HUAC, May 24, 1949, 405.

12. "Letter to Fred Jones," Paul Crouch Papers, Box 1, Hoover Institution Archives.

13. "Merry-Go-Round in Miami," Paul Crouch Papers, Box 11, Hoover Institution Archives; "FBI files 1–14," Paul Crouch FBI Files, James Larkin Pearson Library.

14. Schrecker, *Many Are the Crimes*, 228; "FBI files, January 9, 1948," Paul Crouch FBI Files, James Larkin Pearson Library.

15. "FBI files, January 8, 1948," Paul Crouch FBI Files, James Larkin Pearson Library.

16. Ibid; "Merry-Go-Round in Miami," Paul Crouch Papers, Box 1, Hoover Institution Archives.

17. "FBI files, May 15, 1948," Paul Crouch FBI Files, James Larkin Pearson Library.

18. "FBI files, June 21, 1948," Paul Crouch FBI Files, James Larkin Pearson Library.

19. Ibid.

20. Steinberg, *The Great "Red Menace,"* 162–63.

21. Ibid., 165; Caute, *The Great Fear*, 187.

22. Belfrage, *The American Inquisition*, 105–6; Sabin, *Red Scare in Court*, 110, 112.

23. Rovere, "The Kept Witnesses," 64.

24. Sabin, *Red Scare in Court*, 110; DeVoto, "The Ex-Communists," 61; Hofstader, *The Paranoid Style in American Politics and other Essays*, 35.

25. Crouch, "The Anatomy of a Front," 7–8.

26. Ibid., 11, 13.

27. Brown, *Standing against Dragons*, 120.

28. *Testimony of Paul Crouch*, HUAC, May 6, 1949, 181, 214.

29. Ibid., 194–97

30. Ibid., 190–92, 197.

31. Ibid., 198.

32. Ibid., 206.

33. Ibid., 201–2. The Venona files later confirmed that Nelson was sent to California with the task of gathering information on the atomic bomb. See Haynes and Klehr, *Venona*, 230.

34. Ibid., 215, 216.

35. Ibid., 211.

36. Ibid., 218–19.

37. Ibid., appendix.

38. *Journal Patriot*, May 19, 1949; *St. Louis Post Dispatch*, May 18, 1949.

39. *Fort Worth Star Telegram*, May 21, 1949; *Miles City Star*, June 12, 1949; *Honolulu Star Bulletin*, December 29, 1949.

40. "Merry-Go-Round in Miami," Paul Crouch Papers, Box 1, Hoover Institution Archives; *Miami Daily News*, May 8, 1949.

41. *Miami Daily News*, May 9, 1949.

42. Ibid.; Lichtenstein, "Putting Labor's House in Order," 8.

43. *Miami Daily News*, May 10, 1949.

44. Ibid.

45. Ibid., May 13, 1949; Schrecker, *Many Are the Crimes*, 137–38.

46. *Miami Daily News*, May 14, 1949.

47. "*Miami Daily News*, undated, as published in an unnamed Nashville paper, 'Negro Revolt Task Assigned to SCHW,'" Paul Crouch Papers, Box 5, Hoover Institution Archives; "*Miami Daily News*, undated, as published in *Pittsburgh Sunday Telegraph*,

'Reds Plotting Aggression Against US for 20 Years,'" Paul Crouch Papers, Box 5, Hoover Institution Archives.

48. *Miami Daily News*, May 17, 1949.

49. Ibid., May 20, 1949.

50. Ibid., May 18, 1949; Lichtenstein, "Putting Labor's House in Order," 7; "HB Fletcher to DM Ladd," May 26, 1949, June 3, 1949, File 61–6547–206; FBI FOIA.

51. *The Christian Science Monitor*, May 25, 1949.

52. *New York Times*, May 17, 1949.

53. Ibid.

54. Caute, *The Great Fear*, 230.

55. *Hearings Regarding Clarence Hiskey*, HUAC, May 24, 1949, 384–85. Arthur Adams began spying in 1938, but the FBI only became aware of him in 1944. He fled the United States in 1946 and died in the USSR in 1970. For his espionage efforts, he was buried with honors in the Novodevichy Cemetery in Moscow. For more on Adams see Knight, *How the Cold War Began*, 159–60.

56. *New York Times*, May 25, 1949.

57. Schrecker, *No Ivory Tower*, 133–34.

58. *Hearings Regarding Clarence Hiskey*, HUAC, May 24, 1949, 386, 394–95.

59. Ibid., 399.

60. Ibid., 400–402.

61. Schrecker, *No Ivory Tower*, 286.

62. *Hearings Regarding Steve Nelson*, HUAC, June 8, 1949, v, vii.

63. Ibid.

64. Carroll, *The Odyssey of the American Lincoln Brigade*, 132–33, 159.

65. *Annual Report of the* House *Committee on Un-American Activities for the Year 1949*, March 15, 1950, 6.

66. *Hearings Regarding Steve Nelson*, HUAC, June 8, 1949, vii.

67. Ibid., 151, 153.

68. Carroll, *The Odyssey of the American Lincoln Brigade*, 295–96.

69. Nelson, *The 13th Juror*, 172–73.

70. Belfrage, *The American Inquisition*, 152.

71. Ibid.

72. Nelson, *The 13th Juror*, 230; Lichtman and Cohen, *Deadly Farce*, 150.

Chapter 7. Professional Informant, 1950–1951

1. *Congressional Record*, 82nd Congress, 1st session (June 14, 1951), 6602.

2. McCarthy, *America's Retreat from Victory*, 171–72.

3. Hofstader, *The Paranoid Style in American Politics and Other Essays*, 25–26.

4. Schrecker, *Many Are the Crimes*, 93, 94, 98; Klehr and Haynes, "Communists and the CIO: From the Soviet Archives," 445.

5. Klehr and Haynes, "Communists and the CIO: From the Soviet Archives," 446.

6. "Calling the Turn on Harry Bridges," Paul Crouch Papers, Box 1, Hoover Institution Archives; *New York Times*, December 16, 1949.

7. *Washington Post*, January 4, 1950; *New York Times*, December 16 and 22, 1949.

8. "Unknown, undated," Paul Crouch Papers, Box 13, Hoover Institution Archives.

9. *New York Times*, December 17, 1949.

10. *San Francisco Examiner*, December 20, 1949; *New York Times*, December 20, 1949; "Unknown, undated," Paul Crouch Papers, Box 12, Hoover Institution Archives.

11. *New York Times*, December 21, 1949; "Unknown, December 1949," Paul Crouch Papers, Box 12, Hoover Institution Archives; Belfrage, *The American Inquisition*, 113.

12. "Unknown, December 1949," Paul Crouch Papers, Box 12, Hoover Institution Archives; *New York Times*, December 17 and 21, 1949.

13. *Washington Post*, December 21, 1949.

14. *New York Times*, December 21, 1949.

15. Belfrage, *The American Inquisition*, 121, 181; "I break with the Communist Party," Paul Crouch Papers, Box 1, Hoover Institution Archives.

16. *Testimony of Paul Crouch*, HUAC, May 6, 1949, 205.

17. "Observations on the Present International Situation and Role of American Communists in Event of War, June 26, 1950," Paul Crouch Papers, Box 1, Hoover Institution Archives.

18. Ibid.

19. Ibid.

20. "The Cold War Becomes Hot," Paul Crouch Papers, Box 1, Hoover Institution Archives.

21. Ibid.

22. "The case against Dean Acheson," Paul Crouch Papers, Box 1, Hoover Institution Archives.

23. Caute, *The Great Fear*, 127; Brown, *Standing against Dragons*, 122.

24. *Journal Patriot*, March 8, 1951.

25. Purcell, *White Collar Radicals*, 149.

26. Ibid.

27. *Washington Post*, January 5, 1951.

28. *New York Journal-American*, January 5, 1951.

29. Purcell, *White Collar Radicals*, 159; *New York Post*, January 4, 1951.

30. Purcell, *White Collar Radicals*, 159–61.

31. Sabin, *Red Scare in Court*, 142–44.

32. Ibid., 143–44.

33. Ibid., 145.

34. Ibid., 145–46

35. Ibid., 263–64, 322, 328, 345, 351.

36. Crouch, "Soviet Underground, U.S.A.," 337.

37. Ibid., 339.

38. Ibid., 336–39.

39. Heale, *American Anti-Communism*, 158.

40. "Statement by Paul Crouch," Paul Crouch Papers, Box 16, Hoover Institution Archives.

41. "Testimony to Senate Subcommittee, May 8 and 9, 1951," Paul Crouch Papers, Box 1, Hoover Institution Archives.

42. "Speech given to Senate Subcommittee, May 8, 1951," Paul Crouch Papers, Box 6, Hoover Institution Archives; "Letter to Joe McCarthy," Paul Crouch Papers, Box 1, Hoover Institution Archives.

43. "Letter to Subcommittee on Internal Security, Committee on the Judiciary, September 1, 1951," Paul Crouch Papers, Box 1, Hoover Institution Archives.

44. *Official Report of Proceedings before the Subversive Activities Control Board*, June 26, 1951.

45. Ibid., July 7, 1951, 3227.

46. Subversive Activities Control Board Docket No. 51-101 Report No. 7 (July 25, 1951).

47. *Official Report of Proceedings before the Subversive Activities Control Board*, July 12, 1951, 3504, 3540, 3739.

48. Ibid., July 23, 1951, 3649–50, 4079–80.

49. *Communist Party of the United States of America v. Subversive Activities Control Board*, 123.

50. Caute, *The Great Fear*, 171–73.

51. "Letter from Crouch to Department of Justice entitled 'Subject: Legislation dealing with subversive Communist Activities,' August 17, 1951," Paul Crouch Papers, Box 6, Hoover Institution Archives.

52. Ibid.

53. Ibid.

54. "The Role of Ex-Communists in National Defense," Paul Crouch Papers, James Larkin Pearson Library.

55. Green, *Battling the Plantation Mentality*, 188.

56. "*Memphis Appeal*, undated," Paul Crouch Papers, Box 6, Hoover Institution Archives; *Memphis Press-Scimitar*, October 26, 1951.

57. Asch, *The Senator and the Sharecropper*, 138–40.

58. "Communism—Infiltration of the Armed Forces and What It Means in the Korean Situation," Paul Crouch Papers, Box 1, Hoover Institution Archives; "Kiwan-o-gram, Kiwanis Club of LA," Paul Crouch Papers, Box 1, Hoover Institution Archives; "Letter from James Newman, September 16, 1952," Paul Crouch Papers, Box 16, Hoover Institution Archives; "The Communist Use of Women," Paul Crouch Papers, Box 1, Hoover Institution Archives.

Chapter 8. Limelight, 1952–1953

1. Caute, *The Great Fear*, 201–2.

2. Steinberg, *The Great "Red Menace,"* 240.

3. *Baltimore Post News*, March 12 and 13, 1952.

4. Pederson, *The Communist Party in Maryland*, 175–77; *New York Times*, March 13, 1952; Steinberg, *The Great "Red Menace,"* 240–41.

5. Holmes, *The Specter of Communism in Hawaii*, 190, 208; *Honolulu Advertiser*, November 18, 1952 and January 1, 1953; *New York Times*, November 14 and 15, 1952.

6. *Honolulu Star Bulletin*, November 21, 1952; *Honolulu Advertiser*, November 21, 1952.

7. *Honolulu Record*, June 11, 1953.

8. Holmes, *The Specter of Communism in Hawaii*, 211; Caute, *The Great Fear*, 202, 208.

9. "Memo to INS, October 22, 1951," Paul Crouch Papers, Box 1, Hoover Institution Archives.

10. "Unknown testimony about the infiltration of the Hawaiian Democratic Party by the Communists," Paul Crouch Papers, Box 2, Hoover Institution Archives.

11. "Crouch Figures on Hawaii," Paul Crouch Papers, Box 1, Hoover Institution Archives.

12. *New York Times*, July 4, 1953.

13. "Recommendations by Paul Crouch on Methods for Dealing with Communist Danger in Hawaii in Testimony before the Senate Committee on Interior and Insular Affairs, July 3," Paul Crouch Papers, Box 1, Hoover Institution Archives.

14. "Letter from Crouch to Eisenhower, July 1952," Paul Crouch Papers, Box 6, Hoover Institution Archives.

15. "Letter to Robert Woytych, January 12, 1953," Paul Crouch Papers, Box 6, Hoover Institution Archives.

16. "Letter to Robert Woytych, July 28, 1953," Paul Crouch Papers, Box 16, Hoover Institution Archives.

17. "Letter to the president, undated," Paul Crouch Papers, Box 16, Hoover Institution Archives.

18. "Unknown, undated," Paul Crouch Papers, Box 11, Hoover Institution Archives.

19. "Letter to the president, undated," Paul Crouch Papers, Box 16, Hoover Institution Archives.

20. Ibid.

21. Ibid.

22. "Communism in Latin America," Paul Crouch Papers, Box 1, Hoover Institution Archives.

23. Ibid.

24. Ibid.

25. Ibid.

26. Ibid.

27. "Affidavit, February 1952," Paul Crouch Papers, Box 16, Hoover Institution Archives.

28. Storrs, "Red Scare Politics and the Suppression of Popular Front Feminism," 500, 502, 506; *Washington Daily News*, January 9, 1953.

29. Storrs, "Red Scare Politics and the Suppression of Popular Front Feminism," 491; *Washington Daily News*, October 10, 1952.

30. *Washington Post*, January 9, 1953.

31. "*Times Herald*, undated, 1952," Paul Crouch Papers, Box 6, Hoover Institution Archives.

32. "FBI files, October 17 and November 3, 1952 and January 21, 1953," Paul Crouch FBI Files, James Larkin Pearson Library; "Payment voucher, November 25, 1952," Paul Crouch Papers, Box 16, Hoover Institution Archives.

33. Lynn, *Charlie Chaplin and His Times*, 391–92.

34. Ibid., 393–94.

35. Ibid., 394–95.

36. *Seattle Post Intelligencer*, May 9, 1953.

37. Hughes and Beckwith, *On the Harbor*, 115–17; *Seattle Post Intelligencer*, April 30 and May 6, 1953.

38. "Unknown and undated," Paul Crouch Papers, Box 10, Hoover Institution Archives; *Seattle Post Intelligencer*, April 30 and May 2, 1953.

39. "FBI files, October 1 and 8, 1953," Paul Crouch FBI Files, James Larkin Pearson Library.

40. "The Miami Formula," *Nation*, January 22, 1955.

41. Ibid.

42. Caute, *The Great Fear*, 230.

43. "The Press: Deportation Order," *Time*, July 20, 1953; *Washington Post*, February 17, 1953; "Absurd," *Time*, July 19, 1954; *Chicago Sun Times*, February 15, 1953; "Letter to Robert Woytych, February 19, 1953," Paul Crouch Papers, Box 1, Hoover Institution Archives; "Letter to Robert Woytych, February 20, 1953," Paul Crouch Papers, Box 1, Hoover Institution Archives.

44. *New York Times*, June 24, 1954; *Washington Post and Times Herald*, June 25, 1954.

45. "Letter from Thomas Finucane, June 25, 1954," Paul Crouch Papers, Box 16, Hoover Institution Archives.

46. *Washington Post and Times Herald*, June 29, 1954.

47. "Unknown and undated," Paul Crouch Papers, Box 10, Hoover Institution Archives.

Chapter 9. Atomic Secrets, 1953–1954

1. Schrecker, *No Ivory Tower*, 75, 136.

2. Bird and Sherwin, *American Prometheus*, 167.

3. Herken, *Brotherhood of the Bomb*, 61.

4. Ibid., 96–97.

5. Ibid.

6. Bird and Sherwin, *American Prometheus*, 190.

7. Ibid., 189.

8. Herken, *Brotherhood of the Bomb*, 98.

9. Ibid., 100–101.

10. Ibid., 144.

11. Schrecker, *No Ivory Tower*, 136, 141–42.

12. Ibid., 142.

13. *Hearings Regarding Communist Infiltration of Radiation Laboratory and Atomic Bomb Project at the University of California, Berkeley*, HUAC, 800, 802.

14. "Testimony to Senate Subcommittee, May 8 and 9, 1951," Paul Crouch Papers, Box 1, Hoover Institution Archives; "Speech given to Senate Subcommittee, May 8, 1951," Paul Crouch Papers, Box 6, Hoover Institution Archives; "Letter to Joe

McCarthy, undated," Paul Crouch Papers, Box 1, Hoover Institution Archives; *Testimony of Philip A. Bart and Marcel Scherer*, HUAC, June 21, 1950, 2651.

15. "Scientist 'X' Dismissed by Minnesota," *Bulletin of the Atomic Scientists*, August 1951, 240; *Washington Post*, May 18, 1951.

16. Bird and Sherwin, *American Prometheus*, 459.

17. McMillan, *The Ruin of J. Robert Oppenheimer and the Birth of the Modern Arms Race*, 149.

18. Ibid., 149–50.

19. *Washington Post*, February 26 and 27, 1953.

20. Ibid., March 6, 1953.

21. *Washington Daily News*, March 5, 1953.

22. Herken, *Brotherhood of the Bomb*, 333.

23. "Sworn Statement of Paul Crouch to US Senate Subcommittee on Internal Security," Paul Crouch Papers, Box 1, Hoover Institution Archives.

24. "Undated statement by Sylvia Crouch," Paul Crouch Papers, Box 8, Hoover Institution Archives.

25. McMillan, *The Ruin of J. Robert Oppenheimer*, 297n12; "FBI files, January 8, 1954," Paul Crouch FBI Files, James Larkin Pearson Library; *Executive Session of the Senate Permanent Subcommittee on Investigations of the Committee on Government Operations*, volume 3, 1834, 1835, 1837.

26. Ibid., 1838.

27. Ibid., 1839, 1841.

28. Ibid.

29. Bird and Sherwin, *American Prometheus*, 104, 124, 135, 136, 160.

30. Alsop and Alsop, *We Accuse!: The Story of the Miscarriage of American Justice in the Case of J. Robert Oppenheimer*, 3.

31. Bird and Sherwin, *American Prometheus*, 118–20, 195.

32. Herken, *Brotherhood of the Bomb*, 107–14.

33. Ibid., 198.

34. Bird and Sherwin, *American Prometheus*, 440.

35. *Washington Post*, May 11, 1950.

36. Bird and Sherwin, *American Prometheus*, 439; *Washington Post*, May 10, 1950.

37. *New York Times*, May 10, 1950.

38. "*Honolulu Record*, 'Portrait of a Fanatic: Paul Crouch,'" Paul Crouch Papers, Box 6, Hoover Institution Archives.

39. Bird and Sherwin, *American Prometheus*, 439.

40. Ibid., 440–41; *Winston-Salem Sentinel*, April 19, 1954.

41. Bird and Sherwin, *American Prometheus*, 456.

42. Ibid., 457, 475.

43. "Memo from Crouch to Roy Cohn, May 21, 1953," Paul Crouch Papers, Box 6, Hoover Institution Archives.

44. "Statement of Paul Crouch, undated," Paul Crouch Papers, Box 16, Hoover Institution Archives.

45. "Suggested Witnesses Regarding Dr. J. Robert Oppenheimer and Background

of Communist Party Activities Facilitating Soviet Atomic Espionage," Paul Crouch Papers, Box 6, Hoover Institution Archives.

46. Ibid.

47. Bird and Sherwin, *American Prometheus*, 442–43; Schrecker, *Many Are the Crimes*, 165.

48. Alsop and Alsop, *We Accuse!: The Story of the Miscarriage of American Justice in the Case of J. Robert Oppenheimer*, 9–10.

49. Polenberg, *In the Matter of J. Robert Oppenheimer*, xx, xxv, xxvi.

50. *Winston-Salem Sentinel*, April 19, 1954.

51. Simpson, "The Re-Trial of the Oppenheimer Case," 387, 388.

52. Bird and Sherwin, *American Prometheus*, 549.

53. Haynes and Klehr, *Venona*, 330; Schecter and Schecter, *Sacred Secrets*, 225.

Chapter 10. "Let Me at Him!" 1954

1. Marx, *Das Kapital*, 284.

2. Horne, *Communist Front? The Civil Rights Congress, 1946–1956*; Borstelmann, *The Cold War and the Color Line*; Dudziak, *Cold War Civil Rights*.

3. *Times Picayune*, March 9, 1954; Salmond, "'The Great Southern Commie Hunt,'" 437–38.

4. Krueger, *And Promises to Keep*, 29–31.

5. Barnard, *Outside the Magic Circle*, 256.

6. Salmond, "'The Great Southern Commie Hunt,'" 438.

7. *Times Picayune*, March 18, 1954.

8. *Hearings on Subversive Influence in Southern Conference Education Fund, Inc.*, March 18, 1954, 11.

9. Belfrage, *The American Inquisition*, 222n.

10. *Hearings on Subversive Influence in Southern Conference Education Fund, Inc.*, March 18, 1954, 11–13.

11. Ibid., 15.

12. Ibid., 15–16.

13. Ibid., 13–14.

14. Ibid., 16–17, 23; Salmond, "'The Great Southern Commie Hunt,'" 440; "*New Orleans States Item*, March 19, 1954," Paul Crouch Paper, Box 7, Hoover Institution Archives.

15. *Hearings on Subversive Influence in Southern Conference Education Fund, Inc.*, March 18, 1954, 23–29.

16. Krueger, *And Promises to Keep*, 105; *Hearings on Subversive Influence in Southern Conference Education Fund, Inc.*, March 18, 1954, 31–36, 43.

17. *Hearings on Subversive Influence in Southern Conference Education Fund, Inc.*, March 18, 1954, 44, 46.

18. Barnard, *Outside the Magic Circle*, 261.

19. Ibid.

20. Salmond, *A Southern Rebel*, 233.

21. *Hearings on Subversive Influence in Southern Conference Education Fund, Inc.*, March 18, 1954, 48, 49, 52.

22. Ibid., 51–52.

23. Ibid., 50–52, 53–54, 59.

24. Ibid., 62, 64.

25. *Hearings on Subversive Influence in Southern Conference Education Fund, Inc.*, March 19, 1954, 84–85.

26. Ibid., 84–90.

27. Barnard, *Outside the Magic Circle*, 259–60; "The Reminiscences of Clifford Durr," Columbia University Oral History Collection, part 3, 295.

28. *Hearings on Subversive Influence in Southern Conference Education Fund, Inc.*, March 19, 1954, 90, 91.

29. Ibid., 91–92.

30. Ibid., 92, 93.

31. "*New Orleans States Item*, March 19, 1954," Paul Crouch Papers, Box 7, Hoover Institution Archives.

32. Salmond, "'The Great Southern Commie Hunt,'" 441.

33. *Hearings on Subversive Influence in Southern Conference Education Fund, Inc.*, March 19, 1954, 94.

34. Ibid., 95.

35. Salmond, *A Southern Rebel*, 5–26, 55, 83, 163, 222. The concert went on nonetheless.

36. Ibid., 229–30.

37. *Hearings on Subversive Influence in Southern Conference Education Fund, Inc.*, March 19, 1954, 101, 102–4.

38. Ibid., 118, 119.

39. Ibid., 120, 121, 122.

40. Ibid., 127, 132.

41. Ibid., 133–39.

42. Brown, *Standing against Dragons*, 98–99; *Hearings on Subversive Influence in Southern Conference Education Fund, Inc.*, March 19, 1954, 139–42, 143–44.

43. *Hearings on Subversive Influence in Southern Conference Education Fund, Inc.*, March 19, 1954, 144, 145–48.

44. Ibid., 152.

45. "*New Orleans States Item*, March 20, 1954," Paul Crouch Papers, Box 7, Hoover Institution Papers.

46. Barnard, *Outside the Magic Circle*, 263–64.

47. Salmond, "'The Great Southern Commie Hunt,'" 445; *Washington Post*, March 21, 1954; *New York Times*, March 21, 1954.

48. "*New Orleans States Item*, March 20, 1954," Paul Crouch Papers, Box 7, Hoover Institution Archives.

49. Barnard, *Outside the Magic Circle*, 264; Virginia Durr, Columbia Oral History Collection, part 3, 171–74.

50. Barnard, *Outside the Magic Circle*, 258, 261.

51. Ibid., 261.

52. Belfrage, *The American Inquisition*, 222.

53. Fariello, *Red Scare*, 488–89.

54. *Daily Worker*, March 24, 1954; *New Orleans States Item*, March 21, 1954; *Nation*, April 3, 1954.

55. *New York Times*, March 25, 1954.

56. *Hearings on Subversive Influence in Southern Conference Education Fund, Inc.*, Appendix, 167, 168.

57. Brown, *Standing against Dragons*, 133; Salmond, *A Southern Rebel*, 269, 287; Salmond, "'The Great Southern Commie Hunt,'" 446–50.

58. *Hearings on Subversive Influence in Southern Conference Education Fund, Inc.*, Report, v.

59. Ibid., viii.

60. Brown, *Standing against Dragons*, 132.

61. Krueger, *And Promises to Keep*, 89, 169, 176, 181.

62. Ibid., 178.

63. Labovitz, *Being Red in Philadelphia*, 79; *New York Times*, July 31, 1953.

64. Labovitz, *Being Red in Philadelphia*, 84.

65. Ibid., 85.

66. Ibid., 87.

67. Ibid., 86.

68. Ibid., 84–85; "*The Evening Bulletin*, April 12, 1954," Paul Crouch Papers, Box 9, Hoover Institution Archives.

69. Labovitz, *Being Red in Philadelphia*, 90.

70. Ibid., 91.

71. Ibid., 91, 92; *Washington Post and Times Herald*, April 27, 1954.

72. Steinberg, *The Great "Red Menace,"* 236; Labovitz, *Being Red in Philadelphia*, 92.

73. Labovitz, *Being Red in Philadelphia*, 129.

Chapter 11. "Is Paul Crouch Reliable?" 1954

1. "*The Militant* (undated)," Paul Crouch Papers, Box 2, Hoover Institution Archives; *Daily Worker*, April 27, 1954; Caute, *The Great Fear*, 128.

2. *Daily Worker*, June 27, 1954.

3. *Honolulu Record*, April 15, 1954.

4. "The Informer on the Stand," *Nation*, April 10, 1954.

5. Ibid.; *Testimony of Paul Crouch*, May 6, 1949, HUAC, 215.

6. *Washington Post*, February 17, 1953.

7. "Letter to editor, unknown, undated," Paul Crouch Papers, Box 16, Hoover Institution Archives.

8. "Communist Infiltration of the American Armed Forces, March 1953," Paul Crouch Papers, Box 1, Hoover Institution Archives.

9. Ibid.; *New York Times*, May 28, 1954.

10. Belfrage, *The American Inquisition*, 208.

11. *Washington Daily News*, July 1, 1954.

12. "Letter from Thomas Daily, May 3, 1954," Paul Crouch Papers, Box 1, Hoover Institution Archives.

13. *New York Herald Tribune*, April 19, 1954.

14. Ibid.

15. *Washington Post and Times Herald*, April 16, 1954.

16. *Winston-Salem Sentinel*, April 19, 1954.

17. "Letter from Crouch to the NY Herald Tribune and the Alsops, April 19, 1954," Paul Crouch Papers, Box 7, Hoover Institution Archives.

18. "Letter from Crouch to Everett Walker, April 20, 1954," Paul Crouch Papers, Box 8, Hoover Institution Archives.

19. *Washington Post*, July 4, 1954.

20. *New York Herald Tribune*, May 19, 1954; *Washington Post and Times Herald*, May 19, 1954.

21. "FBI files, April 16, May 18, and May 28, 1954," Paul Crouch FBI Files, James Larkin Pearson Library.

22. *Washington Post and Times Herald*, June 29 and July 2, 1954.

23. "Copy of NY Supreme Court lawsuit," Paul Crouch Papers, Box 5, Hoover Institution Archives.

24. *Daily Worker*, December 14, 1954.

25. "Letter to Brownell, June 8, 1954," Paul Crouch Papers, Box 16, Hoover Institution Archives.

26. "FBI files, May 29, 1954," Paul Crouch FBI Files, James Larkin Pearson Library.

27. "FBI files, June 2, 1954," Paul Crouch FBI Files, James Larkin Pearson Library.

28. "FBI files, July 7, 1954," Paul Crouch FBI Files, James Larkin Pearson Library; *Washington Daily News*, July 14, 1954; Lichtman and Cohen, *Deadly Farce*, 143.

29. *Washington Post and Times Herald*, July 2, 1954.

30. "Letter to J Edgar Hoover, June 28, 1954," Paul Crouch Papers, Box 1, Hoover Institution Archives.

31. Belfrage, *The American Inquisition*, 228.

32. "Unknown and undated," Paul Crouch Papers, Box 1, Hoover Institution Archives; "FBI files, June 18, 1954," Paul Crouch FBI Files, James Larkin Pearson Library.

33. *New York Times*, July 10, 1954.

34. Ibid., July 9, 1954.

35. *Atlantic Monthly*, May 1941, 594–97.

36. "Stewart Alsop was an Ex-Marxist," Paul Crouch Papers, Box 1, Hoover Institution Archives.

37. *Washington Post and Times Herald*, July 15, 1954.

38. *Miami Herald*, July 31, 1954.

39. *National Republic*, June 1954.

40. "Letter from J. Gerald Brennan to Brownell, August 8, 1954," Paul Crouch Papers, Box 8, Hoover Institution Archives.

41. "VFW Fact Sheet on Un-American Activities, Vol. 1 No. 5 August 16, 1954," Paul Crouch Papers, Box 16, Hoover Institution Archives.

42. "National Committee for the Vindication of Paul Crouch" (emphasis in original source), Paul Crouch Papers, Box 16, Hoover Institution Archives.

43. *Washington Post and Times Herald*, July 5, 1954; *Nation*, July 17, 1954.

44. *New Republic*, July 19, 1954.

45. *Miami Herald*, May 25, 1955.

46. "The Crouch Appendix from the Board of immigration Appeals, U.S. Department of Justice in the Matter of Jacob Burck," Paul Crouch Papers, Box 2, Hoover Institution Archives.

47. Ibid.; "Copies of *Union Record* and *Dade County News*," Paul Crouch Papers, Box 5, Hoover Institution Archives.

48. "The Crouch Appendix from the Board of immigration Appeals, U.S. Department of Justice in the Matter of Jacob Burck," Paul Crouch Papers, Box 2, Hoover Institution Archives. See letters from W. B. Sandlin July 20, 1953, Adelaide Sanchez July 20, 1953, Rollin Rodgers July 17, 1953, and Rose Camner July 18, 1953.

49. Ibid.

50. "Letter to J. Edgar Hoover, June 28, 1954," Paul Crouch Papers, Box 8, Hoover Institution Archives.

51. Martin, *The Billy Graham Story*, 101, 115, 166.

52. "NBC Today Show, July 22, 1954," Paul Crouch Papers, Box 2, Hoover Institution Archives.

53. "Christianform pamphlet," Paul Crouch Papers, Box 16, Hoover Institution Archives.

54. "*For God and Freedom, the Voice of Christianform*, vol. V, no. 2, June 1, 1954," Paul Crouch Papers, Box 8, Hoover Institution Archives.

55. "Undated and untitled speech," Paul Crouch Papers, Box 16, Hoover Institution Archives.

56. "Undated and untitled speech," Paul Crouch Papers, Box 16, Hoover Institution Archives.

57. "Federation of Former Communists," Paul Crouch Papers, Box 2, Hoover Institution Archives.

58. Schrecker, *Many Are the Crimes*, 85.

59. "NBC Today Show, July 22, 1954," Paul Crouch Papers, Box 2, Hoover Institution Archives.

60 Ibid.

61. Ibid.

62. "Letter from Crouch to Brownell, July 6, 1954," Paul Crouch Papers, Box 8, Hoover Institution Archives; "Paul Crouch Replies to the Smear Attacks by Communists, Fellow Travelers, and Others: The Facts about the charges against him and the reasons for these accusations" (emphasis in original source), Paul Crouch Papers, Box 8, Hoover Institution Archives.

63. "*Honolulu Star Bulletin*, February 23, undated," Paul Crouch Papers, Box 16, Hoover Institution Archives.

64. "Page 14, separated from the rest of the material, untitled and dated" (emphasis in original source), Paul Crouch Papers, Box 16, Hoover Institution Archives; "Broken Chains, Chapter 31, page 17," Paul Crouch Papers, Box 17, Hoover Institution Archives.

65. "Letter from T. O'Conor Sloane III" (emphasis in original source), Paul Crouch

Papers, Box 8, Hoover Institution Archives; "Letter from Duquesne University, March 17, 1953," Paul Crouch Papers, Box 10, Hoover Institution Archives.

66. "Names of Members of the Communist Party" (emphasis in original source), Paul Crouch Papers, Box 4, Hoover Institution Archives.

67. Lichtman and Cohen, *Deadly Farce*, 132, 205–6.

Chapter 12. "A Lonely and Despised Man," 1955 and Beyond

1. Schrecker, *Many Are the Crimes*, 312.

2. Rovere, "The Kept Witnesses."

3. "Letter to Congressman Francis Walter, February 7, 1955," Paul Crouch Papers, Box 1, Hoover Institution Archives.

4. *Strategy and Tactics of World Communism*, 247, 249.

5. Lichtman and Cohen, *Deadly Farce*, 29, 152.

6. "Letter to Drew Pearson, February 20, 1955," Paul Crouch Papers, James Larkin Pearson Library; "Letter to Drew Pearson, March 3, 1955," Paul Crouch Papers, Box 8, Hoover Institution Archives.

7. "Letter to Drew Pearson, May 9, 1955," Paul Crouch Papers, Box 8, Hoover Institution Archives.

8. Rovere, *The American Establishment*, 119.

9. Rovere, "The Kept Witnesses," 29.

10. Ibid., 31–32; Rovere, *The American Establishment*, 125.

11. Rovere, "The Kept Witnesses," 29, 32, 34.

12. Lichtman and Cohen, *Deadly Farce*, 143.

13. "Letter to James Eastland, April 28, 1955," Paul Crouch Papers, Box 6, Hoover Institution Archives.

14. "Letter from Sylvia Crouch to the FBI, July 5, 1955," Paul Crouch Papers, Box 1, Hoover Institution Archives.

15. "Letter from Sylvia Crouch to the FBI, July 7, 1955," Paul Crouch Papers, Box 1, Hoover Institution Archives.

16. "Letter from Sylvia to Pearson July 21, 1955" (emphasis in original source), Paul Crouch Papers, James Larkin Pearson Library.

17. "Unsigned letter from Portland, Oregon September 3, 1955," Paul Crouch Papers, James Larkin Pearson Library.

18. "Letter from Crouch to unknown, September 7, 1955," Paul Crouch Papers, James Larkin Pearson Library.

19. "Letter from Ellis Rubin to Tanya Hartley, November 30, 1955," Paul Crouch Papers, Box 16, Hoover Institution Archives.

20. Belfrage, *The American Inquisition*, 235; *Journal Patriot*, November 21 and 28, 1955; *North Wilkesboro Hustler*, November 23 and 30, 1955.

21. *Daily Worker*, November 21, 1955; Salmond, "'The Great Southern Commie Hunt,'" 450–51; Durr, "A Noted Victim of Paul Crouch Writes the Informer's Obituary," 3.

22. "Deposition of Sylvia Crouch by Florida Legislative Investigation Committee, January 7, 1958," Paul Crouch Papers, Box 1, Hoover Institution Archives. Among

the names she named were: Leonard Patterson, Manning Johnson, Jack McMichael, Charles Smolikoff, Jack Strong, Irving Gold, Shirley Gold, Gail and Carol Gropper, George Nelson, James Nimmo, Nat Ross, Don West, Michael Shantzek, Phil Shepsky, Leo Sheiner, Frances and Carolyn Stevens.

23. Barnard, *Outside the Magic Circle*, 270.

24. Barrett, *William Z. Foster and the Tragedy of American Radicalism*, 242.

25. Caute, *The Great Fear*, 54; Draper, *American Communism and Soviet Russia*, 213.

26. Haynes and Klehr, *Venona*, 9; Navasky, "Cold War Ghosts"; Schrecker, *Many Are the Crimes*; Schrecker, "Comments on John Earl Haynes' The Cold War Debate Continues."

27. Schrecker, *Many Are the Crimes*, 353; Caute, *The Great Fear*, 138.

28. Steinberg, *The Great "Red Menace,"* 279–80.

29. Heale, *American Anti-Communism*, 195–96; Caute, *The Great Fear*, 208.

30. Belfrage, *The American Inquisition*, 274; Lichtman and Cohen, *Deadly Farce*, 2, 4.

31. Heale, *American Anti-Communism*, 163; Schrecker, *Many Are the Crimes*, 45; Lichtman and Cohen, *Deadly Farce*, 12.

32. Laird, *Into Tibet*; Mayers, *George Kennan and the Dilemmas of US Foreign Policy*.

33. Hoffer, *True Believer*, 152–53.

34. Holmes, *The Specter of Communism in Hawaii*, 79.

35. Caute, *The Great Fear*, 137.

36. Schrecker, *Many Are the Crimes*, 45, 76.

37. Belfrage, *The American Inquisition*, 108; Rovere, *The American Establishment*, 288.

BIBLIOGRAPHY

Primary Sources

Annual Report of the Committee on Un-American Activities for the year 1949. Committee on Un-American Activities. House of Representatives. March 15, 1950.

Barnard, Hollinger F. *Outside the Magic Circle: The Autobiography of Virginia Foster Durr*. Tuscaloosa: University of Alabama Press, 1985.

Civil Rights Congress. *We Charge Genocide: The Historic Petition to the United Nations for Relief From a Crime of the United States Government Against the Negro People*. New York: International Publishers, 1951.

Communist. Chicago, Ill.: Workers Communist Party (1927–1944).

Communist Activities Among Aliens and National Groups. Hearings before the Subcommittee on Immigration and Naturalization of the Committee on the Judiciary. United States Senate. Eighty-First Congress. First Session. 1932.

The Communist Party of the United States of America: What It Is, How It Works. A Handbook for Americans. Subcommittee to Investigate the Administration of the Internal Security Act and other Internal Security Laws of the Committee on the Judiciary. United States Senate. December 21, 1955.

Communist Party of the United States of America *v. Subversive Activities Control Board* United States Supreme Court, 351 U.S. 115 (1956).

Congressional Record. Eighty-Second Congress. First Session. June 14, 1951.

Daily Worker. Chicago, Ill.: Daily Worker Publishing Co. (1924–1957).

Department of Justice Appropriations Bill for 1948: Hearings Before the Subcommittee of the Committee on Appropriations. House of Representatives. Eightieth Congress. First Session. 1947.

Durr, Clifford. *The Reminiscences of Clifford Durr*. Columbia University Oral History Collection. pt. 3, no. 200 (1977).

Durr, Virginia. *The Reminiscences of Virginia Foster Durr*. Columbia University Oral History Collection. pt. 3 (1974).

XIth Plenum of the Executive Committee of the Communist International: Theses, Resolutions, and Decisions. London: Modern Books, 1967.

Executive Session of the Senate Permanent Subcommittee on Investigations of the Committee on Government Operations. Volume 3. Eighty-Third Congress. First Session. 1953.

Files of the Communist Party of the United States of America in the Comintern Archives. New York: IDC Publishers, 1999. Microfilm.

Hearings before the Subcommittee to Investigate the Administration of the Internal Security Act and Other Internal Security Laws of the Committee on the Judiciary. United States Senate. Eighty-Third Congress. Second Session on Subversive Influence in Southern Conference Education Fund, Inc. March 18, 19, and 20, 1954.

Hearings Regarding Clarence Hiskey Including Testimony of Paul Crouch. Hearing before the Committee on Un-American Activities. House of Representatives. Eighty-First Congress. First Session. May 24, 1949.

Hearings Regarding Communist Infiltration of Radiation Laboratory and Atomic Bomb Project at the University of California, Berkeley, Calif.—Vol. II. Hearings before the Committee on Un-American Activities. House of Representatives. Eighty-First Congress. First Session. August 26, 1949, July 1, September 10, 1948, August 14 and September 14 and 27, 1949.

Hearings Regarding Steve Nelson. Hearings before the Committee on Un-American Activities. House of Representatives. Eighty-First Congress. First Session. June 8, 1949.

Junius Scales Papers 4879. Southern Historical Collection. Wilson Library. University of North Carolina. Chapel Hill, North Carolina.

Labor Defender. Chicago, Ill.: International Labor Defense (1926–1937).

New South. Birmingham, Al.: CPUSA (1937).

Official Report of Proceedings before the Subversive Activities Control Board. Part 1. Reel 10. (June–July 1951).

Paul Crouch FBI files. James Larkin Pearson Library, Learning Resources Center, Wilkes Community College. Wilkesboro, North Carolina.

Paul Crouch Letters. James Larkin Pearson Correspondence, Learning Resources Center, Wilkes Community College. Wilkesboro, North Carolina.

Paul Crouch Papers. Hoover Institution Archives. Palo Alto, California.

Paul Crouch Papers. James Larkin Pearson Library, Learning Resources Center, Wilkes Community College. Wilkesboro, North Carolina.

President's Committee on Civil Rights. *To Secure These Rights.* Washington, D.C.: Government Printing Office, 1947.

Scope of Soviet Activity in the United States. Hearings before the Subcommittee to Investigate the Administration of the Internal Security Act and Other Internal Security Laws of the Committee on the Judiciary. United States Senate. Eighty-Fourth Congress. Second Session. December 5 and 6, 1956.

Southern Worker. Birmingham, Al.: CPUSA (1930–1937).

Strategy and Tactics of World Communism (The Significance of the Matusow Case). Hearing before the Subcommittee to Investigate the Administration of the Internal Security Act and Other Internal Security Laws of the Committee on the Judiciary. United States Senate. Eighty-Fourth Congress. First Session. February 28, 1955.

Subversive Activities Control Board Docket No. 51–101. Report No. 7 (July 25, 1951).

Testimony of Philip A. Bart (General Manager of Freedom of the Press, Publishers of the Daily Worker, Official Organ of the Communist Party) and Marcel Scherer (Coordina-

tor, New York Labor Conference for Peace, and Formerly District Representative of District 4, United Electrical, Radio, and Machine Workers of America, CIO). Hearing before the Committee on Un-American Activities. House of Representatives. Eighty-First Congress. Second Session. June 21, 1950.

Testimony of Paul Crouch. Hearings before the Committee on Un-American Activities. House of Representatives. Eighty-First Congress. First Session. May 6, 1949.

Theodore Draper research files. Manuscript, Archives, and Rare Book Library, Emory University. Atlanta, Georgia.

U.S. Military Intelligence Reports. *Surveillance of Radicals in the United States, 1917–1941.* Reel 21. Frederick, Md.: University Publications of America.

The World Situation and Economic Struggle: Theses of the Tenth Plenum ECCI. London: Communist Party of Great Britain, 1929.

Young Worker. Chicago, Ill.: Young Communist League of America (1927–1936).

Secondary Sources

Allen, James. "The Black Belt: Area of Negro Majority." *The Communist* XIII, no. 6 (June 1934): 581–99.

Alsop, Stewart. "Wanted: A Faith to Fight For." *The Atlantic Monthly* 167, no. 7 (May 1941): 594–97.

Alsop, Joseph, and Stewart Alsop. *We Accuse!: The Story of the Miscarriage of American Justice in the Case of J. Robert Oppenheimer.* 1955.

Arendt, Hannah. "The Ex-Communist." *Commonweal* 157, no. 24 (March 20, 1953): 595–99.

Asch, Chris. *The Senator and the Sharecropper: The Freedom Struggles of James O. Eastland and Fannie Lou Hammer.* New York: W. W. Norton, 2008.

Axel, Peter. "Scientist 'X' Dismissed by Minnesota." *Bulletin of the Atomic Scientists* VII, nos. 7–8 (August 1951): 240.

Barrett, James. *William Z. Foster and the Tragedy of American Radicalism.* Urbana: University of Illinois Press, 1999.

Bass, John. "Bolsheviks on the Bluff: A History of Memphis Communists and Their Labor and Civil Rights Contributions, 1930–1957." PhD dissertation. University of Memphis, 2009.

Belfrage, Cedric. *The American Inquisition, 1945–1960.* Indianapolis, Ind.: Bobbs-Merrill, 1973.

Bentley, Elizabeth. *Out of Bondage: The Story of Elizabeth Bentley.* New York: Devin-Adir Company, 1951.

Bird, Kai, and Martin Sherwin. *American Prometheus: The Triumph and Tragedy of J. Robert Oppenheimer.* New York: Vintage, 2006.

Borstelmann, Thomas. *The Cold War and the Color Line: American Race Relations in the Global Arena.* Cambridge, Mass.: Harvard University Press, 2001.

Brown, Louise Fargo. "Portrait of an Informer: A 17th Century Moral." *The Nation* (April 3, 1954): 272–74.

Brown, Sarah. *Standing against Dragons: Three Southern Lawyers in the Era of Fear.* Baton Rouge: Louisiana State University Press, 1998.

Budenz, Louis Francis. *This Is My Story*. New York: Whittlesey House, 1947.

———. "The Informer on the Stand." *The Nation* (April 10, 1954): 302–6.

Carroll, Peter N. *The Odyssey of the Abraham Lincoln Brigade: Americans in the Spanish Civil War*. Palo Alto, Calif.: Stanford University Press, 1994.

Carter, Dan T. *The Politics of Rage: George Wallace, The Origins of the New Conservatism, and the Transformation of American Politics*. Second Edition. Baton Rouge: Louisiana State University Press, 2000.

Caute, David. *The Great Fear: The Anti-Communist Purge Under Truman and Stalin*. New York: Simon and Schuster, 1978.

Ceplair, Larry. *Anti-Communism in Twentieth-Century America: A Critical History*. New York: Praeger, 2011.

Chambers, Whittaker. *Witness*. Washington, D.C.: Regnery Publishing, 1952.

Cherney, Robert. William Issel, and Kiernan Walsh Taylor, eds. *American Labor and the Cold War: Grassroots Politics and Postwar Political Culture*. New Brunswick, N.J.: Rutgers University Press, 2004.

Crossman, Richard H. ed. *The God that Failed*. New York: Columbia University Press, 2001.

Crouch, John. *Historical Sketches of Wilkes County*. 1902.

Crouch, Paul. "Anatomy of a Front." *Plain Talk Magazine* (March 1949): 7–13.

———. "Soviet Underground, U.S.A." *The Freeman* (February 16, 1951): 336–39.

DeVoto, Bernard. "The Ex-Communists." *Atlantic Monthly* 187, no. 2 (February 1951).

Dilling, Elizabeth. *The Red Network: A "Who's Who and Handbook of Radicalism for Patriots*. Chicago, Ill.: Ayer Company, 1934.

Donner, Frank. "The Miami Formula: Grassroots McCarthyism." *The Nation* (January 22, 1955): 65–71.

Draper, Theodore. *American Communism and Soviet Russia*. New York: Penguin Books, 1960.

Dudziak, Mary. *Cold War Civil Rights: Race and the Image of American Democracy*. Princeton, N.J.: Princeton University Press, 2000.

Durr, Clifford. "A Noted Victim of Paul Crouch Writes the Informer's Obituary." *I. F. Stone's Weekly* (December 12, 1955): 193.

Fariello, Griffin. *Red Scare: Memories of the American Inquisition*. New York: Avon Books, 1995.

Gilmore, Glenda Elizabeth. *Defying Dixie: The Radical Roots of Civil Rights, 1919–1950*. New York: W. W. Norton, 2008.

Ginzburg, Benjamin. *Rededication to Freedom*. New York: Simon and Schuster, 1959.

Green, Laurie. *Battling the Plantation Mentality: Memphis and the Black Freedom Struggle*. Chapel Hill: University of North Carolina Press, 2007.

Griggs, William. "McCarthy's Witches." *New American* (June 16, 2003): 14–15.

Haynes, John Earl, and Harvey Klehr. *Venona: Decoding Soviet Espionage in America*. New Haven, Conn.: Yale University Press, 1999.

Heale, M. J. *American Anti-Communism: Combating the Enemy Within, 1830–1970*. Baltimore, Md.: Johns Hopkins University Press, 1990.

Herken, Gregg. *Brotherhood of the Bomb: The Tangled Lives and Loyalties of Robert Oppenheimer, Ernest Lawrence, and Edward Teller*. New York: Holt Paperback, 2002.

Hoffer, Eric. *True Believer: Thoughts on the Nature of Mass Movements*. New York: Harper Perennial Classics, 2002.

Hofstader, Richard. *The Paranoid Style in American Politics and Other Essays*. Cambridge, Mass.: Harvard University Press, 1965.

Holmes, Michael T. *The Specter of Communism in Hawaii*. Honolulu: University of Hawaii Press, 1994.

Horne, Gerald. *Communist Front? The Civil Rights Congress, 1946–1956*. Rutherford, N.J.: Farleigh Dickinson University Press, 1987.

Hughes, John C. and Ryan Teague Beckwith. *On the Harbor: From Black Friday to Nirvana*. Las Vegas, Nev.: Stephens Press, 2005.

Isserman, Maurice. *Which Side Were You On?: The American Communist Party during the Second World War*. Urbana: University of Illinois Press, 1993.

Kelley, Robin. *Hammer and Hoe: Alabama Communists During the Great Depression*. Chapel Hill: University of North Carolina Press, 1990.

Kern, Gary. *A Death in Washington: Walter G. Krivitsky and the Stalin Terror*. New York: Enigma Books, 2004.

Kessler, Lauren. *Clever Girl: Elizabeth Bentley, the Spy Who Ushered in the McCarthy Era*. New York: Harper Collins, 2003.

Klehr, Harvey. *The Heyday of American Communism: The Depression Decade*. New York: Basic Books, 1984.

Klehr, Harvey, and John Earl Haynes. *The American Communist Movement, Storming Heaven Itself*. New York: Twayne Publishers, 1992.

———. "Communists and the CIO: From the Soviet Archives." *Labor History* 35 (1994): 442–46.

Knight, Amy. *How the Cold War Began: The Gouzenko Affair and the Hunt for Soviet Spies*. Toronto, Ontario: McClelland and Stewart, Ltd., 2005.

Korstad, Robert. *Civil Rights Unionism: Tobacco Workers and the Struggle for Democracy in the Mid-Twentieth Century South*. Chapel Hill: University of North Carolina Press, 2003.

Krueger, Thomas. *And Promises to Keep: The Southern Conference for Human Welfare, 1938–1948*. Nashville, Tenn.: Vanderbilt University Press, 1967.

Labovitz, Sherman. *Being Red in Philadelphia: A Memoir of the McCarthy Era*. Philadelphia, Pa.: Camino Books, 1998.

Laird, Thomas. *Into Tibet: The CIA's First Atomic Spy and His Secret Expedition to Lhasa*. New York: Grove Press, 2002.

Larrowe, Charles. *Harry Bridges: The Rise and Fall of Radical Labor in the United States*. Lawrence Hill and Co., 1977.

Lewis, Earl. *In Their Own Interests: Race, Class, and Power in Twentieth Century Norfolk*. Berkeley: University of California Press, 1991.

Liberman, Robbie and Lang, Clarence. eds. *Anticommunism and the African American Freedom Movement: "Another Side of the Story."* New York: Palmgrave MacMillian, 2009.

Lichtenstein, Alex. "Putting Labor's House in Order: The Transport Workers Union and Labor Anti-Communism in Miami during the 1940s." *Labor History* 139, no. 1 (1998): 7–23.

Lichtman, Robert M., and Ronald D. Cohen. *Deadly Farce: Harvey Matusow and the Informer System in the McCarthy Era*. Urbana: University of Illinois Press, 2004.

Lynn, Kenneth. *Charlie Chaplin and His Times*. New York: Simon and Schuster, 1997.

Marlowe, Alex. "McBride versus Smith: Philadelphia Court Drama." *The Nation* (July 17, 1954): 48–49.

Martin, William. *The Billy Graham Story: A Prophet with Honour.* London: Hutchinson, 1992.

Marx, Karl. *Das Kapital*. New York: International Publishers, 1967.

Matusow, Harvey. *False Witness*. New York: Cameron and Khan, 1955.

Mayers, David. *George Kennan and the Dilemmas of US Foreign Policy*. New York: Oxford University Press, 1990.

McCarthy, Joseph. *America's Retreat from Victory: The Story of George Catlett Marshall*. New York: Devin-Adir Company, 1951.

———. *McCarthyism: The Fight For America*. New York: Devin-Adir Company, 1952.

McCullough, David. *Truman*. New York: Simon and Schuster, 1992.

McMillan, Priscilla J. *The Ruin of J. Robert Oppenheimer and the Birth of the Modern Arms Race*. New York: Viking, 2005.

Merry, Robert. *Taking on the World: Joseph and Stewart Alsop—Guardians of the American Century*. Create Space, 2012.

Metzger, Delbert E. "Duty of the Lawyer: The Defense of Heresy." *The Nation* (May 1, 1954): 380–82.

Mouledous, Joseph C. "From Browderism to Peaceful Co-Existence: An Analysis of Developments in the Communist Position on the American Negro." *Phylon* (1st Qtr., 1964): 79–90.

Navasky, Victor S. *Naming Names*. New York: Hill and Wang, 2003.

———. "Cold War Ghosts." *Nation* (July 16, 2001).

Nelson, Steve. *The 13th Juror: The Inside Story of My Trial*. New York: Masses and Mainstream Publications, 1955.

Oakley, J. Ronald. *God's Country: America in the Fifties*. New York: Barricade Books, 1990.

Olmsted, Kathryn S. *Red Spy Queen: A Biography of Elizabeth Bentley*. Chapel Hill: University of North Carolina Press, 2002.

Olney, Warren. "The Use of Former Communists as Witnesses." *Vital Speeches of the Day* 20, no. 21 (August 15, 1954).

Oshinsky, David M. *A Conspiracy So Immense: The World of Joe McCarthy*. New York: Oxford University Press, 1983.

Ottanelli, Fraser. *The Communist Party of the United States: From the Depression to World War II*. New Brunswick, N.J.: Rutgers University Press, 1991.

Packer, Herbert. *Ex-Communist Witnesses: Four Studies in Fact Finding*. Palo Alto, Calif.: Stanford University Press, 1962.

Papanikolas, Helen Z. "Unionism, Communism and the Great Depression: The Carbon County Coal Strike." *Utah Historical Quarterly* 41, no. 3 (Summer 1973): 256–300.

Pederson, Vernon L. *The Communist Party in Maryland, 1919–57*. Urbana: University of Illinois Press, 2001.

Polenberg, Richard, ed. *In the Matter of J. Robert Oppenheimer: The Security Clearance Hearings*. Ithaca, N.Y.: Cornell University Press, 2001.

Purcell, Aaron. *White Collar Radicals: TVA's Knoxville Fifteen, the New Deal, and the McCarthy Era*. Knoxville: University of Tennessee Press, 2009.

Record, Wilson. "The Development of the Communist Position on the Negro Question in the United States." *The Phylon Quarterly* (3rd Qtr., 1958): 306–26.

Reinecke, John. *The Filipino Piecemeal Sugar Strike of 1924–1925*. Honolulu: Social Science Research Institute, University of Hawaii, 1995.

Rovere, Richard. "The Kept Witnesses." *Harper's* (May 1955): 25–34.

———. *The American Establishment and Other Reports, Opinions, and Speculations*. New York: Harcourt, Brace, and World, 1962.

Ryan, James. *Earl Browder: The Failure of American Communism*. Tuscaloosa: University of Alabama Press, 1997.

Sabin, Arthur. *Red Scare in Court: New York versus the International Workers Order*. Philadelphia: University of Pennsylvania Press, 1993.

Salmond, John. "'The Great Southern Commie Hunt': Aubrey Williams, the Southern Conference Educational Fund, and the Internal Security Subcommittee." *South Atlantic Quarterly* (Autumn 1978): 433–52.

———. *Conscience of a Lawyer: Clifford J. Durr and American Civil Liberties, 1899–1975*. Tuscaloosa: University of Alabama Press, 1990.

———. *Gastonia, 1929: The Story of the Loray Mill Strike*. Chapel Hill: University of North Carolina Press, 1995.

———. *The General Textile Strike of 1934*. Columbia: University of Missouri Press, 2002.

———. *Southern Rebel: The Life and Times of Aubrey Willis Williams, 1890–1965*. Chapel Hill: University of North Carolina Press, 2009.

Schecter, Jarrold, and Leona Schecter. *Sacred Secrets: How Soviet Intelligence Operations Changed American History*. Washington, D.C.: Potomac Books, 2003.

Schrecker, Ellen. *No Ivory Tower: McCarthyism and the Universities*. New York: Oxford University Press, 1986.

———. *Many Are the Crimes: McCarthyism in America*. Princeton, N.J.: Princeton University Press, 1998.

———. "Comments on John Earl Haynes' The Cold War Debate Continues: A Traditionalist View of Historical Writing on Domestic Communism and Anti-Communism." *Journal of Cold War Studies* 2, no. 1 (Winter 2000): 76–115.

Shelton, William. "Paul Crouch, Informer." *New Republic* 131, no. 3 (July 19, 1954).

Shogan, Robert. *No Sense of Decency—The Army McCarthy Hearings: A Demagogue Falls and Television Takes Charge of American Politics*. Chicago: Ivan R. Dee, 2009.

Simpson, Alan. "The Re-Trial of the Oppenheimer Case." *Bulletin of Atomic Scientists* (December 1954): 387.

Smith, Sharon. *Subterranean Fire: A History of Working Class Radicalism in the United States*. Chicago: Haymarket Books, 2006.

Solomon, Mark. *The Cry Was Unity, Communists and African Americans, 1917–1936*. Jackson: University Press of Mississippi, 1998.

Starobin, Joseph. *American Communism in Crisis, 1943–1957*. Cambridge, Mass.: Harvard University Press, 1972.

Steinberg, Peter L. *The Great "Red Menace": United States Prosecution of American Communists, 1947–1952*. Westport, Conn.: Greenwood Press, 1984.

Stern, Phillip. *The Oppenheimer Case*. New York: Harper and Row, 1969.

Storrs, Landon. "Red Scare Politics and the Suppression of Popular Front Feminism: The Loyalty Investigation of Mary Dublin Keyserling." *Journal of American History* 90, no. 2 (September 2003): 491–524.

Talbert, Roy. *Negative Intelligence: The Army and the American Left, 1917–1941*. Jackson: University Press of Mississippi, 1991.

Taylor, Gregory S. *The History of the North Carolina Communist Party*. Columbia: University of South Carolina Press, 2009.

Weissman, David. "The Proceedings to Disbar Leo Sheiner." *Lawyers Guild Review* 16 (Winter 1956): 137–48.

Wheen, Francis. *Strange Days Indeed: The 1970s, the Golden Age of Paranoia*. New York: BBS/Public Affairs, 2010.

Woods, Jeff. *Black Struggle Red Scare: Segregation and Anti-Communism in the South, 1948–1968*. Baton Rouge: Louisiana State University Press, 2004.

INDEX

GREGORY S. TAYLOR is associate professor of modern American history at Chowan University. He is the author of *The History of the North Carolina Communist Party*.